WORKING PAPERS

to accompany

FINANCIAL ACCOUNTING

8TH EDITION

JERRY J. WEYGANDT Ph.D., C.P.A.
Arthur Andersen Alumni Professor of Accounting
University of Wisconsin—Madison
Madison, Wisconsin

PAUL D. KIMMEL Ph.D., C.P.A.
Associate Professor of Accounting
University of Wisconsin—Milwaukee
Milwaukee, Wisconsin

DONALD E. KIESO Ph.D., C.P.A.
KPMG Peat Marwick Emeritus Professor of Accountancy
Northern Illinois University
DeKalb, Illinois

Prepared by
Dick D. Wasson, M.B.A., C.P.A.
Southwestern College
San Diego State University
University of Phoenix

John Wiley & Sons, Inc.

COVER PHOTO: ©Bill Stevenson/Aurora Photos, Inc.

ISBN-13   978-1-118-10298-5

Printed in the United States of America

10 9 8 7 6 5 4 3 2 1

Printed and bound by Courier-Westford

CONTENTS

Working Paper templates are provided for end-of-chapter brief exercises, Do it! exercises, exercises, problems, and broadening your perspective problems. Working Paper templates are not provided for solutions that are textual in nature.

BE1-1

		Assets	Liabilities	Stockholders' Equity	
1	(a)	$ 9 0 0 0 0	$ 5 0 0 0 0	$	1
2					2
3	(b)		4 5 0 0 0	7 0 0 0 0	3
4					4
5	(c)	9 4 0 0 0		6 0 0 0 0	5
6					6
7	**BE1-4** See next page				7
8					8
9	**BE1-10**				9

10	**Grande Company**	10
11	Balance Sheet	11
12	December 31, 2014	12
13	Assets	13
14		14
15		15
16		16
17		17
18		18
19	Liabilities and Stockholders' Equity	19
20		20
21		21
22		22
23		23
24		24
25		25
26		26
27		27
28		28
29		29
30		30

Chapter 1 Brief Exercises Concluded

Solve Accounting Equation

BE1-4

	Assets =	Liabilities +	Common Stock +	Stockolders' Equity		
				Revenues -	Retained Earnings	
					Expenses -	Dividends
(a)						
1						
2						
3						
4						
(b)						
5						
6						
7						
8						
9						
(c)						
10						
11						
12						
13						
14						
15						
16						
17						
18						
19						
20						

	Assets	=	Liabilities	+	Stockholders' Equity				
	Cash +	Accounts Receivable	Accounts Payable +	Common Stock +	Retained Earnings			
					Revenues -	Expenses -	Dividends
1							
2 (1)							
3							
4 (2)							
5							
6 (3)							
7							
8 (4)							
9							
10							
11							
12							
13							
14							
15							
16							
17							
18							
19							
20							
21							
22							
23							

1	(a)	1
2		2
3		3
4		4
5		5
6		6
7	(b)	7
8		8
9		9
10		10
11		11
12		12
13		13
14		14
15		15
16		16
17		17
18	(c)	18
19		19
20		20
21		21
22		22
23		23
24		24
25		25
26		26
27		27
28		28
29		29
30		30
31		31
32		32
33		33
34		34
35		35
36		36
37		37
38		38
39		39
40		40

(a)

1	1.
2	
3	2.
4	
5	3.
6	
7	4.
8	
9	5.
10	
11	6.
12	
13	7.
14	
15	8.
16	
17	9.
18	
19	10.
20	
21	
22	
23	
24	
25	

(b)

(c)

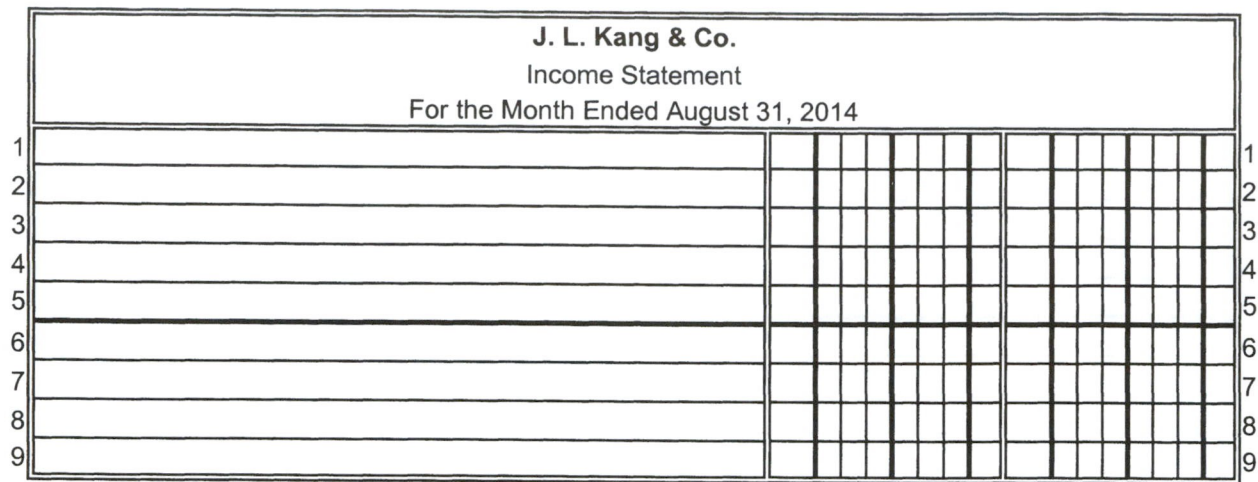

J. L. Kang & Co.

Income Statement

For the Month Ended August 31, 2014

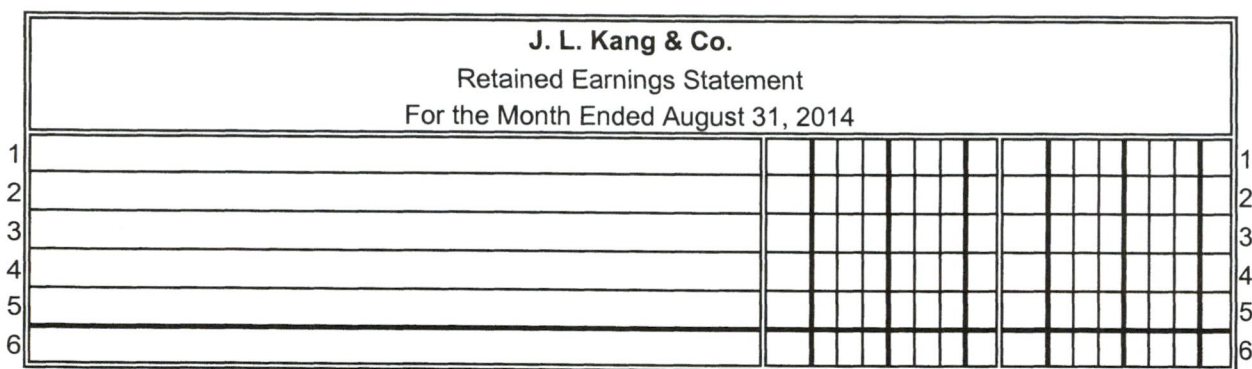

J. L. Kang & Co.

Retained Earnings Statement

For the Month Ended August 31, 2014

J. L. Kang & Co.

Balance Sheet

August 31, 2014

Assets

Liabilities and Stockholders' Equity

1	(a)									1
2										2
3										3
4										4
5										5
6										6
7										7
8										8
9										9
10										10
11	(b)									11
12										12
13										13
14										14
15										15
16										16
17										17
18										18
19										19
20										20
21	(c)									21
22										22
23										23
24										24
25										25
26										26
27										27
28										28
29										29
30										30
31										31
32										32
33										33
34										34
35										35
36										36
37										37
38										38
39										39
40										40

1	(a)	1
2		2
3		3
4		4
5		5
6	(b)	6
7		7
8		8
9		9
10		10
11		11
12		12
13		13
14		14
15		15
16		16
17		17
18		18
19		19
20		20
21	(c)	21
22		22
23		23
24		24
25		25
26	(d)	26
27		27
28		28
29		29
30		30
31		31
32		32
33		33
34		34
35		35
36		36
37		37
38		38
39		39
40		40

Karen Weigel Co.

Income Statement

For the Year Ended December 31, 2014

1			
2			
3			
4			
5			
6			
7			
8			
9			
10			

Karen Weigel Co.

Retained Earnings Statement

For the Year Ended December 31, 2014

1		
2		
3		
4		
5		
6		
7		
8		
9		
10		

E1-13

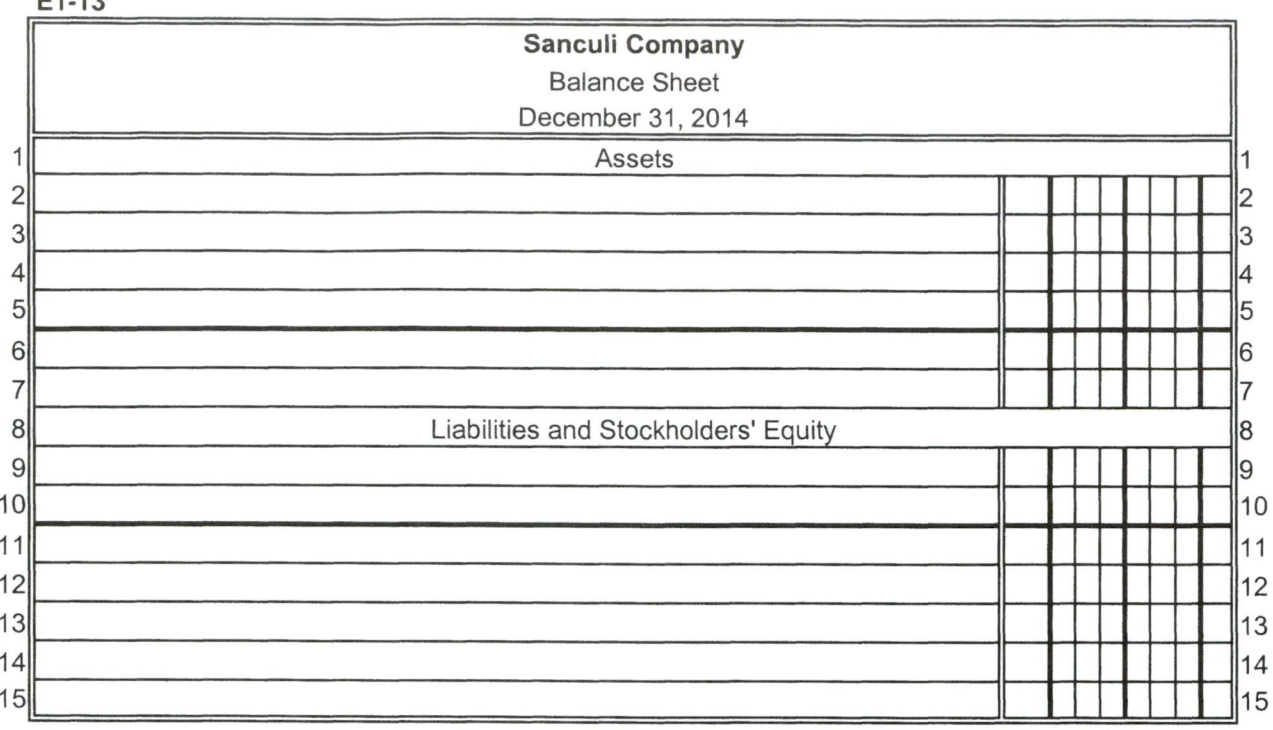

	Sanculi Company		
	Balance Sheet		
	December 31, 2014		
1	Assets		1
2			2
3			3
4			4
5			5
6			6
7			7
8	Liabilities and Stockholders' Equity		8
9			9
10			10
11			11
12			12
13			13
14			14
15			15

E1-15

	Donna Marie Cruise Company		
	Income Statement		
	For the Year Ended December 31, 2014		
1			1
2			2
3			3
4			4
5			5
6			6
7			7
8			8
9			9
10			10

(a)

1										1
2										2
3										3
4										4
5										5
6										6
7										7
8										8
9										9
10										10

(b)

Bear Park

Balance Sheet

December 31, 2014

	Assets				
1					1
2					2
3					3
4					4
5					5
6					6
7					7
8	Liabilities and Stockholders' Equity				8
9					9
10					10
11					11
12					12
13					13
14					14
15					15
16					16
17					17
18					18
19					19
20					20
21					21
22					22

Williams and Douglas, Attorneys at Law
Retained Earnings Statement
For the Year Ended December 31, 2014

1		
2		
3		
4		
5		
6		
7		
8		
9		
10 Supporting Computations		
11		
12		
13		
14		
15		
16		
17		
18		
19		
20		
21		
22		
23		
24		
25		
26		
27		
28		
29		
30		
31		
32		
33		
34		
35		
36		
37		
38		
39		
40		

Belleview Company

Statement of Cash Flows

For the Year Ended December 31, 2014

	1																				

Problem 1-1A

Kinney's Repair Inc.

You will find this working paper at the end of this work book

(a) (Continued)

Key to Retained Earnings Column:

(b)

Problem 1-2A

Donahue Veterinary Clinic

You will find this working paper at the end of this work book

(a) (Continued)

Key to chnges in Retained Ernings:

1	1
2	2
3	3
4	4
5	5
6	6
7	7
8	8

(b)

Donahue Veterinary Clinic
Income Statement
For the Month Ended September 30, 2014

1 Revenues	1
2	2
3	3
4	4
5 Expenses	5
6	6
7	7
8	8
9	9
10 Net Income (Loss)	10

Donahue Veterinary Clinic
Retained Earnings Statement
For the Month Ended September 30, 2014

1	1
2	2
3	3
4	4
5	5
6	6

(b) (Continued)

Donahue Veterinary Clinic

Balance Sheet

September 30, 2014

	Assets										
1											
2											
3											
4											
5											
6											
7											
8											
9											
10											
11	Liabilities and Stockholders' Equity										
12											
13											
14											
15											
16											
17											
18											
19											
20											
21											
22											
23											
24											
25											
26											
27											
28											
29											
30											

(a)

Blue Sky Flying School
Income Statement
For the Month Ended May 31, 2014

1	Revenues			
2				
3				
4				
5	Expenses			
6				
7				
8				
9				
10				
11				
12				
13				
14	Net Income (Loss)			
15				
16				
17				
18				
19				
20				

Blue Sky Flying School
Retained Earnings Statement
For the Month Ended May 31, 2014

1			
2			
3			
4			
5			
6			
7			
8			
9			
10			

(a) Continued

Blue Sky Flying School
Balance Sheet
May 31, 2014

	Assets											
1	Assets											1
2												2
3												3
4												4
5												5
6												6
7												7
8												8
9												9
10	Liabilities and Stockholders' Equity											10
11												11
12												12
13												13
14												14
15												15
16												16
17												17
18												18
19												19
20												20

(b)

Blue Sky Flying School
Income Statement
For the Month Ended May 31, 2014

1	Revenues											1
2												2
3												3
4	Expenses											4
5												5
6												6
7												7
8												8
9												9
10												10
11												11
12	Net Income (Loss)											12
13												13
14												14
15												15

(b) Concluded

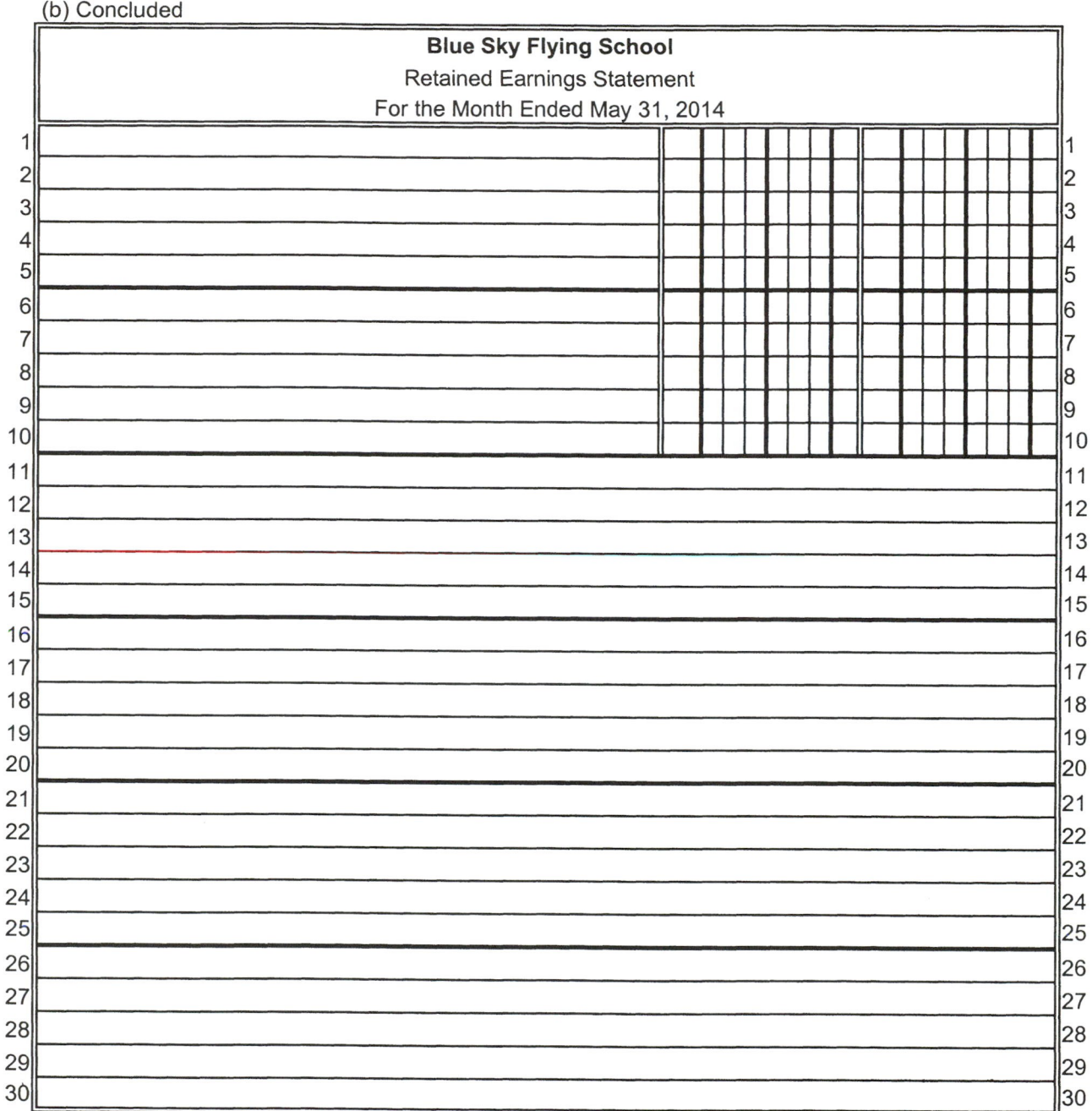

Blue Sky Flying School

Retained Earnings Statement

For the Month Ended May 31, 2014

Problem 1-4A

Stiner Deliveries

You will find this working paper at the end of this work book

(a) (Continued)

Key to Retained Earnings Column

	1
	2
	3
	4

(b)

Stiner Deliveries

Income Statement

For the Month Ended June 30, 2014

Revenues			
Expenses			
Net income (loss)			

(c)

Stiner Deliveries

Balance Sheet

June 30, 2014

Assets			
Liabilities and Stockholders' Equity			

(a)

	Crosby Company	Stills Company	Nash Company	Young Company	
1	January 1, 2014				1
2	Assets	$ 75000	$ 110000		$ 150000	2
3	Liabilities	50000		75000		3
4	Stockholders' equity		60000	45000	100000	4
5	December 31, 2014					5
6	Assets		137000	200000		6
7	Liabilities	55000	75000		80000	7
8	Stockholders' equity	40000		130000	140000	8
9	Stockholders' equity					9
10	changes in year					10
11	Add'l investment		15000	10000	15000	11
12	Dividends	10000		14000	10000	12
13	Total revenues	350000	420000		500000	13
14	Total expenses	330000	385000	342000		14
15						15

(b)

Stills Company
Retained Earnings Statement
For the Year Ended December 31, 2014

1			1
2			2
3			3
4			4
5			5
6			6
7			7
8			8
9			9
10			10

(c)

11		11
12		12
13		13
14		14
15		15
16		16
17		17
18		18
19		19
20		20

Problem 1-1B

Holiday Travel Agency

You will find this working paper at the end of this work book

(a) (Continued)

Key to Retained Earnings Column:

1		1
2		2
3		3
4		4
5		5
6		6
7		7
8	(b)	8
9		9
10		10
11		11
12		12
13		13
14		14
15		15
16		16
17		17
18		18
19		19
20		20

Problem 1-2B

Mandy Arnold, Attorney at Law

You will find this working paper at the end of this work book

(a) (Continued)

Key to changes in Retained Earnings column:

1	1
2	2
3	3
4	4
5	5
6	6

(b)

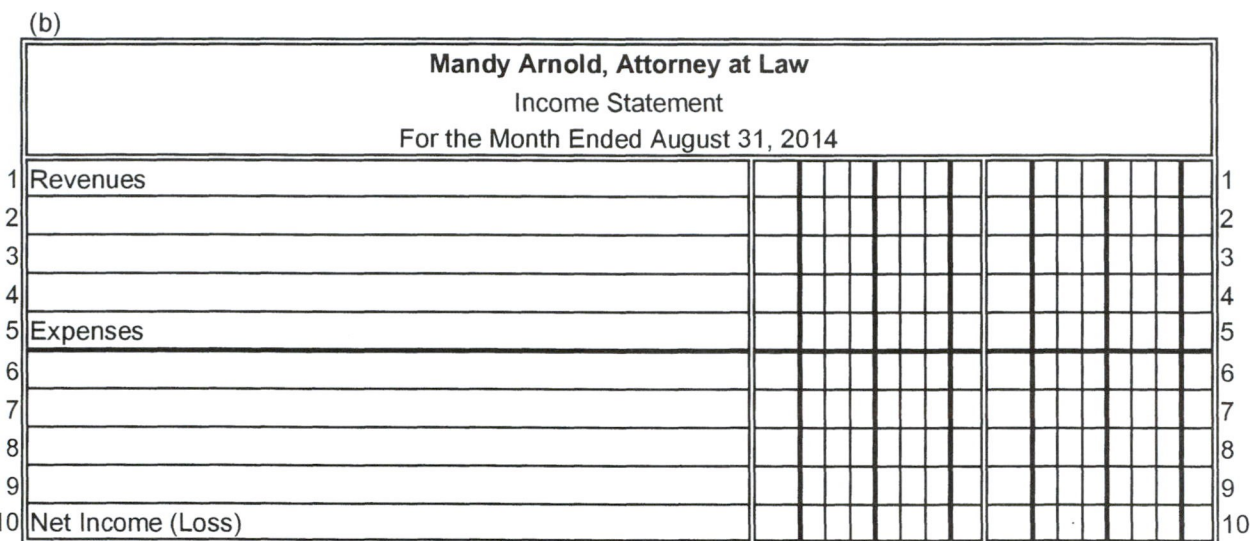

Mandy Arnold, Attorney at Law
Income Statement
For the Month Ended August 31, 2014

1 Revenues		1
2		2
3		3
4		4
5 Expenses		5
6		6
7		7
8		8
9		9
10 Net Income (Loss)		10

Mandy Arnold, Attorney at Law
Retained Earnings Statement
For the Month Ended August 31, 2014

1		1
2		2
3		3
4		4
5		5
6		6

(b) (Continued)

	Mandy Arnold, Attorney at Law		
	Balance Sheet		
	August 31, 2014		
Assets			
Liabilities and Stockholders' Equity			

(a)

Angelic Cosmetics Co.
Income Statement
For the Month Ended June 30, 2014

1 Revenues			1
2			2
3			3
4			4
5 Expenses			5
6			6
7			7
8			8
9			9
10			10
11			11
12			12
13			13
14 Net Income (Loss)			14
15			15
16			16
17			17
18			18
19			19
20			20

Angelic Cosmetics Co.
Retained Earnings Statement
For the Month Ended June 30, 2014

1		1
2		2
3		3
4		4
5		5
6		6
7		7
8		8
9		9
10		10

(a) Continued

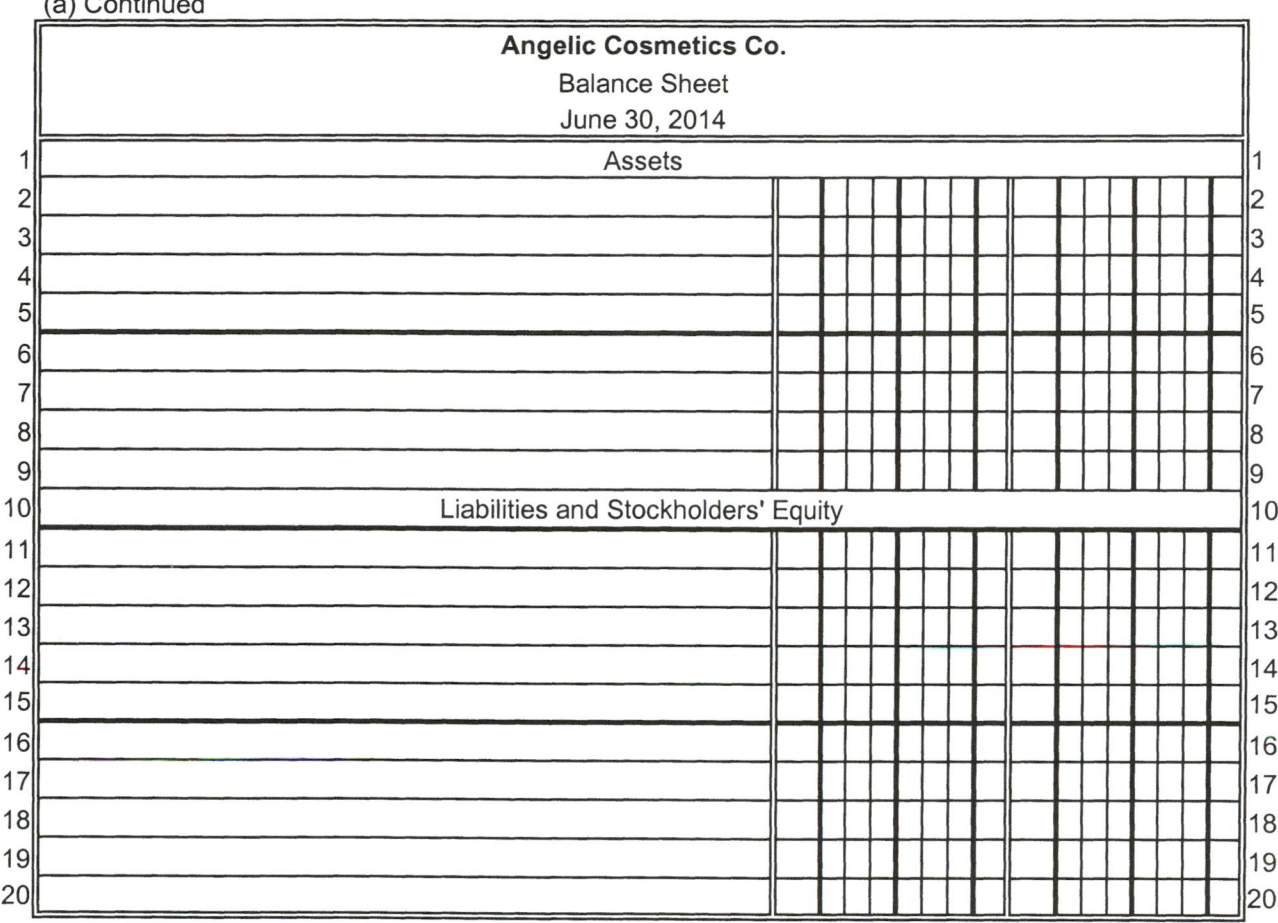

Angelic Cosmetics Co.

Balance Sheet

June 30, 2014

	Assets						
1							1
2							2
3							3
4							4
5							5
6							6
7							7
8							8
9							9
10	Liabilities and Stockholders' Equity						10
11							11
12							12
13							13
14							14
15							15
16							16
17							17
18							18
19							19
20							20

(b)

Angelic Cosmetics Co.

Income Statement

For the Month Ended June 30, 2014

1	Revenues						1
2							2
3							3
4	Expenses						4
5							5
6							6
7							7
8							8
9							9
10							10
11							11
12	Net Income (Loss)						12
13							13
14							14
15							15

(b) Concluded

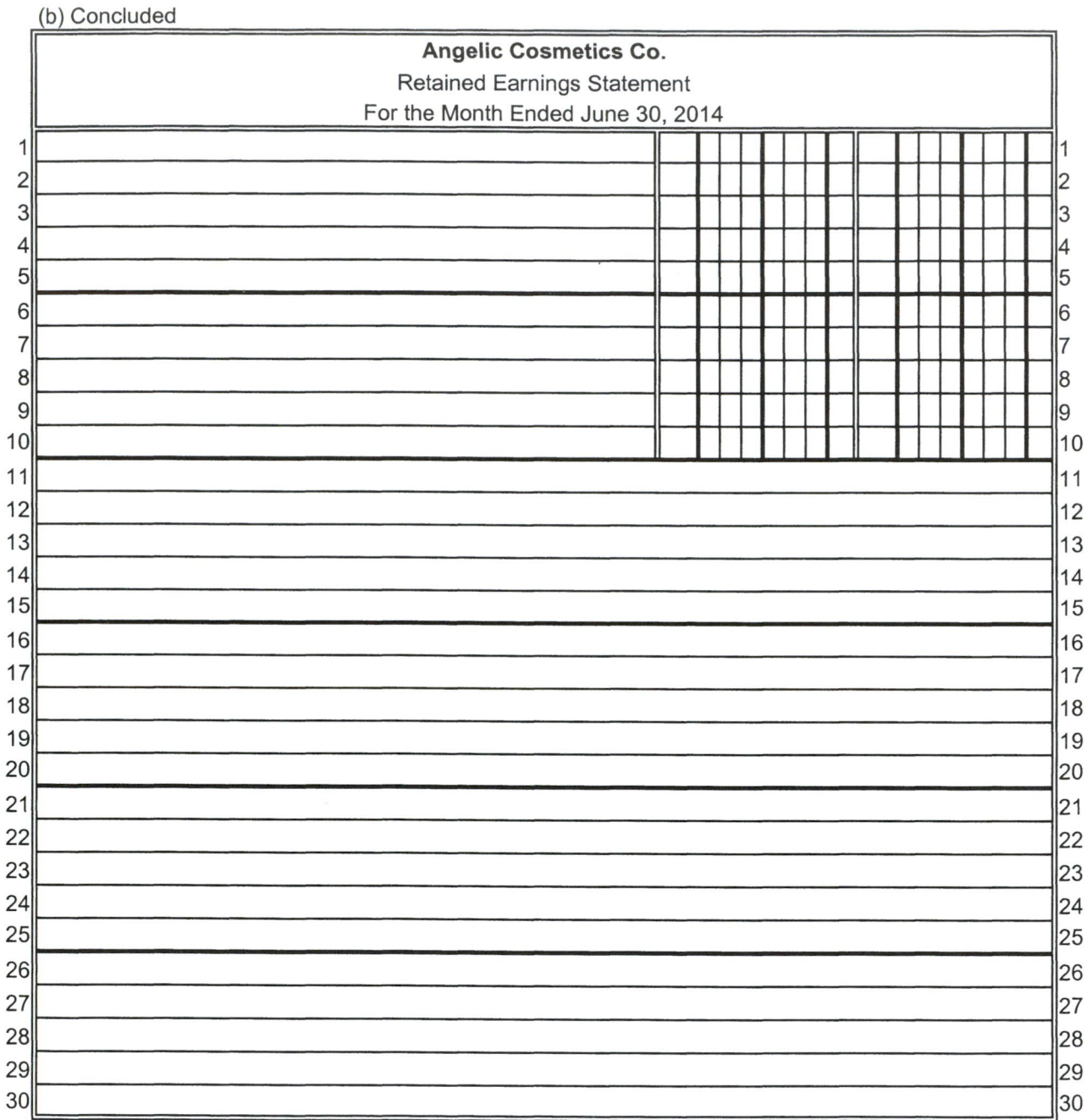

Angelic Cosmetics Co.
Retained Earnings Statement
For the Month Ended June 30, 2014

Problem 1-4B

Paulis Consulting

You will find this working paper at the end of this work book

(a) (Continued)

Key to Retained Earnings Column

1	1
2	2
3	3
4	4

(b)

Paulis Consulting

Income Statement

For the Month Ended May 31, 2014

1	Revenues		1
2			2
3			3
4	Expenses		4
5			5
6			6
7			7
8			8
9			9
10	Net income (loss)		10

(c)

Paulis Consulting

Balance Sheet

May 31, 2014

1	Assets		1
2			2
3			3
4			4
5			5
6			6
7			7
8	Liabilities and Stockholders' Equity		8
9			9
10			10
11			11
12			12
13			13
14			14
15			15
16			16

(a)

	John Company	Paul Company	George Company	Ringo Company	
1 January 1, 2014					1
2 Assets	$ 70 000	$ 90 000		$ 150 000	2
3 Liabilities	50 000		75 000		3
4 Stockholders' equity		50 000	54 000	100 000	4
5 December 31, 2014					5
6 Assets		117 000	180 000		6
7 Liabilities	55 000	79 000		80 000	7
8 Stockholders' equity	40 000		100 000	145 000	8
9 Stockholders' equity					9
10 changes in year					10
11 Add'l investment		8 000	10 000	15 000	11
12 Dividends	10 000		12 000	10 000	12
13 Total revenues	350 000	390 000		500 000	13
14 Total expenses	335 000	400 000	360 000		14
15					15

(b)

John Company	
Retained Earnings Statement	
For the Year Ended December 31, 2014	
1		1
2		2
3		3
4		4
5		5
6		6
7		7
8		8
9		9
10		10

11 (c)	11
12	12
13	13
14	14
15	15
16	16
17	17
18	18
19	19
20	20

1	(a)	1
2		2
3		3
4		4
5		5
6	(b)	6
7		7
8		8
9		9
10		10
11	(c)	11
12		12
13		13
14		14
15		15
16	(d) Net sales - 2008:	16
17		17
18	2009:	18
19		19
20	2010:	20
21		21
22		22
23		23
24		24
25		25
26	(e)	26
27		27
28		28
29		29
30		30
31		31
32		32
33		33
34		34
35		35
36		36
37		37
38		38
39		39
40		40

	PepsiCo	Coca-Cola
(a) (in millions)		
1. Total assets		
2. Accounts receivable (net)		
3. Net sales		
4. Net income		

(b)

(a)

1	1
2	2
3	3
4	4
5	5

(b)

Chip-Shot Driving Range Company

Balance Sheet

March 31, 2014

	Assets		
1			1
2			2
3			3
4			4
5			5
6			6
7			7
8			8
9			9
10			10
11	Liabilities and Stockholders' Equity		11
12			12
13			13
14			14
15			15
16			16
17			17
18			18
19			19
20			20
21			21
22			22
23			23
24			24
25			25
26			26
27			27
28			28
29			29
30			30

	(c)	
1		1
2		2
3		3
4		4
5		5
6		6
7		7
8		8
9		9
10		10
11		11
12		12
13		13
14		14
15	(d)	15
16		16
17		17
18		18
19		19
20		20
21		21
22		22
23		23
24		24
25		25
26		26
27		27
28		28
29		29
30		30
31		31
32		32
33		33
34		34
35		35
36		36
37		37
38		38
39		39
40		40

1	1
2	2
3	3
4	4
5	5
6	6
7	7
8	8
9	9
10	10
11	11
12	12
13	13
14	14
15	15
16	16
17	17
18	18
19	19
20	20
21	21
22	22
23	23
24	24
25	25
26	26
27	27
28	28
29	29
30	30
31	31
32	32
33	33
34	34
35	35
36	36
37	37
38	38
39	39
40	40

New York Company
Balance Sheet
December 31, 2014

	Assets						
1							1
2							2
3							3
4							4
5							5
6							6
7							7
8							8
9	Liabilities and Stockholders' Equity						9
10							10
11							11
12							12
13							13
14							14
15							15
16							16
17							17
18							18
19							19
20							20
21							21
22							22
23							23
24							24
25							25
26							26
27							27
28							28
29							29
30							30
31							31
32							32
33							33
34							34
35							35
36							36
37							37
38							38
39							39
40							40

BE2-3

		Account Titles	Debit	Credit	
1	June 1				1
2					2
3					3
4	2				4
5					5
6					6
7	3				7
8					8
9					9
10	12				10
11					11
12					12

BE2-6

	Date	Account Titles	Debit	Credit	
14					14
15	Aug. 1				15
16					16
17					17
18	4				18
19					19
20					20
21	16				21
22					22
23					23
24	27				24
25					25
26					26
27					27
28					28
29					29
30					30
31					31
32					32
33					33
34					34
35					35
36					36
37					37
38					38
39					39
40					40

BE2-7

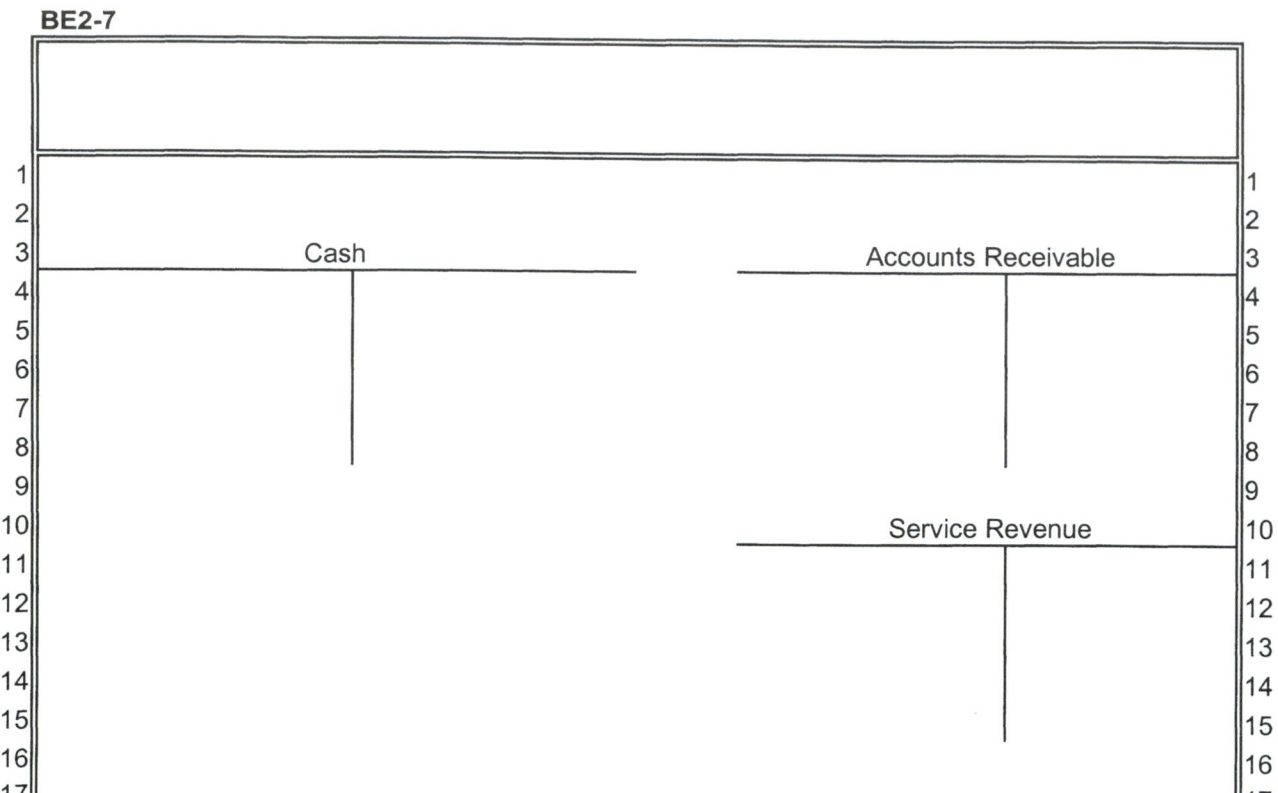

BE2-8

Cash

Date	Explanation	Ref	Debit	Credit	Balance

Accounts Receivable

Date	Explanation	Ref	Debit	Credit	Balance

Service Revenue

Date	Explanation	Ref	Debit	Credit	Balance

BE2-9

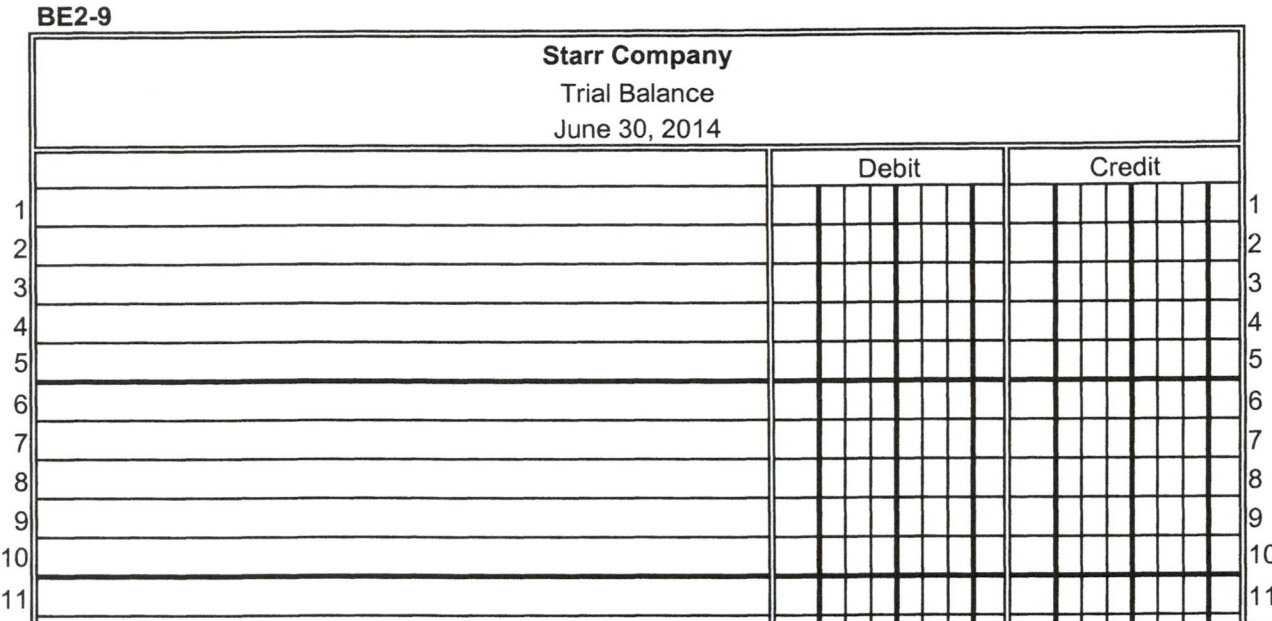

Starr Company Trial Balance June 30, 2014	Debit	Credit
1		
2		
3		
4		
5		
6		
7		
8		
9		
10		
11		
12		

BE2-10

Cheng Company Trial Balance December 31, 2014	Debit	Credit
1		
2		
3		
4		
5		
6		
7		
8		
9		
10		
11		

DO IT! 2-2

	Activity	Account Titles	Debit	Credit	
1					1
2					2
3					3
4					4
5					5
6					6
7					7
8					8
9					9
10					10

DO IT! 2-3

Cash

11	11
12	12
13	13
14	14
15	15
16	16
17	17
18	18
19	19
20	20
21	21
22	22
23	23
24	24
25	25

		Debit	Credit
Chillin' Company			
Trial Balance			
December 31, 2014			
1			
2			
3			
4			
5			
6			
7			
8			
9			
10			
11			
12			
13			
14			
15			
16			
17			
18			
19			
20			
21			
22			
23			
24			
25			
26			
27			
28			
29			
30			
31			
32			
33			
34			
35			
36			
37			
38			
39			
40			

General Journal   J1

	Date	Account Titles	Ref.	Debit	Credit	
1	Jan. 2					1
2						2
3						3
4	3					4
5						5
6						6
7	9					7
8						8
9						9
10	11					10
11						11
12						12
13	16					13
14						14
15						15
16	20					16
17						17
18						18
19	23					19
20						20
21						21
22	28					22
23						23
24						24

E2-5

	Date	Account Titles	Ref.	Debit	Credit	
1	Oct. 1					1
2						2
3						3
4	2					4
5						5
6	3					6
7						7
8						8
9	6					9
10						10
11						11
12	27					12
13						13
14						14
15	30					15
16						16
17						17

E2-6

	(a)					
1	1.					1
2						2
3	2.					3
4						4
5	3.					5
6						6
7	(b)	Account Titles		Debit	Credit	7
8	1.					8
9						9
10						10
11	2.					11
12						12
13						13
14	3.					14
15						15
16						16
17						17
18						18

	(a)		Assets =	Liabilities +	Owners' Equity	
1	1.					1
2						2
3	2.					3
4						4
5	3.					5
6						6
7	4.					7
8						8
9						9
10	(b)	Account Titles		Debit	Credit	10
11	1.					11
12						12
13						13
14	2.					14
15						15
16						16
17	3.					17
18						18
19						19
20	4.					20
21						21
22						22
23						23

(a)

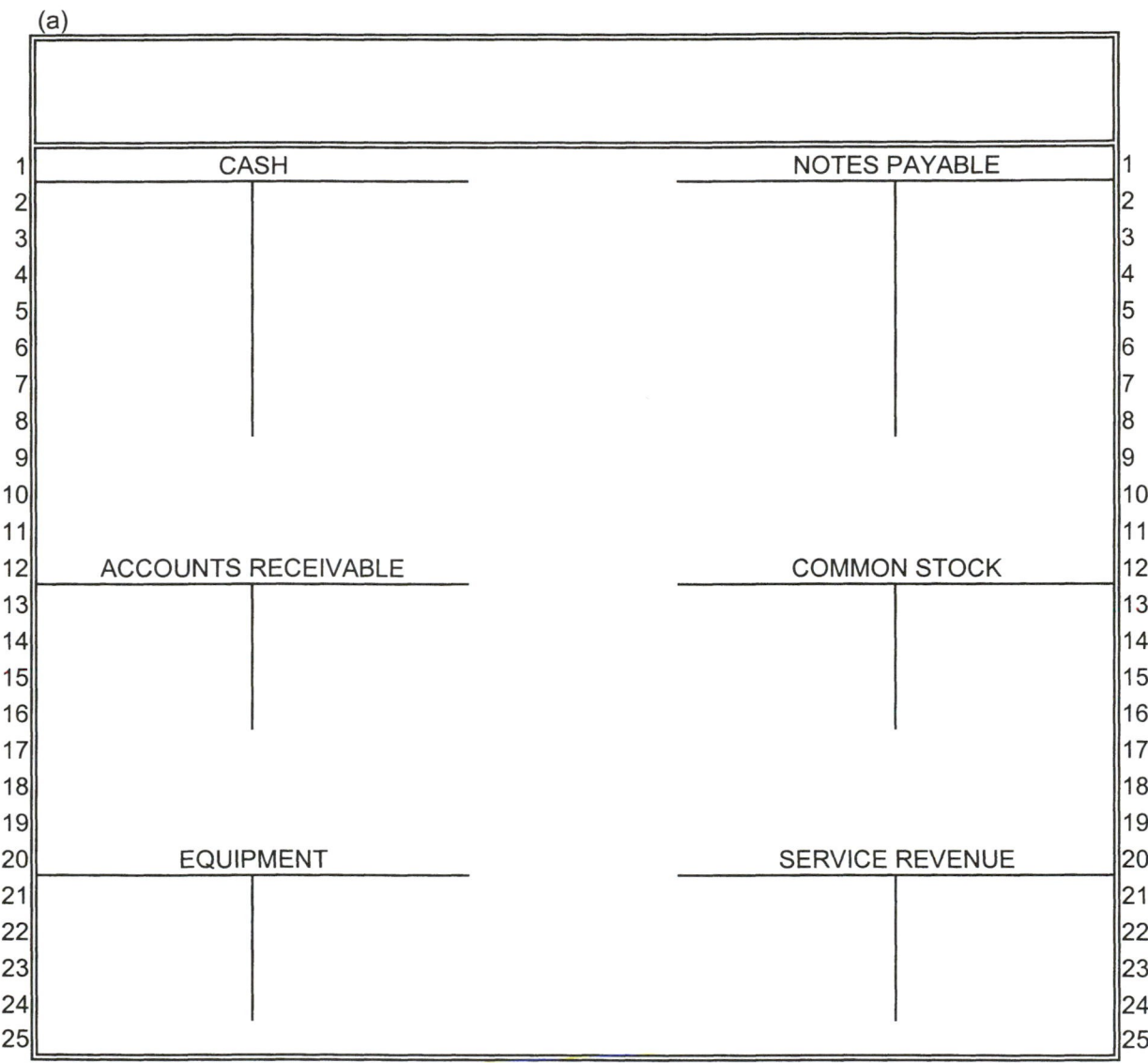

CASH	NOTES PAYABLE
ACCOUNTS RECEIVABLE	COMMON STOCK
EQUIPMENT	SERVICE REVENUE

(b)

Roberta Mendez, Investment Broker
Trial Balance
August 31, 2014

	Debit	Credit
1		
2		
3		
4		
5		
6		
7		
8		
9		
10		

(a)   General Journal

	Date	Account Titles	Ref.	Debit	Credit	
1	Apr. 1					1
2						2
3						3
4						4
5	12					5
6						6
7						7
8						8
9	15					9
10						10
11						11
12						12
13	25					13
14						14
15						15
16						16
17	29					17
18						18
19						19
20						20
21	30					21
22						22
23						23
24						24
25						25
26						26

(b)

Padre Landscaping Company
Trial Balance
April 30, 2014

		Debit	Credit	
1				1
2				2
3				3
4				4
5				5
6				6
7				7
8				8
9				9

(a) General Journal

	Date	Account Titles	Debit	Credit	
1	Oct. 1				1
2					2
3					3
4					4
5	10				5
6					6
7					7
8					8
9	10				9
10					10
11					11
12					12
13	20				13
14					14
15					15
16					16
17	20				17
18					18
19					19
20					20

(b)

Sparks Co.
Trial Balance
October 31, 2014

		Debit	Credit	
1				1
2				2
3				3
4				4
5				5
6				6
7				7
8				8
9				9
10				10
11				11
12				12
13				13

(a)   General Journal   J1

	Date	Account Titles	Ref.	Debit	Credit	
1	Sept. 1					1
2						2
3						3
4	5					4
5						5
6						6
7						7
8	25					8
9						9
10						10
11	30					11
12						12

(b)

Cash   No. 101

Date	Explanation	Ref.	Debit	Credit	Balance

Equipment   No. 157

Date	Explanation	Ref.	Debit	Credit	Balance

Accounts Payable   No. 201

Date	Explanation	Ref.	Debit	Credit	Balance

Common Stock   No. 311

Date	Explanation	Ref.	Debit	Credit	Balance

Dividends   No. 332

Date	Explanation	Ref.	Debit	Credit	Balance

Tempus Fugit Delivery Service Trial Balance July 31, 2014	Debit	Credit
1		
2		
3		
4		
5		
6		
7		
8		
9		
10		
11		
12		
13		
14		
15		
16		
17		

General Journal   J1

	Date	Account Titles	Ref.	Debit	Credit	
1	Apr. 1					1
2						2
3						3
4						4
5	4					5
6						6
7						7
8						8
9	8					9
10						10
11						11
12						12
13	11					13
14						14
15						15
16						16
17	12					17
18						18
19	13					19
20						20
21						21
22						22
23	17					23
24						24
25						25
26						26
27	20					27
28						28
29						29
30						30
31	25					31
32						32
33						33
34						34
35	30					35
36						36
37						37
38						38
39	30					39
40						40
41						41

(a)   General Journal   J1

	Date	Account Titles	Ref.	Debit	Credit	
1	May 1					1
2						2
3						3
4						4
5	2					5
6						6
7	3					7
8						8
9						9
10						10
11	7					11
12						12
13						13
14						14
15	11					15
16						16
17						17
18						18
19	12					19
20						20
21						21
22						22
23	17					23
24						24
25						25
26						26
27	31					27
28						28
29						29
30						30
31	31					31
32						32
33						33
34						34
35						35
36						36
37						37
38						38
39						39
40						40

(b)

Cash

No. 101

Date	Explanation	Ref.	Debit	Credit	Balance

Accounts Receivable

No. 112

Date	Explanation	Ref.	Debit	Credit	Balance

Supplies

No. 126

Date	Explanation	Ref.	Debit	Credit	Balance

Accounts Payable

No. 201

Date	Explanation	Ref.	Debit	Credit	Balance

Unearned Service Revenue

No. 209

Date	Explanation	Ref.	Debit	Credit	Balance

Common Stock

No. 311

Date	Explanation	Ref.	Debit	Credit	Balance

(b) (Continued)

Service Revenue   No. 400

Date	Explanation	Ref.	Debit	Credit	Balance

Salaries and Wages Expense   No. 726

Date	Explanation	Ref.	Debit	Credit	Balance

Rent Expense   No. 729

Date	Explanation	Ref.	Debit	Credit	Balance

(c)

Kara Shin, Inc. Trial Balance May 31, 2014		
	Debit	Credit
1 Cash		
2 Accounts Receivable		
3 Supplies		
4 Accounts Payable		
5 Unearned Service Revenue		
6 Common Stock		
7 Service Revenue		
8 Salaries and Wages Expense		
9 Rent Expense		
10		
11		

(a) & (c)

Cash				Common Stock	
Bal.	8,000			Bal.	30,000
				Retained Earnings	
				Bal.	11,000
Accounts Receivable				Dividends	
Bal.	15,000				
Supplies				Service Revenue	
Bal.	13,000				
Prepaid Rent				Advertising Expense	
Bal.	3,000				
Equipment				Miscellaneous Expense	
Bal.	21,000				
				Salaries and Wages Expense	
Accounts Payable					
		Bal.	19,000		

(b)   General Journal   J1

Date	Account Titles	Debit	Credit
1.			
2.			
3.			
4.			
5.			
6.			
7.			
8.			
9.			

(d)

	Byte Repair Service, Inc. Trial Balance January 31, 2014	Debit	Credit	
1	Cash			1
2	Accounts Receivable			2
3	Supplies			3
4	Prepaid Rent			4
5	Equipment			5
6	Accounts Payable			6
7	Common Stock			7
8	Retained Earnings			8
9	Dividends			9
10	Service Revenue			10
11	Advertising Expense			11
12	Miscellaneous Expense			12
13	Salaries and Wages Expense			13
14	Totals			14
15				15
16				16
17				17
18				18

	Garland Company				
	Trial Balance				
	May 31, 2014				
		Debit		Credit	
1					
2					
3					
4					
5					
6					
7					
8					
9					
10					
11					
12					
13					
14					
15					
16	Journal Entry Aids:				
17					
18					
19					
20					
21					
22					
23					
24					
25					
26					
27					
28					
29					
30					
31					
32					
33					
34					
35					
36					
37					
38					
39					
40					

(a) and (c)

Cash   No. 101

Date	Explanation	Ref.	Debit	Credit	Balance
Apr. 1	Balance	√			6 0 0 0

Accounts Receivable   No. 112

Date	Explanation	Ref.	Debit	Credit	Balance

Prepaid Rentals   No. 136

Date	Explanation	Ref.	Debit	Credit	Balance

Land   No. 140

Date	Explanation	Ref.	Debit	Credit	Balance
Apr. 1	Balance	√			1 0 0 0 0

Buildings   No. 145

Date	Explanation	Ref.	Debit	Credit	Balance
Apr. 1	Balance	√			8 0 0 0

Equipment   No. 157

Date	Explanation	Ref.	Debit	Credit	Balance
Apr. 1	Balance	√			6 0 0 0

Accounts Payable   No. 201

Date	Explanation	Ref.	Debit	Credit	Balance
Apr. 1	Balance	√			2 0 0 0

(a) and (c) (Continued)

Mortgage Payable   No. 275

Date	Explanation	Ref.	Debit	Credit	Balance
Apr. 1	Balance	√			8 0 0 0

Common Stock   No. 311

Date	Explanation	Ref.	Debit	Credit	Balance
Apr. 1	Balance	√			2 0 0 0 0

Service Revenue   No. 405

Date	Explanation	Ref.	Debit	Credit	Balance

Rent Revenue   No. 406

Date	Explanation	Ref.	Debit	Credit	Balance

Advertising Expense   No. 610

Date	Explanation	Ref.	Debit	Credit	Balance

Salaries and Wages Expense   No. 726

Date	Explanation	Ref.	Debit	Credit	Balance

Rent Expense   No. 729

Date	Explanation	Ref.	Debit	Credit	Balance

(b)   General Journal   J1

	Date	Account Titles	Ref.	Debit	Credit	
1	Apr. 2					1
2						2
3						3
4						4
5	3					5
6						6
7	9					7
8						8
9						9
10						10
11	10					11
12						12
13						13
14						14
15						15
16						16
17	11					17
18						18
19	12					19
20						20
21						21
22						22
23	20					23
24						24
25						25
26						26
27	25					27
28						28
29						29
30						30
31	29					31
32						32
33						33
34						34
35	30					35
36						36
37						37
38						38
39	30					39
40						40
41						41

(d)

Classic Theater Trial Balance April 30, 2014	Debit	Credit	
1 Cash			1
2 Accounts Receivable			2
3 Prepaid Rentals			3
4 Land			4
5 Buildings			5
6 Equipment			6
7 Accounts Payable			7
8 Mortgage Payable			8
9 Common Stock			9
10 Service Revenue			10
11 Rent Revenue			11
12 Advertising Expense			12
13 Salaries and Wages Expense			13
14 Rent Expense			14
15 Totals			15
16			16
17			17

General Journal J1

	Date	Account Titles	Ref.	Debit	Credit	
1	Mar. 1					1
2						2
3						3
4						4
5	3					5
6						6
7						7
8						8
9						9
10						10
11	5					11
12						12
13						13
14						14
15	6					15
16						16
17						17
18						18
19	10					19
20						20
21						21
22						22
23	18					23
24						24
25						25
26						26
27	19					27
28						28
29						29
30						30
31	25					31
32						32
33						33
34						34
35	30					35
36						36
37						37
38						38
39						39
40						40

General Journal   J1

	Date	Account Titles	Ref.	Debit	Credit	
1	Mar. 30					1
2						2
3						3
4						4
5	31					5
6						6
7						7
8						8
9						9
10						10
11						11
12						12
13						13
14						14
15						15
16						16
17						17
18						18
19						19
20						20
21						21
22						22
23						23
24						24
25						25
26						26
27						27
28						28
29						29
30						30
31						31
32						32
33						33
34						34
35						35
36						36
37						37
38						38
39						39
40						40

(a)   General Journal   J1

	Date	Account Titles	Ref.	Debit	Credit	
1	Apr. 1					1
2						2
3						3
4						4
5	1					5
6						6
7	2					7
8						8
9						9
10						10
11	3					11
12						12
13						13
14						14
15						15
16	10					16
17						17
18						18
19						19
20	11					20
21						21
22						22
23						23
24	20					24
25						25
26						26
27						27
28	30					28
29						29
30						30
31						31
32	30					32
33						33
34						34
35						35
36						36
37						37
38						38
39						39
40						40

(b)

Cash   No. 101

Date	Explanation	Ref.	Debit	Credit	Balance

Accounts Receivable   No. 112

Date	Explanation	Ref.	Debit	Credit	Balance

Supplies   No. 126

Date	Explanation	Ref.	Debit	Credit	Balance

Accounts Payable   No. 201

Date	Explanation	Ref.	Debit	Credit	Balance

Unearned Service Revenue   No. 209

Date	Explanation	Ref.	Debit	Credit	Balance

Common Stock   No. 311

Date	Explanation	Ref.	Debit	Credit	Balance

(b) (Continued)

Service Revenue   No. 400

Date	Explanation	Ref.	Debit	Credit	Balance

Salaries and Wages Expense   No. 726

Date	Explanation	Ref.	Debit	Credit	Balance

Rent Expense   No. 729

Date	Explanation	Ref.	Debit	Credit	Balance

(c)

Judi Dench, Dentist
Trial Balance
April 30, 2014

		Debit	Credit	
1	Cash			1
2	Accounts Receivable			2
3	Supplies			3
4	Accounts Payable			4
5	Unearned Service Revenue			5
6	Common Stock			6
7	Service Revenue			7
8	Salaries and Wages Expense			8
9	Rent Expense			9
10	Totals			10
11				11

(a)   General Journal

	Trans.	Account Titles	Debit	Credit	
1	1.				1
2					2
3					3
4	2.				4
5					5
6	3.				6
7					7
8					8
9	4.				9
10					10
11					11
12					12
13	5.				13
14					14
15					15
16	6.				16
17					17
18					18
19	7.				19
20					20
21					21
22	8.				22
23					23
24					24
25					25
26	9.				26
27					27
28					28
29	10.				29
30					30
31					31
32	11.				32
33					33
34					34
35	12.				35
36					36
37					37
38					38
39					39
40					40

(b)

Cash		Accounts Payable

Accounts Receivable		Common Stock

Supplies		Service Revenue

Prepaid Insurance		Salaries and Wages Expense

Prepaid Rent		Utilities Expense

Equipment		

(c)

Chamberlain Services Trial Balance May 31, 2014	Debit	Credit	
1 Cash			1
2 Accounts Receivable			2
3 Supplies			3
4 Prepaid Insurance			4
5 Prepaid Rent			5
6 Equipment			6
7 Accounts Payable			7
8 Common Stock			8
9 Service Revenue			9
10 Salaries and Wages Expense			10
11 Utilities Expense			11
12 Totals			12

Ron Salem Co. Trial Balance June 30, 2014	Debit	Credit
1		
2		
3		
4		
5		
6		
7		
8		
9		
10		
11		
12		
13		
14		
15		
16 Journal Entry Aids:		
17		
18		
19		
20		
21		
22		
23		
24		
25		
26		
27		
28		
29		
30		
31		
32		
33		
34		
35		
36		
37		
38		
39		
40		

(a) and (c)

Cash   No. 101

Date	Explanation	Ref.	Debit	Credit	Balance
Mar. 1	Balance	√			8 0 0 0

Accounts Receivable   No. 112

Date	Explanation	Ref.	Debit	Credit	Balance

Land   No. 140

Date	Explanation	Ref.	Debit	Credit	Balance
Mar. 1	Balance	√			2 1 0 0 0

Buildings   No. 145

Date	Explanation	Ref.	Debit	Credit	Balance
Mar. 1	Balance	√			1 0 0 0 0

Equipment   No. 157

Date	Explanation	Ref.	Debit	Credit	Balance
Mar. 1	Balance	√			8 0 0 0

Accounts Payable   No. 201

Date	Explanation	Ref.	Debit	Credit	Balance
Mar. 1	Balance	√			7 0 0 0

Common Stock   No. 311

Date	Explanation	Ref.	Debit	Credit	Balance
Mar. 1	Balance	√			4 0 0 0 0

(a) and (c) (Continued)

Service Revenue   No. 405

Date	Explanation	Ref.	Debit	Credit	Balance

Rent Revenue   No. 406

Date	Explanation	Ref.	Debit	Credit	Balance

Advertising Expense   No. 610

Date	Explanation	Ref.	Debit	Credit	Balance

Salaries and Wages Expense   No. 727

Date	Explanation	Ref.	Debit	Credit	Balance

Rent Expense   No. 729

Date	Explanation	Ref.	Debit	Credit	Balance

(b)

General Journal

J1

	Date	Account Titles	Ref.	Debit	Credit	
1	Mar. 2					1
2						2
3						3
4						4
5						5
6	3					6
7						7
8	9					8
9						9
10						10
11						11
12	10					12
13						13
14						14
15						15
16	11					16
17						17
18	12					18
19						19
20						20
21						21
22	20					22
23						23
24						24
25						25
26	20					26
27						27
28						28
29						29
30	31					30
31						31
32						32
33						33
34						34
35						35
36						36
37						37
38						38
39						39
40						40

(b) (Cont)   General Journal   J1

	Date	Account Titles	Ref.	Debit	Credit	
1	Mar. 31					1
2						2
3						3
4						4
5						5
6						6
7	31					7
8						8
9						9
10						10
11						11
12						12
13						13
14						14
15						15
16						16

(d)

Russo Theater
Trial Balance
March 31, 2014

		Debit	Credit	
1	Cash			1
2	Accounts Receivable			2
3	Land			3
4	Buildings			4
5	Equipment			5
6	Accounts Payable			6
7	Common Stock			7
8	Service Revenue			8
9	Rent Revenue			9
10	Advertising Expense			10
11	Salaries and Wages Expense			11
12	Rent Expense			12
13	Totals			13
14				14
15				15
16				16
17				17

(a)

	Date	Account Titles	Debit	Credit	
1	May 1				1
2					2
3					3
4	5				4
5					5
6					6
7	7				7
8					8
9					9
10	14				10
11					11
12					12
13	15				13
14					14
15					15
16	20				16
17					17
18					18
19	30				19
20					20
21					21
22	31				22
23					23
24					24
25					25

(b)

1		1
2		2
3		3
4		4
5		5

(c)

	1									1	
1											2
2											3
3											4
4											5
5											6
6											7
7											8
8											9
9											10
10											

(d)

	1									1	
1											2
2											3
3											4
4											5
5											6
6											7
7											8
8											9
9											10
10											

BE3-3

	Date	Account Titles	Debit	Credit	
1	Dec. 31				1
2					2
3					3
4					4
5					5
6		Supplies	Supplies Expense		6
7					7
8					8
9					9
10					10

BE3-4

	Date	Account Titles	Debit	Credit	
11					11
12	Date	Account Titles	Debit	Credit	12
13	Dec. 31				13
14					14
15					15
16					16
17		Depreciation Expense	Accum. Depreciation - Equipment		17
18					18
19					19
20					20
21					21
22	Balance Sheet:				22
23					23
24					24
25					25
26					26

BE3-5

	Date	Account Titles	Debit	Credit	
27					27
28	Date	Account Titles	Debit	Credit	28
29	July 1				29
30					30
31					31
32	Dec. 31				32
33					33
34					34
35					35
36		Prepaid Insurance	Insurance Expense		36
37					37
38					38
39					39
40					40

BE3-6

	Date	Account Titles	Debit	Credit	
1	July 1				1
2					2
3					3
4					4
5	Dec. 31				5
6					6
7					7
8					8
9					9
10					10

11	Unearned Service Revenue	Service Revenue
12		
13		
14		
15		

BE3-7

	Date	Account Titles	Debit	Credit	
17	Date	Account Titles	Debit	Credit	17
18	Dec. 31				18
19					19
20					20
21	31				21
22					22
23					23
24	31				24
25					25
26					26
27					27
28					28
29					29
30					30
31					31
32					32
33					33
34					34
35					35
36					36
37					37
38					38
39					39
40					40

BE3-9

	Lopez Company				
	Income Statement				
	For the Year Ended December 31, 2014				
1				1
2				2
3				3
4				4
5				5
6				6
7				7
8				8
9				9
10				10
11				11
12				12
13				13
14				14

BE3-10

	Lopez Company				
	Retained Earnings Statement				
	For the Year Ended December 31, 2014				
19				19
20				20
21				21
22				22
23				23
24				24
25				25

*BE3-11

	Date	Account Titles	Debit	Credit	
28	(a)				28
29	Apr. 30				29
30					30
31					31
32					32
33	(b)				33
34	Apr. 30				34
35					35
36					36
37					37
38					38
39					39
40					40

DO IT! 3-2

Trans	Account Titles	Debit	Credit
1.			
2.			
3.			
4.			

DO IT! 3-3

Trans	Account Titles	Debit	Credit
1.			
2.			
3.			

(a)

Net income is computed as follows:

1				1
2				2
3				3
4				4
5				5
6				6
7				7
8				8
9				9
10				10
11				11
12				12
13				13
14				14
15				15
16				16

(b)   Total assets and liabilities are computed as follows:

Assets:

18	Assets:			18
19				19
20				20
21				21
22				22
23				23
24				24
25				25
26				26

Liabilities:

28				28
29				29
30				30
31				31
32				32
33				33
34				34
35				35

(c)

36			36
37			37
38			38
39			39
40			40

E3-3

E3-7

	Date	Account Titles	Debit	Credit	
1	Mar. 31				1
2					2
3					3
4					4
5	31				5
6					6
7					7
8	31				8
9					9
10					10
11	31				11
12					12
13					13
14	31				14
15					15
16					16

Item	Account Titles	Debit	Credit
1.			
2.			
3.			
4.			
5.			
6.			
7.			

E3-8

	Date	Account Titles	Debit	Credit	
1	Jan. 31				1
2					2
3					3
4	31				4
5					5
6					6
7	31				7
8					8
9					9
10	31				10
11					11
12					12
13	31				13
14					14
15					15
16	31				16
17					17

E3-9

	Date	Account Titles	Debit	Credit	
1	Oct. 31				1
2					2
3					3
4	31				4
5					5
6					6
7	31				7
8					8
9					9
10	31				10
11					11
12					12
13	31				13
14					14
15					15
16	31				16
17					17
18					18
19	31				19
20					20

E3-10

	Midland Co.						
	Income Statement						
	For the Month Ended July 31, 2014						
1	Revenues:						1
2							2
3	Expenses:						3
4							4
5							5
6							6
7							7
8							8
9							9
10							10

E3-11

	Answer	Computation		
1	(a)			1
2				2
3				3
4				4
5				5
6	(b)			6
7				7
8				8
9				9
10				10
11				11
12				12
13				13
14	(c)			14
15				15
16				16
17				17
18				18
19				19
20				20
21				21
22				22
23				23
24				24
25				25

	Date	Account Titles	Debit	Credit	
1	(a)				1
2	July 10				2
3					3
4					4
5	14				5
6					6
7					7
8	15				8
9					9
10					10
11	20				11
12					12
13					13
14					14
15					15
16	(b)				16
17	July 31				17
18					18
19					19
20	31				20
21					21
22					22
23	31				23
24					24
25					25
26	31				26
27					27
28					28
29					29
30					30
31					31
32					32
33					33
34					34
35					35
36					36
37					37
38					38
39					39
40					40

E3-13

	Date	Account Titles	Debit	Credit	
1	Aug. 31				1
2					2
3					3
4	31				4
5					5
6					6
7	31				7
8					8
9					9
10	31				10
11					11
12					12
13					13
14	31				14
15					15
16					16
17	31				17
18					18
19					19
20					20

E3-14

Matusiak Company

Income Statement

For the Year Ended August 31, 2014

1	Revenues:			1
2				2
3				3
4				4
5	Expenses:			5
6				6
7				7
8				8
9				9
10				10
11				11
12				12
13				13
14				14
15				15

Matusiak Company
Retained Earnings Statement
For the Year Ended August 31, 2014

1		1
2		2
3		3
4		4

Matusiak Company
Balance Sheet
August 31, 2014

	Assets		
1	Assets		1
2			2
3			3
4			4
5			5
6			6
7			7
8			8
9			9
10	Liabilities and Stockholders' Equity		10
11			11
12			12
13			13
14			14
15			15
16			16
17			17
18			18
19			19
20			20
21			21
22			22
23			23

	Account Titles	Debit	Credit	
1	(a)			1
2	1.			2
3				3
4				4
5	2.			5
6				6
7				7
8	3.			8
9				9
10				10
11				11
12				12
13				13
14				14
15	4.			15
16				16
17				17
18	5.			18
19				19
20				20
21				21
22	(b)			22
23				23
24				24
25				25
26				26
27				27
28				28
29				29
30				30
31				31
32				32
33				33
34				34
35				35
36				36
37				37
38				38
39				39
40				40

E3-16

1	(a)			1
2				2
3				3
4				4
5				5
6				6
7	(b)			7
8				8
9				9
10				10
11				11
12	(c)			12
13				13
14				14
15				15
16				16
17				17
18				18
19				19
20				20
21				21
22				22
23				23
24				24
25				25

*E3-17

		Account Titles	Debit	Credit	
1	1.				1
2					2
3					3
4	2.				4
5					5
6					6
7	3.				7
8					8
9					9
10					10

(a)

	Date	Account Titles	Debit	Credit	
1	Jan. 2				1
2					2
3					3
4	10				4
5					5
6					6
7	15				7
8					8
9					9

(b)

	Date	Account Titles	Debit	Credit	
11					11
12	Jan. 31				12
13					13
14					14
15	31				15
16					16
17					17
18	31				18
19					19

CASH

PREPAID INSURANCE   INSURANCE EXPENSE

SUPPLIES   SUPPLIES EXPENSE

UNEARNED SERVICE REVENUE   SERVICE REVENUE

(c)

1	Prepaid Insurance										1
2	Supplies										2
3	Unearned Service Revenue										3
4	Service Revenue										4
5	Insurance Expense										5
6	Supplies Expense										6
7											7
8											8
9											9
10											10

(a)   General Journal   J3

	Date	Account Titles	Ref.	Debit	Credit	
1	2014					1
2	June 30					2
3						3
4						4
5	30					5
6						6
7						7
8	30					8
9						9
10						10
11	30					11
12						12
13						13
14	30					14
15						15
16						16
17	30					17
18						18
19						19
20	30					20
21						21
22						22
23						23
24						24
25						25
26						26
27						27
28						28
29						29
30						30
31						31
32						32
33						33
34						34
35						35
36						36
37						37
38						38
39						39
40						40

(b)

Cash   No. 101

Date	Explanation	Ref.	Debit	Credit	Balance
2014					
June 30	Balance	√			6 2 0 0

Accounts Receivable   No. 112

Date	Explanation	Ref.	Debit	Credit	Balance
2014					
June 30	Balance	√			6 0 0 0

Supplies   No. 126

Date	Explanation	Ref.	Debit	Credit	Balance
2014					
June 30	Balance	√			2 0 0 0

Prepaid Insurance   No. 130

Date	Explanation	Ref.	Debit	Credit	Balance
2014					
June 30	Balance	√			3 0 0 0

Equipment   No. 157

Date	Explanation	Ref.	Debit	Credit	Balance
2014					
June 30	Balance	√			1 4 4 0 0

Accumulated Depreciation - Equipment   No, 158

Date	Explanation	Ref.	Debit	Credit	Balance

Accounts Payable   No. 201

Date	Explanation	Ref.	Debit	Credit	Balance
2014					
June 30	Balance	√			4 7 0 0

(b) (Continued)

Unearned Service Revenue   No. 209

Date	Explanation	Ref.	Debit	Credit	Balance
2014					
June 30	Balance	√			4 0 0 0

Salaries and Wages Payable   No. 212

Date	Explanation	Ref.	Debit	Credit	Balance

Common Stock   No. 311

Date	Explanation	Ref.	Debit	Credit	Balance
2014					
June 30	Balance	√			2 0 0 0 0

Service Revenue   No. 400

Date	Explanation	Ref.	Debit	Credit	Balance
2014					
June 30	Balance	√			7 9 0 0

Supplies Expense   No. 631

Date	Explanation	Ref.	Debit	Credit	Balance

Depreciation Expense   No. 711

Date	Explanation	Ref.	Debit	Credit	Balance

(b) (Continued)

Insurance Expense   No. 722

Date	Explanation	Ref.	Debit	Credit	Balance

Salaries and Wages Expense   No. 726

Date	Explanation	Ref.	Debit	Credit	Balance
2014					
June 30	Balance	√			4 0 0 0

Rent Expense   No. 729

Date	Explanation	Ref.	Debit	Credit	Balance
2014					
June 30	Balance	√			1 0 0 0

Utilities Expense   No. 732

Date	Explanation	Ref.	Debit	Credit	Balance

(c)

Cuono Company Adjusted Trial Balance June 30, 2014	Debit	Credit	
1	Cash			1
2	Accounts Receivable			2
3	Supplies			3
4	Prepaid Insurance			4
5	Equipment			5
6	Accumulated Depreciation - Equipment			6
7	Accounts Payable			7
8	Unearned Service Revenue			8
9	Salaries and Wages Payable			9
10	Common Stock			10
11	Service Revenue			11
12	Supplies Expense			12
13	Depreciation Expense			13
14	Insurance Expense			14
15	Salaries and Wages Expense			15
16	Rent Expense			16
17	Utilities Expense			17
18	Totals			18

(a)

General Journal   J1

	Date	Account Titles	Ref.	Debit	Credit	
1	Aug. 31					1
2						2
3						3
4	31					4
5						5
6						6
7	31					7
8						8
9						9
10	31					10
11						11
12						12
13	31					13
14						14
15						15
16	31					16
17						17
18						18
19	31					19
20						20
21						21
22	31					22
23						23
24						24
25						25
26						26

(b)

Cash   No. 101

Date	Explanation	Ref.	Debit	Credit	Balance
Aug. 31	Balance	√			1 9 6 0 0

Accounts Receivable   No. 112

Date	Explanation	Ref.	Debit	Credit	Balance

(b) (Continued)

Supplies — No. 126

Date	Explanation	Ref.	Debit	Credit	Balance
Aug. 31	Balance	√			3 3 0 0

Prepaid Insurance — No. 130

Date	Explanation	Ref.	Debit	Credit	Balance
Aug.31	Balance	√			6 0 0 0

Land — No. 140

Date	Explanation	Ref.	Debit	Credit	Balance
Aug.31	Balance	√			2 5 0 0 0

Buildings — No. 143

Date	Explanation	Ref.	Debit	Credit	Balance
Aug. 31	Balance	√			1 2 5 0 0 0

Accumulated Depreciation - Buildings — No. 144

Date	Explanation	Ref.	Debit	Credit	Balance

Equipment — No. 157

Date	Explanation	Ref.	Debit	Credit	Balance
Aug. 31	Balance	√			2 6 0 0 0

Accumulated Depreciation - Equipment — No. 158

Date	Explanation	Ref.	Debit	Credit	Balance

Accounts Payable — No. 201

Date	Explanation	Ref.	Debit	Credit	Balance
Aug. 31	Balance	√			6 5 0 0

Unearned Rent Revenue — No. 209

Date	Explanation	Ref.	Debit	Credit	Balance
Aug. 31	Balance	√			7 4 0 0

Salaries and Wages Payable — No. 212

Date	Explanation	Ref.	Debit	Credit	Balance

(b) (Continued)

Interest Payable   No. 230

Date	Explanation	Ref.	Debit	Credit	Balance

Mortgage Payable   No. 275

Date	Explanation	Ref.	Debit	Credit	Balance
Aug. 31	Balance	√			8 0 0 0 0

Common Stock   No. 311

Date	Explanation	Ref.	Debit	Credit	Balance
Aug. 31	Balance	√			1 0 0 0 0 0

Dividends   No. 332

Date	Explanation	Ref.	Debit	Credit	Balance
Aug. 31	Balance	√			5 0 0 0

Rent Revenue   No. 429

Date	Explanation	Ref.	Debit	Credit	Balance
Aug. 31	Balance	√			8 0 0 0 0

Maintenance and Repairs Expense   No. 622

Date	Explanation	Ref.	Debit	Credit	Balance

Supplies Expense   No. 631

Date	Explanation	Ref.	Debit	Credit	Balance

Depreciation Expense   No. 711

Date	Explanation	Ref.	Debit	Credit	Balance
Aug. 31	Balance	√			3 6 0 0

Interest Expense   No. 718

Date	Explanation	Ref.	Debit	Credit	Balance

Insurance Expense   No. 722

Date	Explanation	Ref.	Debit	Credit	Balance

(b) (Continued)

Salaries and Wages Expense   No. 726

Date	Explanation	Ref.	Debit	Credit	Balance
Aug. 31	Balance	√			5 1 0 0 0

Utilities Expense   No. 732

Date	Explanation	Ref.	Debit	Credit	Balance
Aug. 31	Balance	√			9 4 0 0

(c)

	Lazy River Resort, Inc. Adjusted Trial Balance August 31, 2014	Debit	Credit	
1	Cash			1
2	Accounts Receivable			2
3	Supplies			3
4	Prepaid Insurance			4
5	Land			5
6	Buildings			6
7	Accumulated Depreciation - Buildings			7
8	Equipment			8
9	Accumulated Depreciation - Equipment			9
10	Accounts Payable			10
11	Unearned Rent Revenue			11
12	Salaries and Wages Payable			12
13	Interest Payable			13
14	Mortgage Payable			14
15	Common Stock			15
16	Dividends			16
17	Rent Revenue			17
18	Maintenance and Repairs Expense			18
19	Supplies Expense			19
20	Depreciation Expense			20
21	Interest Expense			21
22	Insurance Expense			22
23	Salaries and Wages Expense			23
24	Utilities Expense			24
25	Totals			25
26				26

(d)

Lazy River Resort, Inc.

Income Statement

For the Three Months Ended August 31, 2014

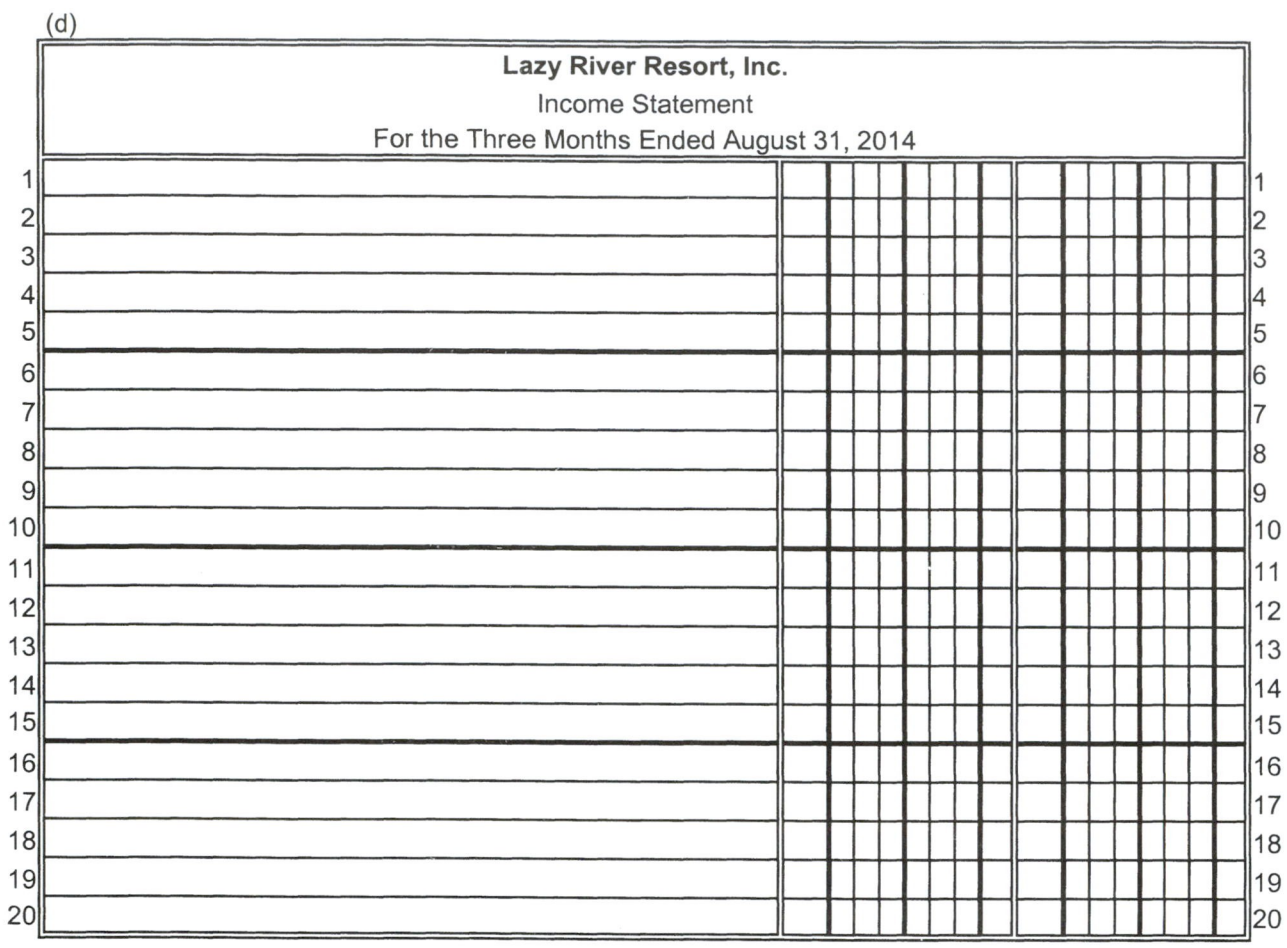

Lazy River Resort, Inc.

Retained Earnings Statement

For the Three Months Ended August 31, 2014

(d) (Continued)

Lazy River Resort, Inc.
Balance Sheet
August 31, 2014

	Assets					
1						
2						
3						
4						
5						
6						
7						
8						
9						
10						
11						
12						
13						
14						
15						
16	Liabilities and Stockholders' Equity					
17						
18						
19						
20						
21						
22						
23						
24						
25						
26						
27						
28						
29						
30						
31						
32						
33						
34						
35						
36						
37						
38						
39						
40						

(a)

	Date	Accounts Titles	Debit	Credit	
1	Dec. 31				1
2					2
3					3
4	31				4
5					5
6					6
7	31				7
8					8
9					9
10	31				10
11					11
12					12
13	31				13
14					14
15					15
16	31				16
17					17
18					18
19	31				19
20					20
21					21

(b)

Costello Advertising Agency, Inc.
Income Statement
For the Year Ended December 31, 2014

1				1
2				2
3				3
4				4
5				5
6				6
7				7
8				8
9				9
10				10
11				11
12				12
13				13
14				14

(b) (Continued)

Costello Advertising Agency, Inc.		
Retained Earnings Statement		
For the Year Ended December 31, 2014		

Costello Advertising Agency, Inc.		
Balance Sheet		
December 31, 2014		
Assets		
Liabilities and Stockholders' Equity		

(c)

(1)

(2)

General Journal

	Date	Accounts Titles	Debit	Credit	
1	1.				1
2	Dec. 31				2
3					3
4					4
5					5
6	2.				6
7	Dec. 31				7
8					8
9					9
10					10
11	3.				11
12	Dec. 31				12
13					13
14					14
15					15
16	4.				16
17	Dec. 31				17
18					18
19					19
20					20
21					21
22					22
23					23
24					24
25					25
26					26
27					27
28					28
29					29
30					30
31					31
32					32
33					33
34					34
35					35
36					36
37					37
38					38
39					39
40					40

(a), (c) and (e)

Cash   No. 101

Date	Explanation	Ref.	Debit	Credit	Balance
Sept. 1	Balance	√			4 8 8 0

Accounts Receivable   No. 112

Date	Explanation	Ref.	Debit	Credit	Balance
Sept. 1	Balance	√			3 5 2 0

Supplies   No. 126

Date	Explanation	Ref.	Debit	Credit	Balance
Sept. 1	Balance	√			2 0 0 0

Equipment   No. 153

Date	Explanation	Ref.	Debit	Credit	Balance
Sept. 1	Balance	√			1 8 0 0 0

Accumulated Depreciation - Equipment   No. 154

Date	Explanation	Ref.	Debit	Credit	Balance
Sept. 1	Balance	√			2 1 0 0

Accounts Payable   No. 201

Date	Explanation	Ref.	Debit	Credit	Balance
Sept. 1	Balance	√			3 4 0 0

(a), (c) and (e) (Continued)

Unearned Service Revenue   No. 209

Date	Explanation	Ref.	Debit	Credit	Balance
Sept. 1	Balance	√			1 4 0 0

Salaries and Wages Payable   No. 212

Date	Explanation	Ref.	Debit	Credit	Balance
Sept. 1	Balance	√			5 0 0

Common Stock   No. 311

Date	Explanation	Ref.	Debit	Credit	Balance
Sept. 1	Balance	√			1 0 0 0 0

Retained Earnings   No. 320

Date	Explanation	Ref.	Debit	Credit	Balance
Sept. 1	Balance	√			1 1 0 0 0

(a), (c) and (e) (Continued)

Service Revenue   No. 407

Date	Explanation	Ref.	Debit	Credit	Balance

Supplies Expense   No. 631

Date	Explanation	Ref.	Debit	Credit	Balance

Depreciation Expense   No. 711

Date	Explanation	Ref.	Debit	Credit	Balance

Salaries and Wages Expense   No. 726

Date	Explanation	Ref.	Debit	Credit	Balance

Rent Expense   No. 729

Date	Explanation	Ref.	Debit	Credit	Balance

(b)   General Journal   J1

Date	Account Titles	Ref.	Debit	Credit
Sept. 8				
10				
12				
15				
17				
20				
22				
25				
27				
29				

(d) & (f)

Beck Equipment Repair, Inc.
Trial Balances
September 30, 2014

	(d) Before Adjustment		(f) After Adjustment		
	Dr.	Cr.	Dr.	Cr.	
1 Cash					1
2 Accounts Receivable					2
3 Supplies					3
4 Equipment					4
5 Accum. Depreciation-Equipment					5
6 Accounts Payable					6
7 Unearned Service Revenue					7
8 Salaries and Wages Payable					8
9 Common Stock					9
10 Retained Earnings					10
11 Service Revenue					11
12 Depreciation Expense					12
13 Supplies Expense					13
14 Salaries and Wages Expense					14
15 Rent Expense					15
16 Totals					16
17					17
18					18
19					19
20					20
21					21

(e)   General Journal   J1

	Date	Account Titles	Ref	Debit	Credit	
1	1.					1
2	Sept. 30					2
3						3
4						4
5						5
6						6
7	2.					7
8	Sept. 30					8
9						9
10						10
11						11
12						12
13	3.					13
14	Sept. 30					14
15						15
16						16
17						17
18						18
19	4.					19
20	Sept. 30					20
21						21
22						22
23						23
24						24
25						25

(g)

Beck Equipment Repair, Inc.

Income Statement

For the Month Ended September 30, 2014

Beck Equipment Repair, Inc.

Retained Earnings Statement

For the Month Ended September 30, 2014

(g) (Continued)

Beck Equipment Repair, Inc.				
Balance Sheet				
September 30, 2014				
Assets				
Liabilities and Stockholders' Equity				

(a)

	Date	Account Titles	Debit	Credit	
1	1.				1
2	June 30				2
3					3
4					4
5					5
6	2.				6
7	June 30				7
8					8
9					9
10					10
11	3.				11
12	June 30				12
13					13
14					14
15					15
16	4.				16
17	June 30				17
18					18
19					19
20					20
21	5.				21
22	June 30				22
23					23
24					24
25					25
26	6.				26
27	June 30				27
28					28
29					29
30					30
31					31
32					32
33					33
34					34
35					35
36					36
37					37
38					38
39					39
40					40

(b)

Alpha Graphics Company, Inc. Adjusted Trial Balance June 30, 2014	Debit	Credit
1		
2		
3		
4		
5		
6		
7		
8		
9		
10		
11		
12		
13		
14		
15		
16		
17		
18		
19		
20		
21		
22		
23		
24		
25		

(c)

Alpha Graphics Company, Inc.

Income Statement

For the Six Months Ended June 30, 2014

1				
2				
3				
4				
5				
6				
7				
8				
9				
10				
11				
12				
13				
14				
15				
16				
17				
18				
19				
20				

Alpha Graphics Company, Inc.

Retained Earnings Statement

For the Six Months Ended June 30, 2014

1		
2		
3		
4		
5		
6		
7		

(c) (Continued)

Alpha Graphics Company, Inc.

Balance Sheet

June 30, 2014

	Assets				
1					
2					
3					
4					
5					
6					
7					
8					
9					
10					
11					
12					
13	Liabilities and Stockholders' Equity				
14					
15					
16					
17					
18					
19					
20					
21					
22					
23					
24					
25					
26					
27					

(a)   General Journal   J4

	Date	Account Titles	Ref.	Debit	Credit	
1	2014					1
2	May 31					2
3						3
4						4
5	31					5
6						6
7						7
8						8
9	31					9
10						10
11						11
12						12
13	31					13
14						14
15						15
16						16
17	31					17
18						18
19						19
20						20
21	31					21
22						22
23						23
24						24
25	31					25
26						26
27						27
28						28
29						29
30						30
31						31
32						32
33						33
34						34
35						35
36						36
37						37
38						38
39						39
40						40

(b)

Cash   No. 101

Date	Explanation	Ref.	Debit	Credit	Balance
2014					
May 31	Balance	√			7 7 0 0

Accounts Receivable   No. 112

Date	Explanation	Ref.	Debit	Credit	Balance
2014					
May 31	Balance	√			4 0 0 0

Supplies   No. 126

Date	Explanation	Ref.	Debit	Credit	Balance
2014					
May 31	Balance	√			1 5 0 0

Prepaid Insurance   No. 130

Date	Explanation	Ref.	Debit	Credit	Balance
2014					
May 31	Balance	√			2 4 0 0

Equipment   No. 157

Date	Explanation	Ref.	Debit	Credit	Balance
2014					
May 31	Balance	√			1 2 0 0 0

Accumulated Depreciation - Equipment   No. 158

Date	Explanation	Ref.	Debit	Credit	Balance

Accounts Payable   No. 201

Date	Explanation	Ref.	Debit	Credit	Balance
2014					
May 31	Balance	√			4 5 0 0

(b) (Continued)

Unearned Service Revenue   No. 209

Date	Explanation	Ref.	Debit	Credit	Balance
2014					
May 31	Balance	√			2 6 0 0

Salaries and Wages Payable   No. 212

Date	Explanation	Ref.	Debit	Credit	Balance

Common Stock   No. 311

Date	Explanation	Ref.	Debit	Credit	Balance
2014					
May 31	Balance	√			1 6 0 0 0

Service Revenue   No. 400

Date	Explanation	Ref.	Debit	Credit	Balance
2014					
May 31	Balance	√			8 5 0 0

Supplies Expense   No. 631

Date	Explanation	Ref.	Debit	Credit	Balance

Depreciation Expense   No. 711

Date	Explanation	Ref.	Debit	Credit	Balance

(b) (Continued)

Insurance Expense   No. 722

Date	Explanation	Ref.	Debit	Credit	Balance

Salaries and Wages Expense   No. 726

Date	Explanation	Ref.	Debit	Credit	Balance
2014					
May 31	Balance	√			3 0 0 0

Rent Expense   No. 729

Date	Explanation	Ref.	Debit	Credit	Balance
2014					
May 31	Balance	√			1 0 0 0

Utilities Expense   No. 736

Date	Explanation	Ref.	Debit	Credit	Balance

(c)

Vektek Consulting, Inc. Adjusted Trial Balance May 31, 2014	Debit	Credit
1 Cash		
2 Accounts Receivable		
3 Supplies		
4 Prepaid Insurance		
5 Equipment		
6 Accumulated Depreciation - Equipment		
7 Accounts Payable		
8 Unearned Service Revenue		
9 Salaries and Wages Payable		
10 Common Stock		
11 Service Revenue		
12 Salaries and Wages Expense		
13 Rent Expense		
14 Depreciation Expense		
15 Insurance Expense		
16 Utilities Expense		
17 Supplies Expense		
18 Totals		

(a) General Journal J1

	Date	Account Titles	Ref.	Debit	Credit	
1	May 31					1
2						2
3						3
4	31					4
5						5
6						6
7	31					7
8						8
9						9
10	31					10
11						11
12						12
13	31					13
14						14
15						15
16	31					16
17						17
18						18
19	31					19
20						20
21						21
22						22
23						23
24						24
25						25
26						26

(b)

Cash No. 101

Date	Explanation	Ref.	Debit	Credit	Balance
May 31	Balance	√			2 5 0 0

Supplies No. 126

Date	Explanation	Ref.	Debit	Credit	Balance
May 31	Balance	√			1 5 2 0

(b) (Continued)

Prepaid Insurance No. 130

Date	Explanation	Ref.	Debit	Credit	Balance
May 31		√			2 4 0 0

Land No. 140

Date	Explanation	Ref.	Debit	Credit	Balance
May 31	Balance	√			1 4 0 0 0

Buildings No. 141

Date	Explanation	Ref.	Debit	Credit	Balance
May 31	Balance	√			5 8 0 0 0

Accumulated Depreciation - Buildings No. 142

Date	Explanation	Ref.	Debit	Credit	Balance

Equipment No. 157

Date	Explanation	Ref.	Debit	Credit	Balance
May 31	Balance	√			1 5 0 0 0

Accumulated Depreciation - Equipment No. 158

Date	Explanation	Ref.	Debit	Credit	Balance

Accounts Payable No. 201

Date	Explanation	Ref.	Debit	Credit	Balance
May 31	Balance	√			4 8 0 0

Unearned Rent Revenue No. 209

Date	Explanation	Ref.	Debit	Credit	Balance
May 31	Balance	√			3 3 0 0

Salaries and Wages Payable No. 212

Date	Explanation	Ref.	Debit	Credit	Balance

Interest Payable No. 230

Date	Explanation	Ref.	Debit	Credit	Balance

(b) (Continued)

Mortgage Payable   No. 275

Date	Explanation	Ref.	Debit	Credit	Balance
May 31	Balance	√			38000

Common Stock   No. 311

Date	Explanation	Ref.	Debit	Credit	Balance
May 31	Balance	√			40000

Rent Revenue   No. 429

Date	Explanation	Ref.	Debit	Credit	Balance
May 31	Balance	√			12300

Advertising Expense   No. 610

Date	Explanation	Ref.	Debit	Credit	Balance
May 31	Balance	√			780

Supplies Expense   No. 631

Date	Explanation	Ref.	Debit	Credit	Balance

Depreciation Expense   No. 711

Date	Explanation	Ref.	Debit	Credit	Balance

Interest Expense   No. 718

Date	Explanation	Ref.	Debit	Credit	Balance

Insurance Expense   No. 722

Date	Explanation	Ref.	Debit	Credit	Balance

Salaries and Wages Expense   No. 726

Date	Explanation	Ref.	Debit	Credit	Balance
May 31	Balance	√			3300

Utilities Expense   No. 732

Date	Explanation	Ref.	Debit	Credit	Balance

(c)

Badger Motel, Inc. Adjusted Trial Balance May 31, 2014	Debit	Credit
1 Cash		
2 Supplies		
3 Prepaid Insurance		
4 Land		
5 Buildings		
6 Accumulated Depreciation - Buildings		
7 Equipment		
8 Accumulated Depreciation - Equipment		
9 Accounts Payable		
10 Unearned Rent Revenue		
11 Salaries and Wages Payable		
12 Interest Payable		
13 Mortgage Payable		
14 Common Stock		
15 Rent Revenue		
16 Advertising Expense		
17 Supplies Expense		
18 Depreciation Expense		
19 Interest Expense		
20 Insurance Expense		
21 Salaries and Wages Expense		
22 Utilities Expense		
23 Totals		
24		
25		
26		
27		

(d)

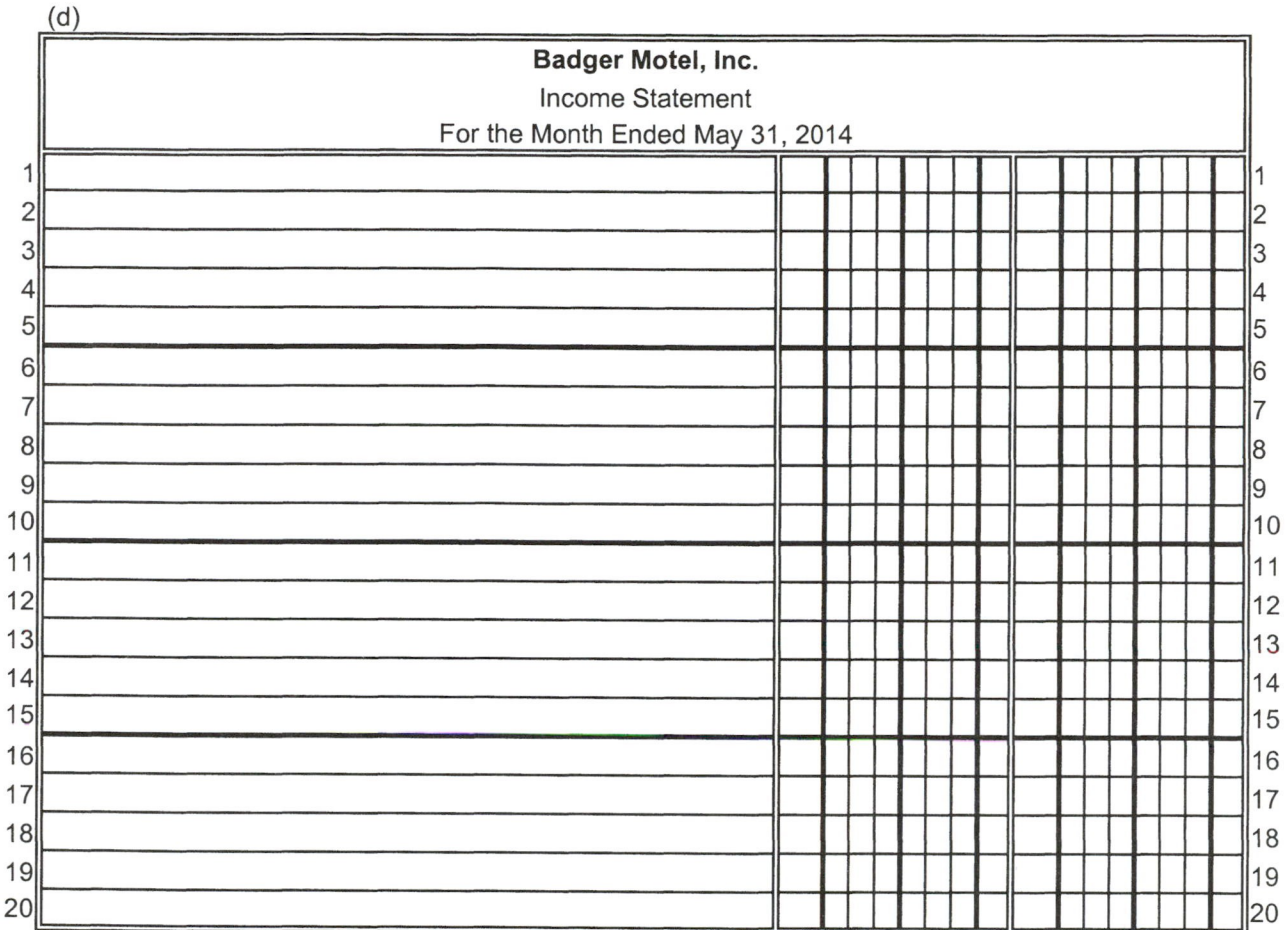

Badger Motel, Inc.

Income Statement

For the Month Ended May 31, 2014

Badger Motel, Inc.

Retained Earnings Statement

For the Month Ended May 31, 2014

(d) (Continued)

	Badger Motel, Inc.								
	Balance Sheet								
	May 31, 2014								
1	Assets								1
2									2
3									3
4									4
5									5
6									6
7									7
8									8
9									9
10									10
11									11
12									12
13									13
14									14
15									15
16	Liabilities and Stockholders' Equity								16
17									17
18									18
19									19
20									20
21									21
22									22
23									23
24									24
25									25
26									26
27									27
28									28
29									29
30									30
31									31
32									32
33									33
34									34
35									35
36									36
37									37
38									38
39									39
40									40

(a)

	Date	Accounts Titles	Debit	Credit	
1	Sept. 30				1
2					2
3					3
4	30				4
5					5
6					6
7	30				7
8					8
9					9
10	30				10
11					11
12					12
13	30				13
14					14
15					15
16	30				16
17					17
18					18
19	30				19
20					20
21					21

(b)

Medina Co., Inc.

Income Statement

For the Quarter Ended September 30, 2014

1	Revenues:		1
2			2
3			3
4			4
5	Expenses:		5
6			6
7			7
8			8
9			9
10			10
11			11
12			12
13			13
14			14

(b) (Continued)

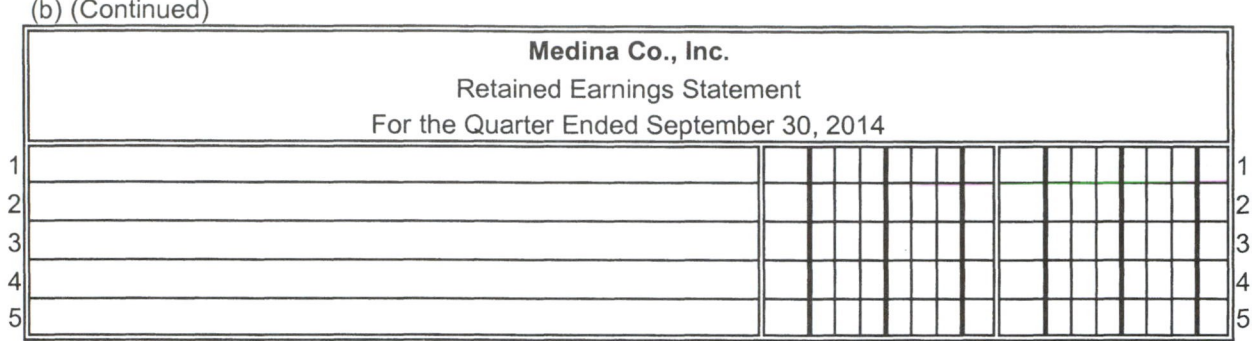

Medina Co., Inc.
Retained Earnings Statement
For the Quarter Ended September 30, 2014

1		1
2		2
3		3
4		4
5		5

Medina Co., Inc.
Balance Sheet
September 30, 2014

	Assets	
1		1
2		2
3		3
4		4
5		5
6		6
7		7
8		8
9		9
10	Liabilities and Stockholders' Equity	10
11		11
12		12
13		13
14		14
15		15
16		16
17		17
18		18
19		19
20		20
21		21
22		22

(c)

1		1
2		2
3		3
4		4

General Journal

Date	Accounts Titles	Debit	Credit
1.			
Dec. 31			
2.			
Dec. 31			
3.			
Dec. 31			
4.			
Dec. 31			

(a), (c) and (e)

Cash   No. 101

Date	Explanation	Ref.	Debit	Credit	Balance
Nov. 1	Balance	√			2400

Accounts Receivable   No. 112

Date	Explanation	Ref.	Debit	Credit	Balance
Nov. 1	Balance	√			4450

Supplies   No. 126

Date	Explanation	Ref.	Debit	Credit	Balance
Nov. 1	Balance	√			1800

Equipment   No. 157

Date	Explanation	Ref.	Debit	Credit	Balance
Nov. 1	Balance	√			16000

Accumulated Depreciation - Equipment   No. 158

Date	Explanation	Ref.	Debit	Credit	Balance
Nov. 1	Balance	√			2000

Accounts Payable   No. 201

Date	Explanation	Ref.	Debit	Credit	Balance
Nov. 1	Balance	√			2600

(a), (c) and (e) (Continued)

Unearned Service Revenue No. 209

Date	Explanation	Ref.	Debit	Credit	Balance
Nov. 1	Balance	√			1 3 6 0

Salaries and Wages Payable No. 212

Date	Explanation	Ref.	Debit	Credit	Balance
Nov. 1	Balance	√			7 0 0

Common Stock No. 311

Date	Explanation	Ref.	Debit	Credit	Balance
Nov. 1	Balance	√			1 0 0 0 0

Retained Earnings No. 320

Date	Explanation	Ref.	Debit	Credit	Balance
Nov. 1	Balance	√			7 9 9 0

(a), (c) and (e) (Continued)

Service Revenue   No. 400

Date	Explanation	Ref.	Debit	Credit	Balance

Supplies Expense   No. 631

Date	Explanation	Ref.	Debit	Credit	Balance

Depreciation Expense   No. 711

Date	Explanation	Ref.	Debit	Credit	Balance

Salaries and Wages Expense   No. 726

Date	Explanation	Ref.	Debit	Credit	Balance

Rent Expense   No. 729

Date	Explanation	Ref.	Debit	Credit	Balance

(b)   General Journal   J1

	Date	Account Titles	Ref	Debit	Credit	
1	Nov. 8					1
2						2
3						3
4						4
5	10					5
6						6
7						7
8	12					8
9						9
10						10
11	15					11
12						12
13						13
14	17					14
15						15
16						16
17	20					17
18						18
19						19
20	22					20
21						21
22						22
23	25					23
24						24
25						25
26	27					26
27						27
28						28
29	29					29
30						30
31						31
32						32
33						33
34						34
35						35

(d) & (f)

Samone Equipment Repair, Inc.
Trial Balances
November 30, 2014

	(d) Before Adjustment		(f) After Adjustment	
	Dr.	Cr.	Dr.	Cr.
1 Cash				
2 Accounts Receivable				
3 Supplies				
4 Equipment				
5 Accum. Depreciation-Equipment				
6 Accounts Payable				
7 Unearned Service Revenue				
8 Salaries and Wages Payable				
9 Common Stock				
10 Retained Earnings				
11 Service Revenue				
12 Depreciation Expense				
13 Supplies Expense				
14 Salaries and Wages Expense				
15 Rent Expense				
16 Totals				
17				
18				
19				
20				
21				

(e)

General Journal

J1

	Date	Account Titles	Ref	Debit	Credit	
1	1.					1
2	Nov. 30					2
3						3
4						4
5						5
6						6
7	2.					7
8	Nov. 30					8
9						9
10						10
11						11
12						12
13	3.					13
14	Nov. 30					14
15						15
16						16
17						17
18						18
19	4.					19
20	Nov. 30					20
21						21
22						22
23						23
24						24
25						25

(g)

Samone Equipment Repair, Inc.
Income Statement
For the Month Ended November 30, 2014

1			1
2			2
3			3
4			4
5			5
6			6
7			7
8			8
9			9
10			10
11			11
12			12
13			13
14			14
15			15

Samone Equipment Repair, Inc.
Retained Earnings Statement
For the Month Ended November 30, 2014

1		1
2		2
3		3
4		4
5		5
6		6
7		7
8		8
9		9
10		10
11		11

(g) (Continued)

Samone Equipment Repair, Inc.
Balance Sheet
November 30, 2014

	Assets					
1						
2						
3						
4						
5						
6						
7						
8						
9						
10						
11	Liabilities and Stockholders' Equity					
12						
13						
14						
15						
16						
17						
18						
19						
20						
21						
22						

	PepsiCo	Coca-Cola
1 Increase (decrease) from 2009 to 2010 in:		
2		
3		
4 (a) Property, plant, and equipment, net		
5		
6		
7		
8 (b) Selling, general, and administrative expenses		
9		
10		
11		
12 (c) Long-term debt (obligations)		
13		
14		
15		
16 (d) Net income		
17		
18		
19		
20 (e) Cash and cash equivalents		
21		
22		
23		
24		
25		
26		
27		
28		
29		
30		
31		
32		
33		
34		
35		
36		
37		
38		
39		

(a)

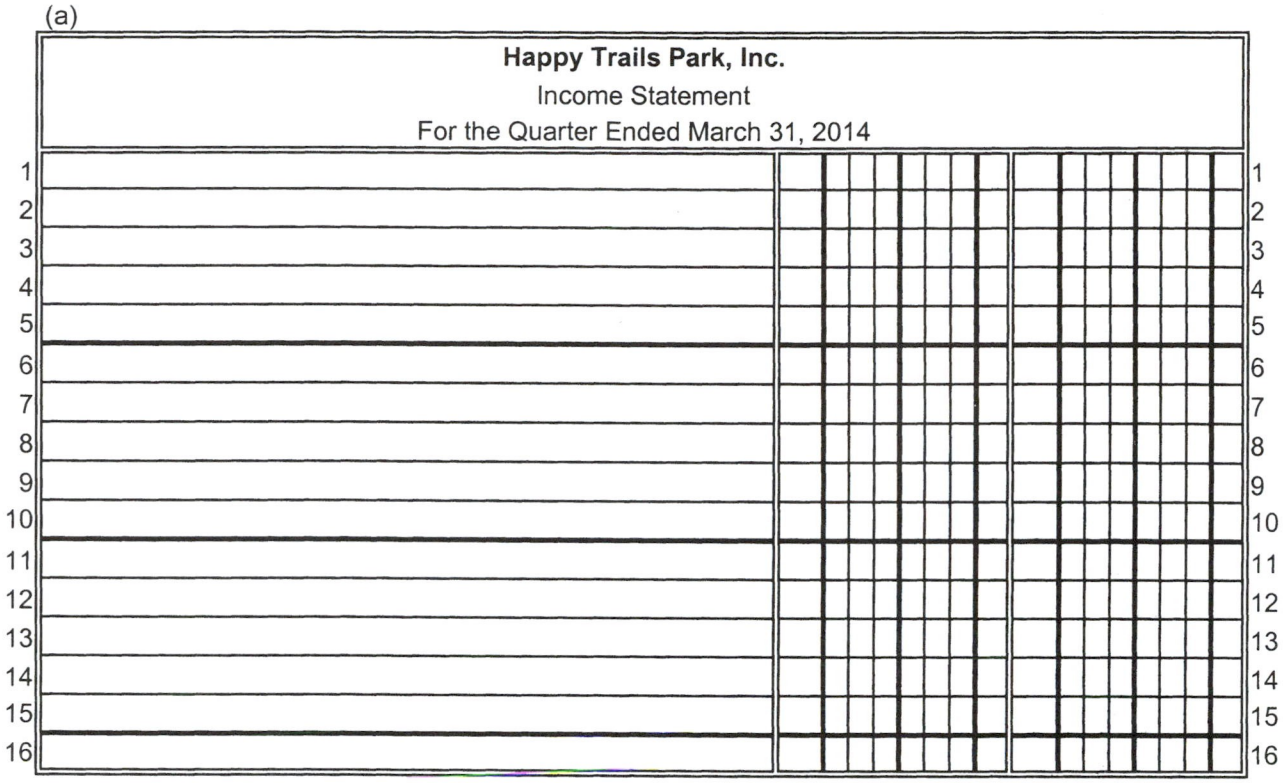

	Happy Trails Park, Inc. Income Statement For the Quarter Ended March 31, 2014		
1			
2			
3			
4			
5			
6			
7			
8			
9			
10			
11			
12			
13			
14			
15			
16			

(b)

1	
2	
3	
4	
5	
6	
7	
8	
9	
10	
11	
12	
13	
14	
15	
16	
17	
18	

Brief Exercise 4-2

Keo Company

You will find this working paper at the end of this work book

BE4-4

	Date	Account Titles	Debit	Credit	
1	Dec. 31				1
2					2
3					3
4	31				4
5					5
6					6
7					7
8	31				8
9					9
10					10
11	31				11
12					12
13					13
14					14

BE4-6

	Date	Account Titles	Debit	Credit	
1	July 31				1
2					2
3					3
4	31				4
5					5
6					6

Service Revenue

	Date	Explanation	Ref.	Debit	Credit	Balance	
1	7/31	Balance	√			19200	1
2							2

Salaries and Wages Exp(

	Date	Explanation	Ref.	Debit	Credit	Balance	
1	7/31	Balance	√			8800	1
2							2

Maintenance and Repairs

	Date	Explanation	Ref.	Debit	Credit	Balance	
1	7/31	Balance	√			2500	1
2							2

BE4-9

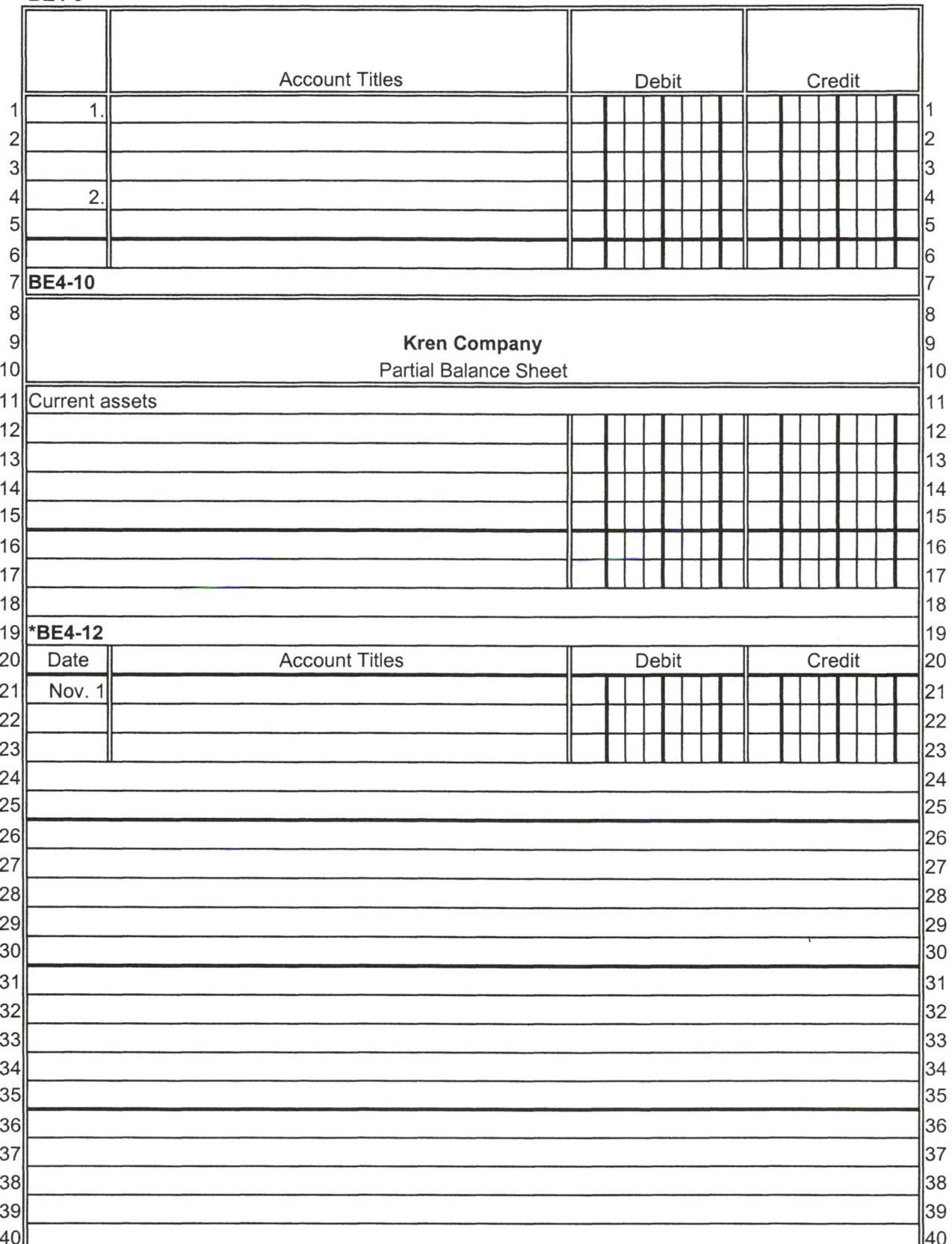

		Account Titles	Debit	Credit	
1	1.				1
2					2
3					3
4	2.				4
5					5
6					6

BE4-10

Kren Company

Partial Balance Sheet

Current assets

*BE4-12

Date	Account Titles	Debit	Credit
Nov. 1			

DO IT! 4-2

	Date	Account Titles	Debit	Credit	
1	Dec. 31				1
2					2
3					3
4	31				4
5					5
6					6
7					7
8	**DO IT! 4-3**				8
9		**Pahl Company**			9
10		Partial Balance Sheet			10
11		December 31, 2014			11
12					12
13					13
14					14
15					15
16					16
17					17
18					18
19					19
20					20
21					21
22					22
23					23
24					24
25					25
26					26
27					27
28					28
29					29
30					30
31					31
32					32
33					33
34					34
35					35

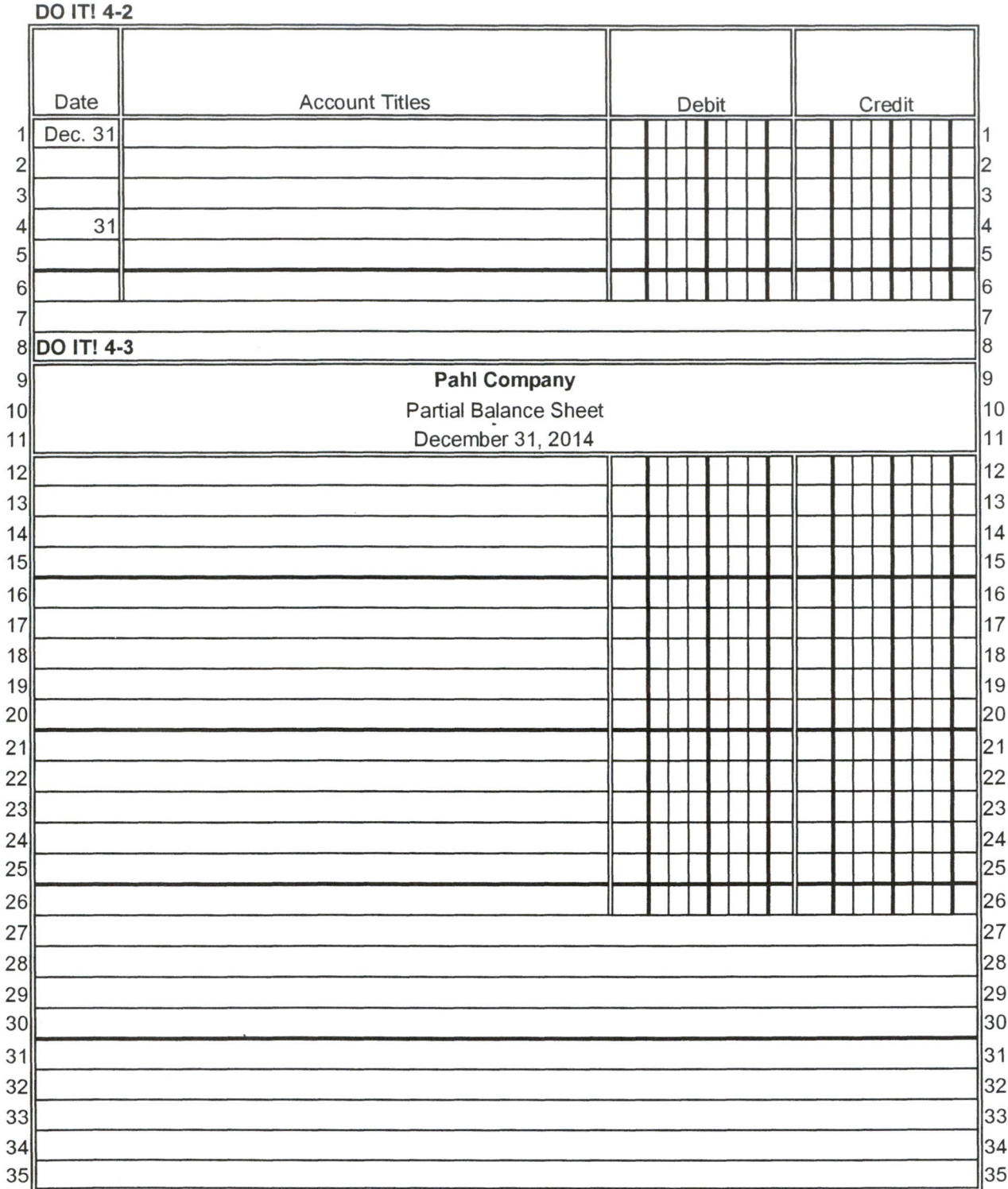

Exercise 4-1

Cajon Company

You will find this working paper at the end of this work book

Albanese Company

(Partial) Worksheet

For the Month Ended April 30, 2014

	Account Titles	Adjusted Trial Balance Dr.	Adjusted Trial Balance Cr.	Income Statement Dr.	Income Statement Cr.	Balance Sheet Dr.	Balance Sheet Cr.
1	Cash	17442					
2	Accounts Receivable	7840					
3	Prepaid Rent	2280					
4	Equipment	23000					
5	Accumulated Depr. - Equipment		4800				
6	Notes Payable		5700				
7	Accounts Payable		5672				
8	Common Stock		22000				
9	Retained Earnings		4000				
10	Dividends	3000					
11	Service Revenue		12590				
12	Salaries and Wages Expense	9840					
13	Rent Expense	760					
14	Depreciation Expense	600					
15	Interest Expense	57					
16	Interest Payable		57				
17	Totals	54819	54819				
18	Net Income						
19	Totals						
20							
21							

Albanese Company		
Income Statement		
For the Month Ended April 30, 2014		

1			
2			
3			
4			
5			
6			
7			
8			
9			
10			
11			
12			
13			
14			
15			
16			
17			
18			

Albanese Company	
Retained Earnings Statement	
For the Month Ended April 30, 2014	

1	
2	
3	
4	
5	
6	

(Continued)

Albanese Company
Balance Sheet
April 30, 2014

	Assets								
1									1
2									2
3									3
4									4
5									5
6									6
7									7
8									8
9									9
10									10
11									11
12									12
13	Liabilities and Stockholders' Equity								13
14									14
15									15
16									16
17									17
18									18
19									19
20									20
21									21
22									22
23									23
24									24
25									25
26									26

(a)

	Date	Account Titles	Debit	Credit	
1	Apr. 30				1
2					2
3					3
4	30				4
5					5
6					6
7					7
8					8
9					9
10	30				10
11					11
12					12
13	30				13
14					14
15					15

(b)

INCOME SUMMARY	RETAINED EARNINGS

(c)

Albanese Company

Post-Closing Trial Balance

April 30, 2014

		Debit	Credit	
1				1
2				2
3				3
4				4
5				5
6				6
7				7
8				8
9				9
10				10
11				11

(a)

	Account Titles	Debit	Credit	
1				1
2				2
3				3
4				4
5				5
6				6
7				7
8				8
9				9
10				10
11				11
12	.			12

(b)

		Income Statement		Balance Sheet		
		Debit	Credit	Debit	Credit	
1	Accounts Receivable					1
2	Prepaid Insurance					2
3	Accum. Depr.-Equip.					3
4	Sal. & Wages Pay					4
5	Service Revenue					5
6	Sal. & Wages Exp					6
7	Insurance Expense					7
8	Depr. Expense					8
9						9

Exercise 4-6

Freeman Company

(a)

	Account Titles	Trial Balance		Adjustments		Adjusted Trial Balance		
		Debit	Credit	Debit	Credit	Debit	Credit	
1	Accounts Receivable					34000		1
2	Prepaid Insurance	26000				18000		2
3	Supplies	7000						3
4	Accumulated Depreciation-Equip.		12000					4
5	Salaries and Wages Payable						5000	5
6	Service Revenue		88000				95000	6
7	Insurance Expense							7
8	Depreciation Expense					10000		8
9	Supplies Expense					4700		9
10	Salaries and Wages Expense					49000		10

(b)

	Account Titles	Debit	Credit	
1				1
2				2
3				3
4				4
5				5
6				6
7				7
8				8
9				9
10				10
11				11
12				12
13				13
14				14

(a)

Account Titles	Debit	Credit
1		
2		
3		
4		
5		
6		
7		
8		
9		
10		
11		
12		
13		
14		
15		

(b)

Lanza Company

Post-Closing Trial Balance

June 30, 2014

Account Titles	Debit	Credit
1		
2		
3		
4		
5		
6		
7		
8		
9		
10		

(a) General Journal J15

	Date	Account Titles	Ref.	Debit	Credit	
1	July 31					1
2						2
3						3
4						4
5	31					5
6						6
7						7
8						8
9						9
10	31					10
11						11
12						12
13	31					13
14						14

(b)

Retained Earnings No. 320

Date	Explanation	Ref.	Debit	Credit	Balance
July 31	Balance	√			2 0 2 6 0

Income Summary No. 350

Date	Explanation	Ref.	Debit	Credit	Balance

(c)

Roth Company

Post-Closing Trial Balance

July 31, 2014

		Debit	Credit	
1				1
2				2
3				3
4				4
5				5
6				6
7				7
8				8

(a)

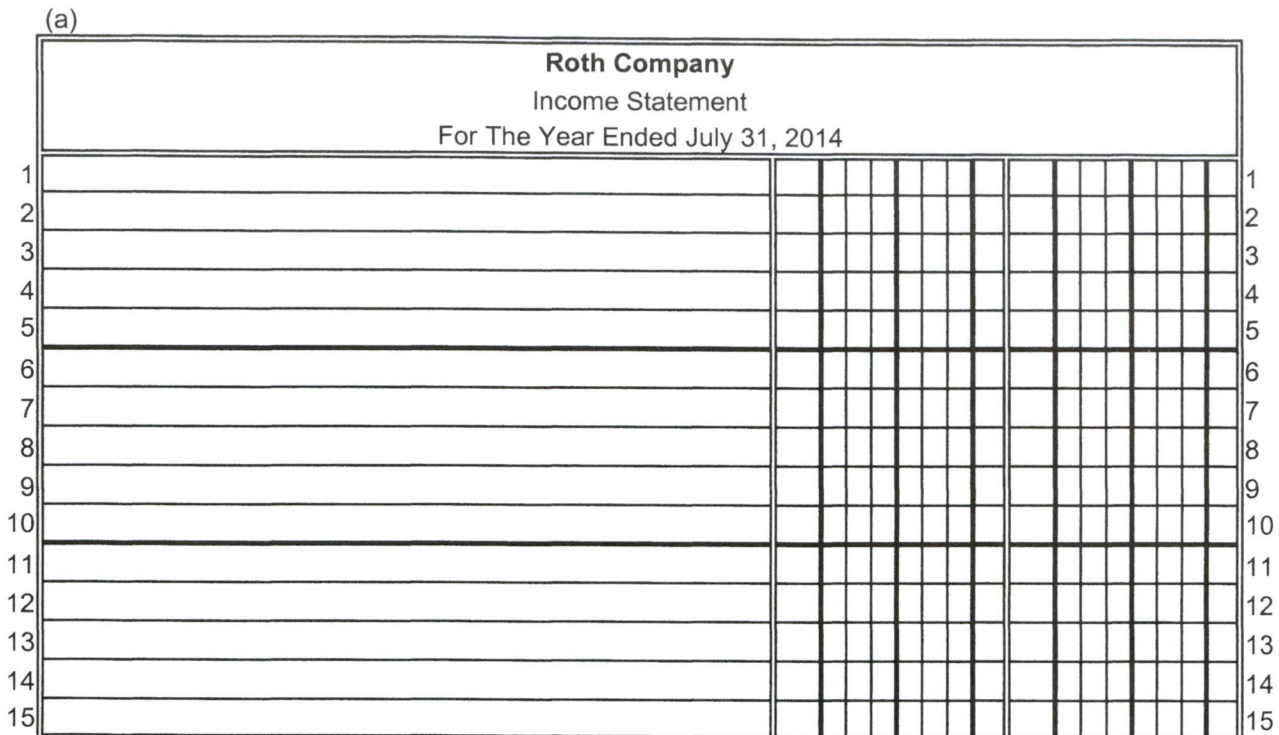

(b) (Continued)

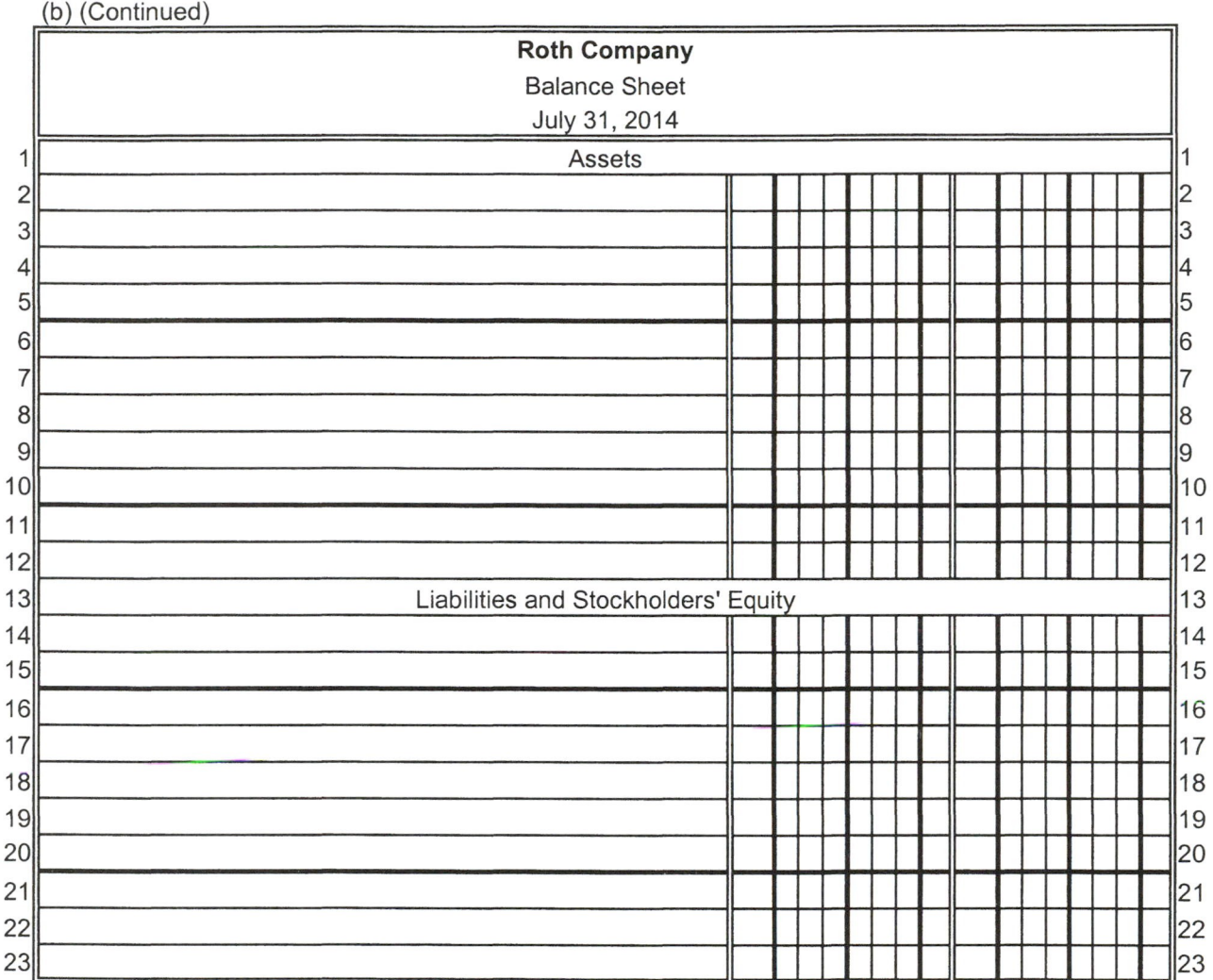

Roth Company
Balance Sheet
July 31, 2014

	Assets						
1							1
2							2
3							3
4							4
5							5
6							6
7							7
8							8
9							9
10							10
11							11
12							12
13	Liabilities and Stockholders' Equity						13
14							14
15							15
16							16
17							17
18							18
19							19
20							20
21							21
22							22
23							23

E4-11

	Date	Account Titles	Debit	Credit	
1	(a)				1
2	June 30				2
3					3
4					4
5	30				5
6					6
7					7
8					8
9					9
10	30				10
11					11
12					12
13	30				13
14					14

(b)

INCOME SUMMARY

E4-13

	Date	Account Titles	Debit	Credit	
1	1.				1
2					2
3					3
4	2.				4
5					5
6					6
7					7
8	3.				8
9					9
10					10

		Account Titles	Debit	Credit	
1	(a)				1
2	1.				2
3					3
4					4
5					5
6					6
7					7
8	2.				8
9					9
10					10
11					11
12					12
13					13
14	3.				14
15					15
16					16
17					17
18					18
19					19
20	(b)				20
21	1.				21
22					22
23					23
24	2.				24
25					25
26					26
27					27
28	3.				28
29					29
30					30
31					31
32					32
33					33
34					34
35					35
36					36
37					37
38					38
39					39
40					40

(a)

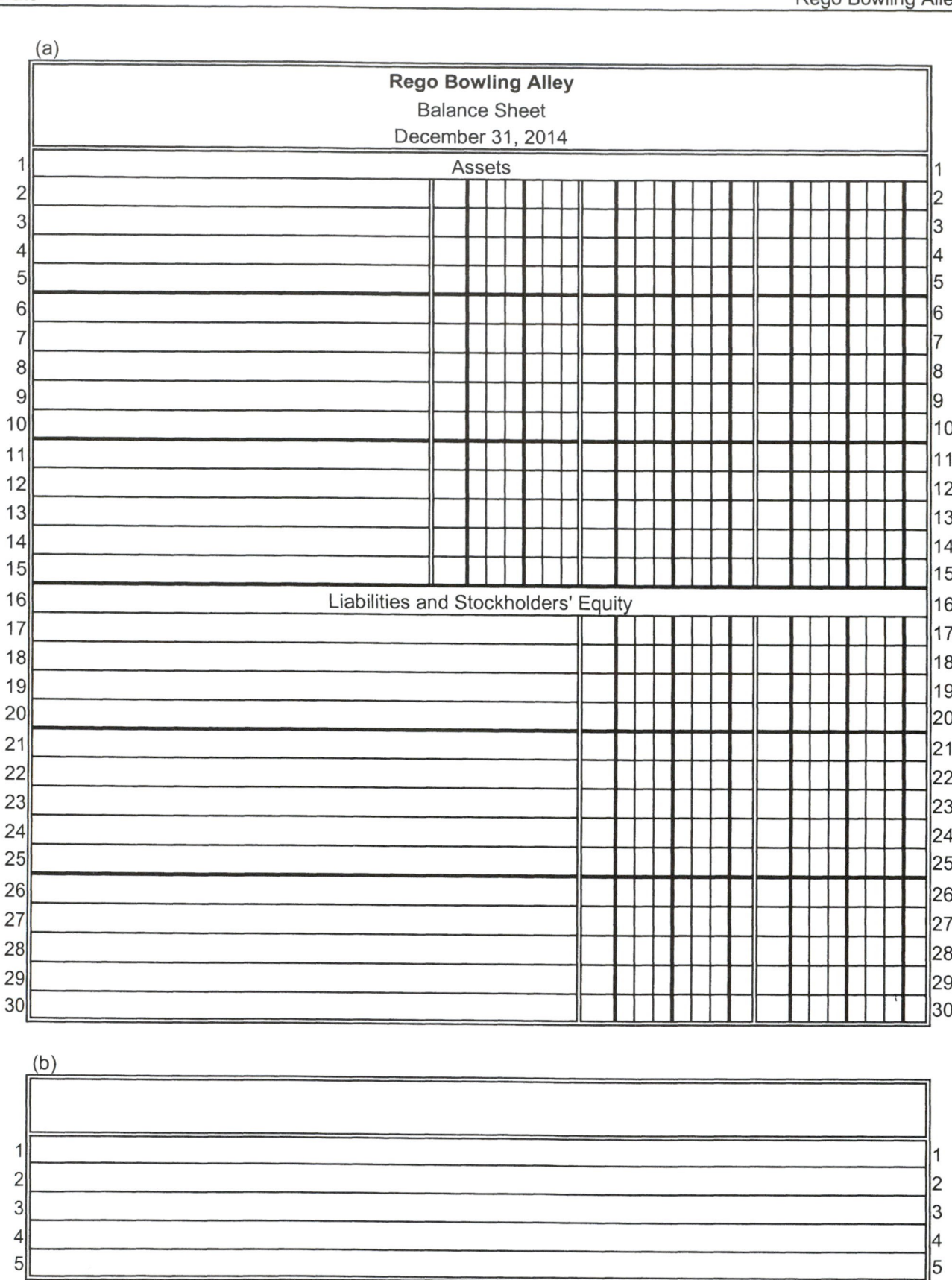

Rego Bowling Alley
Balance Sheet
December 31, 2014

Assets

Liabilities and Stockholders' Equity

(b)

	Sexton Company
	Balance Sheet
	December 31, 2014
	(in thousands)

	Assets							
1								
2								
3								
4								
5								
6								
7								
8								
9								
10								
11								
12								
13								
14								
15								
16	Liabilities and Stockholders' Equity							
17								
18								
19								
20								
21								
22								
23								
24								
25								
26								
27								
28								
29								
30								

(a)

	Emjay Company Income Statement For The Year Ended July 31, 2014			
1	Revenues:				1
2					2
3					3
4					4
5					5
6	Expenses:				6
7					7
8					8
9					9
10					10
11					11
12					12
13					13
14					14
15					15

	Emjay Company Retained Earnings Statement For The Year Ended July 31, 2014			
1					1
2					2
3					3
4					4
5					5

(b) (Continued)

Emjay Company
Balance Sheet
July 31, 2014

	Assets										
1											1
2											2
3											3
4											4
5											5
6											6
7											7
8											8
9											9
10											10
11											11
12											12
13	Liabilities and Stockholders' Equity										13
14											14
15											15
16											16
17											17
18											18
19											19
20											20
21											21
22											22
23											23
24											24
25											25

	Date	Account Titles	Debit	Credit	
1	(a)				1
2	Dec. 31				2
3					3
4					4
5	Jan. 6				5
6					6
7					7
8					8
9	(b)				9
10	Dec. 31				10
11					11
12					12
13	Jan. 1				13
14					14
15					15
16	6				16
17					17
18					18
19					19
20					20

(a) & (b)

	Date	Account Titles	Debit	Credit	
1	Dec. 31				1
2					2
3					3
4					4
5	31				5
6					6
7					7
8					8
9	Jan. 1				9
10					10
11					11
12	1				12
13					13
14					14
15					15

(c) & (e)

ACCOUNTS RECEIVABLE

Dec 31 Bal   24,500

SERVICE REVENUE

Dec 31 Bal   93,800

INTEREST PAYABLE

Dec 31 Bal   1,300

INTEREST EXPENSE

Dec 31 Bal   8,300

(d)

	Date	Account Titles	Debit	Credit	
31	Date	Account Titles	Debit	Credit	31
32		(1)			32
33	Jan. 10				33
34					34
35					35
36		(2)			36
37	15				37
38					38
39					39
40					40

Problem 4-1A

Sherlock Holmes, P.I., Inc.

You will find this working paper at the end of this work book

(b)

Sherlock Holmes, P.I., Inc.
Income Statement
For the Quarter Ended March 31, 2014

1			
2			
3			
4			
5			
6			
7			
8			
9			
10			
11			
12			
13			
14			
15			

Sherlock Holmes, P.I., Inc.
Retained Earnings Statement
For the Quarter Ended March 31, 2014

1	
2	
3	
4	
5	
6	
7	
8	
9	
10	

(b) (Continued)

Sherlock Holmes, P.I., Inc.
Balance Sheet
March 31, 2014

Assets

Liabilities and Stockholders' Equity

(c)

General Journal

	Date	Account Titles	Debit	Credit	
1		Adjusting Entries			1
2	Mar. 31				2
3					3
4					4
5	31				5
6					6
7					7
8	31				8
9					9
10					10
11	31				11
12					12
13					13
14	31				14
15					15

(d)

General Journal

	Date	Account Titles	Debit	Credit	
1		Closing Entries			1
2	Mar. 31				2
3					3
4					4
5	31				5
6					6
7					7
8					8
9					9
10					10
11					11
12					12
13					13
14					14
15	31				15
16					16
17					17
18	31				18
19					19

(a)

Watson Company
Worksheet (Partial)
For the Year Ended December 31, 2014

	Account		Adjusted Trial Balance		Income Statement		Balance Sheet	
	No.	Titles	Dr.	Cr.	Dr.	Cr.	Dr.	Cr.
1	101	Cash	17800					
2	112	Accounts Receivable	14400					
3	126	Supplies	2300					
4	130	Prepaid Insurance	4400					
5	151	Equipment	46000					
6	152	Accum. Depr. - Equip.		18000				
7	200	Notes Payable		20000				
8	201	Accounts Payable		8000				
9	212	Salaries & Wages Payable		2600				
10	230	Interest Payable		1000				
11	311	Common Stock		15000				
12	320	Retained Earnings		9800				
13	332	Dividends	12000					
14	400	Service Revenue		86200				
15	610	Advertising Expense	10000					
16	631	Supplies Expense	3700					
17	711	Depreciation Expense	6000					
18	722	Insurance Expense	4000					
19	726	Salaries & Wages Expense	39000					
20	905	Interest Expense	1000					
21		Totals	160600	160600				
22		Net Income						
23		Totals						
24								

(b)

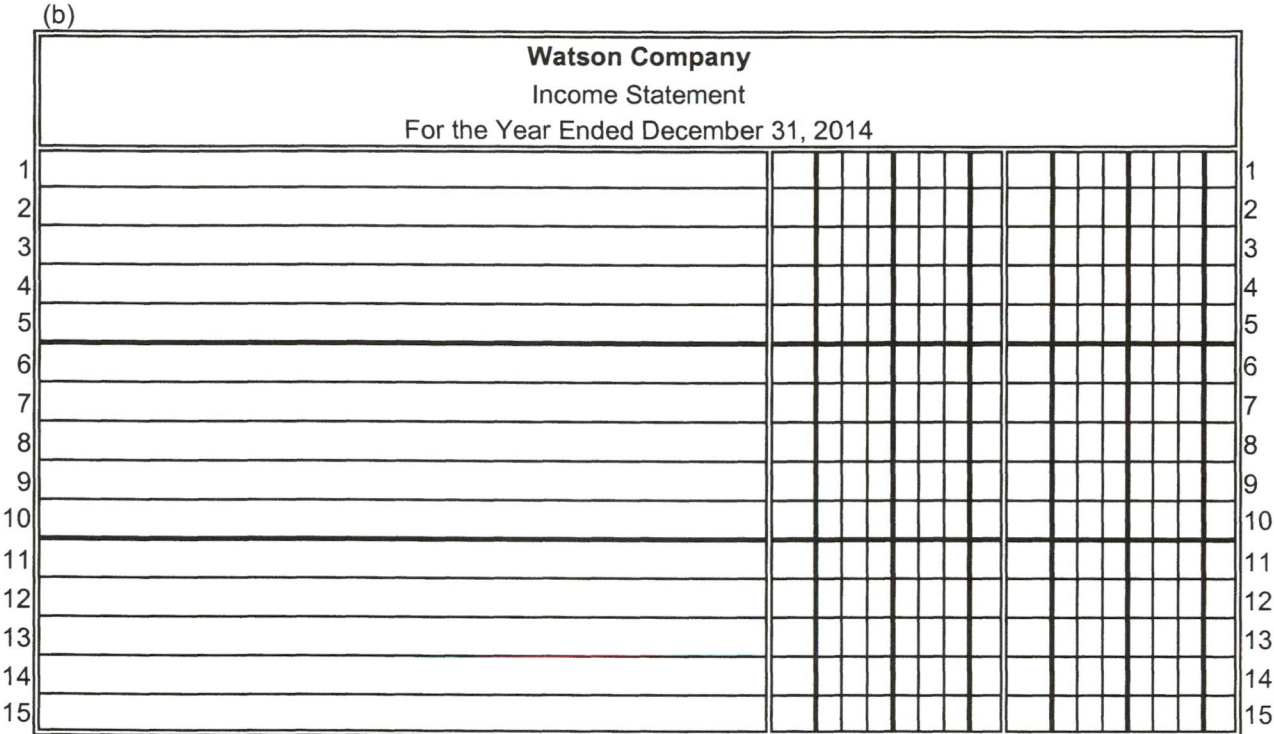

Watson Company					
Income Statement					
For the Year Ended December 31, 2014					

1		1
2		2
3		3
4		4
5		5
6		6
7		7
8		8
9		9
10		10
11		11
12		12
13		13
14		14
15		15

Watson Company	
Retained Earnings Statement	
For the Year Ended December 31, 2014	

1		1
2		2
3		3
4		4
5		5
6		6
7		7
8		8
9		9
10		10

(b) (Continued)

Watson Company
Balance Sheet
December 31, 2014

	Assets												
1													
2													
3													
4													
5													
6													
7													
8													
9													
10													
11													
12													
13													
14													
15													
16	Liabilities and Stockholders' Equity												
17													
18													
19													
20													
21													
22													
23													
24													
25													
26													
27													
28													
29													
30													
31													
32													
33													

(c)

	General Journal				J14

	Date	Account Titles	Ref.	Debit	Credit	
1	Dec. 31					1
2						2
3						3
4	31					4
5						5
6						6
7						7
8						8
9						9
10						10
11						11
12	31					12
13						13
14						14
15	31					15
16						16
17						17
18						18

(d)

Retained Earnings   No.320

Date	Explanation	Ref.	Debit	Credit	Balance
Jan 1	Balance	√			9 8 0 0

Dividends   No. 332

Date	Explanation	Ref.	Debit	Credit	Balance
Dec 31	Balance	√			1 2 0 0 0

Income Summary   No. 350

Date	Explanation	Ref.	Debit	Credit	Balance

(d) (Continued)

Service Revenue   No. 400

Date	Explanation	Ref.	Debit	Credit	Balance
Dec 31	Balance	√			86200

Advertising Expense   No. 610

Date	Explanation	Ref.	Debit	Credit	Balance
Dec 31	Balance	√			10000

Supplies Expense   No. 631

Date	Explanation	Ref.	Debit	Credit	Balance
Dec 31	Balance	√			3700

Depreciation Expense   No. 711

Date	Explanation	Ref.	Debit	Credit	Balance
Dec 31	Balance	√			6000

Insurance Expense   No. 722

Date	Explanation	Ref.	Debit	Credit	Balance
Dec 31	Balance	√			4000

Salaries and WagesExpense   No. 726

Date	Explanation	Ref.	Debit	Credit	Balance
Dec 31	Balance	√			39000

Interest Expense   No. 905

Date	Explanation	Ref.	Debit	Credit	Balance
Dec 31	Balance	√			1000

(e)

Watson Company Post-Closing Trial Balance December 31, 2014	Debit	Credit
1		
2		
3		
4		
5		
6		
7		
8		
9		
10		
11		
12		
13		
14		
15		
16		
17		
18		
19		
20		

(a)

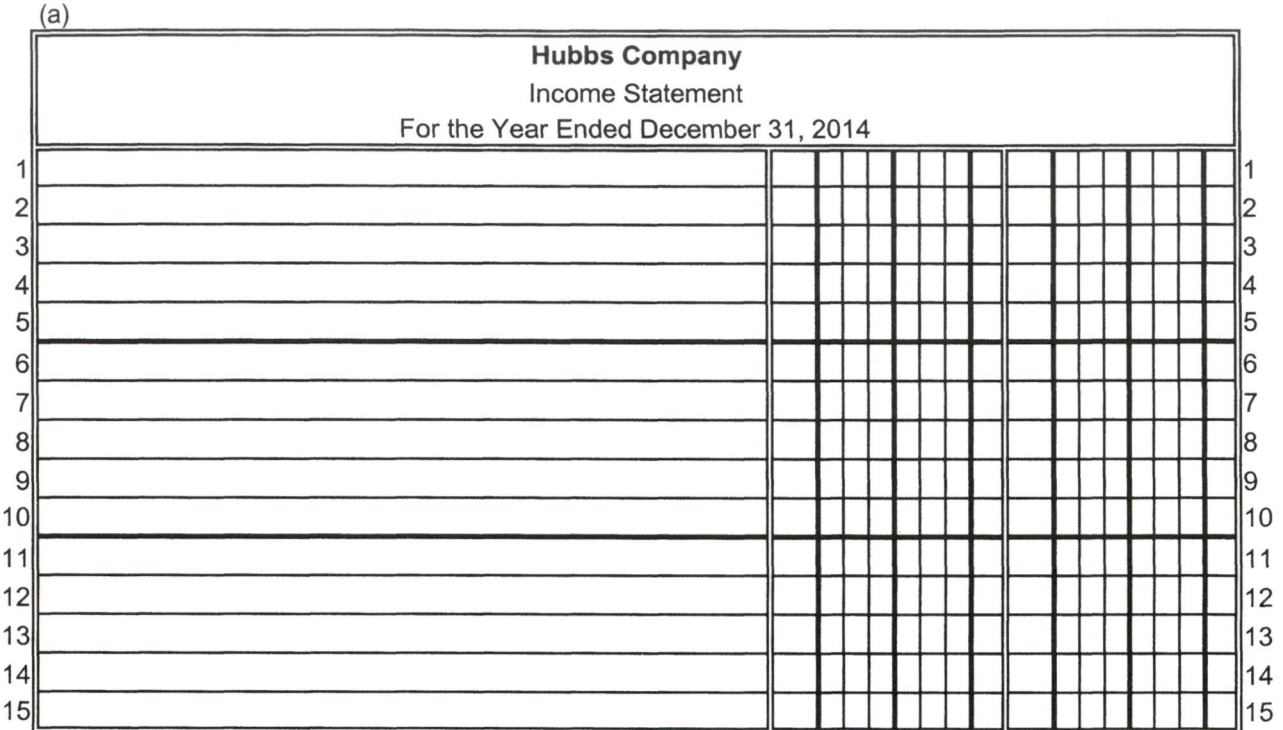

Hubbs Company
Income Statement
For the Year Ended December 31, 2014

Hubbs Company
Retained Earnings Statement
For the Year Ended December 31, 2014

(a) (Continued)

Hubbs Company
Balance Sheet
December 31, 2011

	Assets										
1											1
2											2
3											3
4											4
5											5
6											6
7											7
8											8
9											9
10											10
11											11
12											12
13	Liabilities and Stockholders' Equity										13
14											14
15											15
16											16
17											17
18											18
19											19
20											20
21											21
22											22
23											23
24											24

(b)   General Journal

	Date	Accounts Titles	Ref.	Debit	Credit	
1		Closing Entries				1
2	Dec. 31					2
3						3
4						4
5	31					5
6						6
7						7
8						8
9						9
10						10
11						11
12	31					12
13						13
14						14
15	31					15
16						16
17						17
18						18
19						19
20						20
21						21
22						22
23						23
24						24
25						25

(c)

Retained Earnings	No. 320		Maint. & Repairs Expense	No. 622
	1/1 Bal 9,700		12/31 Bal 4,100	

			Depreciation Expense	No. 711
			12/31 Bal 3,300	

Dividends	No.332		Insurance Expense	No. 722
12/31 Bal 4,000			12/31 Bal 2,200	

Income Summary	No. 350		Salaries & Wages Expense	No. 726
			12/31 Bal 35,200	

			Utilities Expense	No. 732
Service Revenue	No. 400		12/31 Bal 4,000	
	12/31 Bal 47,000			

(d)

Hubbs Company
Post-Closing Trial Balance
December 31, 2014

	Debit	Credit
1		
2		
3		
4		
5		
6		
7		
8		
9		
10		

Problem 4-4A

Excelsior Amusement Park

You will find this working paper at the end of this work book

(b)

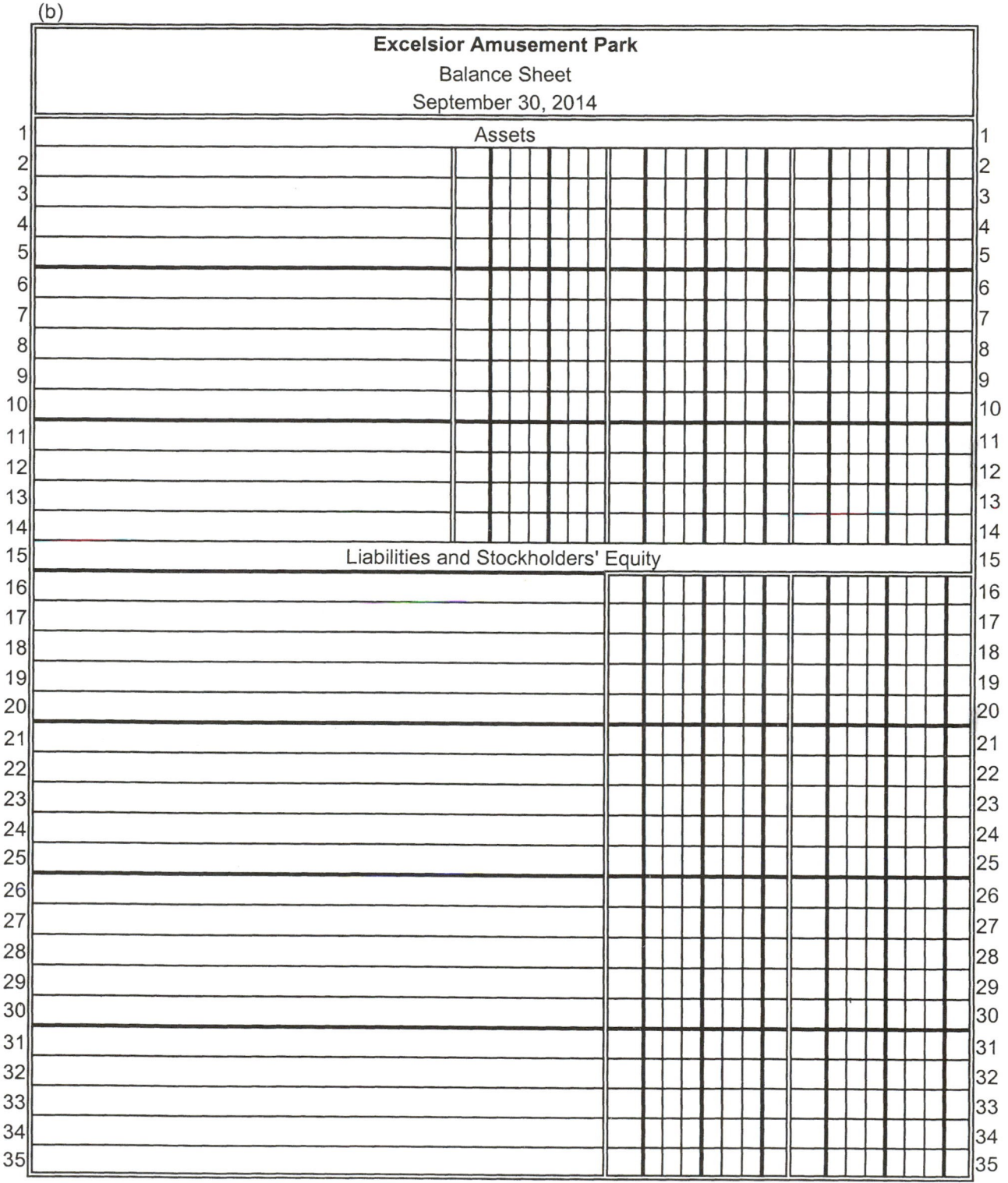

Excelsior Amusement Park

Balance Sheet

September 30, 2014

Assets

Liabilities and Stockholders' Equity

(c) & (d)

	Date	Accounts Titles	Debit	Credit	
1	(c)	Adjusting Entries			1
2	Sept. 30				2
3					3
4					4
5	30				5
6					6
7					7
8	30				8
9					9
10					10
11	30				11
12					12
13					13
14	30				14
15					15
16					16
17	30				17
18					18
19					19
20	(d)	Closing Entries			20
21	Sept. 30				21
22					22
23					23
24	30				24
25					25
26					26
27					27
28					28
29					29
30					30
31					31
32					32
33					33
34					34
35	30				35
36					36
37					37
38	30				38
39					39
40					40

(e)

Excelsior Amusement Park Post-Closing Trial Balance September 30, 2014	Debit	Credit

(a)   General Journal   J1

	Date	Accounts Titles	Ref.	Debit	Credit	
1	Mar. 1					1
2						2
3						3
4	1					4
5						5
6						6
7						7
8	3					8
9						9
10						10
11	5					11
12						12
13						13
14	14					14
15						15
16						16
17	18					17
18						18
19						19
20	20					20
21						21
22						22
23	21					23
24						24
25						25
26	28					26
27						27
28						28
29	31					29
30						30
31						31
32	31					32
33						33
34						34
35						35
36						36
37						37
38						38
39						39
40						40

Problem 4-5A

Fresh Step Carpet Cleaners

You will find this working paper at the end of this work book

(a), (e) and (f)

Cash   No. 101

Date	Explanation	Ref.	Debit	Credit	Balance

Accounts Receivable   No. 112

Date	Explanation	Ref.	Debit	Credit	Balance

Supplies   No. 128

Date	Explanation	Ref.	Debit	Credit	Balance

Prepaid Insurance   No. 130

Date	Explanation	Ref.	Debit	Credit	Balance

Equipment   No. 157

Date	Explanation	Ref.	Debit	Credit	Balance

(a), (e) and (f) (Continued)

Accumulated Depreciation - Equipment   No. 158

Date	Explanation	Ref.	Debit	Credit	Balance

Accounts Payable   No. 201

Date	Explanation	Ref.	Debit	Credit	Balance

Salaries and Wages Payable   No. 212

Date	Explanation	Ref.	Debit	Credit	Balance
			Debit	Credit	Balance

Common Stock   No. 311

Date	Explanation	Ref.	Debit	Credit	Balance

Retained Earnings   No. 320

Date	Explanation	Ref.	Debit	Credit	Balance

Dividends   No. 332

Date	Explanation	Ref.	Debit	Credit	Balance

Income Summary   No. 350

Date	Explanation	Ref.	Debit	Credit	Balance

(a), (e) and (f) (Continued)

Service Revenue   No. 400

Date	Explanation	Ref.	Debit	Credit	Balance

Gasoline Expense   No. 633

Date	Explanation	Ref.	Debit	Credit	Balance

Supplies Expense   No. 634

Date	Explanation	Ref.	Debit	Credit	Balance

Depreciation Expense   No. 711

Date	Explanation	Ref.	Debit	Credit	Balance

Insurance Expense   No. 722

Date	Explanation	Ref.	Debit	Credit	Balance

Salaries and Wages Expense   No. 726

Date	Explanation	Ref.	Debit	Credit	Balance

(d)

Fresh Step Carpet Cleaners

Income Statement

For the Month Ended March 31, 2014

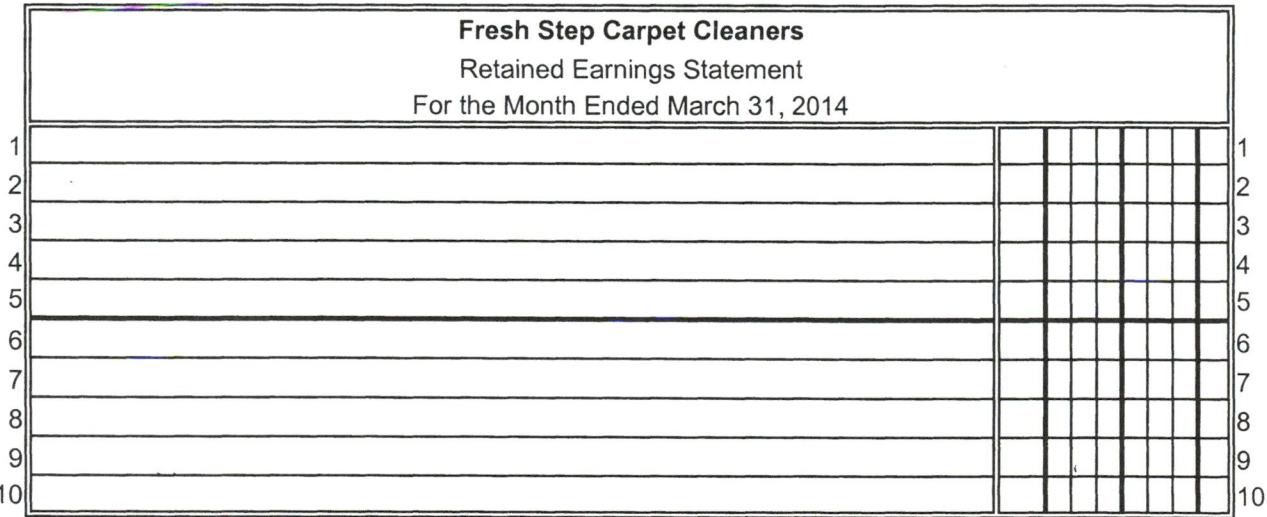

Fresh Step Carpet Cleaners

Retained Earnings Statement

For the Month Ended March 31, 2014

(d) (Continued)

Fresh Step Carpet Cleaners
Balance Sheet
March 31, 2014

	Assets						
1							
2							
3							
4							
5							
6							
7							
8							
9							
10							
11							
12							
13							
14	Liabilities and Stockholders' Equity						
15							
16							
17							
18							
19							
20							
21							
22							
23							
24							
25							
26							
27							

(e)   General Journal   J2

	Date	Accounts Titles	Ref.	Debit	Credit	
1		Adjusting Entries				1
2	Mar. 31					2
3						3
4						4
5	31					5
6						6
7						7
8	31					8
9						9
10						10
11	31					11
12						12
13						13
14	31					14
15						15
16						16

(f)   General Journal   J3

	Date	Account Titles	Ref.	Debit	Credit	
1		Closing Entries				1
2	Mar. 31					2
3						3
4						4
5	31					5
6						6
7						7
8						8
9						9
10						10
11						11
12	31					12
13						13
14						14
15	31					15
16						16
17						17
18						18
19						19

(g)

Fresh Step Carpet Cleaners

Post-Closing Trial Balance

March 31, 2014

	Debit	Credit
1		
2		
3		
4		
5		
6		
7		
8		
9		
10		
11		
12		

Problem 4-6A

Info Cable

You will find this working paper at the end of this work book

(b)

		Debit	Credit	
1	Cash			1
2	Accounts Receivable			2
3	Supplies			3
4	Equipment			4
5	Accumulated Depreciation - Equipment			5
6	Accounts Payable			6
7	Salaries and Wages Payable			7
8	Unearned Service Revenue			8
9	Common Stock			9
10	Retained Earnings			10
11	Service Revenue			11
12	Salaries and Wages Expense			12
13	Advertising Expense			13
14	Miscellaneous Expense			14
15	Depreciation Expense			15
16	Maintenance and Repairs Expense			16
17				17
18				18
19				19
20				20
21				21
22				22
23				23
24				24
25				25
26				26
27				27
28				28
29				29
30				30

Info Cable

Trial Balance

April 30, 2014

Problem 4-1B

Firmament Roofing

You will find this working paper at the end of this work book

(b)

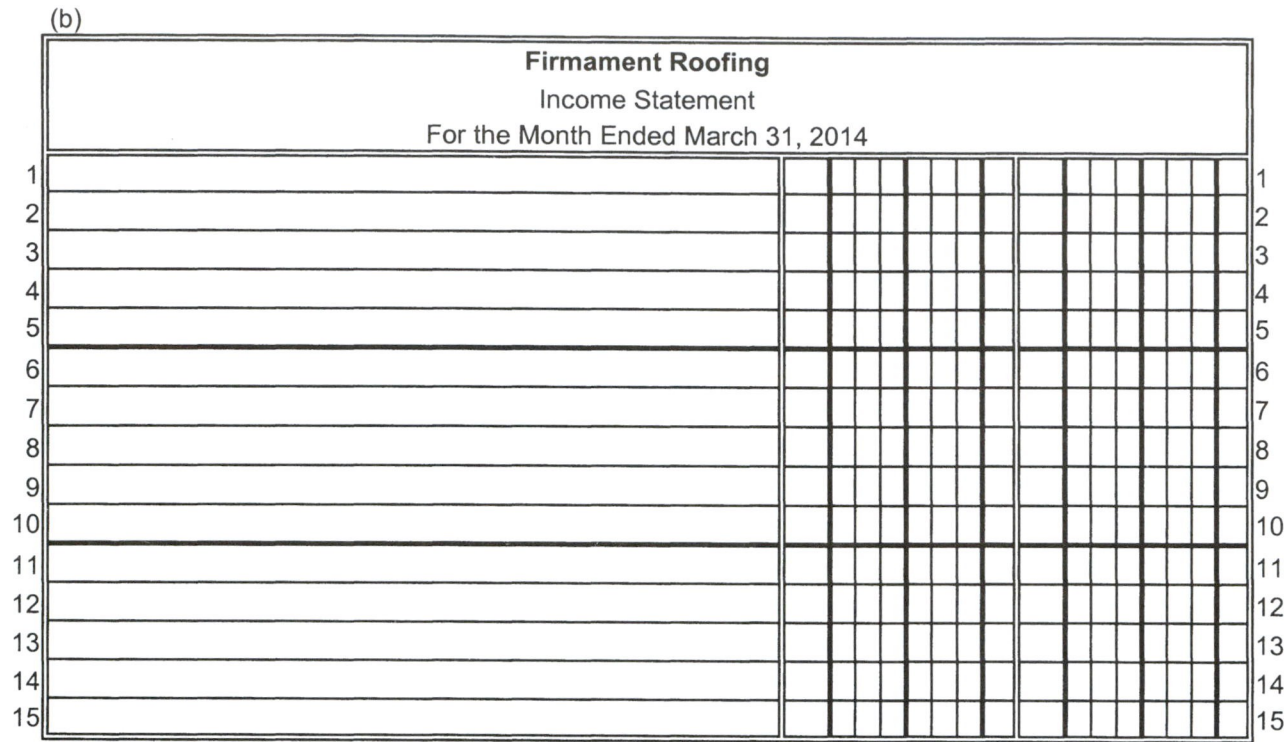

Firmament Roofing

Income Statement

For the Month Ended March 31, 2014

Firmament Roofing

Retained Earnings Statement

For the Month Ended March 31, 2014

(b) (Continued)

Firmament Roofing

Balance Sheet

March 31, 2014

Assets						
Liabilities and Stockholders' Equity						

(c)   General Journal

	Date	Account Titles	Debit	Credit	
1		Adjusting Entries			1
2	Mar. 31				2
3					3
4					4
5	31				5
6					6
7					7
8	31				8
9					9
10					10
11	31				11
12					12
13					13
14					14
15					15

(d)   General Journal

	Date	Account Titles	Debit	Credit	
1		Closing Entries			1
2	Mar. 31				2
3					3
4					4
5	31				5
6					6
7					7
8					8
9					9
10					10
11	31				11
12					12
13					13
14	31				14
15					15
16					16

(a)

Eagle Company
Partial Worksheet
For the Year Ended December 31, 2011

	Account No.	Titles	Adjusted Trial Balance Dr.	Adjusted Trial Balance Cr.	Income Statement Dr.	Income Statement Cr.	Balance Sheet Dr.	Balance Sheet Cr.
1	101	Cash	5300					
2	112	Accounts Receivable	10800					
3	126	Supplies	1500					
4	130	Prepaid Insurance	2000					
5	151	Equipment	27000					
6	152	Accum. Depr. - Equip.		5600				
7	200	Notes Payable		15000				
8	201	Accounts Payable		4600				
9	212	Salaries & Wages Payable		2400				
10	230	Interest Payable		600				
11	311	Common Stock		10000				
12	320	Retained Earnings		4200				
13	332	Dividends	5000					
14	400	Service Revenue		59000				
15	610	Advertising Expense	8400					
16	631	Supplies Expense	4000					
17	711	Depreciation Expense	5600					
18	722	Insurance Expense	3200					
19	726	Salaries & Wages Expense	28000					
20	905	Interest Expense	600					
21		Totals	101400	101400				
22		Net Income						
23		Totals						
24								

(b)

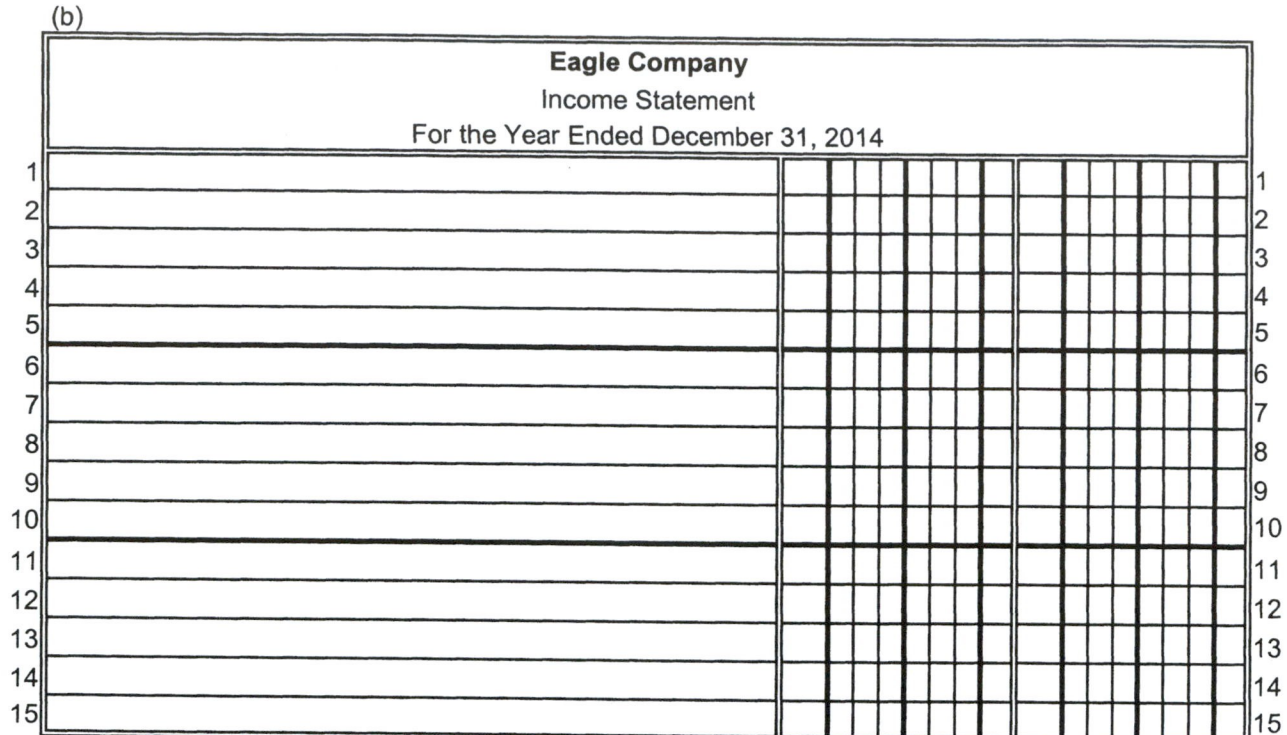

Eagle Company

Income Statement

For the Year Ended December 31, 2014

1		
2		
3		
4		
5		
6		
7		
8		
9		
10		
11		
12		
13		
14		
15		

Eagle Company

Retained Earnings Statement

For the Year Ended December 31, 2014

1	
2	
3	
4	
5	
6	
7	
8	
9	
10	

(b) (Continued)

	Eagle Company									
	Balance Sheet									
	December 31, 2014									
1	Assets									1
2										2
3										3
4										4
5										5
6										6
7										7
8										8
9										9
10										10
11										11
12										12
13										13
14										14
15										15
16	Liabilities and Stockholders' Equity									16
17										17
18										18
19										19
20										20
21										21
22										22
23										23
24										24
25										25
26										26
27										27
28										28
29										29
30										30
31										31
32										32
33										33

(c)

General Journal   J14

	Date	Account Titles	Ref.	Debit	Credit	
1	Dec. 31					1
2						2
3						3
4	31					4
5						5
6						6
7						7
8						8
9						9
10						10
11						11
12	31					12
13						13
14						14
15	31					15
16						16
17						17
18						18

(d)

Retained Earnings   No.320

Date	Explanation	Ref.	Debit	Credit	Balance
Jan 1	Balance	√			4 2 0 0

Dividends   No. 332

Date	Explanation	Ref.	Debit	Credit	Balance
Dec 31	Balance	√			5 0 0 0

Income Summary   No. 350

Date	Explanation	Ref.	Debit	Credit	Balance

(d) (Continued)

Service Revenue   No. 400

Date	Explanation	Ref.	Debit	Credit	Balance
Dec 31	Balance	√			5 9 0 0 0

Advertising Expense   No. 610

Date	Explanation	Ref.	Debit	Credit	Balance
Dec 31	Balance	√			8 4 0 0

Supplies Expense   No. 631

Date	Explanation	Ref.	Debit	Credit	Balance
Dec 31	Balance	√			4 0 0 0

Depreciation Expense   No. 711

Date	Explanation	Ref.	Debit	Credit	Balance
Dec 31	Balance	√			5 6 0 0

Insurance Expense   No. 722

Date	Explanation	Ref.	Debit	Credit	Balance
Dec 31	Balance	√			3 2 0 0

Salaries and Wages Expense   No. 726

Date	Explanation	Ref.	Debit	Credit	Balance
Dec 31	Balance	√			2 8 0 0 0

Interest Expense   No. 905

Date	Explanation	Ref.	Debit	Credit	Balance
Dec 31	Balance	√			6 0 0

(e)

Eagle Company Post-Closing Trial Balance December 31, 2014	Debit	Credit
1			1
2			2
3			3
4			4
5			5
6			6
7			7
8			8
9			9
10			10
11			11
12			12
13			13
14			14
15			15
16			16
17			17
18			18
19			19
20			20

(a)

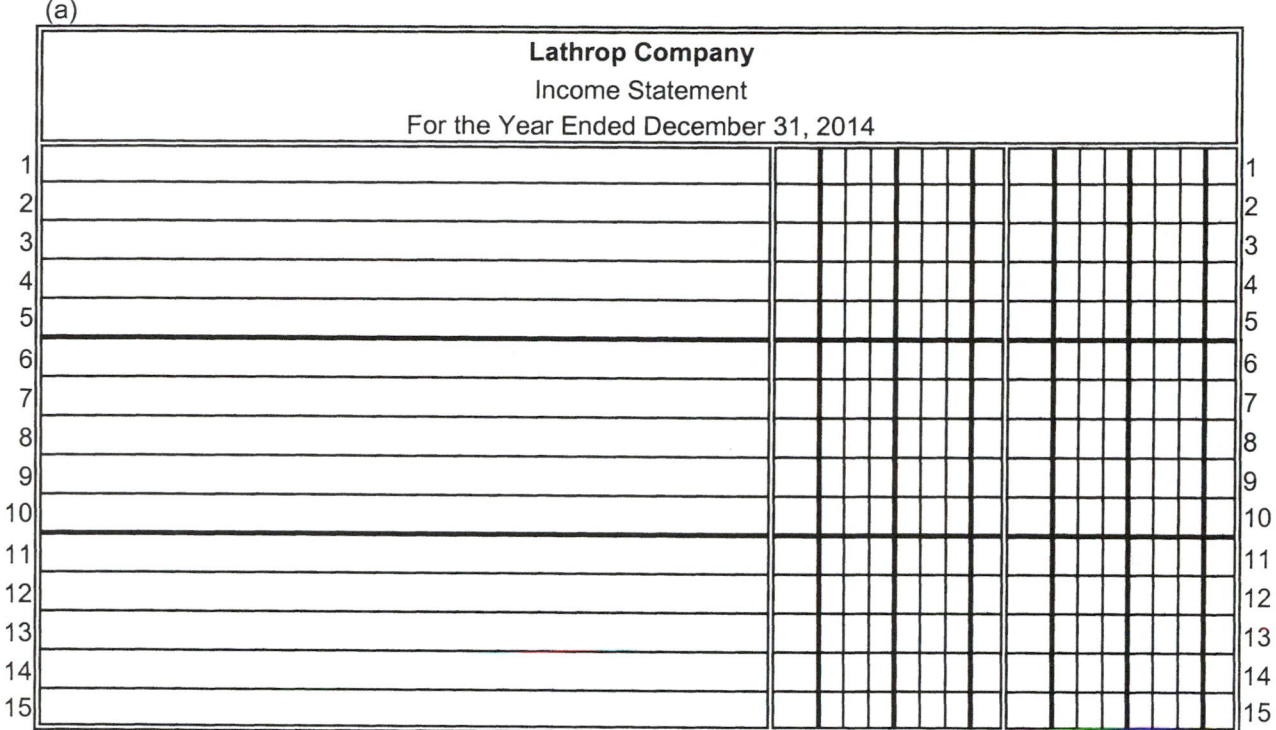

Lathrop Company

Income Statement

For the Year Ended December 31, 2014

Lathrop Company

Retained Earnings Statement

For the Year Ended December 31, 2014

(a) (Continued)

Lathrop Company
Balance Sheet
December 31, 2014

	Assets						
1							
2							
3							
4							
5							
6							
7							
8							
9							
10							
11							
12	Liabilities and Stockholders' Equity						
13							
14							
15							
16							
17							
18							
19							
20							
21							
22							
23							

(b)   General Journal

	Date	Accounts Titles	Ref.	Debit	Credit	
1		Closing Entries				1
2	Dec. 31					2
3						3
4						4
5	31					5
6						6
7						7
8						8
9						9
10						10
11						11
12	31					12
13						13
14						14
15	31					15
16						16
17						17
18						18
19						19
20						20
21						21
22						22
23						23
24						24
25						25

(c)

Retained Earnings	No. 320		
	1/1 Bal	16,400	

Dividends	No. 332		
12/31 Bal	8,000		

Income Summary	No. 350

Service Revenue	No. 400		
	12/31 Bal	56,000	

Maint. & Repairs Expense	No. 622		
12/31 Bal	1,600		

Depreciation Expense	No. 711		
12/31 Bal	3,000		

Insurance Expense	No. 722		
12/31 Bal	1,800		

Salaries & Wages Expense	No. 726		
12/31 Bal	27,000		

Utilities Expense	No. 732		
12/31 Bal	1,400		

(d)

Lathrop Company
Post-Closing Trial Balance
December 31, 2014

	Debit	Credit
1		
2		
3		
4		
5		
6		
7		
8		
9		
10		

Problem 4-4B

Kumar Management Services, Inc.

You will find this working paper at the end of this work book

(b)

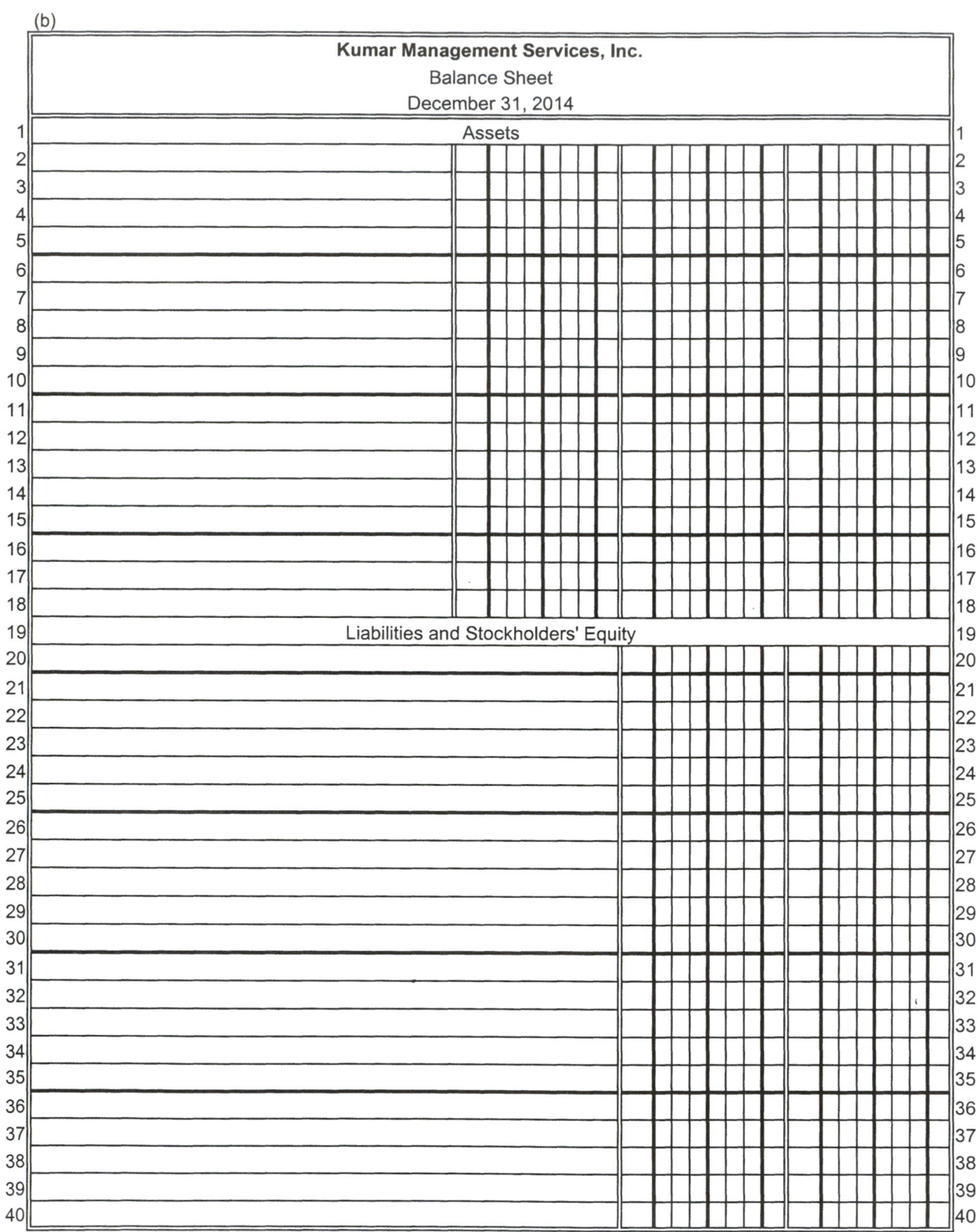

Kumar Management Services, Inc.

Balance Sheet

December 31, 2014

Assets

Liabilities and Stockholders' Equity

	Date	Accounts Titles	Debit	Credit	
1	(c)	Adjusting Entries			1
2	Dec. 31				2
3					3
4					4
5	31				5
6					6
7					7
8	31				8
9					9
10					10
11	31				11
12					12
13					13
14	31				14
15					15
16					16
17					17
18					18
19	(d)	Closing Entries			19
20	Dec. 31				20
21					21
22					22
23					23
24	31				24
25					25
26					26
27					27
28					28
29					29
30					30
31					31
32					32
33	31				33
34					34
35					35
36	31				36
37					37
38					38
39					39
40					40

(e)

Kumar Management Services, Inc.
Post-Closing Trial Balance
December 31, 2014

	Debit	Credit
1		
2		
3		
4		
5		
6		
7		
8		
9		
10		
11		
12		
13		
14		
15		
16		
17		
18		
19		
20		
21		
22		
23		
24		
25		
26		
27		
28		
29		
30		

(a)   General Journal   J1

	Date	Accounts Titles	Ref.	Debit	Credit	
1	July 1					1
2						2
3						3
4	1					4
5						5
6						6
7						7
8	3					8
9						9
10						10
11	5					11
12						12
13						13
14	12					14
15						15
16						16
17	18					17
18						18
19						19
20	20					20
21						21
22						22
23	21					23
24						24
25						25
26	25					26
27						27
28						28
29	31					29
30						30
31						31
32	31					32
33						33
34						34
35						35
36						36
37						37
38						38
39						39

Problem 4-5B

Brennan's Cleaning Services

You will find this working paper at the end of this work book

(a), (e) and (f)

Cash   No. 101

Date	Explanation	Ref.	Debit	Credit	Balance

Accounts Receivable   No. 112

Date	Explanation	Ref.	Debit	Credit	Balance

Supplies   No. 128

Date	Explanation	Ref.	Debit	Credit	Balance

Prepaid Insurance   No. 130

Date	Explanation	Ref.	Debit	Credit	Balance

Equipment   No. 157

Date	Explanation	Ref.	Debit	Credit	Balance

(a), (e) and (f) (Continued)

Accumulated Depreciation - Equipment

No. 158

Date	Explanation	Ref.	Debit	Credit	Balance

Accounts Payable

No. 201

Date	Explanation	Ref.	Debit	Credit	Balance

Salaries and Wages Payable

No. 212

Date	Explanation	Ref.	Debit	Credit	Balance

Common Stock

No. 311

Date	Explanation	Ref.	Debit	Credit	Balance

Retained Earnings

No. 320

Date	Explanation	Ref.	Debit	Credit	Balance

Dividends

No. 332

Date	Explanation	Ref.	Debit	Credit	Balance

Income Summary

No. 350

Date	Explanation	Ref.	Debit	Credit	Balance

(a), (e) and (f) (Continued)

Service Revenue   No. 400

Date	Explanation	Ref.	Debit	Credit	Balance

Gasoline Expense   No. 633

Date	Explanation	Ref.	Debit	Credit	Balance

Supplies Expense   No. 634

Date	Explanation	Ref.	Debit	Credit	Balance

Depreciation Expense   No. 711

Date	Explanation	Ref.	Debit	Credit	Balance

Insurance Expense   No. 722

Date	Explanation	Ref.	Debit	Credit	Balance

Salaries and Wages Expense   No. 726

Date	Explanation	Ref.	Debit	Credit	Balance

(d)

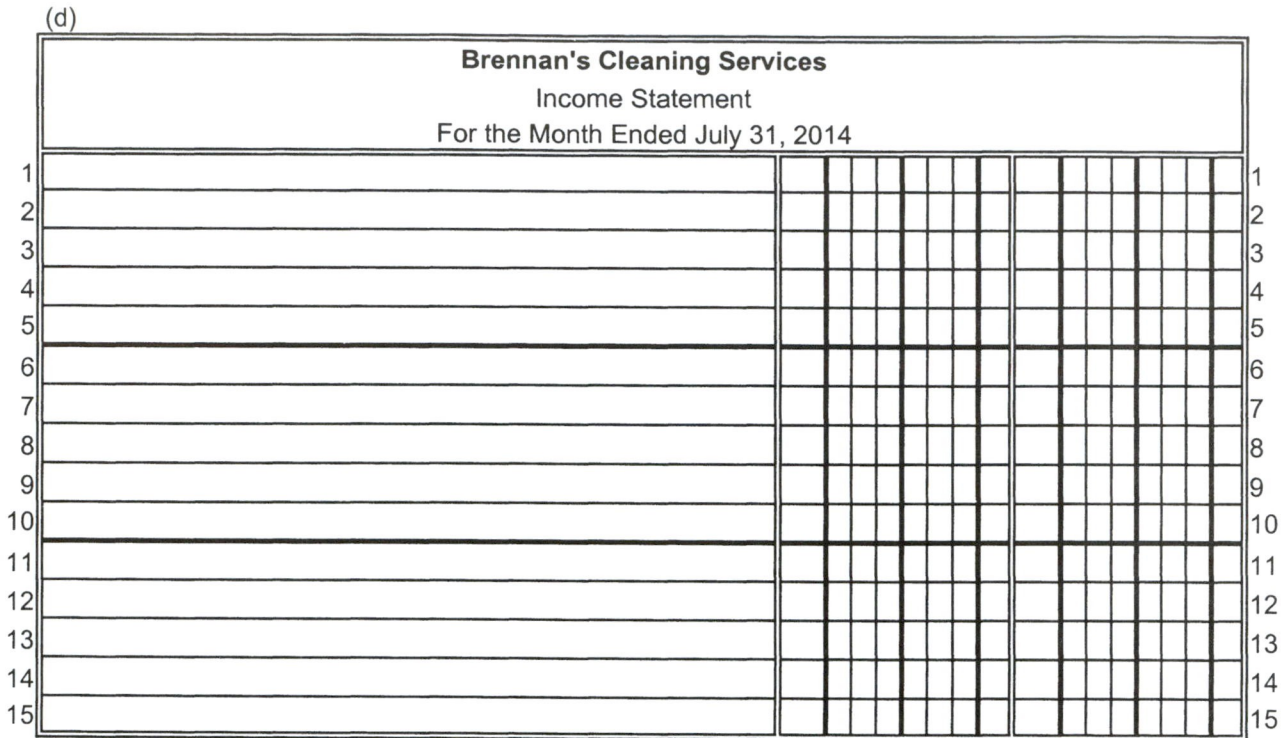

Brennan's Cleaning Services
Income Statement
For the Month Ended July 31, 2014

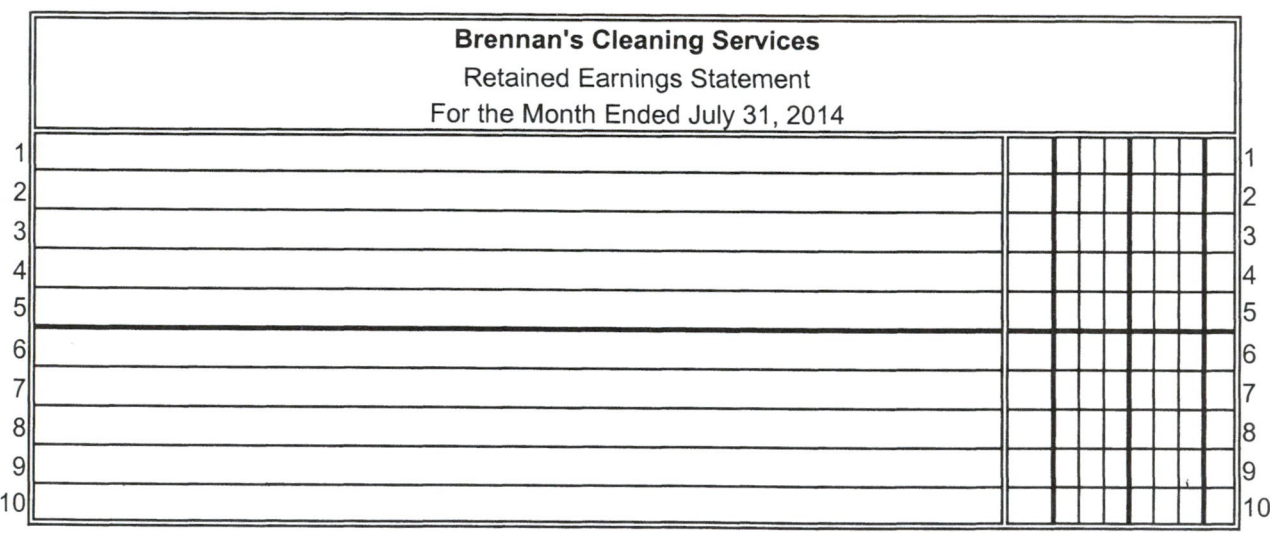

Brennan's Cleaning Services
Retained Earnings Statement
For the Month Ended July 31, 2014

(d) (Continued)

Brennan's Cleaning Services
Balance Sheet
July 31, 2014

Assets						
Liabilities and Stockholders' Equity						

(e) General Journal J2

	Date	Accounts Titles	Ref.	Debit	Credit	
1		Adjusting Entries				1
2	July 31					2
3						3
4						4
5	31					5
6						6
7						7
8	31					8
9						9
10						10
11	31					11
12						12
13						13
14	31					14
15						15
16						16

(f) General Journal J3

	Date	Account Titles	Ref.	Debit	Credit	
1		Closing Entries				1
2	July 31					2
3						3
4						4
5	31					5
6						6
7						7
8						8
9						9
10						10
11						11
12	31					12
13						13
14						14
15	31					15
16						16
17						17
18						18
19						19

(g)

Brennan's Cleaning Services Post-Closing Trial Balance July 31, 2014	Debit	Credit
1		
2		
3		
4		
5		
6		
7		
8		
9		
10		
11		
12		

(a) General Journal J1

	Date	Accounts Titles	Ref.	Debit	Credit	
1	July 1					1
2						2
3						3
4	1					4
5						5
6						6
7						7
8	3					8
9						9
10						10
11	5					11
12						12
13						13
14	12					14
15						15
16						16
17	18					17
18						18
19						19
20	20					20
21						21
22						22
23	21					23
24						24
25						25
26	25					26
27						27
28						28
29	31					29
30						30
31						31
32	31					32
33						33
34						34
35						35
36						36
37						37
38						38
39						39
40						40

Comprehensive Problem Ch 2 - 4

Mary's Maids Cleaning Service

You will find this working paper at the end of this work book

(a), (e) and (f)

Cash   No. 101

Date	Explanation	Ref.	Debit	Credit	Balance

Accounts Receivable   No. 112

Date	Explanation	Ref.	Debit	Credit	Balance

Supplies   No. 128

Date	Explanation	Ref.	Debit	Credit	Balance

Prepaid Insurance   No. 130

Date	Explanation	Ref.	Debit	Credit	Balance

Equipment   No. 157

Date	Explanation	Ref.	Debit	Credit	Balance

Accumulated Depreciation - Equipment   No. 158

Date	Explanation	Ref.	Debit	Credit	Balance

(a), (e) and (f) (Continued)

Accounts Payable   No. 201

Date	Explanation	Ref.	Debit	Credit	Balance

Salaries and Wages Payable   No. 212

Date	Explanation	Ref.	Debit	Credit	Balance

Common Stock   No. 311

Date	Explanation	Ref.	Debit	Credit	Balance

Retained Earnings   No. 320

Date	Explanation	Ref.	Debit	Credit	Balance

Dividends   No. 332

Date	Explanation	Ref.	Debit	Credit	Balance

Income Summary   No. 350

Date	Explanation	Ref.	Debit	Credit	Balance

(a), (e) and (f) (Continued)

Service Revenue   No. 400

Date	Explanation	Ref.	Debit	Credit	Balance

Gasoline Expense   No. 633

Date	Explanation	Ref.	Debit	Credit	Balance

Supplies Expense   No. 634

Date	Explanation	Ref.	Debit	Credit	Balance

Depreciation Expense   No. 711

Date	Explanation	Ref.	Debit	Credit	Balance

Insurance Expense   No. 722

Date	Explanation	Ref.	Debit	Credit	Balance

Salaries and Wages   No. 726

Date	Explanation	Ref.	Debit	Credit	Balance

(d)

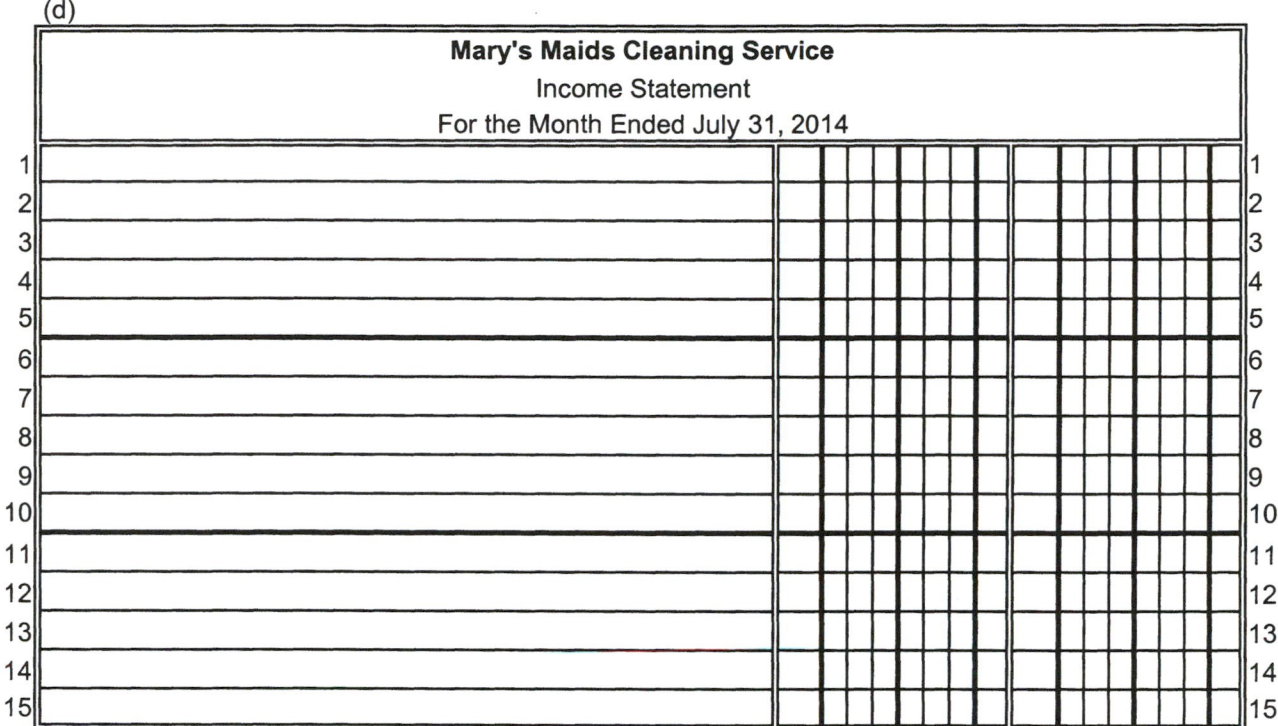

Mary's Maids Cleaning Service

Income Statement

For the Month Ended July 31, 2014

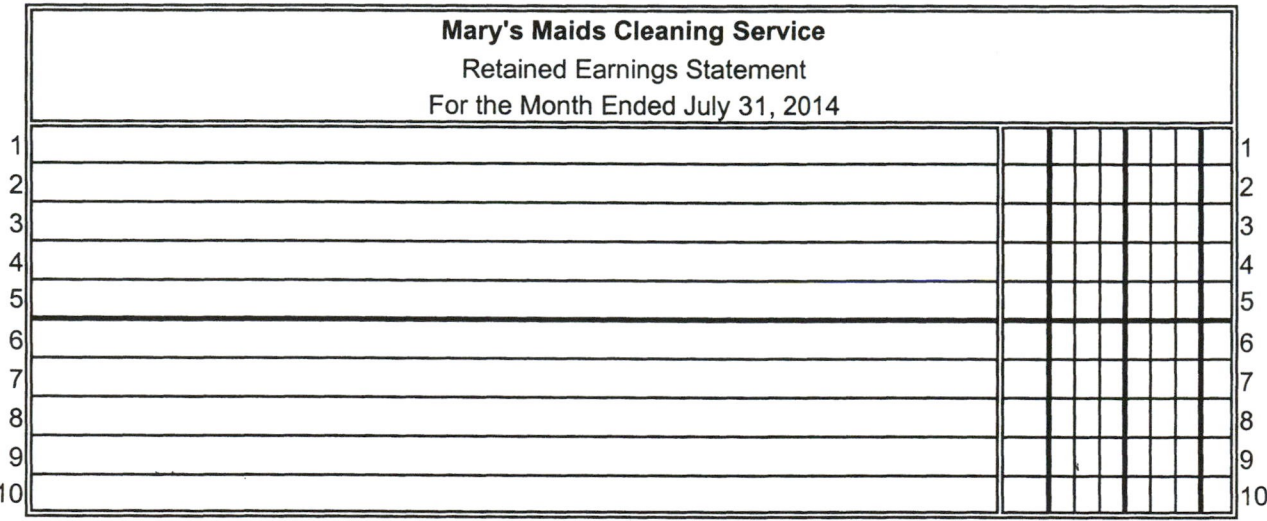

Mary's Maids Cleaning Service

Retained Earnings Statement

For the Month Ended July 31, 2014

(d) (Continued)

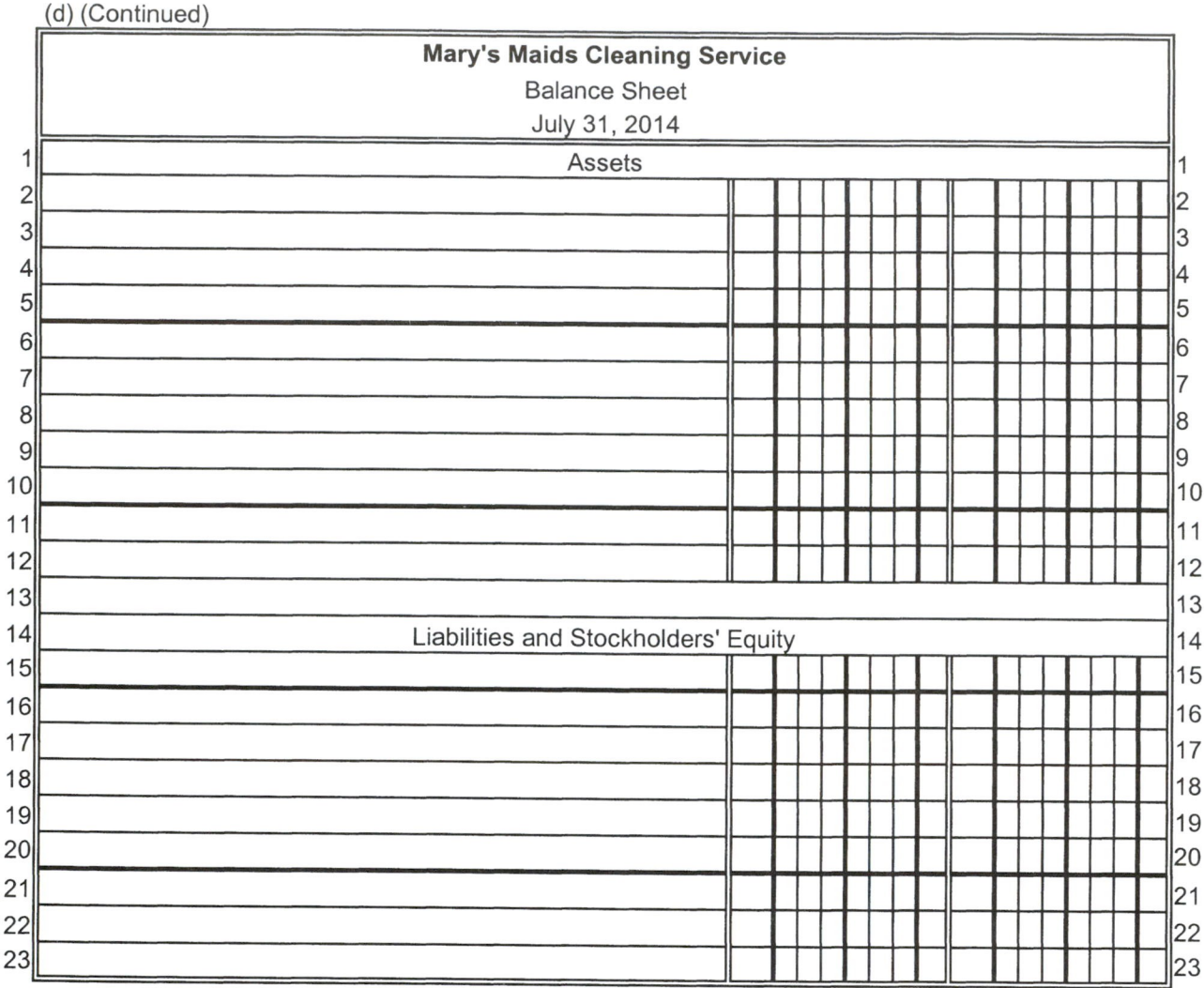

Mary's Maids Cleaning Service

Balance Sheet

July 31, 2014

Assets

Liabilities and Stockholders' Equity

(g)

Mary's Maids Cleaning Service

Post-Closing Trial Balance

July 31, 2014

	Debit	Credit

General Journal   J2

	Date	Accounts Titles	Ref.	Debit	Credit	
1	(e)	Adjusting Entries				1
2	July 31					2
3						3
4						4
5	31					5
6						6
7						7
8	31					8
9						9
10						10
11	31					11
12						12
13						13
14	31					14
15						15
16						16

General Journal   J3

	Date	Account Titles	Ref.	Debit	Credit	
1	(f)	Closing Entries				1
2	July 31					2
3						3
4						4
5	31					5
6						6
7						7
8						8
9						9
10						10
11						11
12	31					12
13						13
14						14
15	31					15
16						16
17						17
18						18
19						19
20						20

	PepsiCo	Coca-Cola
1		
2 (a) (in millions)		
3		
4 1. Total current assets		
5		
6 2. Net property, plant, and equipment		
7		
8 3. Total current liabilities		
9		
10 4. Total stockholders' (shareholders') equity		
11		
12		
13		
14		
15		
16 (b)		

(a)

Everclean Janitorial Service					
Balance Sheet					
December 31, 2014					
Assets					
Liabilities and Stockholders' Equity					

Everclean Janitorial Service		
Retained Earnings Account Detail		
December 31, 2014		
Retained earnings account balance as reported		$ 2 4 0 0 0

(b)

	Assets	
1		1
2		2
3		3
4		4
5		5
6		6
7		7
8		8
9		9
10		10
11		11
12		12
13		13
14		14
15		15
16	Liabilities and Stockholders' Equity	16
17		17
18		18
19		19
20		20
21		21
22		22
23		23
24		24
25		25
26		26
27		27
28		28
29		29
30		30
31		31
32		32
33		33
34		34
35		35
36		36
37		37
38		38
39		39
40		40

IFRS4-3

	Diaz Company			
	Partial Statement of Financial Position			

IFRS4-4

	Zurich Company			
	Partial Statement of Financial Position			
	December 31, 2014			

IFRS4-5

	Rego Bowling Alley									
	Statement of Financial Position									
	December 31, 2014									
	Assets									

Equity and Liabilities

BE5-1

	Sales	Cost of Goods Sold	Gross Profit	Operating Expenses	Net Income
(a)	$ 75000		$ 30000		$ 10800
(b)	108000	55000			29500
(c)		83900	79600	39500	

BE5-2

	Account Titles	Debit	Credit
Giovanni Company			
Gordon Company			

BE5-3

	Account Titles	Debit	Credit
(a)			
(b)			
(c)			

BE5-4

	Account Titles	Debit	Credit
(a)			
(b)			
(c)			

BE5-5

Account Titles	Debit	Credit

BE5-6

Account Titles	Debit	Credit

BE5-7

Piccola Company

Income Statement (Partial)

For the Month Ended October 31, 2014

BE5-10

BE5-11

***BE5-12**

	Account Titles	Debit	Credit
(a)			
(b)			
(c)			

DO IT! 5-1

	Date	Account Titles	Debit	Credit	
1	Oct. 5				1
2					2
3					3
4					4
5	8				5
6					6
7					7
8					8
9					9

DO IT! 5-2

10					10
11	Oct. 5				11
12					12
13					13
14					14
15					15
16					16
17					17
18					18
19	8				19
20					20
21					21
22					22
23					23
24					24
25					25
26					26

DO IT! 5-3

27					27
28	Dec. 31				28
29					29
30					30
31					31
32					32
33	31				33
34					34
35					35
36					36
37					37
38					38
39					39
40					40

E5-2   General Journal

	Date	Account Titles	Debit	Credit	
1	(a)				1
2	Apr. 5				2
3					3
4					4
5	6				5
6					6
7					7
8	7				8
9					9
10					10
11	8				11
12					12
13					13
14	15				14
15					15
16					16
17					17
18	(b)				18
19	May 4				19
20					20
21					21

E5-3

	Date	Account Titles	Debit	Credit	
1	Sept. 6				1
2					2
3					3
4	9				4
5					5
6					6
7	10				7
8					8
9					9
10	12				10
11					11
12					12
13					13
14					14

E5-3 (Continued) General Journal

	Date	Account Titles	Debit	Credit	
1	Sept. 14				1
2					2
3					3
4					4
5					5
6	20				6
7					7
8					8
9					9
10					10
11					11
12					12

E5-4

	Date	Account Titles	Debit	Credit	
1	(a)	Rebecca Company			1
2	June 10				2
3					3
4					4
5	11				5
6					6
7					7
8	12				8
9					9
10					10
11	19				11
12					12
13					13
14					14
15	(b)	Clinton Company			15
16	June 10				16
17					17
18					18
19					19
20					20
21					21
22					22
23					23

E5-4 (Continued)   General Journal

	Date	Account Titles	Debit	Credit	
1	June 12				1
2					2
3					3
4					4
5					5
6	19				6
7					7
8					8
9					9
10					10

E5-5

	Date	Account Titles	Debit	Credit	
1	(a)				1
2	Dec. 3				2
3					3
4					4
5					5
6					6
7					7
8	8				8
9					9
10					10
11	13				11
12					12
13					13
14					14
15					15
16					16
17	(b)				17
18	Jan. 2				18
19					19
20					20
21					21
22					22
23					23
24					24
25					25

E5-6 (a)

	Mendoza Company				
	Income Statement (Partial)				
	For the Year Ended October 31, 2014				
1					1
2					2
3					3
4					4
5					5
6					6

(b)

	Date	Account Titles	Debit	Credit	
1	Oct. 31				1
2					2
3					3
4	31				4
5					5
6					6
7					7

E5-7

	Account Titles	Debit	Credit	
1	(a)			1
2				2
3				3
4	(b)			4
5				5
6				6
7				7
8				8
9				9
10				10
11				11
12				12
13				13
14				14
15				15
16				16
17				17

Section

Date

	Account Titles	Debit	Credit	
1	(a)			1
2				2
3				3
4	(b)			4
5				5
6				6
7				7
8				8
9				9
10				10
11				11
12				12
13				13
14				14
15				15
16				16
17				17
18				18
19				19
20				20
21				21
22				22
23				23
24				24
25				25
26				26
27				27
28				28
29				29
30				30
31				31
32				32
33				33
34				34
35				35
36				36
37				37
38				38
39				39
40				40

(a)

Multi-Step

Bach Company
Income Statement
For the Year Ended March 31, 2014

1			
2			
3			
4			
5			
6			
7			
8			
9			
10			
11			
12			
13			
14			
15			
16			
17			
18			
19			
20			

(b)

1	Gross profit rate =
2	
3	
4	
5	
6	
7	
8	
9	
10	
11	
12	
13	
14	
15	

(a)   Multi-Step

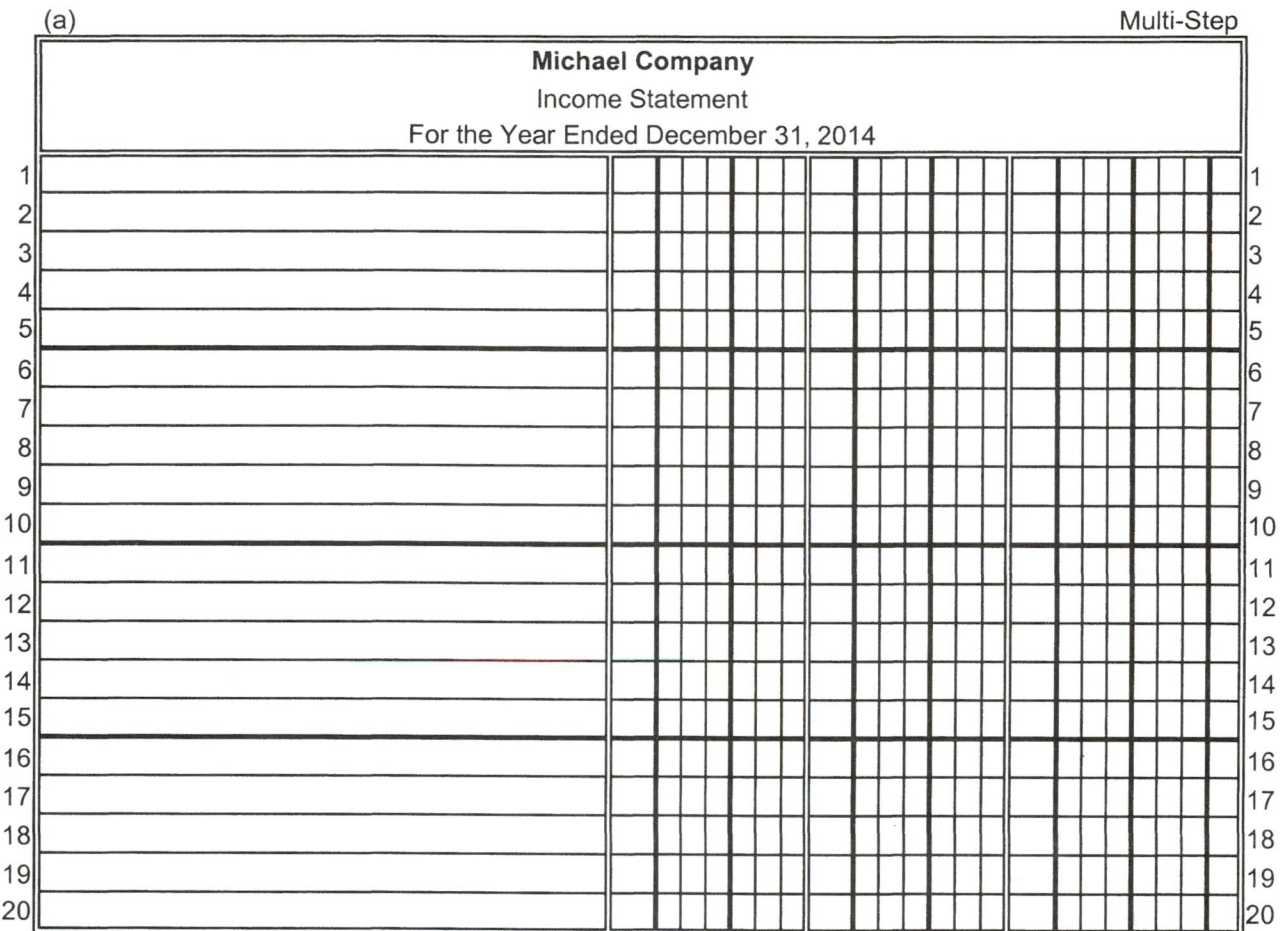

Michael Company
Income Statement
For the Year Ended December 31, 2014

(b)   Single-Step

Michael Company
Income Statement
For the Year Ended December 31, 2014

E5-11

		Account Titles	Debit	Credit	
1	1.				1
2					2
3					3
4	2.				4
5					5
6					6
7					7
8					8
9	3.				9
10					10
11					11
12	4.				12
13					13
14					14
15					15

E5-13

	(a)	Lee Company	Chan Company	
1				1
2	Sales	$ 9 0 0 0 0	$	2
3				3
4	Sales Returns		5 0 0 0	4
5				5
6	Net Sales	8 1 0 0 0	9 8 0 0 0	6
7				7
8	Cost of Goods Sold	5 6 0 0 0		8
9				9
10	Gross Profit		3 7 5 0 0	10
11				11
12	Operating Expenses	1 2 0 0 0		12
13				13
14	Net Income	$	$ 1 5 0 0 0	14
15				15
16	(b) Gross profit rates:			16
17	Lee Company			17
18				18
19	Chan Company			19
20				20

Section

Date   Athena Cosmetics, Harry Grocery and Panama Wholesalers

	Athena Cosmetics	Harry Grocery	Panama Wholesalers	
1				1
2 Sales	$ 9 0 0 0 0		$ 1 2 2 0 0 0	2
3 Sales returns and allowances		5 0 0 0	1 2 0 0 0	3
4 Net sales	8 6 0 0 0	9 5 0 0 0		4
5 Cost of goods sold	5 6 0 0 0			5
6 Gross profit		2 2 0 0 0	2 4 0 0 0	6
7 Operating expenses	1 5 0 0 0		1 8 0 0 0	7
8 Income from operations				8
9 Other expenses and losses	4 0 0 0	3 0 0 0		9
10 Net income		1 1 0 0 0	5 0 0 0	10
11				11
12 Computations:				12
13				13
14				14
15				15
16				16
17				17
18				18
19				19
20				20
21				21
22				22
23				23
24				24
25				25
26				26
27				27
28				28
29				29
30				30
31				31
32				32
33				33
34				34
35				35
36				36
37				37
38				38
39				39
40				40

	Computations (Continued):		
1			1
2			2
3			3
4			4
5			5
6			6
7			7
8			8
9			9
10			10
11			11
12			12
13			13
14			14
15			15
16			16
17			17
18			18
19			19
20			20
21			21
22			22
23			23
24			24
25			25
26			26
27			27
28			28
29			29
30			30
31			31
32			32
33			33
34			34
35			35
36			36
37			37
38			38
39			39
40			40

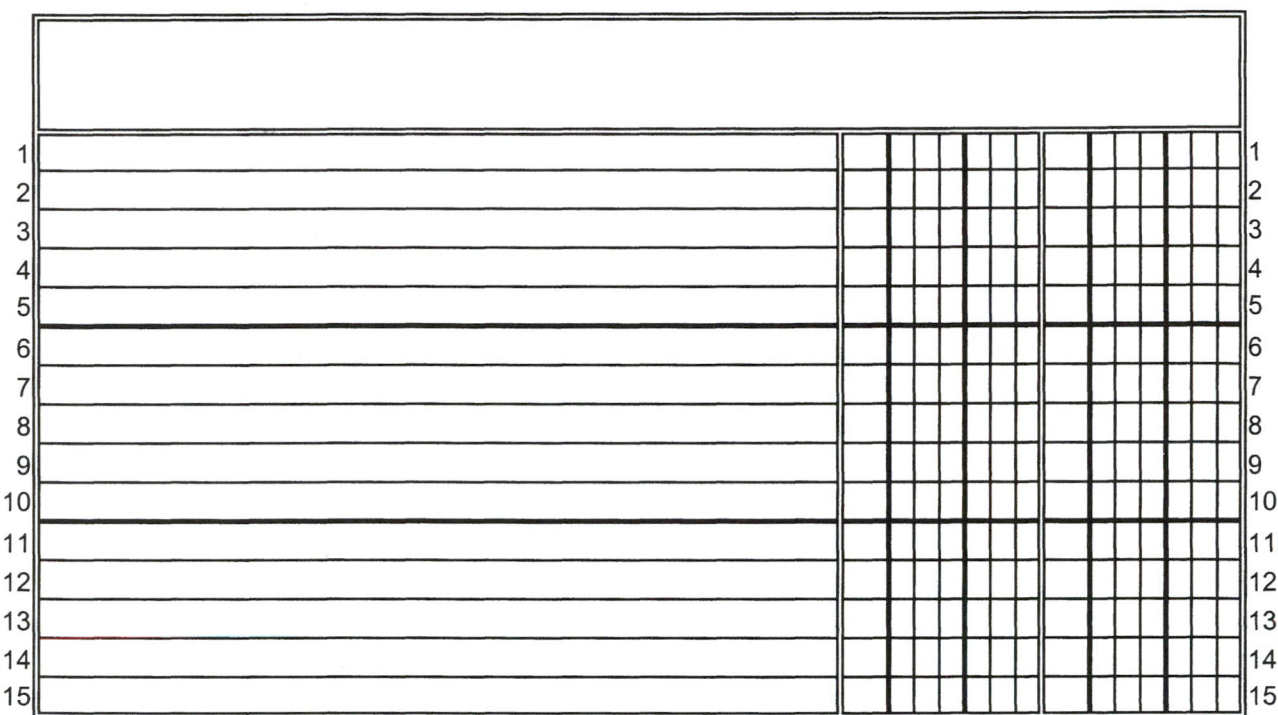

(a)

	1	2	3	4	5	6	7	8	9	10	11	12	13	14	15	16	17	18	19	20	21	22	23	24	25

(b)

	Alpha	Beta	Chi	Decca
1 Beginning inventory	$ 1 5 0	$ 7 0	$ 1 0 0 0	$
2				
3 Purchases	1 6 2 0	1 0 6 0		4 3 5 9 0
4				
5 Purchase returns and				
6 allowances	4 0		2 9 0	
7				
8 Net purchases		1 0 3 0	6 2 1 0	4 1 0 9 0
9				
10 Freight-in	9 5			2 2 4 0
11				
12 Cost of goods purchased		1 2 8 0	7 9 4 0	
13				
14 Cost of goods available for sale	1 8 2 5	1 3 5 0		4 9 5 3 0
15				
16 Ending inventory	3 1 0		1 4 5 0	6 2 3 0
17				
18 Cost of goods sold		1 2 6 0	7 4 9 0	4 3 3 0 0
19				
20				

	Date	Account Titles	Debit	Credit	
1	(a)				1
2	Apr. 5				2
3					3
4					4
5	6				5
6					6
7					7
8	7				8
9					9
10					10
11	8				11
12					12
13					13
14	15				14
15					15
16					16
17					17
18					18
19	(b)				19
20	May 4				20
21					21
22					22
23					23
24					24
25					25

	Date	Account Titles	Debit	Credit	
1	(a)				1
2	Apr. 5				2
3					3
4					4
5	5				5
6					6
7					7
8	7				8
9					9
10					10
11	8				11
12					12
13					13
14	15				14
15					15
16					16
17					17
18					18
19	(b)				19
20	May 4				20
21					21
22					22
23					23
24					24
25					25

Higley Company
Worksheet (Partial)
For the Period Ended May 31, 2014

	Account Titles	Adjusted Trial Balance Dr.	Adjusted Trial Balance Cr.	Income Statement Dr.	Income Statement Cr.	Balance Sheet Dr.	Balance Sheet Cr.	
1	Cash	9 0 0 0						1
2	Inventory	7 6 0 0 0						2
3	Sales		4 6 0 0 0 0					3
4	Sales Returns and Allowances	1 0 0 0 0						4
5	Sales Discounts	9 0 0 0						5
6	Cost of Goods Sold	2 8 8 0 0 0						6
7								7
8								8
9								9
10								10
11								11
12								12
13								13
14								14
15								15

Exercise 5-21

Adelle Company

You will find this working paper at the end of this work book

General Journal

	Date	Account Titles	Debit	Credit	
1	July 1				1
2					2
3					3
4	3				4
5					5
6					6
7					7
8					8
9					9
10	9				10
11					11
12					12
13					13
14	12				14
15					15
16					16
17					17
18	17				18
19					19
20					20
21					21
22					22
23					23
24	18				24
25					25
26					26
27					27
28					28
29					29
30	20				30
31					31
32					32
33	21				33
34					34
35					35
36					36
37					37
38					38
39					39
40					40

General Journal

	Date	Account Titles	Debit	Credit	
1	July 22				1
2					2
3					3
4					4
5					5
6					6
7	30				7
8					8
9					9
10	31				10
11					11
12					12
13					13
14					14
15					15
16					16
17					17
18					18
19					19
20					20
21					21
22					22
23					23
24					24
25					25
26					26
27					27
28					28
29					29
30					30
31					31
32					32
33					33
34					34
35					35
36					36
37					37
38					38
39					39
40					40

(a)   General Journal   J1

	Date	Account Titles	Ref.	Debit	Credit	
1	Apr. 2					1
2						2
3						3
4	4					4
5						5
6						6
7						7
8						8
9						9
10	5					10
11						11
12						12
13	6					13
14						14
15						15
16	11					16
17						17
18						18
19						19
20	13					20
21						21
22						22
23						23
24	14					24
25						25
26						26
27	16					27
28						28
29						29
30	18					30
31						31
32						32
33	20					33
34						34
35						35
36	23					36
37						37
38						38
39						39
40						40

(a) (Continued)   J1

	Date	Account Titles	Ref.	Debit	Credit	
1	Apr. 26					1
2						2
3						3
4	27					4
5						5
6						6
7						7
8	29					8
9						9
10						10
11						11
12						12
13						13
14	30					14
15						15
16						16
17						17
18						18
19						19

(b)

Cash   No. 101

Date	Explanation	Ref.	Debit	Credit	Balance
Apr. 1	Balance	√			8 0 0 0

Accounts Receivable   No. 112

Date	Explanation	Ref.	Debit	Credit	Balance

(b) (Continued)

Inventory   No. 120

Date	Explanation	Ref.	Debit	Credit	Balance

Accounts Payable   No. 201

Date	Explanation	Ref.	Debit	Credit	Balance

Common Stock   No. 311

Date	Explanation	Ref.	Debit	Credit	Balance
Apr. 1	Balance	√			8 0 0 0

Sales   No. 401

Date	Explanation	Ref.	Debit	Credit	Balance

Sales Returns and Allowances   No. 412

Date	Explanation	Ref.	Debit	Credit	Balance

(b) (Continued)

Sales Discounts   No. 414

Date	Explanation	Ref.	Debit	Credit	Balance

Cost of Goods Sold   No. 505

Date	Explanation	Ref.	Debit	Credit	Balance

Freight-out   No. 644

Date	Explanation	Ref.	Debit	Credit	Balance

(c)

	Shmi Distributing Company
	Income Statement (Partial)
	For the Month Ended April 30, 2014

1		
2		
3		
4		
5		
6		
7		
8		
9		
10		

(a)

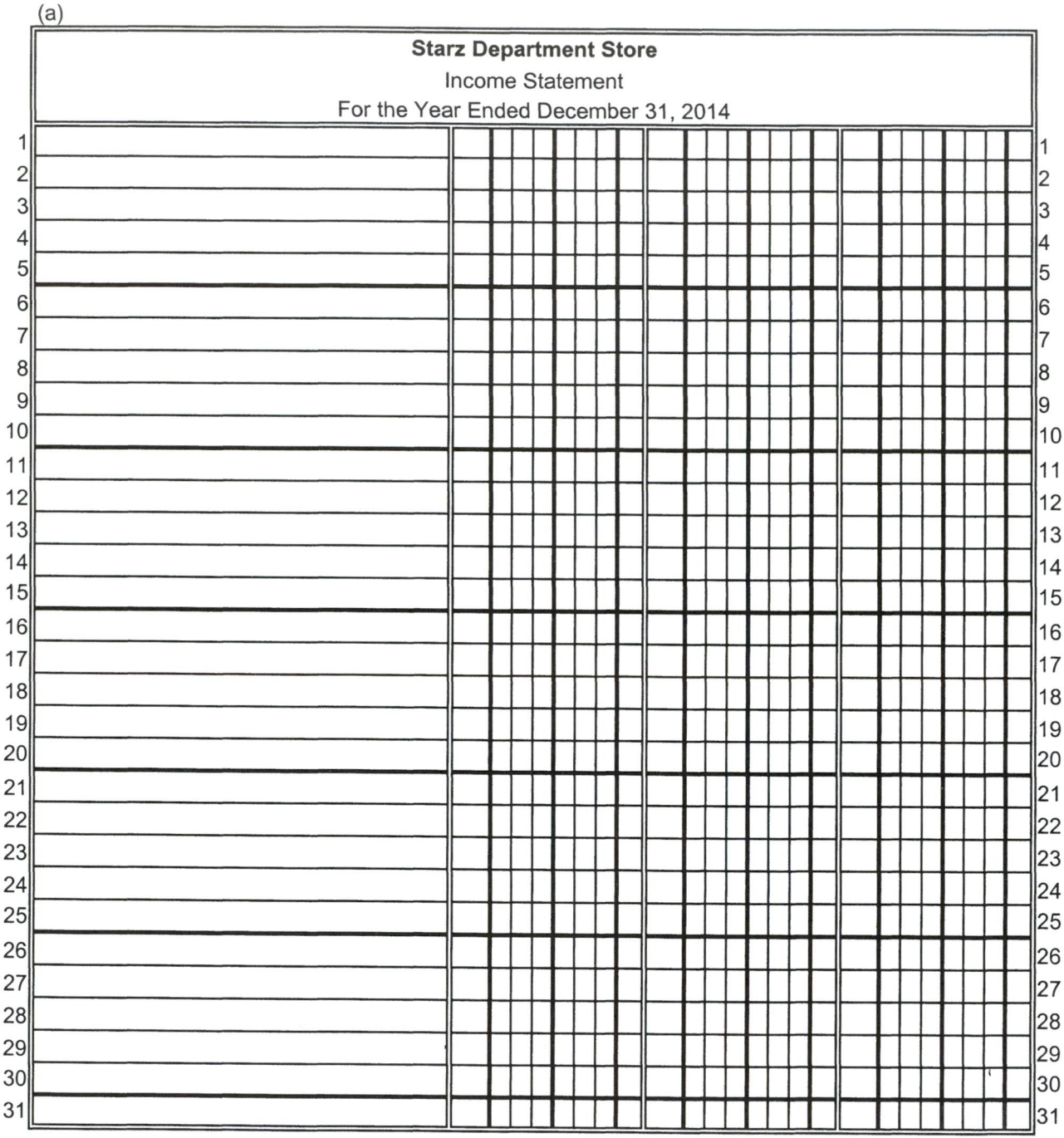

Starz Department Store
Income Statement
For the Year Ended December 31, 2014

Starz Department Store
Retained Earnings Statement
For the Year Ended December 31, 2014

(a) (Continued)

Starz Department Store			
Balance Sheet			
December 31, 2014			

	Assets			
1				
2				
3				
4				
5				
6				
7				
8				
9				
10				
11				
12				
13				
14				
15				
16				
17				
18				
19	Liabilities and Stockholders' Equity			
20				
21				
22				
23				
24				
25				
26				
27				
28				
29				
30				
31				
32				
33				
34				
35				
36				
37				
38				
39				
40				

(b)

General Journal

	Date	Account Titles	Debit	Credit	
1		Adjusting Entries			1
2	Dec. 31				2
3					3
4					4
5	31				5
6					6
7					7
8	31				8
9					9
10					10
11	31				11
12					12
13					13
14	31				14
15					15
16					16
17	31				17
18					18
19					19
20	31				20
21					21
22					22
23					23
24					24
25					25

(c)   General Journal

	Date	Account Titles	Debit	Credit	
1		Closing Entries			1
2	Dec. 31				2
3					3
4					4
5					5
6	31				6
7					7
8					8
9					9
10					10
11					11
12					12
13					13
14					14
15					15
16					16
17					17
18					18
19	31				19
20					20
21					21
22	31				22
23					23
24					24
25					25
26					26
27					27
28					28
29					29
30					30
31					31
32					32
33					33
34					34
35					35

(a)   General Journal   J1

	Date	Account Titles	Ref.	Debit	Credit	
1	Apr. 4					1
2						2
3						3
4	6					4
5						5
6						6
7	8					7
8						8
9						9
10						10
11						11
12						12
13	10					13
14						14
15						15
16	11					16
17						17
18						18
19	13					19
20						20
21						21
22						22
23	14					23
24						24
25						25
26	15					26
27						27
28						28
29	17					29
30						30
31						31
32	18					32
33						33
34						34
35						35
36						36
37						37
38						38
39						39
40						40
41						41

(a) (Continued)   General Journal   J1

	Date	Account Titles	Ref.	Debit	Credit	
1	Apr. 20					1
2						2
3						3
4	21					4
5						5
6						6
7						7
8	27					8
9						9
10						10
11	30					11
12						12
13						13
14						14
15						15
16						16
17						17
18						18
19						19
20						20
21						21
22						22
23						23
24						24
25						25
26						26
27						27
28						28
29						29
30						30
31						31
32						32
33						33
34						34
35						35
36						36
37						37
38						38
39						39
40						40

(b)

Cash   No. 101

Date	Explanation	Ref.	Debit	Credit	Balance
Apr 1	Balance	√			2 2 0 0

Accounts Receivable   No. 112

Date	Explanation	Ref.	Debit	Credit	Balance

Inventory   No. 120

Date	Explanation	Ref.	Debit	Credit	Balance
Apr 1	Balance	√			1 0 0 0

Accounts Payable   No. 201

Date	Explanation	Ref.	Debit	Credit	Balance

(b) (Continued)

Common Stock   No. 311

Date	Explanation	Ref.	Debit	Credit	Balance
Apr 1	Balance	√			4 0 0 0

Sales Revenue   No. 401

Date	Explanation	Ref.	Debit	Credit	Balance

Sales Returns and Allowances   No. 412

Date	Explanation	Ref.	Debit	Credit	Balance

Cost of Goods Sold   No. 505

Date	Explanation	Ref.	Debit	Credit	Balance

(c)

Ackbar's Tennis Shop Trial Balance April 30, 2014	Debit	Credit
1		
2		
3		
4		
5		
6		
7		
8		
9		
10		

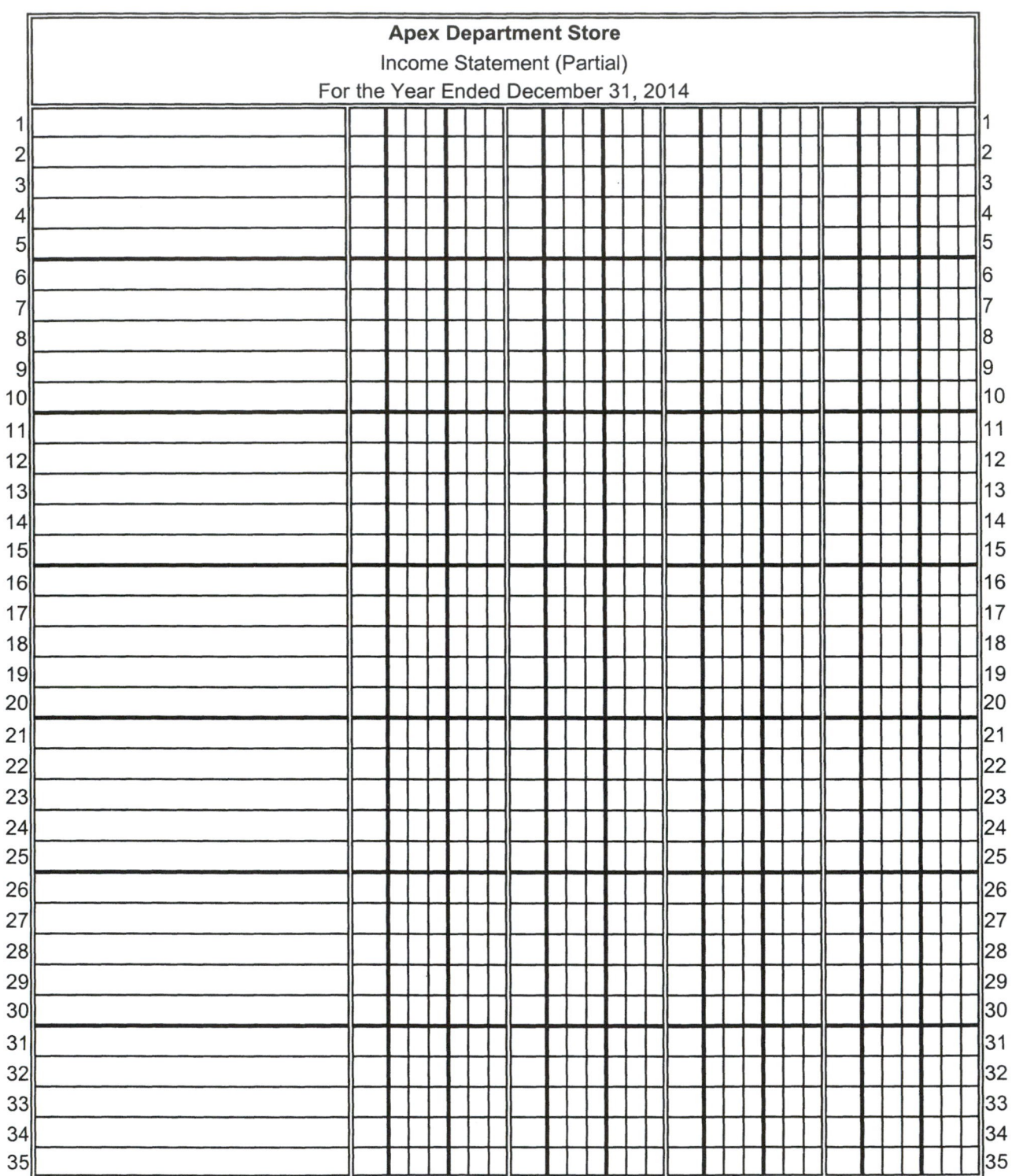

Apex Department Store
Income Statement (Partial)
For the Year Ended December 31, 2014

	2012	2013	2014
(a)			
1 Cost of goods sold:			
2			
3			
4			
5			
6			
7			
8 (b)			
9 Sales revenue			
10			
11			
12			
13 (c)			
14 Beginning accounts payable			
15			
16			
17			
18			
19 (d)			
20 Gross profit rate			
21			

(a)   General Journal

	Date	Account Titles	Debit	Credit	
1	Apr. 4				1
2					2
3					3
4	6				4
5					5
6					6
7	8				7
8					8
9					9
10	10				10
11					11
12					12
13	11				13
14					14
15					15
16	13				16
17					17
18					18
19					19
20	14				20
21					21
22					22
23	15				23
24					24
25					25
26	17				26
27					27
28					28
29	18				29
30					30

(a) (Continued)   General Journal

	Date	Account Titles	Debit	Credit	
1	Apr. 20				1
2					2
3					3
4	21				4
5					5
6					6
7					7
8	27				8
9					9
10					10
11	30				11
12					12
13					13
14					14
15					15
16					16
17					17
18					18
19					19
20					20
21					21
22					22
23					23
24					24
25					25
26					26
27					27
28					28
29					29
30					30

(b)

Cash	**Sales Returns and Allowances**
4/1 Bal. 2,500	
Accounts Receivable	**Purchases**
	Purchase Returns and Allowances
Inventory	
4/1/ Bal. 1,700	
	Purchase Discount
Accounts Payable	
	Freight-in
Common Stock	
4/1/ Bal. 4,200	
Sales Revenue	

(c)

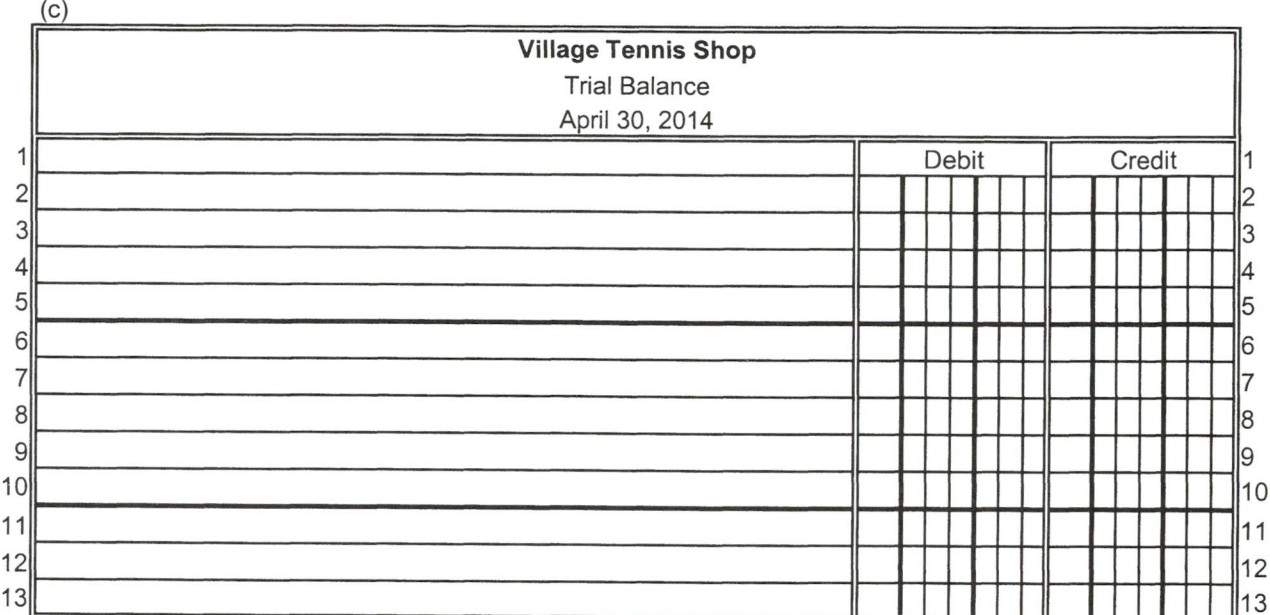

Village Tennis Shop
Trial Balance
April 30, 2014

	Debit	Credit
1		
2		
3		
4		
5		
6		
7		
8		
9		
10		
11		
12		
13		

(d)

Village Tennis Shop
Income Statement (Partial)
For the Month Ended April 30, 2014

1				
2				
3				
4				
5				
6				
7				
8				
9				
10				
11				
12				
13				
14				
15				
16				
17				
18				
19				
20				
21				
22				

Problem 5-8A

Mr. Rosiak Fashion Center

You will find this working paper at the end of this work book

(b)

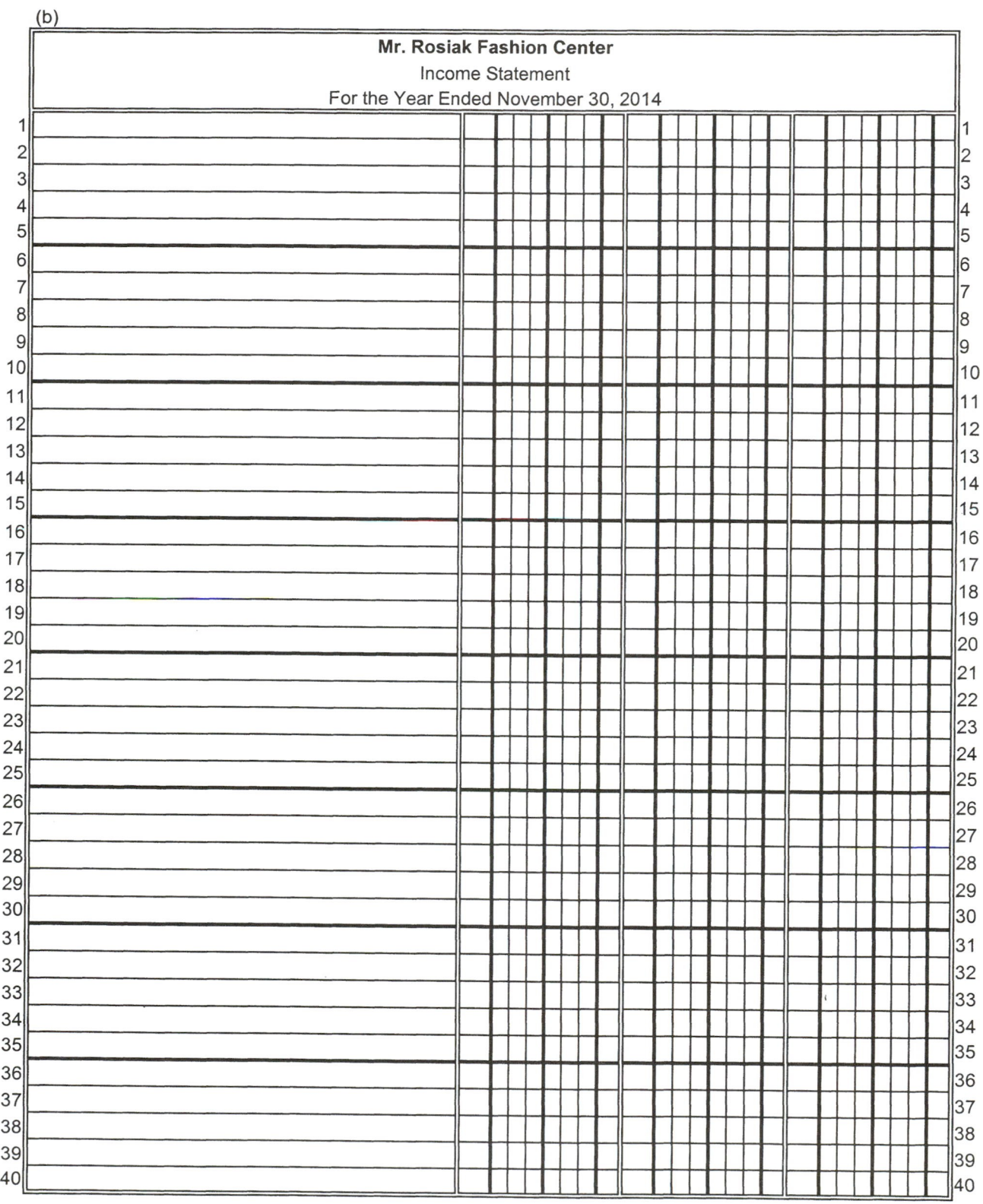

Mr. Rosiak Fashion Center
Income Statement
For the Year Ended November 30, 2014

(b) (Continued)

Mr. Rosiak Fashion Center
Retained Earnings Statement
For the Year Ended November 30, 2014

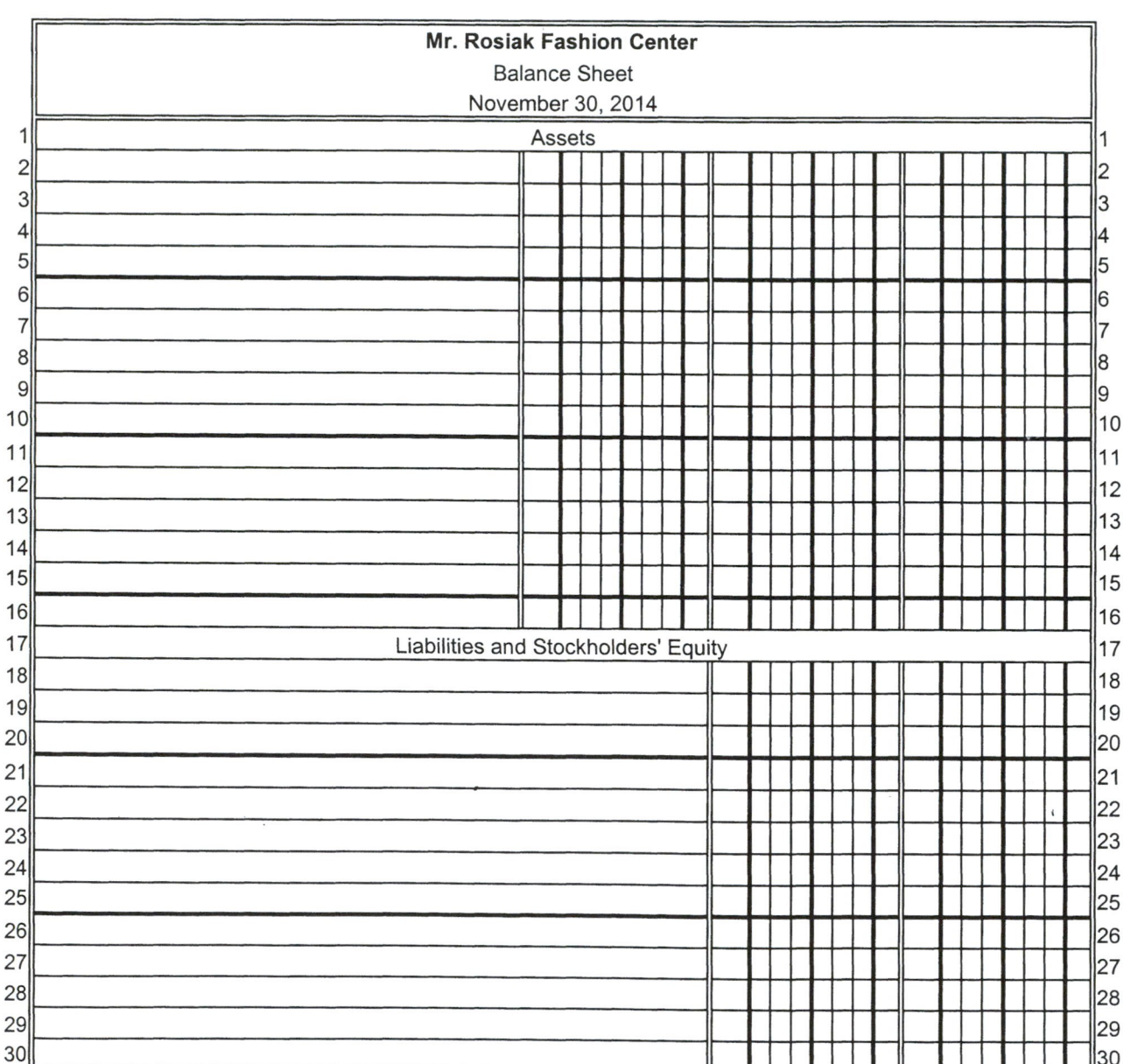

Mr. Rosiak Fashion Center
Balance Sheet
November 30, 2014

Assets

Liabilities and Stockholders' Equity

(c)   General Journal

	Date	Account Titles	Debit	Credit	
1		Adjusting Entries			1
2	Nov. 30				2
3					3
4					4
5	30				5
6					6
7					7
8	30				8
9					9
10					10
11	30				11
12					12
13					13
14	30				14
15					15

(d)

	Date	Account Titles	Debit	Credit	
1		Closing Entries			1
2	Nov. 30				2
3					3
4					4
5	30				5
6					6
7					7
8					8
9					9
10					10
11					11
12					12
13					13
14					14
15					15
16					16
17					17
18					18
19	30				19
20					20
21					21
22	30				22
23					23

(e)

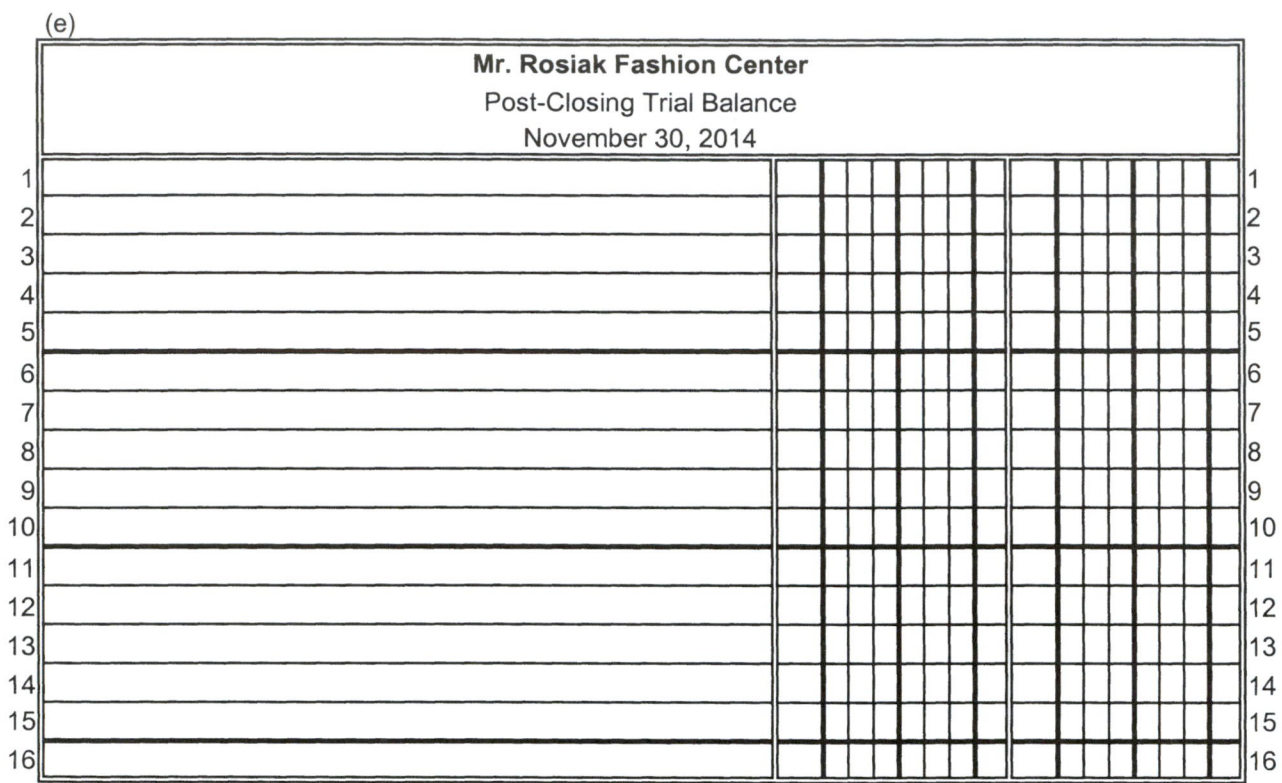

Mr. Rosiak Fashion Center
Post-Closing Trial Balance
November 30, 2014

General Journal

	Date	Account Titles	Debit	Credit	
1	June 1				1
2					2
3					3
4	3				4
5					5
6					6
7					7
8					8
9					9
10	6				10
11					11
12					12
13	9				13
14					14
15					15
16					16
17	15				17
18					18
19					19
20	17				20
21					21
22					22
23					23
24					24
25					25
26	20				26
27					27
28					28
29	24				29
30					30
31					31
32					32
33	26				33
34					34
35					35
36					36
37					37
38					38
39					39
40					40

General Journal

	Date	Account Titles	Debit	Credit	
1	June 28				1
2					2
3					3
4					4
5					5
6					6
7	30				7
8					8
9					9
10					10
11					11
12					12
13					13
14					14
15					15
16					16
17					17
18					18
19					19
20					20
21					21
22					22
23					23
24					24
25					25
26					26
27					27
28					28
29					29
30					30
31					31
32					32
33					33
34					34
35					35
36					36
37					37
38					38
39					39
40					40

(a)   General Journal   J1

	Date	Account Titles	Ref.	Debit	Credit	
1	May 1					1
2						2
3						3
4	2					4
5						5
6						6
7						7
8						8
9						9
10	5					10
11						11
12						12
13	9					13
14						14
15						15
16						16
17	10					17
18						18
19						19
20						20
21	11					21
22						22
23						23
24	12					24
25						25
26						26
27	15					27
28						28
29						29
30	17					30
31						31
32						32
33	19					33
34						34
35						35
36	24					36
37						37
38						38
39						39
40						40

(a) (Continued)   J1

	Date	Account Titles	Ref.	Debit	Credit	
1	May 25					1
2						2
3						3
4	27					4
5						5
6						6
7						7
8						8
9	29					9
10						10
11						11
12						12
13						13
14						14
15	31					15
16						16
17						17
18						18
19						19
20						20

(b)

Cash   No. 101

Date	Explanation	Ref.	Debit	Credit	Balance
May 1	Balance	√			5 0 0 0

Accounts Receivable   No. 112

Date	Explanation	Ref.	Debit	Credit	Balance

(b) (Continued)

Inventory   No. 120

Date	Explanation	Ref.	Debit	Credit	Balance

Supplies   No. 126

Date	Explanation	Ref.	Debit	Credit	Balance

Accounts Payable   No. 201

Date	Explanation	Ref.	Debit	Credit	Balance

Common Stock   No. 311

Date	Explanation	Ref.	Debit	Credit	Balance
May 1	Balance	√			5 0 0 0

Sales   No. 401

Date	Explanation	Ref.	Debit	Credit	Balance

(b) (Continued)

Sales Returns and Allowances   No. 412

Date	Explanation	Ref.	Debit	Credit	Balance

Sales Discounts   No. 414

Date	Explanation	Ref.	Debit	Credit	Balance

Cost of Goods Sold   No. 505

Date	Explanation	Ref.	Debit	Credit	Balance

(c)

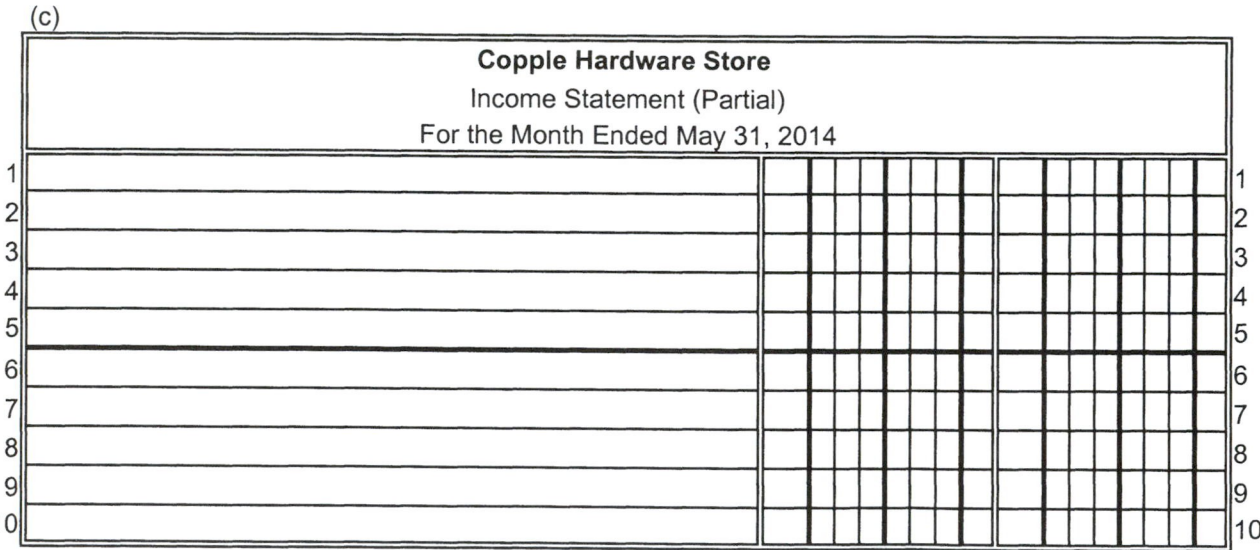

Copple Hardware Store		
Income Statement (Partial)		
For the Month Ended May 31, 2014		

(a)

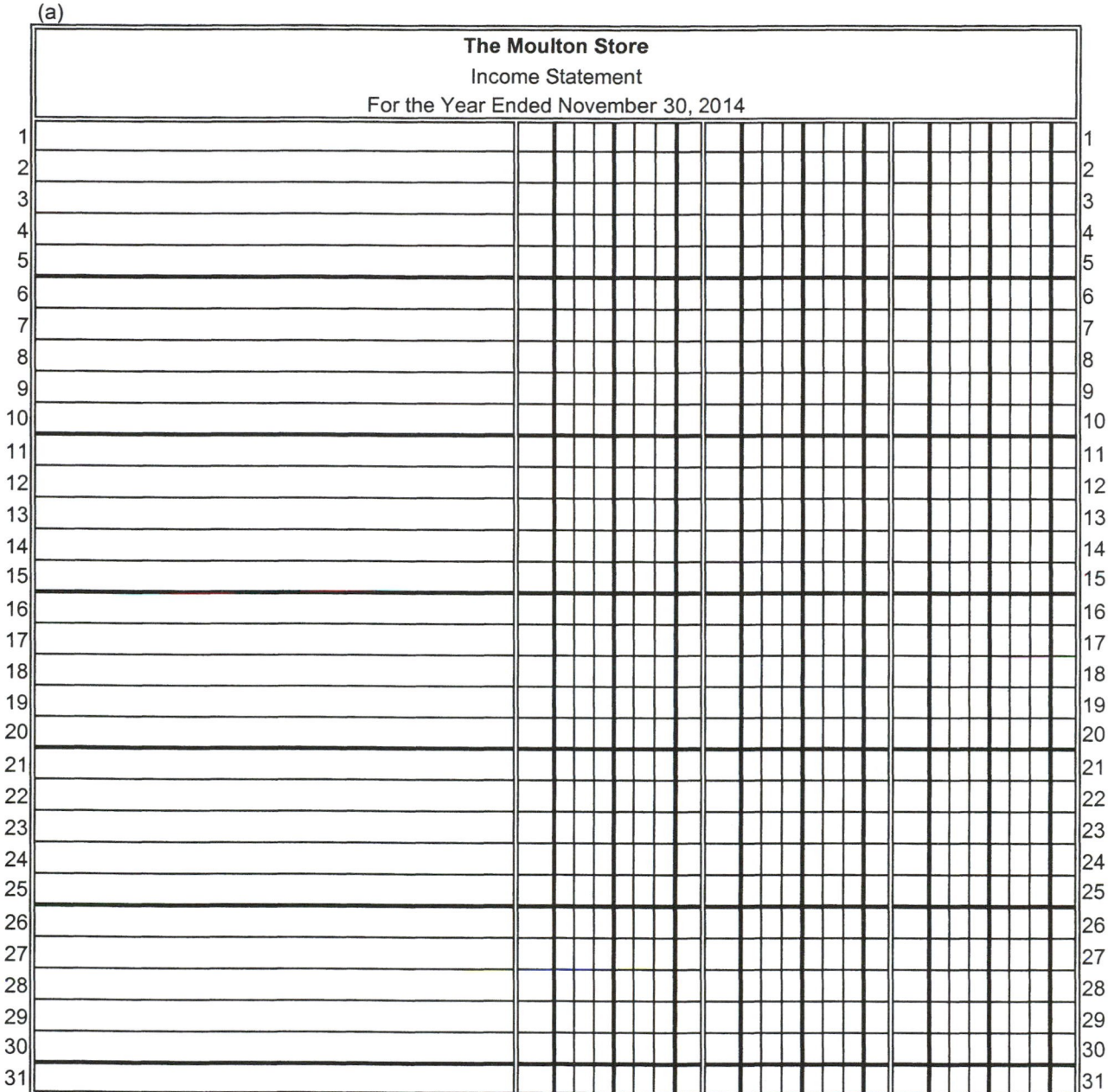

The Moulton Store
Income Statement
For the Year Ended November 30, 2014

The Moulton Store
Retained Earnings Statement
For the Year Ended November 30, 2014

(a) (Continued)

The Moulton Store
Balance Sheet
November 30, 2014

Assets

Liabilities and Stockholders' Equity

(b)   General Journal

Date	Account Titles	Debit	Credit
	Adjusting Entries		
Nov. 30			
30			
30			
30			
30			

(c)   General Journal

	Date	Account Titles	Debit	Credit	
1		Closing Entries			1
2	Nov. 30				2
3					3
4					4
5					5
6	30				6
7					7
8					8
9					9
10					10
11					11
12					12
13					13
14					14
15					15
16					16
17					17
18					18
19					19
20	30				20
21					21
22					22
23	30				23
24					24
25					25
26					26
27					27
28					28
29					29
30					30
31					31
32					32
33					33
34					34
35					35

(a) General Journal J1

	Date	Account Titles	Ref.	Debit	Credit	
1	Apr. 5					1
2						2
3						3
4	7					4
5						5
6						6
7	9					7
8						8
9						9
10	10					10
11						11
12						12
13						13
14						14
15						15
16	12					16
17						17
18						18
19	14					19
20						20
21						21
22						22
23	17					23
24						24
25						25
26	20					26
27						27
28						28
29						29
30						30
31						31
32	21					32
33						33
34						34
35						35
36	27					36
37						37
38						38
39	30					39
40						40
41						41

(b)

Cash   No. 101

Date	Explanation	Ref.	Debit	Credit	Balance
Apr 1	Balance	√			1 8 5 0

Accounts Receivable   No. 112

Date	Explanation	Ref.	Debit	Credit	Balance

Inventory   No. 120

Date	Explanation	Ref.	Debit	Credit	Balance
Apr 1	Balance	√			2 1 5 0

Accounts Payable   No. 201

Date	Explanation	Ref.	Debit	Credit	Balance

(b) (Continued)

Common Stock   No. 311

Date	Explanation	Ref.	Debit	Credit	Balance
Apr 1	Balance	√			4 0 0 0

Sales Revenue   No. 401

Date	Explanation	Ref.	Debit	Credit	Balance

Sales Returns and Allowances   No. 412

Date	Explanation	Ref.	Debit	Credit	Balance

Cost of Goods Sold   No. 505

Date	Explanation	Ref.	Debit	Credit	Balance

(c)

Bill's Discorama
Trial Balance
April 30, 2014

	Debit	Credit
1			1
2			2
3			3
4			4
5			5
6			6
7			7
8			8
9			9
10			10

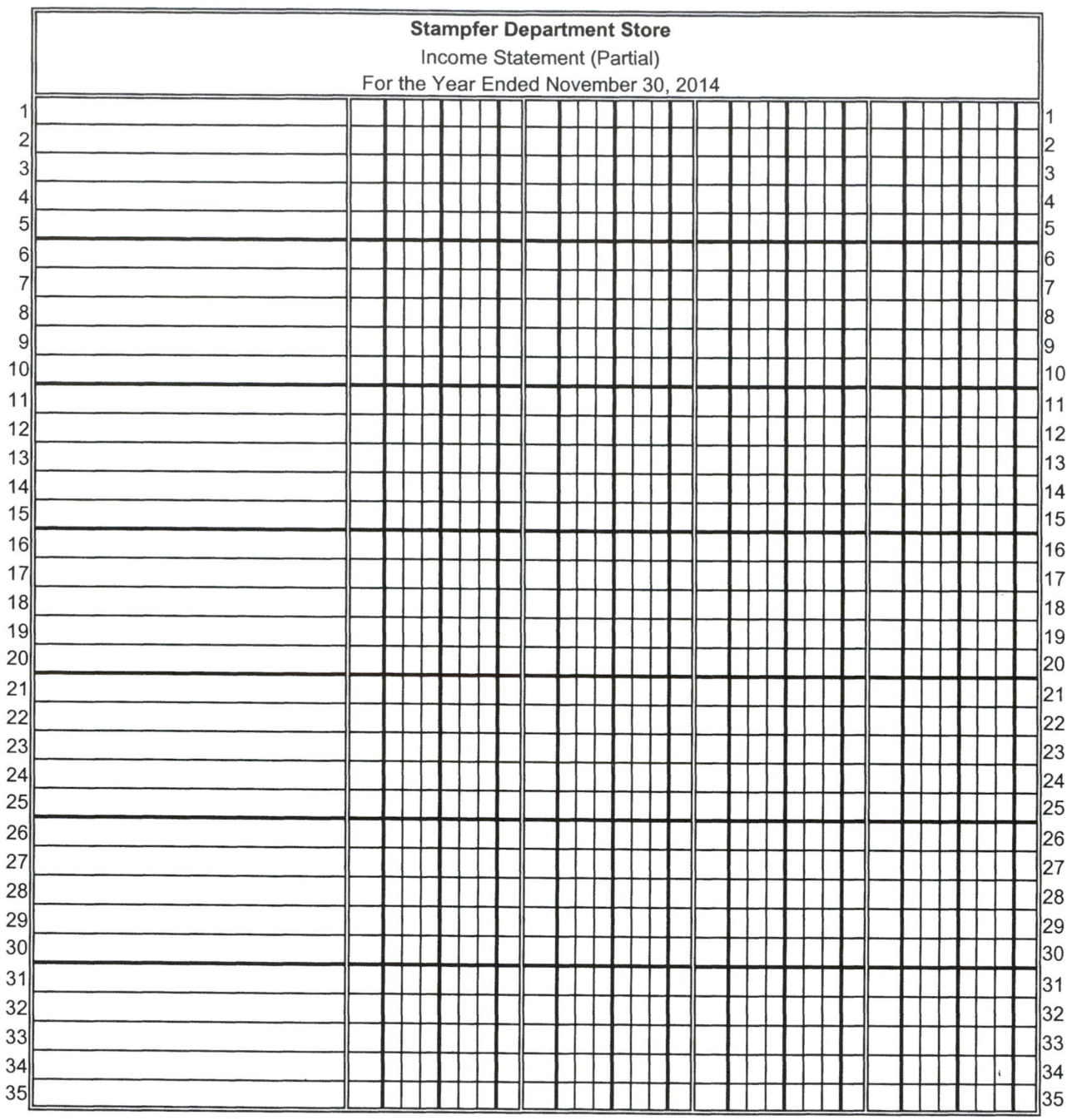

Stampfer Department Store
Income Statement (Partial)
For the Year Ended November 30, 2014

(a)

	2011	2012	2013	2014
Income Statement Data				
Sales		$ 53 300		$ 46 000
Cost of goods sold			13 800	14 300
Gross profit		38 300	35 200	
Operating expenses		35 900		28 600
Net income			2 500	
Balance Sheet Data				
Merchandise inventory	$ 7 200		$ 8 100	
Accounts payable	3 200	3 400	2 500	
Additional Information				
Purchases of merchandise				
inventory on account		14 200		13 200
Cash payments to suppliers				13 600

(b)

		2012	2013	2014
Gross profit rate				
Profit margin ratio				

(a) General Journal

	Date	Account Titles	Debit	Credit	
1	Apr. 5				1
2					2
3					3
4	7				4
5					5
6					6
7	9				7
8					8
9					9
10	10				10
11					11
12					12
13	12				13
14					14
15					15
16	14				16
17					17
18					18
19					19
20	17				20
21					21
22					22
23	20				23
24					24
25					25
26	21				26
27					27
28					28
29					29
30	27				30
31					31
32					32
33	30				33
34					34
35					35
36					36
37					37
38					38
39					39
40					40

(b)

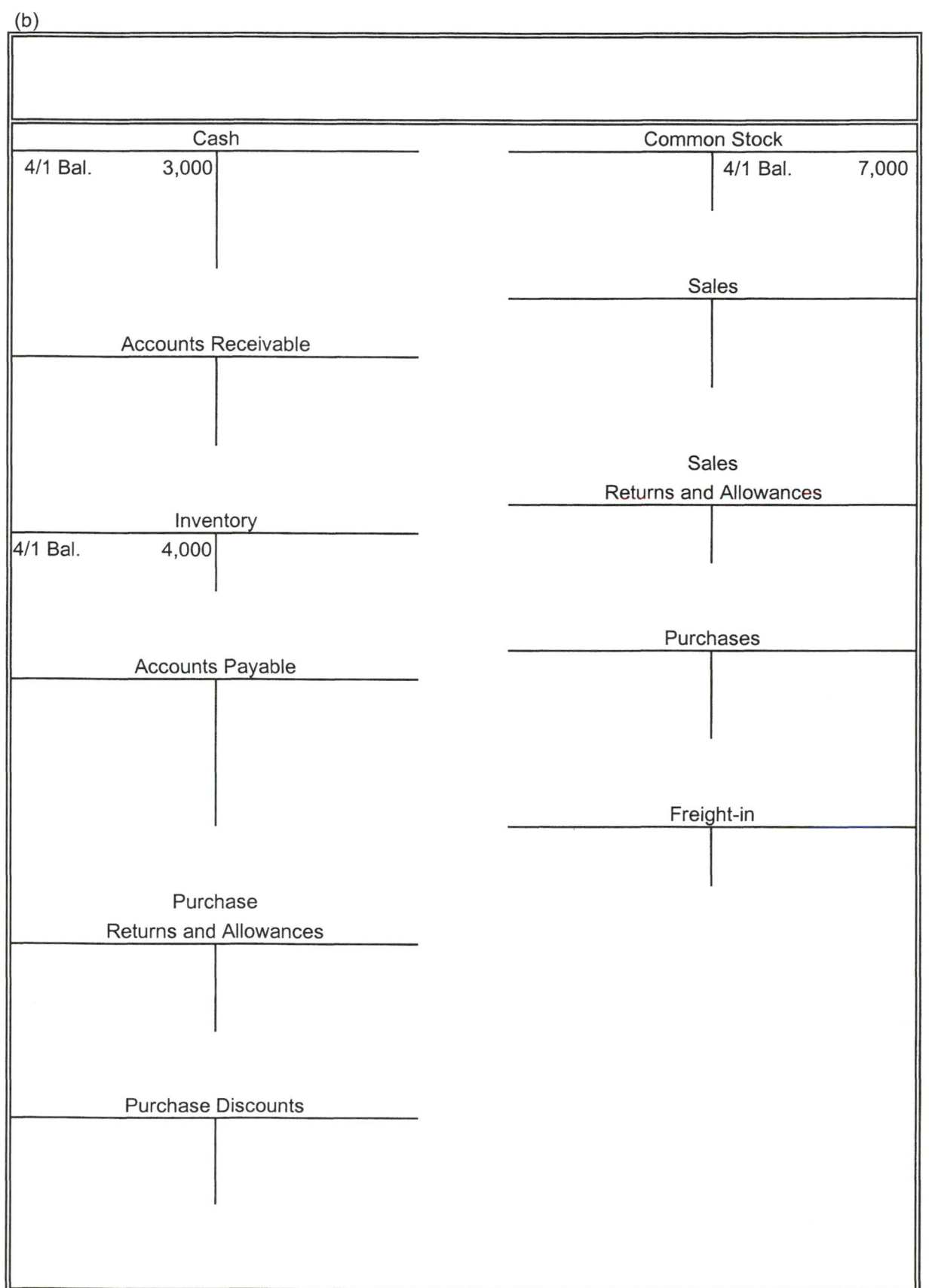

Cash			Common Stock	
4/1 Bal.	3,000		4/1 Bal.	7,000

Accounts Receivable

Sales

Inventory

Sales
Returns and Allowances

4/1 Bal. 4,000

Accounts Payable

Purchases

Freight-in

Purchase
Returns and Allowances

Purchase Discounts

(c)

Tri-State Pro Shop Trial Balance April 30, 2014	Debit	Credit
1		
2		
3		
4		
5		
6		
7		
8		
9		
10		
11		
12		
13		

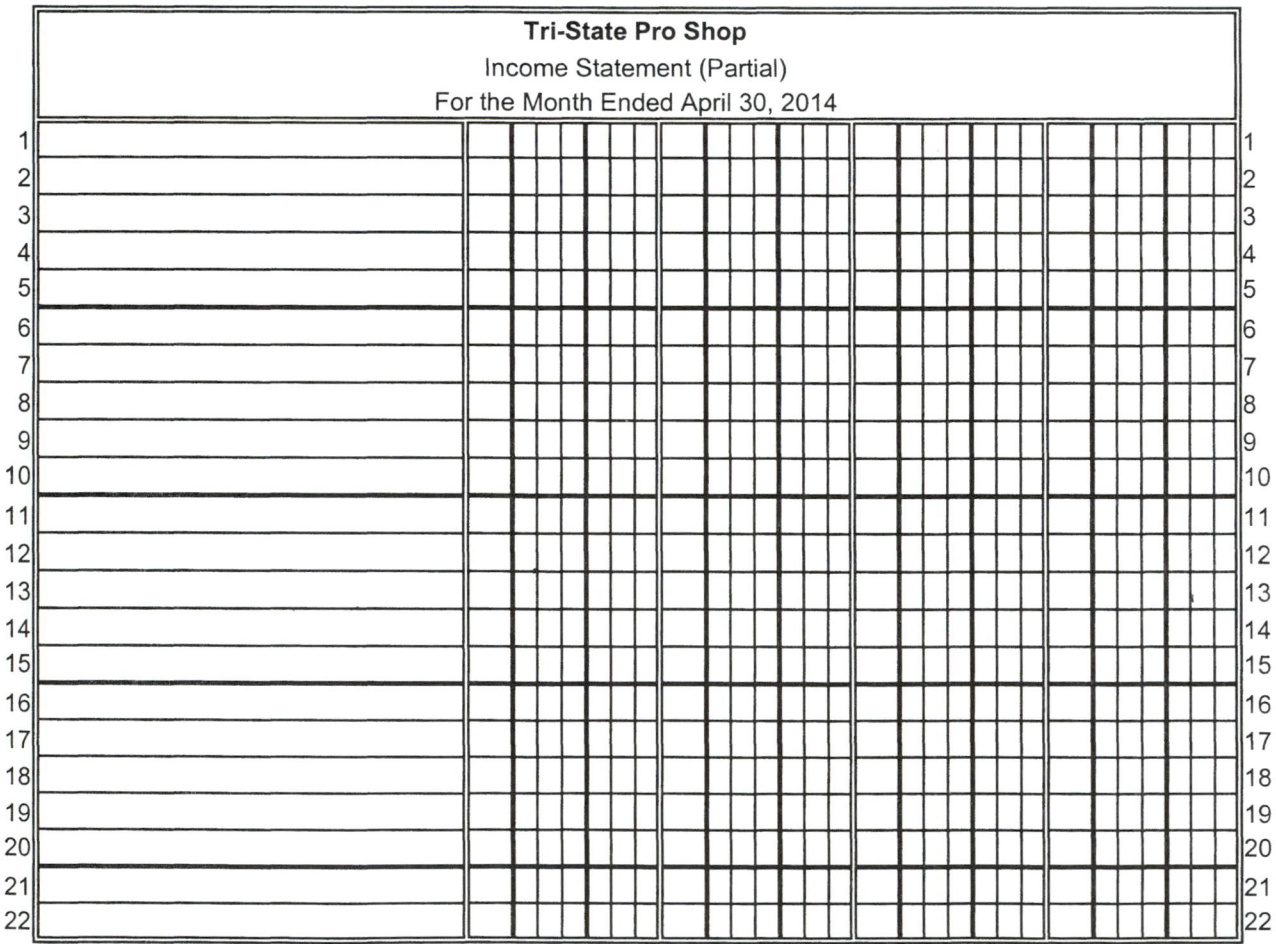

Tri-State Pro Shop Income Statement (Partial) For the Month Ended April 30, 2014				
1				
2				
3				
4				
5				
6				
7				
8				
9				
10				
11				
12				
13				
14				
15				
16				
17				
18				
19				
20				
21				
22				

(a) General Journal

	Date	Account Titles	Debit	Credit	
1	Dec. 6				1
2					2
3					3
4					4
5	8				5
6					6
7					7
8	10				8
9					9
10					10
11					11
12					12
13					13
14	13				14
15					15
16					16
17	15				17
18					18
19					19
20	18				20
21					21
22					22
23					23
24					24
25					25
26	20				26
27					27
28					28
29	23				29
30					30
31					31
32					32
33	27				33
34					34
35					35
36					36
37					37
38					38
39					39
40					40

(c)   General Journal

	Date	Account Titles	Debit	Credit	
1	Dec.31				1
2					2
3					3
4					4
5					5
6					6
7					7
8					8
9					9
10					10
11					11
12					12
13					13
14					14
15					15
16					16
17					17
18					18
19					19
20					20
21					21
22					22
23					23
24					24
25					25
26					26
27					27
28					28
29					29
30					30
31					31
32					32
33					33
34					34
35					35
36					36
37					37
38					38
39					39
40					40

(b) & (c)

Cash		Salaries and Wages Payable	
12/1 Bal 7,200			12/1 Bal 1,000

		Common Stock	
			12/1 Bal 30,000

Accounts Receivable			
12/1 Bal 4,600			

		Retained Earnings	
			12/1 Bal 9,300

Inventory		Sales Revenue	
12/1 Bal 12,000			

Supplies		Sales Discounts	
12/1∧ Ba 1,200			

		Cost of Goods Sold	
Equipment			
12/1 Bal 22,000			

Accumulated Depreciation - Equipment		Depreciation Expense	
	12/1 Bal 2,200		

		Salaries and Wages Expense	

Accounts Payable			
	12/1 Bal 4,500		

		Supplies Expense	

(d)

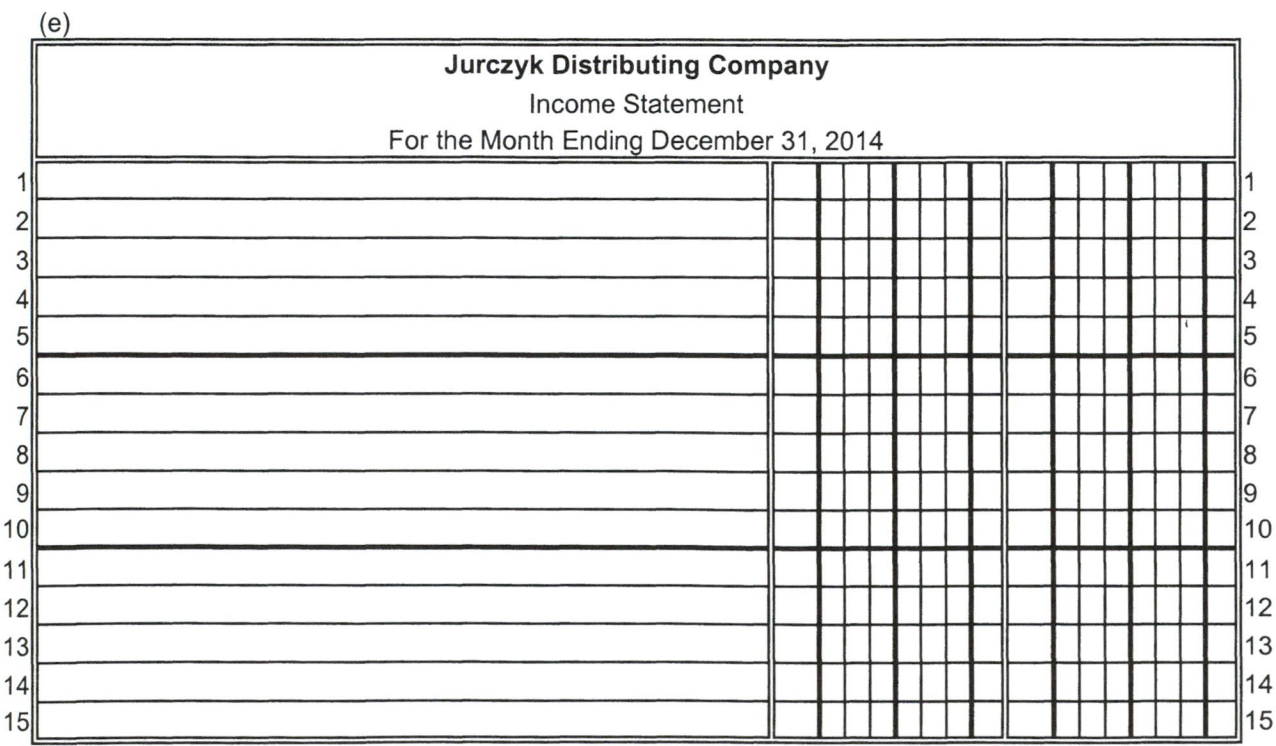

Jurczyk Distributing Company Adjusted Trial Balance December 31, 2014	DR.	CR.

(e)

Jurczyk Distributing Company Income Statement For the Month Ending December 31, 2014		

(d)

Jurczyk Distributing Company
Retained Earnings Statement
For the Month Ended December 31, 2014

1	
2	
3	
4	
5	

Jurczyk Distributing Company
Balance Sheet
December 31, 2014

Assets	
1	
2	
3	
4	
5	
6	
7	
8	
9	
10	
11	
12	
13	

Liabilities and Stockholders' Equity	
14	
15	
16	
17	
18	
19	
20	
21	
22	
23	
24	
25	
26	
27	
28	
29	
30	

	2009		2010
1 (a) (1) Percentage change in sales:			
2			
3			
4			
5			
6			
7			
8			
9 (2) Percentage change in net income:			
10			
11			
12			
13			
14			
15			
16			
17			

	2008	2009	2010
18 (b) Gross profit rate:			
19			
20			
21			
22			
23			
24			
25			
26			
27			
28			
29			
30 (c) Percentage of net income to sales:			
31			
32			
33			
34			
35 Comment:			
36			
37			
38			
39			
40			

	PepsiCo		Coca-Cola
(a)			
(1) 2010 Gross profit			
(2) 2010 Gross profit rate			
(3) 2010 Operating Income			
(4) Percentage change in			
operating income, 2009			
to 2010			
(b)			

(a) (1)   Carrie's changes are implemented

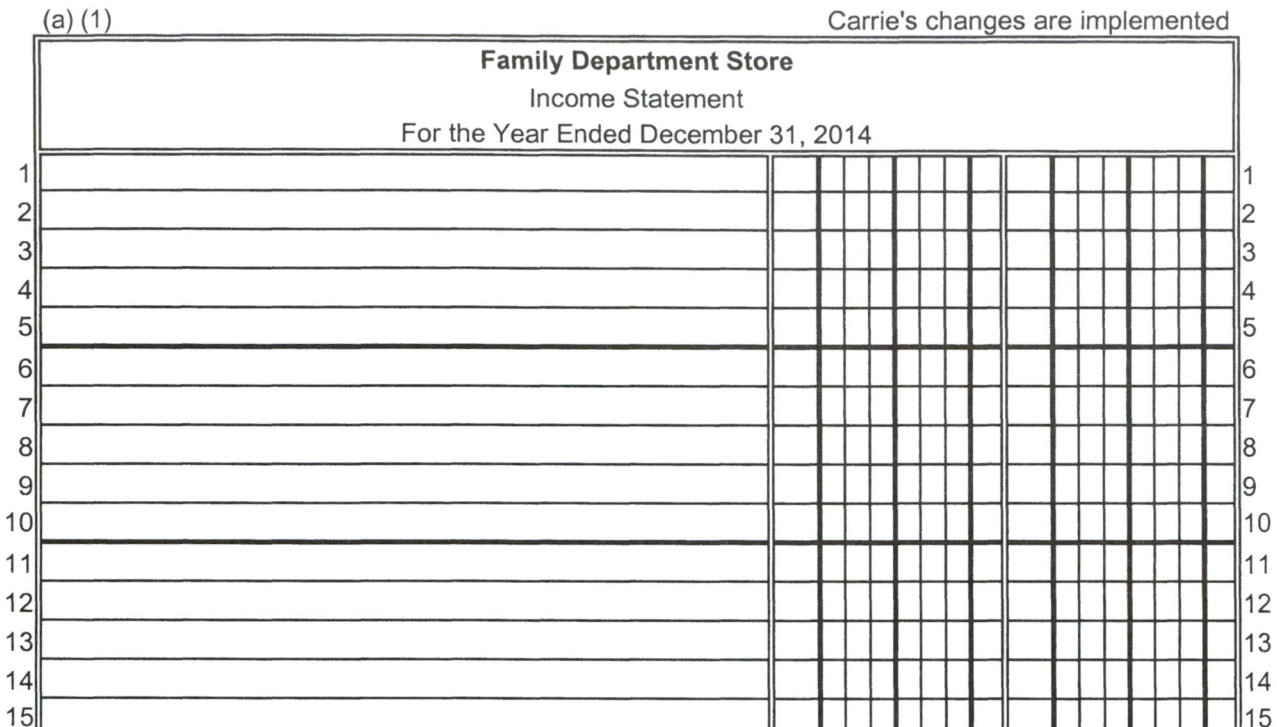

Family Department Store

Income Statement

For the Year Ended December 31, 2014

(2)   Luke's ideas are adopted

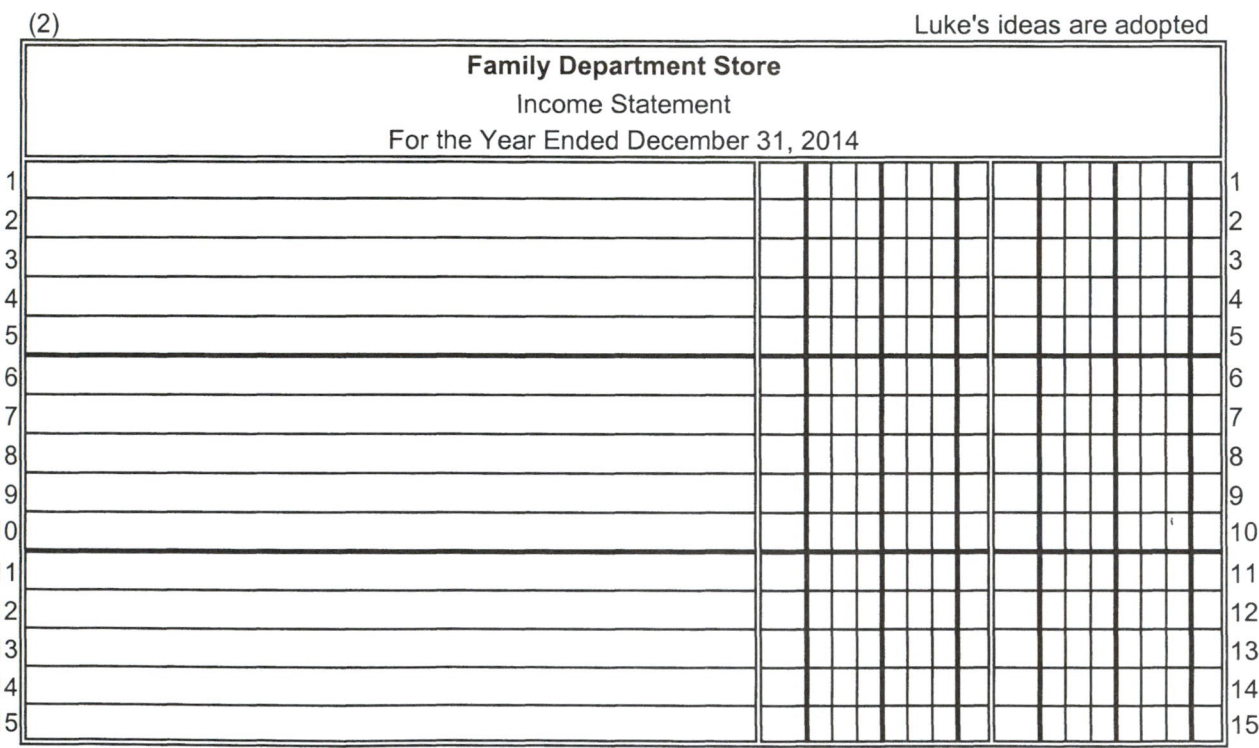

Family Department Store

Income Statement

For the Year Ended December 31, 2014

(b)

1	1
2	2
3	3
4	4
5	5
6	6
7	7
8	8
9	9
10	10

(c)   Both proposals are adopted

Family Department Store

Income Statement

For the Year Ended December 31, 2014

1		1
2		2
3		3
4		4
5		5
6		6
7		7
8		8
9		9
10		10
11		11
12		12
13		13
14		14
15		15
16		16
17		17
18		18
19		19
20		20

	Atlantis Company			
	Comprehensive Income Statement (in thousands of euros)			
	For the Year Ended 2014			

1		1
2		2
3		3
4		4
5		5
6		6
7		7
8		8
9		9
10		10
11		11
12		12
13		13
14		14
15		15
16		16
17		17
18		18
19		19
20		20
21		21
22		22
23		23
24		24
25		25
26		26
27		27
28		28
29		29
30		30

BE6-3

	(a) FIFO			(b) LIFO			
	Units	Unit Cost	Total	Units	Unit Cost	Total	
Ending inventory				Ending inventory			

BE6-4

		Units	Unit Cost	Total	
Average cost per unit					
Ending inventory					

BE6-6

		LIFO	FIFO	
1	Cost of goods sold under:			1
	Purchases			
2				2
3				3
4	Cost of goods available for sale			4
5	Less: Ending inventory			5
6	Cost of goods sold			6
7				7
8				8
9				9
10				10
11				11
12				12
13				13
14				14
15				15

	BE6-7	Cost	Market	LCM	
16					16
17	Inventory categories:				17
18	Cameras				18
19	Camcorders				19
20	DVD players				20
21	Total valuation				21
22					22

	*BE6-11		
23			23
24	(1)		24
25			25
26			26
27			27
28	(2)		28
29			29
30			30
31			31

	*BE6-12	At Cost	At Retail	
32				32
33				33
34				34
35				35
36				36
37	Cost-to-retail ratio:			37
38				38
39	Estimated cost of ending inventory:			39
40				40

*BE6-10

Product E2-D2

(1) FIFO Method

Date	Purchases	Cost of Goods Sold	Balance

(2) LIFO Method

Date	Purchases	Cost of Goods Sold	Balance

(3) Moving-Average-Cost

Date	Purchases	Cost of Goods Sold	Balance

DO IT! 6-1

	1
2	2
3	3
4	4
5	5
6	6

DO IT! 6-2

Cost of goods available for sale:

Ending inventory in units:

Cost of goods sold using:

   (a)   FIFO

   (b)   LIFO

   (c)   Moving-average-cost

E6-1

1	Ending Inventory - physical count	$	2	9	7	0	0	0	1
2									2
3									3
4									4
5									5
6									6
7									7
8									8
9									9
10									10
11									11
12									12
13									13

E6-2

15	Ending inventory - as reported	$	7	4	0	0	0	0	15
16									16
17									17
18									18
19									19
20									20
21									21
22									22
23									23
24									24
25									25
26									26
27									27
28									28
29									29
30									30
31									31
32									32
33									33
34									34
35									35
36									36
37									37
38									38
39									39
40									40

1	(a)					1
2						2
3						3
4						4
5						5
6	(b)					6
7						7
8						8
9						9
10						10
11						11
12						12
13						13
14						14
15						15
16	(c)					16
17						17
18						18
19						19
20						20
21						21
22						22
23						23
24						24
25						25

(a)

	FIFO			
1				
2				
3				
4				
5				
6				
7				
8				

Proof:

	Date	Units	Unit Cost	Total Cost

	LIFO			

Proof:

	Date	Units	Unit Cost	Total Cost

(b)

			FIFO		
1					
2					
3					
4					
5					
6					
7					
8					

Proof:

	Date	Units	Unit Cost	Total Cost

			LIFO		

Proof:

	Date	Units	Unit Cost	Total Cost

1	(a) (1)	FIFO	1
2			2
3			3
4			4
5			5
6			6
7			7
8			8
9			9
10			10
11			11
12			12
13	(2)	LIFO	13
14			14
15			15
16			16
17			17
18			18
19			19
20			20
21			21
22			22
23			23
24	(b)		24
25			25
26			26
27			27
28			28
29			29
30			30
31	(c)		31
32			32
33			33
34			34
35			35
36			36
37			37
38			38
39			39
40			40

1	(a) (1) FIFO	1
2		2
3		3
4		4
5		5
6		6
7		7
8	(2) LIFO	8
9		9
10		10
11		11
12		12
13		13
14		14
15	(3) AVERAGE	15
16		16
17		17
18		18
19		19
20		20
21		21
22	(b)	22
23		23
24		24
25		25
26	(c)	26
27		27
28		28
29		29
30	(d)	30
31		31
32		32
33		33
34		34
35		35
36		36
37		37
38		38
39		39
40		40

E6-8

	Cost of Goods Available for Sale	÷	Total Units Available for Sale	=	Weighted Average Unit Cost	
1	(a)					1
2						2
3	Ending inventory					3
4	Cost of goods sold					4
5						5
6	(b)					6
7						7
8						8
9						9
10	(c)					10
11						11
12						12

E6-9

		Cost	Market	Lower of Cost or Market		
1	Cameras					1
2	Minolta					2
3	Canon					3
4	Total					4
5	Light Meters					5
6	Vivitar					6
7	Kodak					7
8	Total					8
9	Total inventory					9
10						10

E6-10

		Cost	Market	Lower of Cost or Market	'	
1	Cameras					1
2	DVD players					2
3	iPods					3
4	Total inventory					4
5						5
6						6
7						7
8						8

	2013	2014	
1 Beginning inventory			1
2 Cost of goods purchased			2
3 Cost of goods available for sale			3
4 Corrected ending inventory			4
5 Cost of goods sold			5
6			6
7			7
8			8
9			9
10			10
11			11
12			12
13			13
14			14
15			15
16			16
17			17
18			18
19			19
20			20

(a)		2013	2014
1				1
2				2
3				3
4				4
5				5
6				6
7				7
8				8
9				9
10				10
11				11
12				12
13 (b)				13
14				14
15				15
16				16
17				17
18				18
19				19
20				20
21 (c)				21
22				22
23				23
24				24
25				25
26				26
27				27
28				28
29				29
30				30
31				31
32				32
33				33
34				34
35				35
36				36
37				37
38				38
39				39
40				40

*Exercise 6-15

Roselle Appliance

(1) FIFO

Date	Purchases	Cost of Goods Sold	Balance
Jan. 1			
8			
10			
15			

(2) LIFO

Date	Purchases	Cost of Goods Sold	Balance
Jan. 1			
8			
10			
15			

(3) MOVING-AVERAGE-COST

Date	Purchases	Cost of Goods Sold	Balance
Jan. 1			
8			
10			
15			

(a)

1	Cost of goods available for sale:					
2						
3						
4						
5						
6						
7						

FIFO

8	Date	Purchases	Cost of goods sold	Balance
9	June 1			
10	12			
11				
12	15			
13				
14				
15	23			
16				
17	27			
18				
19				
20				

21	Ending inventory =	Cost of goods sold =
22		

(a) (Continued)

LIFO

Date	Purchases	Cost of goods sold	Balance
June 1			
12			
15			
23			
27			

Ending inventory =

Cost of goods sold =

MOVING-AVERAGE COST

Date	Purchases	Cost of goods sold	Balance
June 1			
12			
15			
23			
27			

Ending inventory =

Cost of goods sold =

(b)

(c)

(a)

FIFO

Date	Purchases	Cost of Goods Sold	Balance
1 9/1			
2 9/5			
3 9/12			
4			
5 9/16			
6			
7 9/19			
8			
9 9/26			
10			
11			
12 9/29			
13			
14			
15			

LIFO

Date	Purchases	Cost of Goods Sold	Balance
16			
17			
18 9/1			
19 9/5			
20 9/12			
21			
22 9/16			
23			
24 9/19			
25			
26 9/26			
27			
28			
29 9/29			
30			
31			

(a) (Continued)

MOVING-AVERAGE-COST

Date	Purchases	Cost of Goods Sold	Balance
9/1			
9/5			
9/12			
9/16			
9/19			
9/26			
9/29			

(b)

	Periodic	Perpetual
Ending inventory FIFO		
Ending inventory LIFO		

(c)

(a)

| | 1 | 2 | 3 | 4 | 5 | 6 | 7 | 8 | 9 | 10 | 11 | 12 | 13 | 14 | 15 |
| | 1 | 2 | 3 | 4 | 5 | 6 | 7 | 8 | 9 | 10 | 11 | 12 | 13 | 14 | 15 |

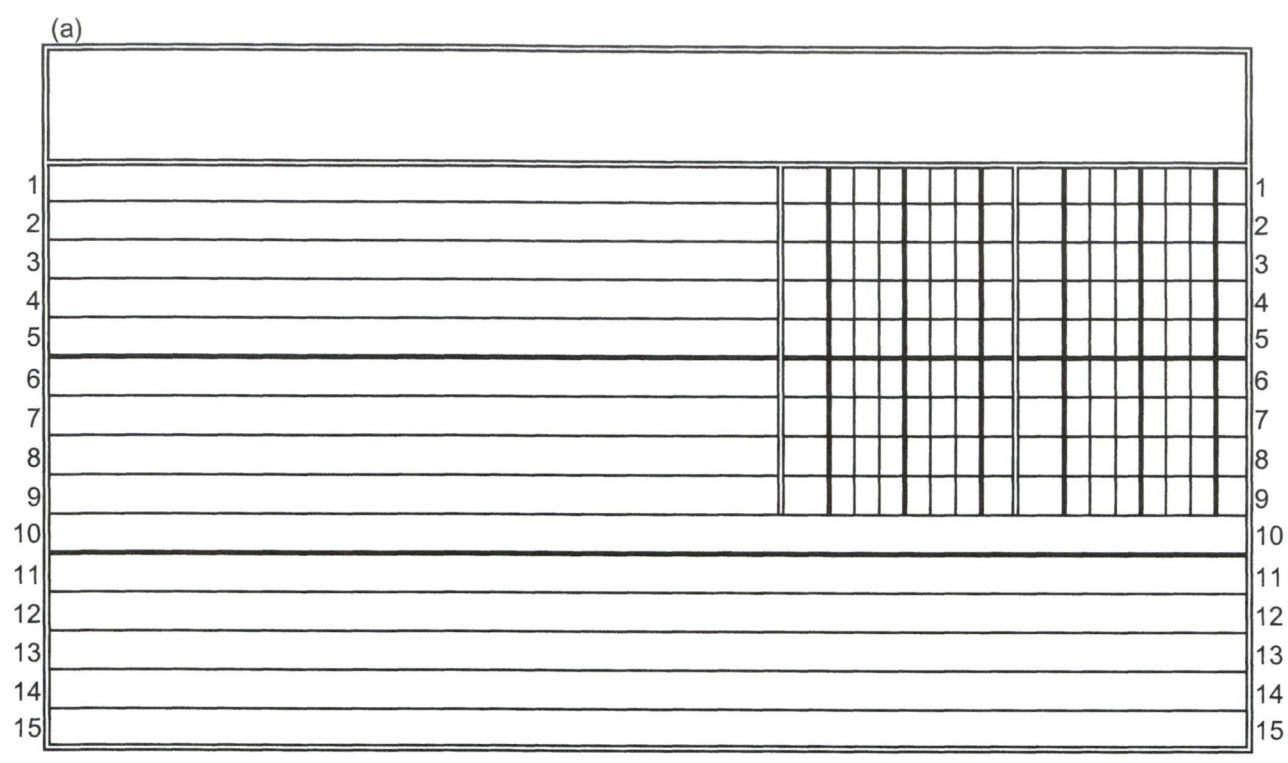

(b)

*E6-19

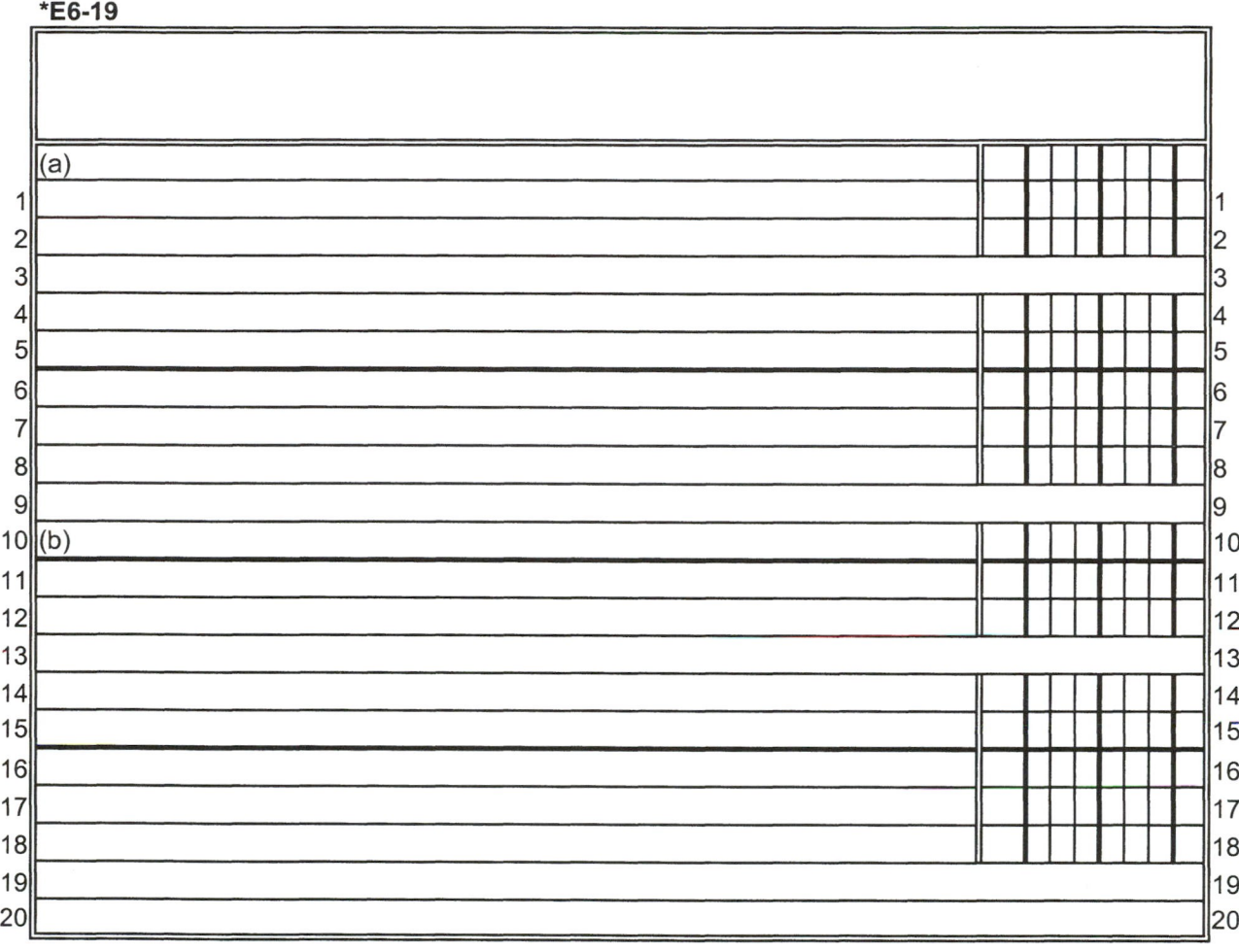

(a)

(b)

*E6-20

	Women's Department		Men's Department	
	Cost	Retail	Cost	Retail
Beginning inventory				
Goods purchased				
Goods avail. for sale				
Net sales				
Ending inv. at retail				
Cost/retail ratio				
Estimated cost of				
ending inventory				

(a)

COST OF GOODS AVAILABLE FOR SALE

	Date	Explanation	Units	Unit Cost	Total Cost	
1	March 1					1
2	5					2
3	13					3
4	21					4
5	26					5
6						6
7						7

(b) **FIFO**

(1) Ending Inventory

	Date		Units	Unit Cost	Total Cost	
10						10
11						11
12						12
13						13
14						14
15						15

(2) Cost of Goods Sold

		Total Cost	
16			16
17			17
18			18
19			19
20			20
21			21

Proof of Cost of Goods Sold

	Date		Units	Unit Cost	Total Cost	
23						23
24						24
25						25
26						26
27						27
28						28
29						29
30						30
31						31
32						32
33						33
34						34
35						35
36						36
37						37
38						38
39						39
40						40

(b) (Continued)

LIFO				
(1)	Ending Inventory			
Date		Units	Unit Cost	Total Cost

(2)	Cost of Goods Sold	

Proof of Cost of Goods Sold				
Date		Units	Unit Cost	Total Cost

Average Cost				
(1)	Ending Inventory			
Average Cost Per Unit		Units	Unit Cost	Total Cost

(2)	Cost of Goods Sold	

(c)

  (1)

  (2)

(a)

COST OF GOODS AVAILABLE FOR SALE

	Date	Explanation	Units	Unit Cost	Total Cost	
1	2/1					1
2	2/20					2
3	5/5					3
4	8/12					4
5	12/8					5
6						6
7						7

(b)   **FIFO**

(1)   Ending Inventory

	Date		Units	Unit Cost	Total Cost	
10						10
11						11
12						12
13						13
14						14
15						15

(2)   Cost of Goods Sold

16		16
17		17
18		18
19		19
20		20
21		21

Proof of Cost of Goods Sold

	Date		Units	Unit Cost	Total Cost	
24						24
25						25
26						26
27						27
28						28

(b) (Continued)

		LIFO			
(1)		Ending Inventory			
Date		Units	Unit Cost	Total Cost	
1					1
2					2
3					3
4					4
5					5

(2)	Cost of Goods Sold		
6			6
7			7
8			8
9			9
10			10
11			11

	Proof of Cost of Goods Sold			
Date		Units	Unit Cost	Total Cost
12				12
13 Date		Units	Unit Cost	Total Cost 13
14				14
15				15
16				16
17				17
18				18
19				19
20				20

	Average Cost			
21				21
(1)	Ending Inventory			
22				22
Average Cost Per Unit	Units	Unit Cost	Total Cost	
23				23
24				24
25				25

(2)	Cost of Goods Sold	
26		26
27		27
28		28
29		29
30		30
31		31

	Proof of Cost of Goods Sold	
32		32
33		33
34		34

(c)

35 (c)		35
36 (1)		36
37		37
38		38
39 (2)		39
40		40

(a)

Red Robin Co.		
Condensed Income Statements		
For the Year Ended December 31, 2014		
	FIFO	LIFO

(b) (1)

(2)

(3)

(4)

(5)

(a)

Cost of Goods Available For Sale

	Date	Explanation	Units	Unit Cost	Total Cost	
1	Oct. 1					1
2	9					2
3	17					3
4	25					4
5						5

Ending Inventory in Units

7					7
8					8
9					9
10					10

Sales Revenue

	Date		Units	Unit Price	Total Sales	
13	Date		Units	Unit Price	Total Sales	13
14	Oct. 11					14
15	22					15
16	29					16
17						17

(1) LIFO

(i) Ending Inventory

	Date		Units	Unit Cost	Total Cost	
21	Date		Units	Unit Cost	Total Cost	21
22						22
23						23
24						24

(ii) Cost of Goods Sold

(iii) Gross Profit

(iv) Gross Profit Rate

(a) (Continued)

(2) (i)	**FIFO** Ending Inventory			
Date		Units	Unit Cost	Total Cost

(ii)	Cost of Goods Sold	

(iii)	Gross Profit	

(iv)	Gross Profit Rate

(3) **Average Cost**

Weighted Average Cost Per Unit

(i)	Ending Inventory	

(ii)	Cost of Goods Sold	

(iii)	Gross Profit	

(a) (Continued)

Average Cost (Continued)

(iv)   Gross Profit Rate

(b)

(a)

	Specific Identification			
(1)	To maximize gross profit			
	Sales Revenue			
Date		Units	Unit Price	Sales Revenue
Mar. 5				
25				
	Cost of Goods Sold			
Date		Units	Unit Cost	Total Cost
Mar. 5				
25				
Sales Revenue				
Cost of Goods Sold				
Gross profit				
(2)	To minimize gross profit			
	Sales Revenue			
Date		Units	Unit Price	Sales Revenue
Mar. 5				
25				
	Cost of Goods Sold			
Date		Units	Unit Cost	Total Cost
Mar. 5				
25				
Sales Revenue				
Cost of Goods Sold				
Gross profit				

(b)

	FIFO				
	Cost of Goods Available for Sale				
Date		Units	Unit Cost	Total Cost	
Mar. 1					
3					
10					

	Units	Unit Cost	Total Cost
Goods available for sale			
Units sold			
Ending inventory			

	Total Cost
Goods available for sale	
Ending inventory	
Cost of goods sold	

	Total Cost
Sales revenue	
Cost of goods sold	
Gross profit	

(c)

	LIFO
Cost of Goods Available for Sale	
Ending inventory	
Cost of goods sold	

Sales revenue	
Cost of goods sold	
Gross profit	

(d)

(a)

	Mumba Inc. Condensed Income Statement For the Year Ended December 31, 2014	FIFO	LIFO
1			
2			
3			
4			
5			
6			
7			
8			
9			
10			
11			
12			
13			
14			

(b)

(a)

	Cost of Goods Available for Sale				
		Units	Unit Cost	Total Cost	
1	Inventory				1
2	Purchases:				2
3	January 2				3
4	January 9				4
5	January 10 return				5
6	Januarty 23				6
7					7
8					8
9	Sales:				9
10					10
11	January 6				11
12	January 9 return				12
13	January 10				13
14	January 30				14
15					15
16					16
17					17
18					18
19					19
20					20
21					21
22					22
23					23
24					24
25					25
26					26
27					27
28					28
29					29
30					30
31					31
32					32
33					33
34					34
35					35
36					36
37					37
38					38
39					39
40					40

(a) (Continued)

LIFO

(1) Date	Purchases	Cost of Goods Sold	Balance
Jan. 1			(150 units @ $19) 2850
2			
6			
9			
9			
10			
10			
23			
30			

(i) Cost of goods sold =

(ii) Ending inventory =

(iii) Gross profit =

(a) (Continued)

FIFO

(2) Date	Purchases	Cost of Goods Sold	Balance	
			(150 units @ $19)	2 8 5 0
Jan. 1				1
2				2
				3
6				4
9				5
				6
9				7
				8
10				9
				10
10				11
				12
23				13
				14
				15
30				16
				17
				18
				19
				20
				21
				22
				23

(i) Cost of goods sold =

(ii) Ending inventory =

(iii) Gross profit =

(a) (Continued)

(3)

Moving Average

Date	Purchases	Cost of Goods Sold	Balance
Jan. 1			(150 units @ $19) 2 8 5 0
2			
6			
9			
9			
10			
10			
23			
30			

(i) Cost of goods sold =

(ii) Ending inventory =

(iii) Gross profit =

(b)

	LIFO	FIFO	Moving Average	
1				1
2				2
3				3
4				4
5				5
6				6
7				7
8				8
9				9
10				10
11				11
12				12
13				13
14				14
15				15
16				16
17				17
18				18
19				19
20				20
21				21
22				22
23				23
24				24
25				25
26				26
27				27
28				28
29				29
30				30
31				31
32				32
33				33
34				34
35				35
36				36
37				37
38				38
39				39
40				40

(a)

FIFO

(1)

Date	Purchases	Cost of Goods Sold	Balance
May 1			
4			
8			
12			
15			
20			
25			

Moving-Average-Cost

(2)

Date	Purchases	Cost of Goods Sold	Balance
May 1			
4			
8			
12			
15			
20			
25			

(a) (Continued)

LIFO

(3) Date	Purchases			Cost of Goods Sold			Balance		
May 1									
4									
8									
12									
15									
20									
25									

(b)

1		
2		
3		
4		

	February
(a)	
Net sales	

14 Gross profit rate	

17 (b)	
18 Net sales	

(a)	Sporting Goods		Jewelry and Cosmetics	
	Cost	Retail	Cost	Retail
2 Beginning inventory				
3 Purchases				
4 Purchase returns				
5 Purchase discounts				
6 Freight-in				
7 Goods available for sale				
8 Net sales				
9 Ending inventory at retail				
10				

11 Cost-to-retail ratio:
12   Sporting goods:
13   Jewelry and cosmetics:
14
15 Estimated ending inventory at cost:
16   Sporting goods:
17   Jewelry and cosmetics:
18
19
20 (b)   Sporting goods:
21
22   Jewelry and cosmetics:
23
24
25

(a)

COST OF GOODS AVAILABLE FOR SALE

	Date	Explanation	Units	Unit Cost	Total Cost
1	Oct. 1				
2	3				
3	9				
4	19				
5	25				
6					
7					

(b)   **FIFO**

(1)   Ending Inventory

	Date		Units	Unit Cost	Total Cost
10					
11					
12					
13					
14					
15					

(2)   Cost of Goods Sold

		Total Cost
16		
17		
18		
19		
20		
21		

Proof of Cost of Goods Sold

	Date		Units	Unit Cost	Total Cost
23					
24					
25					
26					
27					
28					

(b) (Continued)

	LIFO			
(1)	Ending Inventory			
Date		Units	Unit Cost	Total Cost
1				
2				
3				
4				
5				
(2)	Cost of Goods Sold			

Proof of Cost of Goods Sold

Date		Units	Unit Cost	Total Cost

	Average Cost			
(1)	Ending Inventory			
Average Cost Per Unit		Units	Unit Cost	Total Cost
(2)	Cost of Goods Sold			

(c)

(1)

(2)

(a)

COST OF GOODS AVAILABLE FOR SALE

	Date	Explanation	Units	Unit Cost	Total Cost	
1	1/1					1
2	3/15					2
3	7/20					3
4	9/4					4
5	12/2					5
6						6
7						7

(b) **FIFO**

(1) Ending Inventory

	Date		Units	Unit Cost	Total Cost	
10						10
11						11
12						12
13						13
14						14
15						15

(2) Cost of Goods Sold

16				16
17				17
18				18
19				19
20				20
21				21

Proof of Cost of Goods Sold

	Date		Units	Unit Cost	Total Cost	
23						23
24						24
25						25
26						26
27						27
28						28
29						29
30						30
31						31
32						32
33						33
34						34
35						35
36						36
37						37
38						38
39						39
40						40

(b) (Continued)

	LIFO				
(1) Date		Ending Inventory			
			Units	Unit Cost	Total Cost
1					
2					
3					
4					
5					
(2)		Cost of Goods Sold			
7					
8					
9					
10					
11					
12		Proof of Cost of Goods Sold			
Date			Units	Unit Cost	Total Cost
14					
15					
16					
17					
18					
19					
20					

	Average Cost			
(1)	Ending Inventory			
Average Cost Per Unit	Units	Unit Cost		Total Cost
(2)	Cost of Goods Sold			

Proof of Cost of Goods Sold

(c)

(a)

	Gilbert Inc. Condensed Income Statements For the Year Ended December 31, 2014	FIFO	LIFO
1			
2			
3			
4			
5			
6			
7			
8			
9			
10			
11			
12			
13			
14			
15			
16			
17			
18			

(b)   (1)

(2)

(3)

(4)

(5)

(a)

	Cost of Goods Available For Sale			
Date	Explanation	Units	Unit Cost	Total Cost
June 1				
4				
18				
18				
28				

Ending Inventory in Units

Sales Revenue

Date		Units	Unit Price	Total Sales
June 10				
11				
25				

(1) **LIFO**

(i) Ending Inventory

Date		Units	Unit Cost	Total Cost

(ii) Cost of Goods Sold

(iii) Gross Profit

(iv) Gross Profit Rate

(a) (Continued)

(2)   **FIFO**

    (i)   Ending Inventory

Date		Units	Unit Cost	Total Cost

    (ii)   Cost of Goods Sold

    (iii)   Gross Profit

    (iv)   Gross Profit Rate

(3)   **Average Cost**

Weighted Average Cost Per Unit

    (i)   Ending Inventory

    (ii)   Cost of Goods Sold

    (iii)   Gross Profit

(a) (Continued)

Average Cost (Continued)

(iv)   Gross Profit Rate

(b)

(a)

Gas Guzzlers Inc.
Income Statement (Partial)
For the Year Ended December, 31, 2014

	Specific Identification	FIFO	LIFO
1			
2			
3			
4			
5			
6			
7			
8			
9			
10			
11			
12			
13			

14 Specific identification ending inventory consists of:

	Units	Unit Cost	Total Cost
16			
17			
18			
19			
20			

21 FIFO ending inventory consists of:

22			
23			
24			
25			

26 LIFO ending inventory consists of:

27			
28			
29			
30			
31			
32			
33			
34			

35 (b)

36

37

38

39

(a)

	FIFO	LIFO
Creek Co. Condensed Income Statement For the Year Ended December 31, 2014		
1		
2		
3		
4		
5		
6		
7		
8		
9		
10		
11		
12		
13		
14		

(b)

(1)

(2)

(3)

(4)

(5)

(a)

Cost of Goods Available for Sale			
	Units	Unit Cost	Total Cost
Inventory			
Purchases:			
January 5			
January 15			
January 16 return			
January 25			
Sales:			
January 8			
January 10 return			
January 20			

(a) (Continued)

LIFO

(1) Date	Purchases	Cost of Goods Sold	Balance
Jan. 1			(100 @ $14) 1 4 0 0
5			
8			
10			
15			
16			
20			
25			

(i) Cost of goods sold =

(ii) Ending inventory =

(iii) Gross profit =

(a) (Continued)

FIFO

(2) Date	Purchases	Cost of Goods Sold	Balance
Jan. 1			(100 @ $14)
5			
8			
10			
15			
16			
20			
25			

(i) Cost of goods sold =

(ii) Ending inventory =

(iii) Gross profit =

(a) (Continued)

Moving-Average Cost

(3) Date	Purchases	Cost of Goods Sold	Balance
Jan. 1			(100 @ $14) 1400
5			
8			
10			
15			
16			
20			
25			

(i) Cost of goods sold =

(ii) Ending inventory =

(iii) Gross profit =

(b)

	LIFO	FIFO	Moving Average
1			
2			
3			
4			
5			
6			
7			
8			
9			
10			
11			
12			
13			
14			
15			
16			
17			
18			
19			
20			
21			
22			
23			
24			
25			
26			
27			
28			
29			
30			
31			
32			
33			
34			
35			
36			
37			
38			
39			
40			

(a)

FIFO

(1)

Date	Purchases	Cost of Goods Sold	Balance
July 1			
6			
11			
14			
21			
27			

MOVING-AVERAGE-COST

(2)

Date	Purchases	Cost of Goods Sold	Balance
July 1			
6			
11			
14			
21			
27			

(a) (Continued)

LIFO

(3) Date	Purchases			Cost of Goods Sold			Balance		
July 1									
6									
11									
14									
21									
27									

(b)

1		
2		
3		
4		

	November
(a)	
Net sales	
1	
2	
3	
4	
5	
6	
7	
8	
9	
10	
11	
12	
13	
14 Gross profit rate	
15	
16	
17 (b)	
18 Net sales	
19	
20	
21	
22	
23	
24	
25	
26	
27	
28	
29	
30	
31	
32	
33	
34	
35	
36	
37	
38	
39	

(a)	Hardcovers		Paperbacks		
	Cost	Retail	Cost	Retail	
1					1
2 Beginning inventory					2
3 Purchases					3
4 Purchase returns					4
5 Purchase discounts					5
6 Freight-in					6
7 Goods available for sale					7
8 Net sales					8
9 Ending inventory at retail					9
10					10
11 Cost-to-retail ratio:					11
12 Hardcovers:					12
13 Paperbacks:					13
14					14
15 Estimated ending inventory at cost:					15
16 Hardcovers:					16
17 Paperbacks:					17
18					18
19					19
20 (b) Hardcovers:					20
21					21
22 Paperbacks:					22
23					23
24					24
25					25

(a)

	Date	Account Titles	Debit	Credit	
1	Dec 3				1
2					2
3					3
4	5				4
5					5
6					6
7					7
8					8
9					9
10	7				10
11					11
12					12
13					13
14					14
15					15
16	17				16
17					17
18					18
19	22				19
20					20
21					21
22					22
23					23
24					24
25	31				25
26					26
27					27
28					28
29					29
30					30
31					31
32					32
33					33
34					34
35					35
36					36
37					37
38					38
39					39
40					40

(b)   General Ledger

Cash		Retained Earnings	
Bal. 4,650			Bal. 7,000

Accounts Receivable		Sales Revenue	
Bal. 3,900			

Inventory		Cost of Goods Sold	
Bal. 1,950			

Equipment		Salaries and Wages Expense	
Bal. 21,000			

Accumulated Depreciation - Equipment		Depreciation Expense	
	Bal. 1,500		

Accounts Payable		Sales Returns & Allowances	
	Bal. 3,000		

Salaries and Wages Payable	

Common Stock	
	Bal. 20,000

(c)

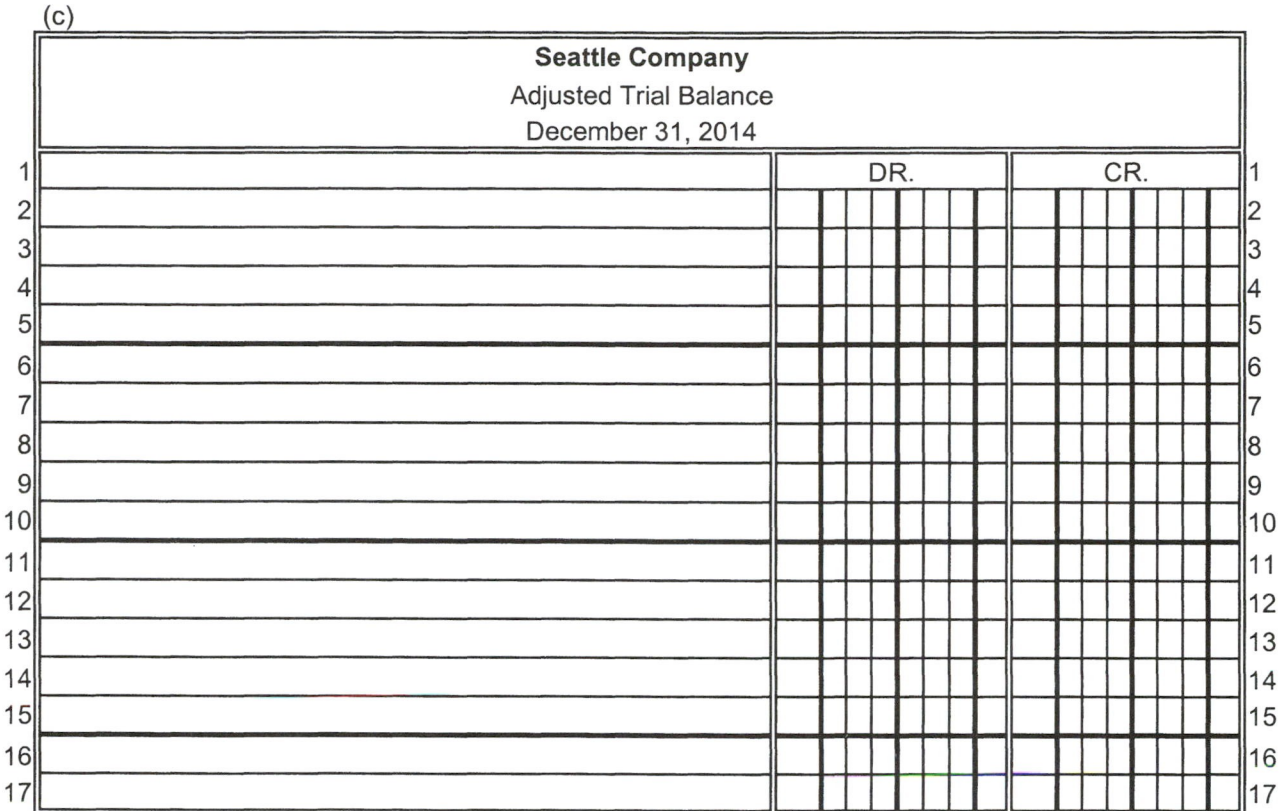

Seattle Company Adjusted Trial Balance December 31, 2014	DR.	CR.
1		
2		
3		
4		
5		
6		
7		
8		
9		
10		
11		
12		
13		
14		
15		
16		
17		

(d)

Seattle Company Income Statement For the Month Ending December 31, 2014		
1		
2		
3		
4		
5		
6		
7		
8		
9		
10		
11		
12		
13		
14		
15		
16		
17		
18		
19		

(d) (Continued)

Seattle Company
Balance Sheet
December 31, 2014

Assets

Liabilities and Stockholders' Equity

(e) FIFO Method

	Date	Explanation	Units	Unit Cost	Cost of Goods Available for Sale	
1						1
2						2
3						3
4						4
5						5

Ending Inventory

	Date		Units	Unit Cost	Total Cost	
6						6
7						7
8						8
9						9
10						10
11						11

Cost of Goods Sold

12			12
13			13
14			14
15			15
16			16

(f) LIFO Method

Ending Inventory

	Date		Units	Unit Cost	Total Cost	
1						1
2						2
3						3
4						4

Cost of Goods Sold

5			5
6			6
7			7
8			8
9			9
10			10
11			11
12			12
13			13
14			14
15			15
16			16
17			17
18			18
19			19

		December 25, 2010	December 26, 2009
1	(a) Inventory (in millions)		
2			
3			
4			
5			
6	(b) Dollar change in inventories between 2009 and 2010:		
7			
8			
9	Percent change in inventories between 2009 and 2010:		
10			
11			
12	2010 inventory as a percent of current assets:		
13			
14			
15			
16	(c)		
17			
18			
19			
20			
21			

		2010	2009	2008
22	(d) PepsiCo (in millions)			
23				
24	Cost of sales			
25				
26				
27	2010 cost of goods sold as a percent of sales:			
28				
29				
30				
31				
32				
33				
34				
35				

		2013	2012
(a) (1)			
(2)			
***(b)**		2013	2012
Net sales			
Gross profit rate			
Average gross profit rate			
***(c) Sales**			

IFRS6-3

	Item No.	Cost		Net Realizable Value		LCNRV	
1	AB	$	1 7 0 0	$	1 4 0 0		1
2	TRX		2 2 0 0		2 3 0 0		2
3	NWA		7 8 0 0		7 1 0 0		3
4	SGH		3 0 0 0		3 7 0 0		4

(c)

BE7-6

		Account Titles	Debit	Credit	
1	1.				1
2					2
3					3
4					4
5	2.				5
6					6
7					7
8					8

BE7-7

	Account Titles	Debit	Credit	
9				9
10				10
11				11
12				12
13				13

BE7-9

	Date	Account Titles	Debit	Credit	
14					14
15	Date	Account Titles	Debit	Credit	15
16	Mar. 20				16
17					17
18					18
19					19
20					20
21					21
22					22

BE7-13

		Credit	
23			23
24			24
25			25
26			26
27			27
28			28
29			29

BE7-14

		Credit	
30			30
31			31
32			32
33			33
34			34
35			35
36			36
37			37
38			38
39			39
40			40

27	Date	Account Titles	Debit	Credit	
1	Aug. 1				1
2					2
3					3
4	30				4
5					5
6					6
7					7
8					8
9					9
10					10
11					11
12					12
13					13
14					14
15					15
16					16
17					17
18					18
19					19
20					20

	Date	Account Titles	Debit	Credit	
1	May 1				1
2					2
3					3
4	June 1				4
5					5
6					6
7					7
8					8
9					9
10	July 1				10
11					11
12					12
13					13
14					14
15	July 10				15
16					16
17					17
18					18
19					19
20					20

E7-8

Date	Account Titles	Debit	Credit
Mar. 1			
15			
20			

E7-9 (a)

Lisa Ceja
Bank Reconciliation
January 31

(b)

Date	Account Titles	Debit	Credit

E7-10

	No.	Amount
1		
2		
3		
4		
5		

E7-11 (a)

Worthy Video Company		
Bank Reconciliation		
July 31		
1		
2		
3		
4		
5		
6		
7		
8		
9		
10		
11		
12		
13		
14		
15		
16		

(b)

	Date	Account Titles	Debit	Credit
1	July 31			
2				
3				
4				
5				
6	31			
7				
8				
9				
10				

(a)

	Wasson Company		
	Bank Reconciliation		
	September 30		
1			
2			
3			
4			
5			
6			
7			
8			
9			
10			
11			
12			
13			
14			
15			
16			
17			
18			
19			
20			

(b)

	Date	Account Titles	Debit	Credit
1	Sept. 30			
2				
3				
4				
5				
6	30			
7				
8				
9	30			
10				
11				
12	30			
13				
14				
15				

1	(a)　　Deposits in transit at July 31:								1
2									2
3									3
4									4
5									5
6									6
7									7
8									8
9									9
10									10
11	(b)　　Outstanding checks at July 31:								11
12									12
13									13
14									14
15									15
16									16
17									17
18									18
19									19
20									20
21	(c)　　Deposits in transit at August 31:								21
22									22
23									23
24									24
25									25
26									26
27									27
28									28
29									29
30									30
31	(d)　　Outstanding checks at August 31:								31
32									32
33									33
34									34
35									35
36									36
37									37
38									38
39									39
40									40

1	(a)	1
2		2
3		3
4		4
5		5
6		6
7		7
8	(b)	8
9		9
10		10
11		11
12		12
13		13
14	(c)	14
15		15
16		16
17		17
18		18
19		19
20		20
21		21
22		22
23		23
24		24
25		25
26		26
27		27
28		28
29		29
30		30
31		31
32		32
33		33
34		34
35		35
36		36
37		37
38		38
39		39
40		40

(a)   General Journal

	Date	Account Titles	Debit	Credit	
1	July 1				1
2					2
3					3
4	15				4
5					5
6					6
7					7
8					8
9					9
10					10
11	31				11
12					12
13					13
14					14
15					15
16					16
17	Aug. 15				17
18					18
19					19
20					20
21					21
22					22
23					23
24	16				24
25					25
26					26
27	31				27
28					28
29					29
30					30
31					31
32					32
33					33
34					34
35					35
36					36
37					37
38					38
39					39
40					40

(b)

Petty Cash

Date	Explanation	Ref.	Debit	Credit	Balance

(c)

(a)

Terrell Company				
Bank Reconciliation				
May 31, 2014				
1				
2				
3				
4				
5				
6				
7				
8				
9				
10				
11				
12				
13				
14				
15				
16				
17				
18				

(b)

General Journal

	Date	Account Titles	Debit	Credit
1	May 31			
2				
3				
4				
5				
6	31			
7				
8				
9	31			
10				
11				
12	31			
13				
14				
15	31			
16				
17				

(a)

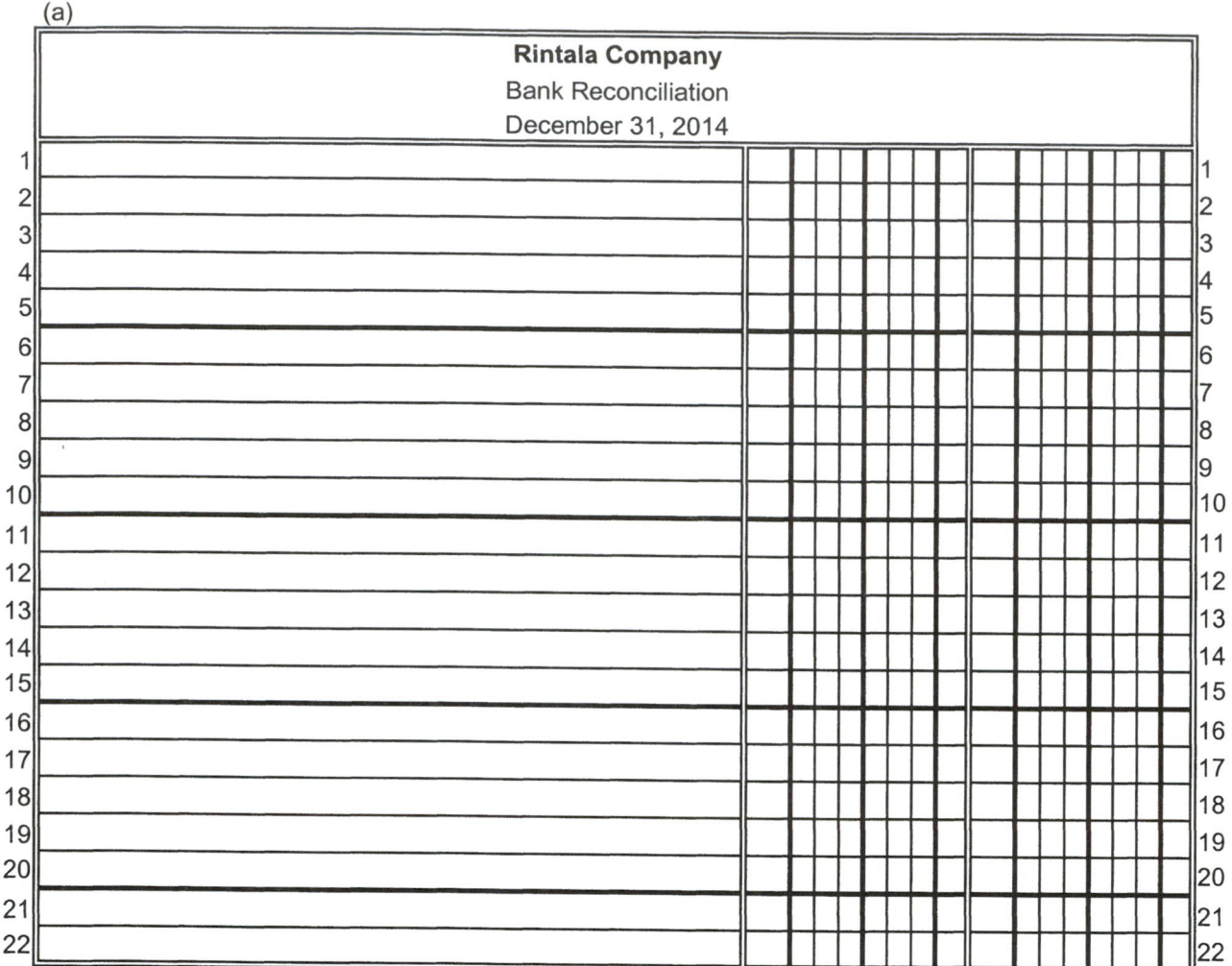

Rintala Company

Bank Reconciliation

December 31, 2014

(b)   General Journal

	Date	Account Titles	Debit	Credit
1	Dec. 31			
2				
3				
4				
5				
6	31			
7				
8				
9	31			
10				
11				
12	31			
13				
14				

(a)

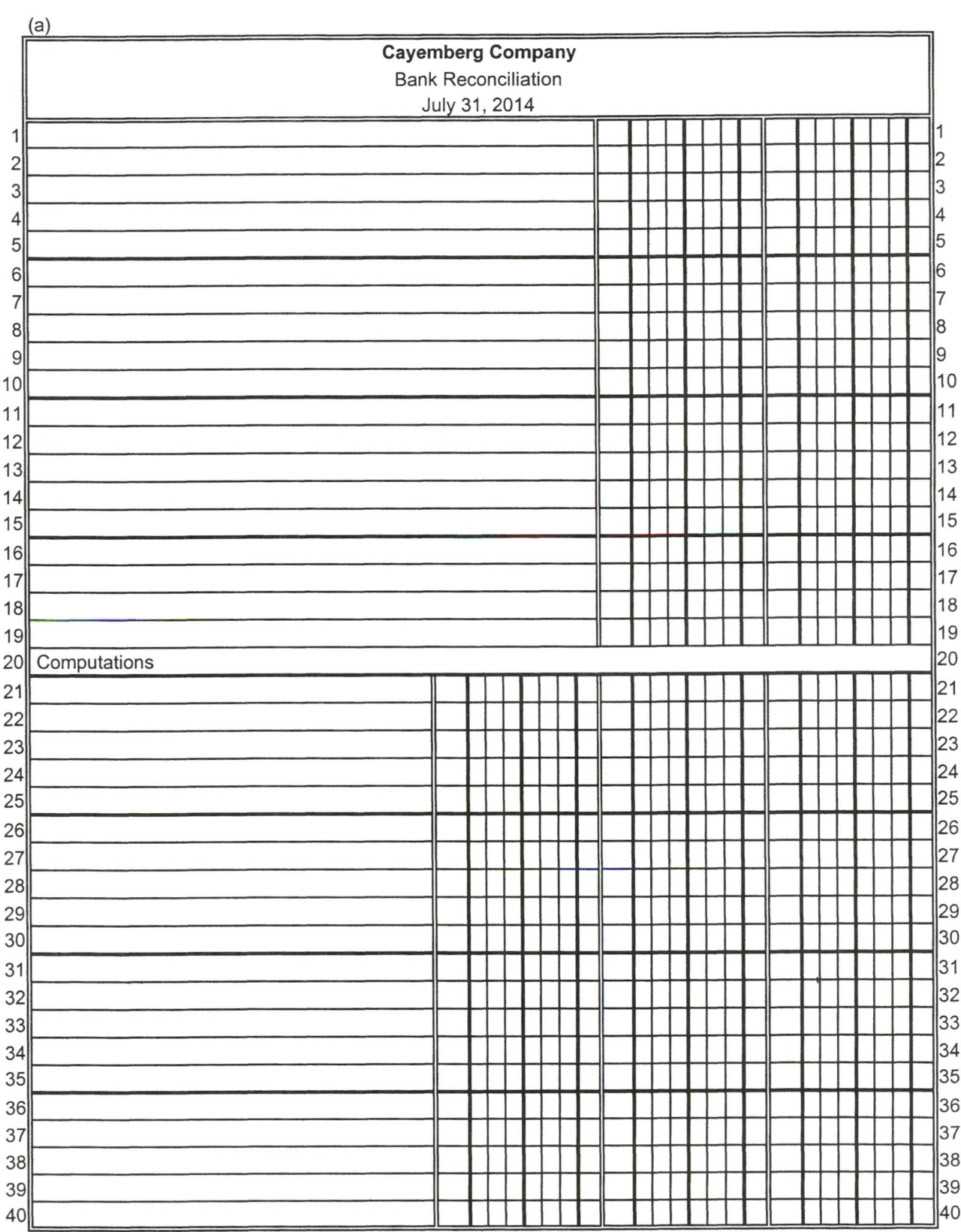

Cayemberg Company
Bank Reconciliation
July 31, 2014

Computations

(b)

General Journal

Date	Account Titles	Debit	Credit
July 31			
31			
31			

(a)

General Journal

	Date	Account Titles	Debit	Credit	
1	July 1				1
2					2
3					3
4	15				4
5					5
6					6
7					7
8					8
9					9
10					10
11	31				11
12					12
13					13
14					14
15					15
16					16
17	Aug. 15				17
18					18
19					19
20					20
21					21
22					22
23					23
24	16				24
25					25
26					26
27	31				27
28					28
29					29
30					30
31					31
32					32
33					33
34					34
35					35
36					36
37					37
38					38
39					39
40					40

(b)

Petty Cash

Date	Explanation	Ref.	Debit	Credit	Balance

(c)

(a)

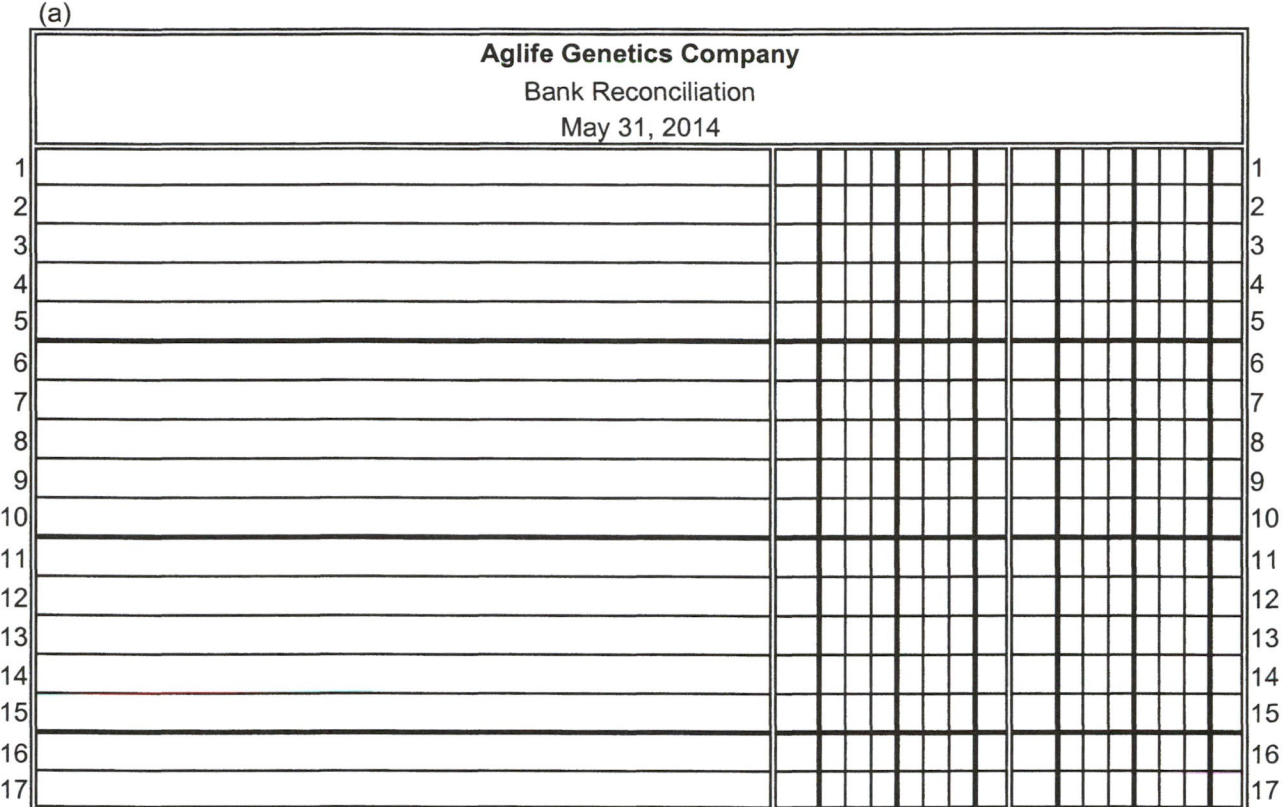

Aglife Genetics Company
Bank Reconciliation
May 31, 2014

(b)   General Journal

	Date	Account Titles	Debit	Credit
1	May 31			
2				
3				
4				
5				
6	31			
7				
8				
9	31			
10				
11				
12	31			
13				
14				
15	31			
16				
17				

(a)

	Goulet Company			
	Bank Reconciliation			
	November 30, 2014			
1				
2				
3				
4				
5				
6				
7				
8				
9				
10				
11				
12				
13				
14				
15				
16				
17				
18				
19				
20				
21				
22				

(b)   General Journal

	Date	Account Titles	Debit	Credit
1	Nov. 30			
2				
3				
4				
5				
6	30			
7				
8				
9	30			
10				
11				
12	30			
13				
14				

(a)

Tizani Company				
Bank Reconciliation				
August 31, 2014				

Computations

(b)

General Journal

	Date	Account Titles	Debit	Credit	
1	Aug. 31				1
2					2
3					3
4					4
5	31				5
6					6
7					7
8	31				8
9					9
10					10
11	31				11
12					12
13					13
14					14
15					15
16					16
17					17
18					18
19					19
20					20

(a)

	Stupendous Company									
	Bank Reconciliation									
	October 31, 2014									
1										1
2										2
3										3
4										4
5										5
6										6
7										7
8										8
9										9
10										10
11										11
12										12
13										13
14										14
15										15
16										16
17										17
18										18
19										19
20										20

21	(b) (1)	21
22		22
23		23
24		24
25	(2)	25
26		26
27		27
28	(3)	28
29		29
30		30
31		31
32		32
33	(c)	33
34		34
35		35
36		36
37		37
38		38
39		39
40		40

	Date	Account Titles	Debit	Credit	
1	Dec. 7				1
2					2
3					3
4	12				4
5					5
6					6
7	17				7
8					8
9					9
10					10
11					11
12					12
13	19				13
14					14
15					15
16	22				16
17					17
18					18
19					19
20	26				20
21					21
22					22
23					23
24	31				24
25					25
26					26
27					27
28					28
29					29
30					30
31					31
32					32
33					33
34					34
35					35
36					36
37					37
38					38
39					39
40					40

(b) & (e)

Cash		Accounts Payable	
12/1 Bal	18,200		12/1 Bal	6,100

		Common Stock	
		12/1 Bal.	50,000

Notes Receivable		Retained Earnings	
12/1 Bal	2,000		12/1 Bal	14,200

		Sales Revenue	

Accounts Receivable		Sales Discounts	
12/1 Bal	7,500		

Inventory		Cost of Goods Sold	
12/1/Bal	16,000		

Prepaid Insurance		Depreciation Expense	
12/1 Bal	1,600		

Equipment		Salaries and Wages Expense	
12/1 Bal.	28,000		

Accumulated Depreciation - Equipment		Insurance Expense	
		12/1 Bal	3,000	

(c)

Westmoreland Company

Bank Reconciliation

December 31, 2014

1	
2	
3	
4	
5	
6	
7	
8	
9	
10	
11	
12	
13	

(d)

	Date	Account Titles	Debit	Credit	
15	Date	Account Titles	Debit	Credit	15
16	Dec. 31				16
17					17
18					18
19	31				19
20					20
21					21
22	31				22
23					23
24					24
25					25
26	31				26
27					27
28					28
29					29
30					30
31					31
32					32
33					33
34					34
35					35
36					36
37					37
38					38
39					39
40					40

(f)

		Debit	Credit	
	Westmoreland Company			
	Trial Balance			
	December 31, 2014			
1		Debit	Credit	1
2	Cash			2
3	Notes Receivable			3
4	Accounts Receivable			4
5	Inventory			5
6	Prepaid Insurance			6
7	Equipment			7
8	Accumulated Depreciation - Equipment			8
9	Accounts Payable			9
10	Common Stock			10
11	Retained Earnings			11
12	Sales Revenue			12
13	Sales Discounts			13
14	Cost of Goods Sold			14
15	Depreciation Expense			15
16	Salaries and Wages Expense			16
17	Insurance Expense			17
18				18
19				19
20				20

(g)

	Westmoreland Company			
	Income Statement			
	For the Month Ending December 31, 2014			
1				1
2				2
3				3
4				4
5				5
6				6
7				7
8				8
9				9
10				10
11				11
12				12
13				13
14				14
15				15

(g)   (Continued)

Westmoreland Company
Balance Sheet
December 31, 2014

Assets			

Liabilities and Stockholders' Equity			

(a) (in millions)	PepsiCo	Coca-Cola
(1) Cash and cash equivalents at year-end 2010		
(2) Increase(decrease) in cash and cash equivalents from 2009 to 2010		
(3) Cash provided by operating activities during year ended Dec. 31, 2010		

(b)

BE8-2

		Account Titles	Debit	Credit	
1	(a)				1
2					2
3					3
4	(b)				4
5					5
6					6
7	(c)				7
8					8
9					9
10					10

	BE8-3	Account Titles	Debit	Credit	
11					11
12	(a)				12
13					13
14					14
15	(b)	Current assets:			15
16					16
17					17
18					18
19					19
20					20
21					21
22					22
23					23

	BE8-4	Account Titles	Debit	Credit	
24					24
25	(a)				25
26					26
27					27

			(1) Before Write-Off	(2) After Write-Off	
28	(b)				28
29					29
30					30
31					31
32					32
33					33
34					34
35					35

BE8-5

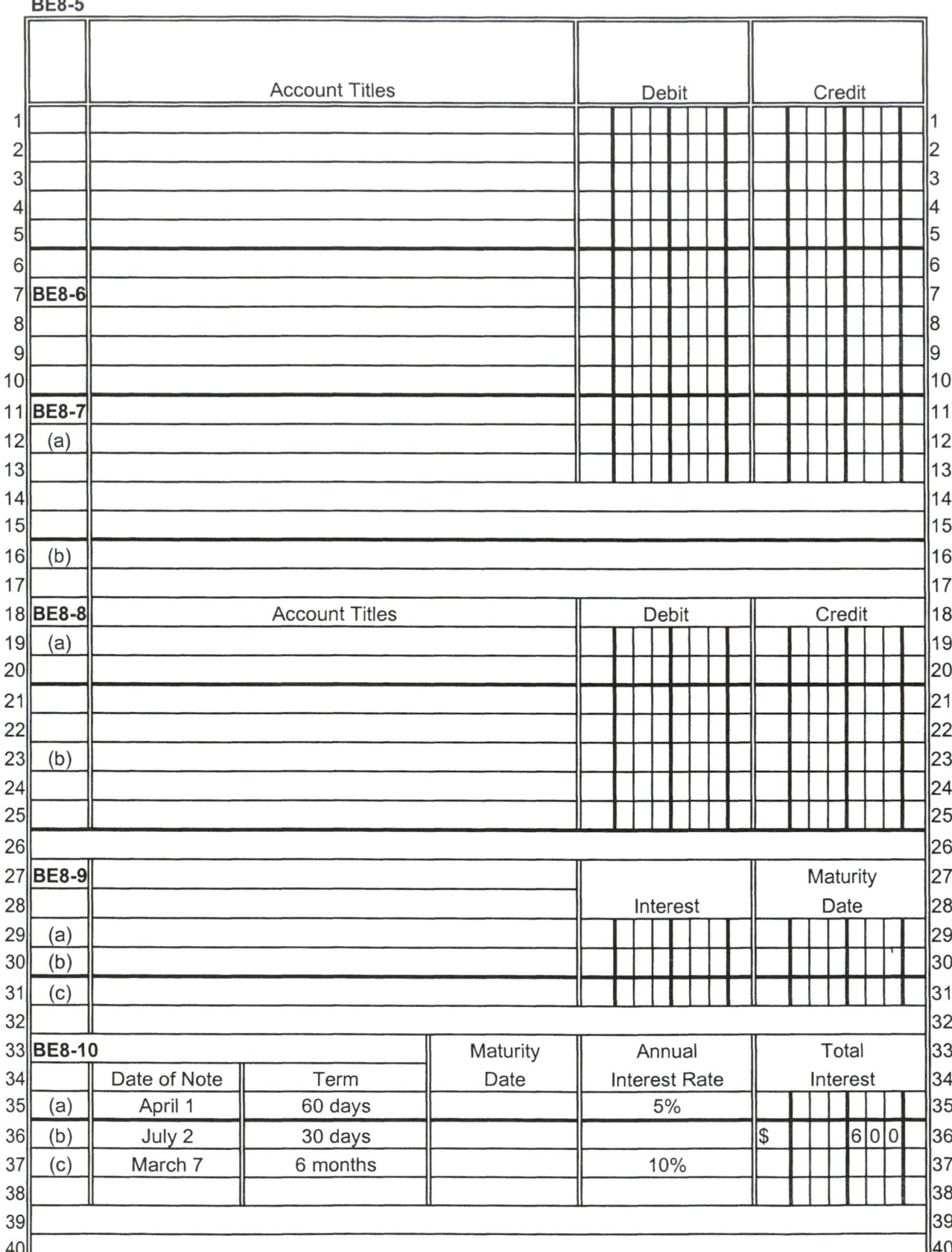

	Account Titles	Debit	Credit
1			
2			
3			
4			
5			
6			
7	**BE8-6**		
8			
9			
10			
11	**BE8-7**		
12	(a)		
13			
14			
15			
16	(b)		
17			

	BE8-8 Account Titles	Debit	Credit
18			
19	(a)		
20			
21			
22			
23	(b)		
24			
25			
26			

	BE8-9	Interest	Maturity Date
27			
28			
29	(a)		
30	(b)		
31	(c)		
32			

BE8-10

	Date of Note	Term	Maturity Date	Annual Interest Rate	Total Interest
35	(a)	April 1	60 days		5%	
36	(b)	July 2	30 days			$ 6 0 0
37	(c)	March 7	6 months		10%	
38						
39						
40						

BE8-11

	Date	Account Titles	Debit	Credit	
1	Date				1
2	Jan. 10				2
3					3
4					4
5					5
6	Feb. 9				6
7					7
8					8
9					9
10					10
11					11
12					12
13					13
14					14
15					15
16					16
17					17
18					18
19					19
20					20
21					21
22					22
23					23
24					24
25					25
26					26
27					27
28					28
29					29
30					30
31					31
32					32
33					33
34					34
35					35
36					36
37					37
38					38
39					39
40					40

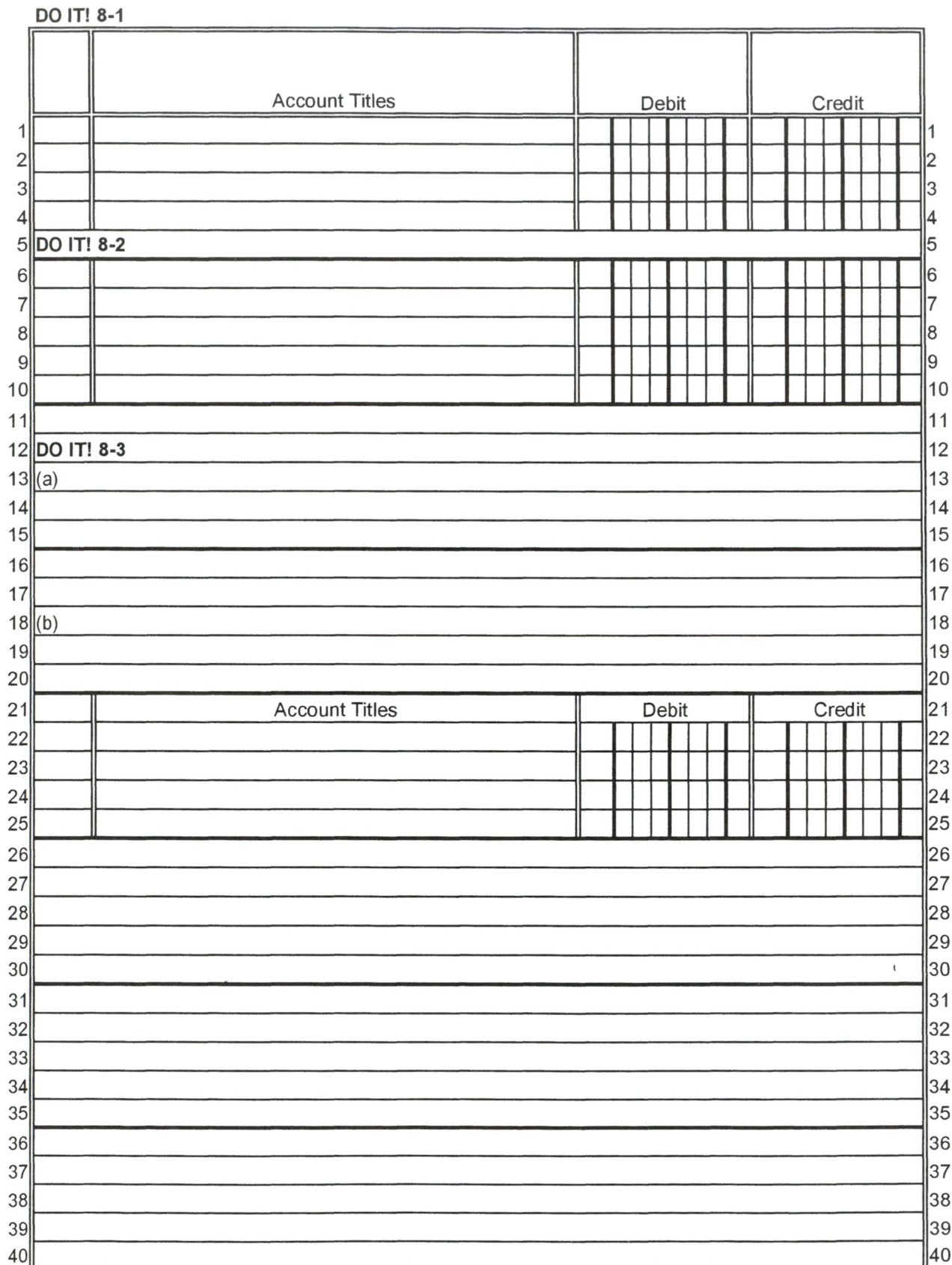

DO IT! 8-1

	Account Titles	Debit	Credit
1			
2			
3			
4			

DO IT! 8-2

		Debit	Credit
5			
6			
7			
8			
9			
10			
11			

DO IT! 8-3

(a)

(b)

	Account Titles	Debit	Credit
21			
22			
23			
24			
25			

E8-1

	Date	Account Titles	Debit	Credit	
1	March 1				1
2					2
3					3
4	3				4
5					5
6					6
7	9				7
8					8
9					9
10					10
11	15				11
12					12
13					13
14	31				14
15					15
16					16
17	**E8-2**				17
18	(a)				18
19	Jan. 6				19
20					20
21					21
22	16				22
23					23
24					24
25					25
26	(b)				26
27	Jan. 10				27
28					28
29					29
30	Feb. 12				30
31					31
32					32
33	Mar. 10				33
34					34
35					35
36					36
37					37
38					38
39					39
40					40

E8-3

	Date	Account Titles	Debit	Credit	
1	(a)				1
2	Dec. 31				2
3					3
4					4
5	(b) (1)				5
6	Dec. 31				6
7					7
8					8
9	(2)				9
10	Dec. 31				10
11					11
12					12
13	(c) (1)				13
14	Dec. 31				14
15					15
16					16
17	(2)				17
18	Dec. 31				18
19					19
20					20

E8-4

	Accounts Receivable	Amount	%	Estimated Uncollectible	
21					21
22	(a)				22
23	Accounts Receivable	Amount	%	Estimated Uncollectible	23
24	1 - 30 days				24
25					25
26	30 - 60 days				26
27					27
28	60 - 90 days				28
29					29
30	Over 90 days				30
31					31
32					32
33					33
34					34
35	(b)				35

	Date	Account Titles	Debit	Credit	
36	Date	Account Titles	Debit	Credit	36
37	Mar. 31				37
38					38
39					39
40					40

E8-5

	Date	Account Titles	Debit	Credit	
1					1
2					2
3					3
4					4
5					5
6					6
7					7
8					8
9					9
10					10
11					11
12					12
13					13
14	**E8-6**				14
15	2013				15
16	Dec. 31				16
17					17
18					18
19					19
20	2014				20
21	May 11				21
22					22
23					23
24					24
25	2014				25
26	Jun. 12				26
27					27
28					28
29					29
30					30
31					31
32					32
33					33

E8-7

	Date	Account Titles	Debit	Credit	
1	(a)				1
2	Mar. 3				2
3					3
4					4
5					5
6					6
7					7
8	(b)				8
9	May 10				9
10					10
11					11
12					12
13					13
14					14
15					15
16	**E8-8**				16
17	(a)				17
18	Apr. 2				18
19					19
20					20
21	May 3				21
22					22
23					23
24	Jun. 1				24
25					25
26					26
27	(b)				27
28	July 4				28
29					29
30					30
31					31
32					32
33					33
34					34
35					35
36					36
37					37
38					38
39					39
40					40

E8-9

	Date	Account Titles	Debit	Credit	
1	(a)				1
2	Jan. 15				2
3					3
4					4
5	20				5
6					6
7					7
8					8
9	Feb 10				9
10					10
11					11
12	15				12
13					13
14					14
15	(b)				15
16					16
17					17

E8-10

	Date	Account Titles	Debit	Credit	
18					18
19	Date	Account Titles	Debit	Credit	19
20	(a)	2014			20
21	Nov. 1				21
22					22
23					23
24	Dec. 11				24
25					25
26					26
27	16				27
28					28
29					29
30	31				30
31					31
32					32
33		Calculation of interest:			33
34					34
35					35
36					36
37	(b)	2015			37
38	Nov. 1				38
39					39
40					40
41					41

E8-11

	Date	Account Titles	Debit	Credit	
1		2014			1
2	May 1				2
3					3
4					4
5	Dec. 31				5
6					6
7					7
8	31				8
9					9
10					10
11		2015			11
12	May 1				12
13					13
14					14
15					15
16					16
17	**E8-12**				17
18	4/1/14				18
19					19
20					20
21	7/1/14				21
22					22
23					23
24	12/31/14				24
25					25
26					26
27					27
28					28
29					29
30	4/1/15				30
31					31
32					32
33					33
34					34
35	5/1/15				35
36					36
37					37
38					38
39					39
40					40

E8-13

	Date	Account Titles	Debit	Credit	
1	(a)				1
2	May 2				2
3					3
4					4
5	(b)				5
6	Nov. 2				6
7					7
8					8
9					9
10	(c)				10
11	Nov. 2				11
12					12
13					13

E8-14

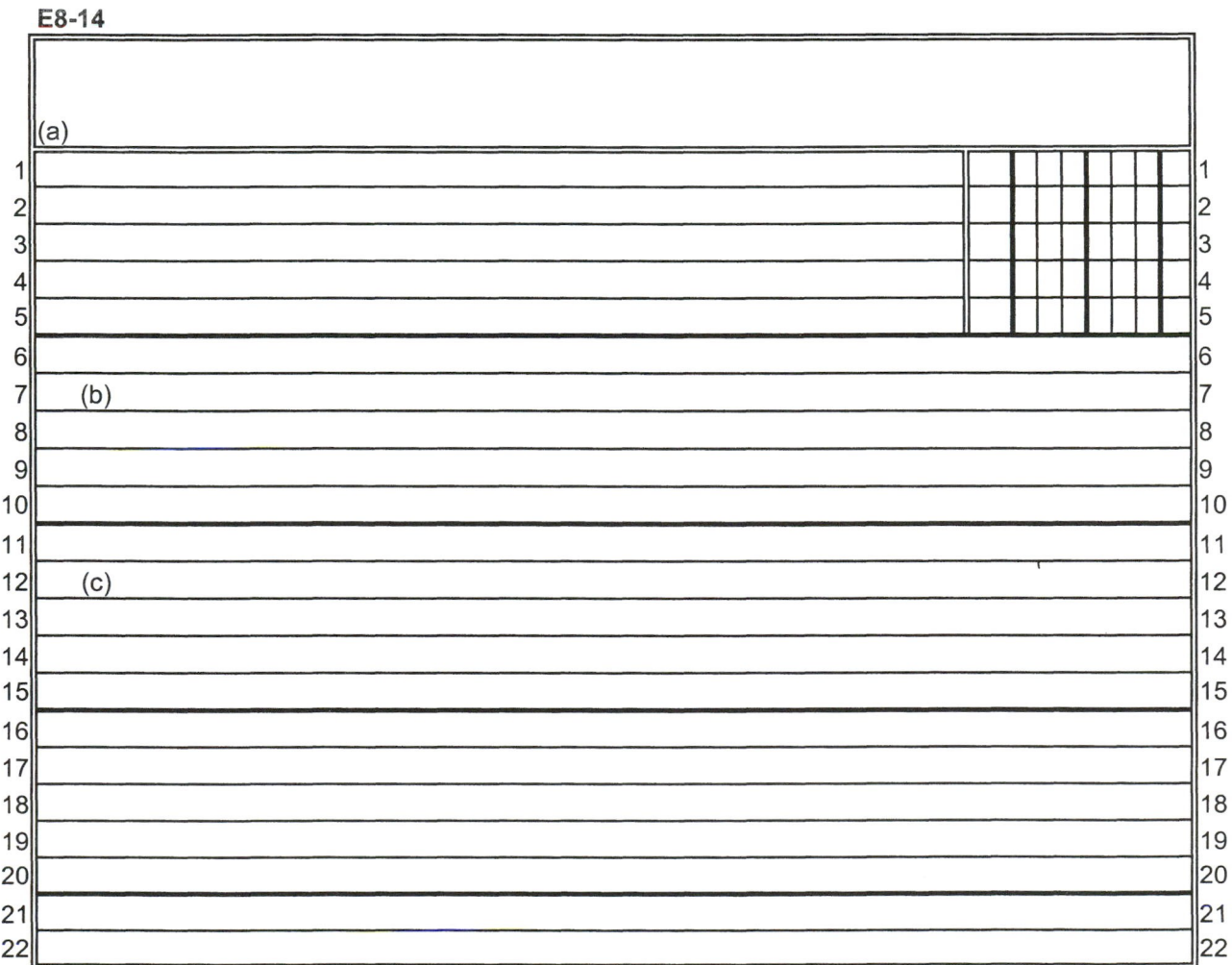

(a)

		Account Titles	Debit	Credit	
1	1.				1
2					2
3					3
4	2.				4
5					5
6					6
7	3.				7
8					8
9					9
10	4.				10
11					11
12					12
13	5.				13
14					14
15					15
16					16
17					17
18					18
19					19
20					20

(b)

Accounts Receivable	
Bal. 960,000	

Allowance for Doubtful Accounts	
	Bal. 70,000

(c)

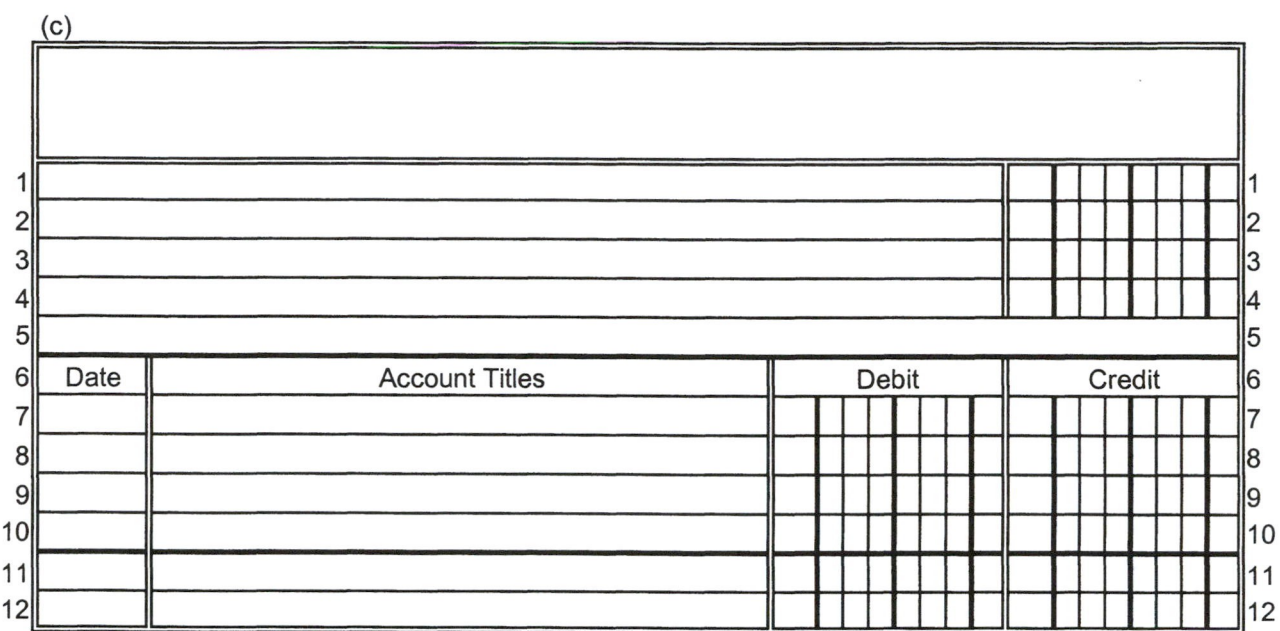

	Date	Account Titles	Debit	Credit	
6					6
7					7
8					8
9					9
10					10
11					11
12					12

(d)

(a), (b), and (c)   General Journal

	Date	Account Titles	Debit	Credit	
1	(a)	2014			1
2	Dec. 31				2
3					3
4					4
5					5
6	(b)	(1) 2015			6
7	Mar. 31				7
8					8
9					9
10					10
11		(2)			11
12	May 31				12
13					13
14					14
15	31				15
16					16
17					17
18					18
19	(c)	2015			19
20	Dec. 31				20
21					21
22					22

(a) & (b)

Bad Debt Expense

	Date	Explanation	Ref.	Debit	Credit	Balance	
1							1
2							2
3							3

Allowance for Doubtful Accounts

	Date	Explanation	Ref.	Debit	Credit	Balance	
1	2014						1
2	Dec. 31	Balance	√			9 0 0 0	2
3							3
4							4
5							5
6							6
7							7

(a)

	Total	Number of Days Outstanding				
		0 - 30	31 - 60	61 - 90	91 - 120	Over 120
1 Accounts receivable	$ 193000	$ 70000	$ 46000	$ 39000	$ 23000	$ 15000
2						
3 % uncollectible		1%	3%	5%	8%	10%
4						
5 Estimated Bad Debts						

	Date	Account Titles	Debit	Credit	
1	(b)				1
2					2
3					3
4	(c)				4
5					5
6					6
7	(d)				7
8					8
9					9
10					10
11					11
12					12
13					13
14					14
15					15

(e)

1		1
2		2
3		3
4		4
5		5

	Date	Account Titles	Debit	Credit	
1	(a)				1
2					2
3					3
4					4
5					5
6	(b) (1)	2014			6
7	Dec. 31				7
8					8
9					9
10	(2)				10
11	Dec. 31				11
12					12
13					13
14					14
15	(c) (1)				15
16	Dec. 31				16
17					17
18					18
19					19
20	(2)				20
21	Dec. 31				21
22					22
23					23
24					24
25					25
26	(d)	2015			26
27					27
28					28
29					29
30					30
31	(e)				31
32					32
33					33
34					34
35					35
36	(f)				36
37					37
38					38
39					39
40					40

(a)

General Journal

	Date	Account Titles	Debit	Credit	
1	Oct. 7				1
2					2
3					3
4	12				4
5					5
6					6
7					7
8	15				8
9					9
10					10
11	15				11
12					12
13					13
14					14
15					15
16	24				16
17					17
18					18
19					19
20					20
21	31				21
22					22
23					23
24					24
25					25
26					26
27					27
28					28
29					29
30					30
31					31
32					32
33					33
34					34
35					35
36					36
37					37
38					38
39					39
40					40

(b)

Notes Receivable

	Date	Explanation	Ref.	Debit	Credit	Balance	
1	Oct 1	Balance	√			31000	1
2							2
3							3
4							4

Accounts Receivable

	Date	Explanation	Ref.	Debit	Credit	Balance	
1							1
2							2
3							3
4							4

Interest Receivable

	Date	Explanation	Ref.	Debit	Credit	Balance	
1	Oct 1	Balance	√			170	1
2							2
3							3
4							4
5							5

(c)

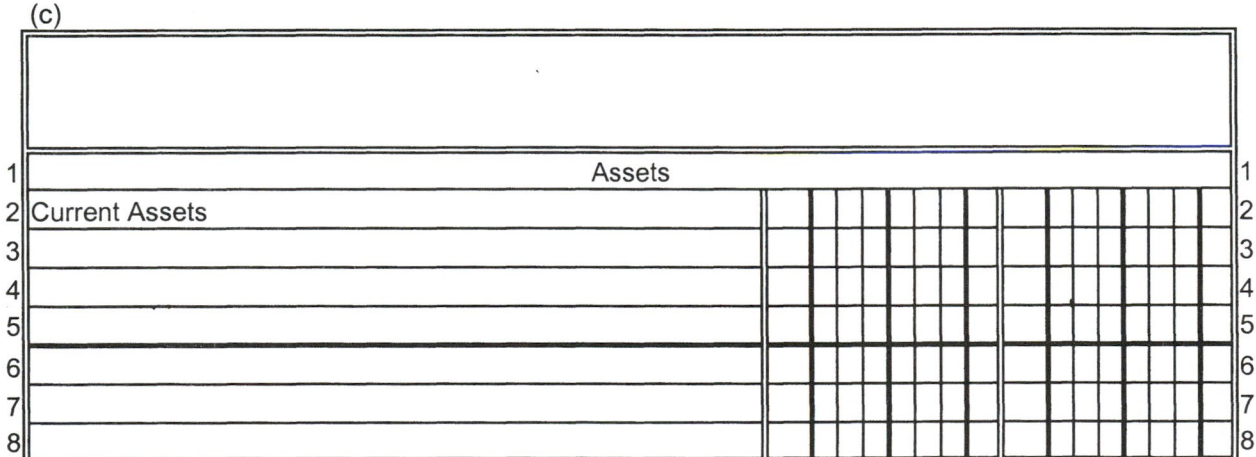

	Assets		
1	Assets		1
2	Current Assets		2
3			3
4			4
5			5
6			6
7			7
8			8

General Journal

	Date	Account Titles	Debit	Credit	
1	Jan. 5				1
2					2
3					3
4	20				4
5					5
6					6
7					7
8	Feb. 18				8
9					9
10					10
11	Apr. 20				11
12					12
13					13
14					14
15	30				15
16					16
17					17
18					18
19	May 25				19
20					20
21					21
22	Aug. 18				22
23					23
24					24
25					25
26	25				26
27					27
28					28
29					29
30	Sept. 1				30
31					31
32					32
33					33
34					34
35					35
36					36
37					37
38					38
39					39
40					40

(a)

		Account Titles	Debit	Credit	
1	1.				1
2					2
3					3
4	2.				4
5					5
6					6
7	3.				7
8					8
9					9
10	4.				10
11					11
12					12
13	5.				13
14					14
15					15
16					16
17					17
18					18
19					19
20					20

(b)

Accounts Receivable

Bal.	220,000	

Allowance for Doubtful Accounts

	Bal.	15,000

(c)

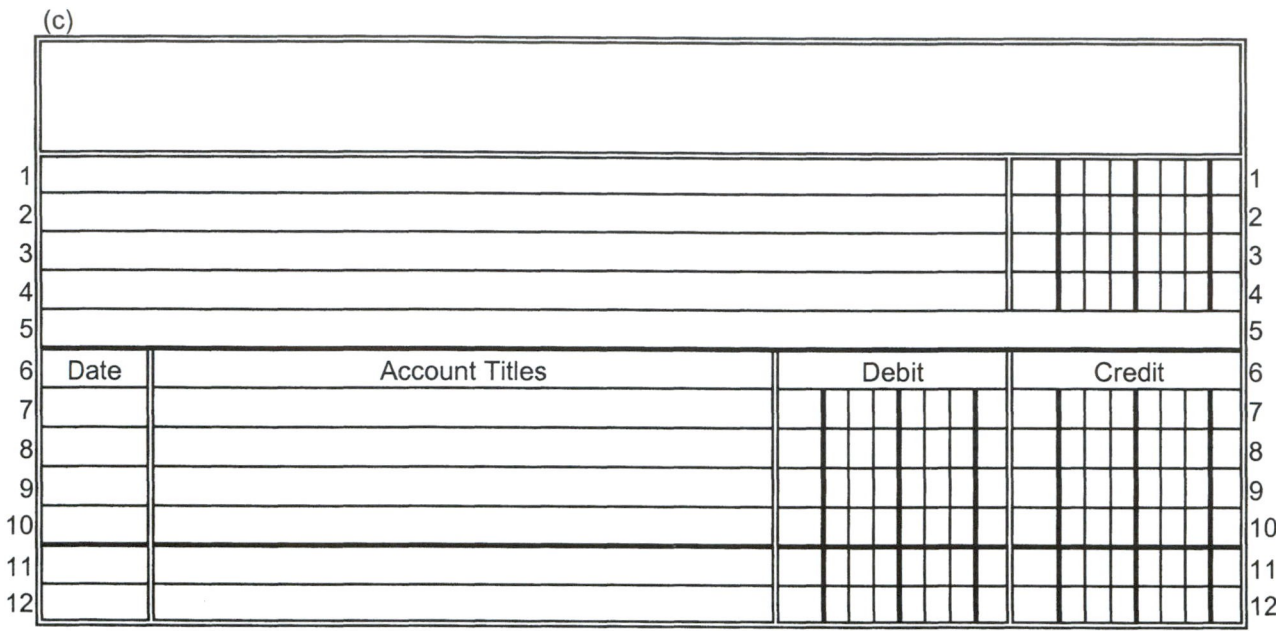

	Date	Account Titles	Debit	Credit	
1					1
2					2
3					3
4					4
5					5
6					6
7					7
8					8
9					9
10					10
11					11
12					12

(d)

Section

Date   Garry Owen Company

(a), (b), and (c)   General Journal

	Date	Account Titles	Debit	Credit	
1	(a)	2014			1
2	Dec. 31				2
3					3
4					4
5					5
6	(b)	(1) 2015			6
7	Mar. 1				7
8					8
9					9
10					10
11		(2)			11
12	May 1				12
13					13
14					14
15	1				15
16					16
17					17
18					18
19	(c)	2015			19
20	Dec. 31				20
21					21
22					22

(a) & (b)

Bad Debt Expense

	Date	Explanation	Ref.	Debit	Credit	Balance	
1							1
2							2
3							3

Allowance for Doubtful Accounts

	Date	Explanation	Ref.	Debit	Credit	Balance	
1	2014						1
2	Dec. 31	Balance	√			1 4 0 0 0	2
3							3
4							4
5							5
6							6
7							7

(a)

	Total	Number of Days Outstanding				
		0 - 30	31 - 60	61 - 90	91 - 120	Over 120
1 Accounts receivable	$ 383000	$ 220000	$ 90000	$ 40000	$ 18000	$ 15000
2						
3 % uncollectible		1%	3%	5%	8%	10%
4						
5 Estimated Bad Debts						

	Date	Account Titles	Debit	Credit	
1	(b)				1
2					2
3					3
4	(c)				4
5					5
6					6
7	(d)				7
8					8
9					9
10					10
11					11
12					12
13					13
14					14
15					15

(e)

1		1
2		2
3		3
4		4
5		5

General Journal

	Date	Account Titles	Debit	Credit	
1	(a) (1)	2014			1
2	Dec. 31				2
3					3
4					4
5					5
6	(2)				6
7	Dec. 31				7
8					8
9					9
10					10
11	(b) (1)				11
12	Dec. 31				12
13					13
14					14
15					15
16	(2)				16
17	Dec. 31				17
18					18
19					19
20	(c)	2015			20
21					21
22					22
23					23
24					24
25	(d)				25
26					26
27					27
28					28
29					29
30					30
31	(e)				31
32	(1)				32
33					33
34					34
35	(2)				35
36					36
37					37

(a)

General Journal

	Date	Account Titles	Debit	Credit	
1	July 5				1
2					2
3					3
4	14				4
5					5
6					6
7					7
8	14				8
9					9
10					10
11	15				11
12					12
13					13
14					14
15					15
16	25				16
17					17
18					18
19					19
20					20
21	31				21
22					22
23					23
24					24
25					25
26					26
27					27
28					28
29					29
30					30
31					31
32					32
33					33
34					34
35					35
36					36
37					37
38					38
39					39
40					40

(b)

Notes Receivable

	Date	Explanation	Ref.	Debit	Credit	Balance	
1	July 1	Balance	√			6 0 0 0 0	1
2							2
3							3
4							4

Accounts Receivable

	Date	Explanation	Ref.	Debit	Credit	Balance	
1							1
2							2
3							3
4							4

Interest Receivable

	Date	Explanation	Ref.	Debit	Credit	Balance	
1	July 1	Balance	√			4 3 5	1
2							2
3							3
4							4
5							5

(c)

	Assets		
1			1
2	Current Assets		2
3			3
4			4
5			5
6			6
7			7
8			8

General Journal

	Date	Account Titles	Debit	Credit	
1	Jan. 5				1
2					2
3					3
4	Feb. 2				4
5					5
6					6
7	12				7
8					8
9					9
10	26				10
11					11
12					12
13	Apr. 5				13
14					14
15					15
16	12				16
17					17
18					18
19					19
20	June 2				20
21					21
22					22
23					23
24	July 5				24
25					25
26					26
27					27
28	15				28
29					29
30					30
31	Oct. 15				31
32					32
33					33
34					34
35					35
36					36
37					37
38					38
39					39
40					40

(a)

	Date	Account Titles	Debit	Credit	
1	Jan. 1				1
2					2
3					3
4					4
5	3				5
6					6
7					7
8	8				8
9					9
10					10
11	11				11
12					12
13					13
14					14
15					15
16					16
17	15				17
18					18
19					19
20					20
21					21
22					22
23					23
24	17				24
25					25
26					26
27	21				27
28					28
29					29
30	24				30
31					31
32					32
33					33
34					34
35					35
36	27				36
37					37
38					38
39	31				39
40					40

(a) (Continued)

	Date	Account Titles	Debit	Credit	
1	Jan. 31				1
2					2
3					3
4	31				4
5					5
6					6
7	31				7
8					8
9					9
10					10

(b)

	Victoria Company Adjusted Trial Balance January 31, 2014	Debit	Credit	
1				1
2				2
3				3
4				4
5				5
6				6
7				7
8				8
9				9
10				10
11				11
12				12
13				13
14				14
15				15
16				16
17				17
18				18
19				19
20				20
21				21
22				22
23				23
24				24
25				25

(b)   Optional T accounts for accounts with multiple transactions

Cash		Supplies	
1/1 Bal. 13,100			

		Accounts Payable	
			1/1 Bal. 8,750

Accounts Receivable		Sales Revenue	
1/1 Bal. 19,780			

Allowance for Doubtful Accounts		Cost of Goods Sold	
	1/1 Bal. 800		

Inventory	
1/1 Bal. 9,400	

(c)

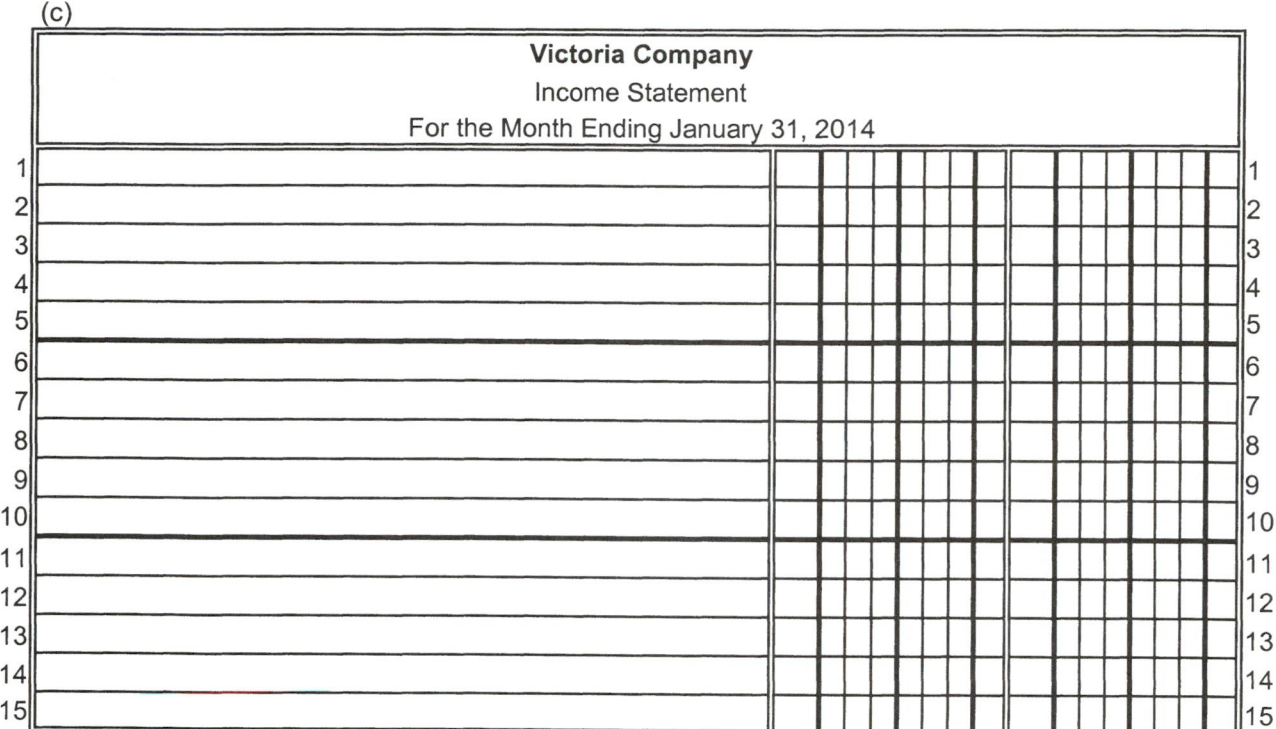

Victoria Company

Income Statement

For the Month Ending January 31, 2014

1					1
2					2
3					3
4					4
5					5
6					6
7					7
8					8
9					9
10					10
11					11
12					12
13					13
14					14
15					15

Victoria Company

Retained Earnings Statement

For the Month Ending January 31, 2014

1		1
2		2
3		3
4		4
5		5
6		6
7		7
8		8
9		9
10		10
11		11
12		12
13		13
14		14
15		15
16		16
17		17
18		18
19		19
20		20

(c)   (Continued)

Victoria Company

Balance Sheet

January 31, 2014

	Assets		
1			
2			
3			
4			
5			
6			
7			
8			
9			
10			
11			
12			
13	Liabilities and Stockholders' Equity		
14			
15			
16			
17			
18			
19			
20			

(a)

CAF Company Accounts Receivable Aging Schedule May 31, 2014				
	Proportion of Total %	Amount in Category	Probability of Non-Collection %	Estimated Uncollectible Amount
Not yet due				
Less than 30 days past due				
30 to 60 days past due				
61 to 120 days past due				
121 to 180 days past due				
Over 180 days past due				
Totals				

(b)

CAF Company Analysis of Allowance for Doubtful Accounts May 31, 2014		
Account Titles	Debit	Credit

(c)

	1. Steps to Improve the Accounts Receivable Situation	2. Risks and Costs Involved	
1			1
2			2
3			3
4			4
5			5
6			6
7			7
8			8
9			9
10			10
11			11
12			12
13			13
14			14
15			15
16			16
17			17
18			18
19			19
20			20
21			21
22			22
23			23
24			24
25			25
26			26
27			27
28			28
29			29
30			30
31			31
32			32
33			33
34			34
35			35
36			36
37			37
38			38
39			39
40			40

(a)	2014	2013	2012
1 Net credit sales			
2			
3			
4			
5			
6			
7			
8			
9			
10			
11			
12			
13			
14			
15			
16 (b) Average accounts receivable			
17			
18			
19			
20			
21			
22			
23			
24			
25			
26			
27			
28			

29 (c)

BE9-5

	Year	Book Value	X	Rate	=	Depreciation
	1					
	2					

BE9-6

Depreciation cost per unit:

		Miles	X	Rate	=	Depreciation
	Year					
	1					
	2					

BE9-7

1			
2			
3			
4			
5			
6			

BE9-8

	Account Titles	Debit	Credit
7			
8	1.		
9			
10			
11	2.		
12			
13			

BE9-9

	Account Titles	Debit	Credit
14			
15	(a)		
16			
17			
18	(b)		
19			
20			
21			

Calculations:

BE9-10

	Account Titles	Debit	Credit	
1				1
2	(a)			2
3				3
4				4
5	(b)			5
6				6
7				7
8				8
9				9
10	Calculations:			10
11				11
12				12
13				13
14				14
15				15
16				16

BE9-11

17	**BE9-11**		17
18	(a)　　Depletion cost per unit =		18
19			19
20			20
21	Depletion expense =		21
22			22
23			23
24			24

	Account Titles	Debit	Credit	
25				25
26				26
27				27
28				28
29	(b)			29
30				30
31				31

	BE9-12 Account Titles	Debit	Credit	
32	**BE9-12**			32
33	(a)			33
34				34
35				35
36	(b)			36
37				37
38				38
39				39
40				40

BE9-13

	Loomis Company		
	Balance Sheet (Partial)		
	December 31, 2014		

1			
2			
3			
4			
5			
6			
7			
8			
9			
10			
11			
12			
13			
14			
15			
16			

*BE9-15

	Account Titles	Debit	Credit

Calculations:

*BE9-16

	Account Titles	Debit	Credit	
1				1
2				2
3				3
4				4
5				5
6				6
7	Calculations:			7
8				8
9				9
10				10
11				11
12				12
13				13
14				14
15				15
16				16
17				17
18				18
19				19
20				20
21				21
22				22
23				23
24				24
25				25
26				26
27				27
28				28
29				29
30				30
31				31
32				32
33				33
34				34
35				35
36				36
37				37
38				38
39				39
40				40

DO IT! 9-1

1				1
2				2
3				3
4				4
5				5
6				6
7				7
8				8
9				9
10				10

DO IT! 9-2

Depreciation expense =

	Account Titles	Debit	Credit	
15				15
16				16
17				17
18				18
19				19

DO IT! 9-4

	Account Titles	Debit	Credit	
21 (a)	Sales of truck for cash at a gain:			21
22				22
23				23
24				24
25				25
26				26
27				27
28				28
29 (b)	Sale of truck for cash at a loss:			29
30				30
31				31
32				32
33				33
34				34
35				35
36				36
37				37
38				38
39				39
40				40

E9-3

1	(a) Cost of land:	
2		
3		
4		
5		
6		
7		
8		
9	(b)	
10		
11		
12		
13		

14 E9-5

15 (a)

16	
17	
18	
19	

(b) Year	Computation		Annual Depreciation Expense	End of Year	
	Units of Activity	Depreciation Cost/Unit		Accumulated Depreciation	Book Value
2014	2 6 0 0 0				
2015	3 2 0 0 0				
2016	2 5 0 0 0				
2017	1 7 0 0 0				

(a)		
1	(1) 2014:	
2		
3	2015:	
4		
5		
6	(2) Calculation of depreciation cost per unit:	
7		
8		
9	2014:	
10		
11	2015:	
12		
13		
14	(3) 2014:	
15		
16	2015:	
17		
18		

(b)	Account Tiles	Debit	Credit
(1)			
(2)	Balance sheet presentation:		

E9-8

		Building	Warehouse
1	(a)		
2			
3			
4			
5			
6			
7			
8			
9			
10	(b)		

	Date	Account Titles	Debit	Credit
11	Date	Account Titles	Debit	Credit
12	Dec. 31			
13				
14				
15				

E9-9

	Date	Account Titles	Debit	Credit
17	Date	Account Titles	Debit	Credit
18	Jan. 1			
19				
20				
21	June 30			
22				
23				
24	30			
25				
26				
27				
28				
29	Dec. 31			
30				
31				
32	31			
33				
34				
35				
36				
37				
38				
39				
40				

		Account Titles	Debit	Credit	
1	(a)				1
2					2
3					3
4					4
5					5
6					6
7	(b)				7
8					8
9					9
10					10
11					11
12					12
13					13
14					14
15					15
16	(c)				16
17					17
18					18
19					19
20					20
21					21
22	(d)				22
23					23
24					24
25					25
26					26
27					27
28					28
29					29
30					30
31					31
32					32
33					33
34					34
35					35
36					36
37					37
38					38
39					39
40					40

E9-11

	Date	Account Titles	Debit	Credit	
1	(a)				1
2	Dec. 31				2
3					3
4					4
5	Calculations				5
6					6
7					7
8					8
9					9
10	(b)				10
11					11
12					12

E9-12

	Date	Account Titles	Debit	Credit	
14	Date	Account Titles	Debit	Credit	14
15	Dec. 31				15
16					16
17					17

E9-13

	Date	Account Titles	Debit	Credit	
19	Date	Account Titles	Debit	Credit	19
20	1/2/14				20
21					21
22					22
23	4/1/14				23
24					24
25					25
26	7/1/14				26
27					27
28					28
29	9/1/14				29
30					30
31					31
32	12/31/14				32
33					33
34					34
35					35
36					36
37	Ending balances, 12/31/14:				37
38	Patent				38
39	Goodwill				39
40	Franchise				40
41	R&D expense				41

_____

		Account Titles	Debit	Credit	
1	(a)				1
2					2
3					3
4					4
5					5
6					6
7	Calculations:				7
8					8
9					9
10					10
11					11
12					12
13					13
14					14
15					15
16					16
17					17
18	(b)	Account Titles	Debit	Credit	18
19					19
20					20
21					21
22					22
23					23
24	Calculations:				24
25					25
26					26
27					27
28					28
29					29
30					30
31					31
32					32
33					33
34					34
35					35
36					36
37					37
38					38
39					39
40					40

	Date	Account Titles	Debit	Credit	
1	(a)				1
2					2
3					3
4					4
5					5
6					6
7	Calculations:				7
8					8
9					9
10					10
11					11
12					12
13					13
14	(b)	Account Titles	Debit	Credit	14
15					15
16					16
17					17
18					18
19					19
20	Calculations:				20
21					21
22					22
23					23
24					24
25					25
26					26
27					27
28					28
29					29
30					30
31					31
32					32
33					33
34					34
35					35
36					36
37					37
38					38
39					39
40					40

	Item	Land	Building	Other Accounts	
				Amount	Account Titles
1						1
2	1.					2
3						3
4	2.					4
5						5
6	3.					6
7						7
8	4.					8
9						9
10	5.					10
11						11
12	6.					12
13						13
14	7.					14
15						15
16	8.					16
17						17
18	9.					18
19						19
20	10.					20
21						21
22						22
23						23
24						24
25						25

	Year	Computation	Accumulated Depreciation, 12/31
(a)		BUS 1	
	2012		
	2013		
	2014		
		BUS 2	
	2012		
	2013		
	2014		
		BUS 3	
	2013		
	2014		

	Year	Depreciation Computation	Expense
(b)		BUS 2	
	(1) 2012		
	(2) 2013		

Total cost of machinery:

(a) (1)

	Account Titles	Debit	Credit

(2) Annual depreciation:

	Account Titles	Debit	Credit

(b) (1)

(2)

	Year	Book Value at Beginning of Year	DDB Rate	Annual Depreciation Expense	Accumulated Depreciation
	2011				
	2012				
	2013				
	2014				

(b) (Continued) and (c)

(b) (3) Depreciation cost per unit:

	Year	Computation	Depreciation Expense
	2014		
	2015		
	2016		
	2017		

(c)

	Year		Depreciation Expense	Accumulated Depreciation	
1	2012				1
2	2013				2
3	2014				3
4	2015				4
5	2016				5
6	2017				6
7	2018				7
8					8
9					9
10					10

11		11
12	Supporting calculations:	12
13		13
14		14
15		15
16		16
17		17
18		18
19		19
20		20
21		21
22		22
23		23
24		24
25		25
26		26
27		27
28		28
29		29
30		30
31		31
32		32
33		33
34		34
35		35
36		36
37		37
38		38
39		39
40		40

(a)   General Journal

	Date	Account Titles	Debit	Credit	
1	Apr. 1				1
2					2
3					3
4	May 1				4
5					5
6					6
7	1				7
8					8
9					9
10					10
11					11
12	Calculations:				12
13					13
14					14
15					15
16					16
17					17
18					18
19	June 1				19
20					20
21					21
22					22
23	July 1				23
24					24
25					25
26	Dec. 31				26
27					27
28					28
29	31				29
30					30
31					31
32	Calculations:				32
33					33
34					34
35					35
36					36
37					37
38					38
39					39
40					40

(b)   General Journal

	Date	Account Titles	Debit	Credit	
1	Dec. 31				1
2					2
3					3
4	31				4
5					5
6					6
7					7
8	Calculations:				8
9					9
10					10
11					11
12					12
13					13
14					14
15					15

(c)

Walton Company

Partial Balance Sheet

December 31, 2014

1			1
2			2
3			3
4			4
5			5
6			6
7			7
8			8
9			9
10			10
11			11
12			12
13			13
14			14
15			15
16			16
17			17
18			18
19			19
20			20

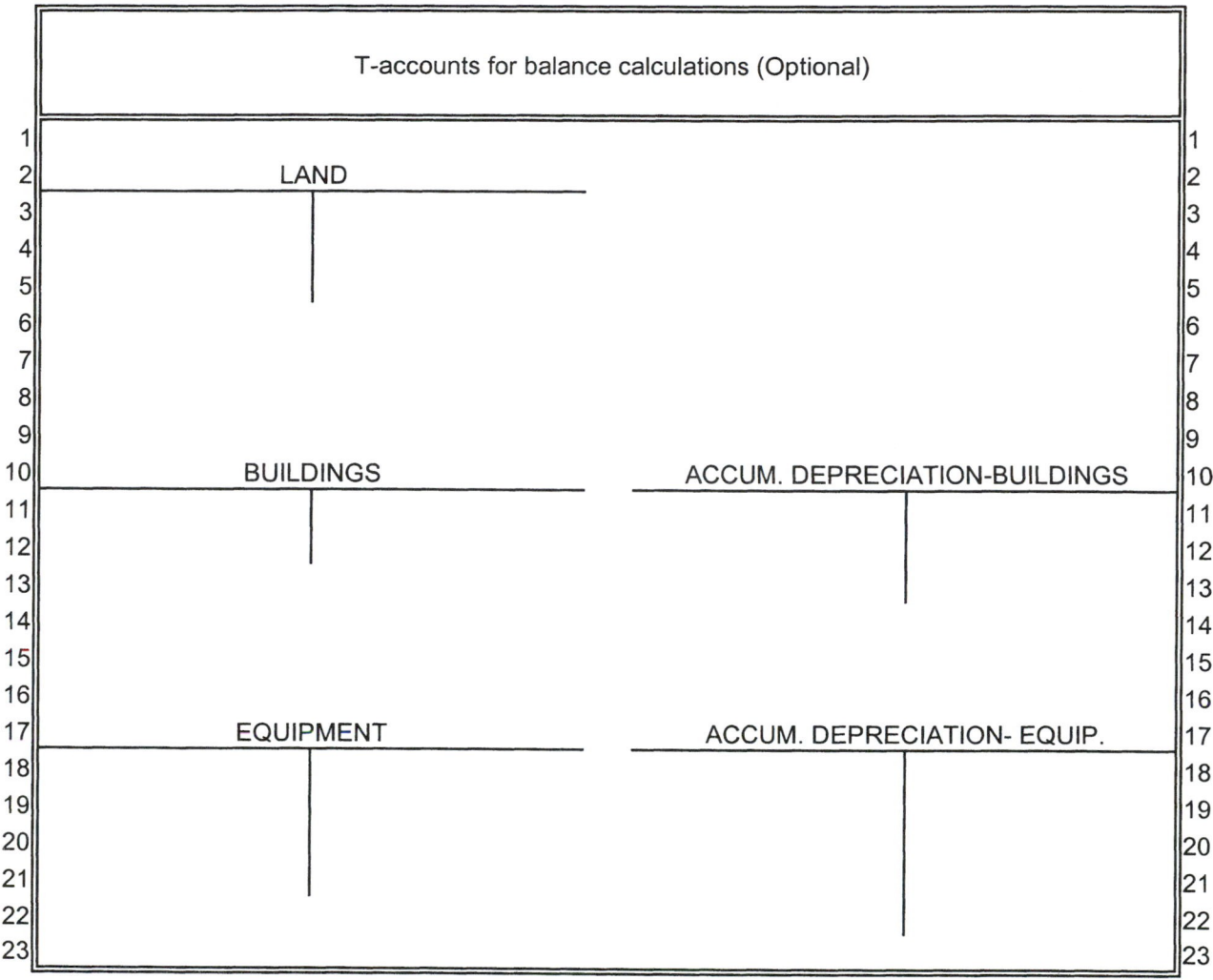

T-accounts for balance calculations (Optional)

LAND

BUILDINGS   ACCUM. DEPRECIATION-BUILDINGS

EQUIPMENT   ACCUM. DEPRECIATION- EQUIP.

	Account Titles	Debit	Credit	
1	(a)			1
2				2
3				3
4				4
5				5
6				6
7				7
8	(b)			8
9				9
10				10
11				11
12				12
13				13
14				14
15				15
16	(c)			16
17				17
18				18
19				19
20				20
21				21
22				22
23				23
24				24
25				25
26				26
27				27
28				28
29				29
30				30
31				31
32				32
33				33
34				34
35				35
36				36
37				37
38				38
39				39
40				40

General Journal

	Date	Account Titles	Debit	Credit	
1	(a)				1
2	Jan. 2				2
3					3
4					4
5	Jan. -				5
6	June				6
7					7
8					8
9	Sept. 1				9
10					10
11					11
12	Oct. 1				12
13					13
14					14
15					15
16	(b)				16
17	Dec. 31				17
18					18
19	31				19
20					20
21					21
22					22
23	(c)	Intangible Assets:			23
24					24
25					25
26					26
27					27
28					28
29					29
30					30
31					31
32					32
33					33
34					34
35					35
36					36
37					37
38					38
39					39
40					40

General Journal

		Account Titles	Debit	Credit	
1	1.				1
2					2
3					3
4					4
5					5
6					6
7					7
8					8
9					9
10	2.				10
11					11
12					12
13					13
14					14
15					15
16					16
17					17
18					18
19					19
20					20
21					21
22					22
23					23
24					24
25					25
26					26
27					27
28					28
29					29
30					30

	Item	Land	Building	Other Accounts	
				Amount	Account Titles
1						1
2	1.					2
3						3
4	2.					4
5						5
6	3.					6
7						7
8	4.					8
9						9
10	5.					10
11						11
12	6.					12
13						13
14	7.					14
15						15
16	8.					16
17						17
18	9.					18
19						19
20	10.					20
21						21
22						22
23						23
24						24
25						25

		Year	Computation	Accumulated Depreciation, 12/31	
1	(a)		MACHINE 1		1
2					2
3		2011			3
4					4
5		2012			5
6					6
7		2013			7
8					8
9		2014			9
10					10
11					11
12			MACHINE 2		12
13					13
14		2012			14
15					15
16		2013			16
17					17
18		2014			18
19					19
20					20
21			MACHINE 3		21
22					22
23		2014			23
24					24
25					25
26					26
27					27
28					28
29					29
30	(b)	Year	Depreciation Computation	Expense	30
31			MACHINE 2		31
32		(1) 2012			32
33					33
34		(2) 2013			34
35					35
36					36
37					37
38					38
39					39
40					40

Total cost of machinery:

(a) (1)

	Account Titles	Debit	Credit

(2) Annual depreciation:

	Account Titles	Debit	Credit

(b) (1)

(2)

Year	Book Value at Beginning of Year	DDB Rate	Annual Depreciation Expense	Accumulated Depreciation
2014				
2015				
2016				
2017				
2018				

(b) (Continued) and (c)

	Year	Computation	Depreciation Expense
(b) (3) Depreciation cost per unit:			
	2014		
	2015		
	2016		
	2017		
	2018		
(c)			

	Year		Depreciation Expense	Accumulated Depreciation	
1	2012				1
2	2013				2
3	2014				3
4	2015				4
5	2016				5
6	2017				6
7	2018				7
8					8
9					9
10					10

11		11
12	Supporting calculations:	12
13		13
14		14
15		15
16		16
17		17
18		18
19		19
20		20
21		21
22		22
23		23
24		24
25		25
26		26
27		27
28		28
29		29
30		30
31		31
32		32
33		33
34		34
35		35
36		36
37		37
38		38
39		39
40		40

(a)

General Journal

	Date	Account Titles	Debit	Credit	
1	Apr. 1				1
2					2
3					3
4	May 1				4
5					5
6					6
7	1				7
8					8
9					9
10					10
11					11
12	Calculations:				12
13					13
14					14
15					15
16					16
17					17
18					18
19	June 1				19
20					20
21					21
22					22
23	July 1				23
24					24
25					25
26	Dec. 31				26
27					27
28					28
29	31				29
30					30
31					31
32	Calculations:				32
33					33
34					34
35					35
36					36
37					37
38					38
39					39
40					40

(b)   General Journal

	Date	Account Titles	Debit	Credit	
1	Dec. 31				1
2					2
3					3
4	31				4
5					5
6					6
7					7
8	Calculations:				8
9					9
10					10
11					11
12					12
13					13
14					14
15					15

(c)

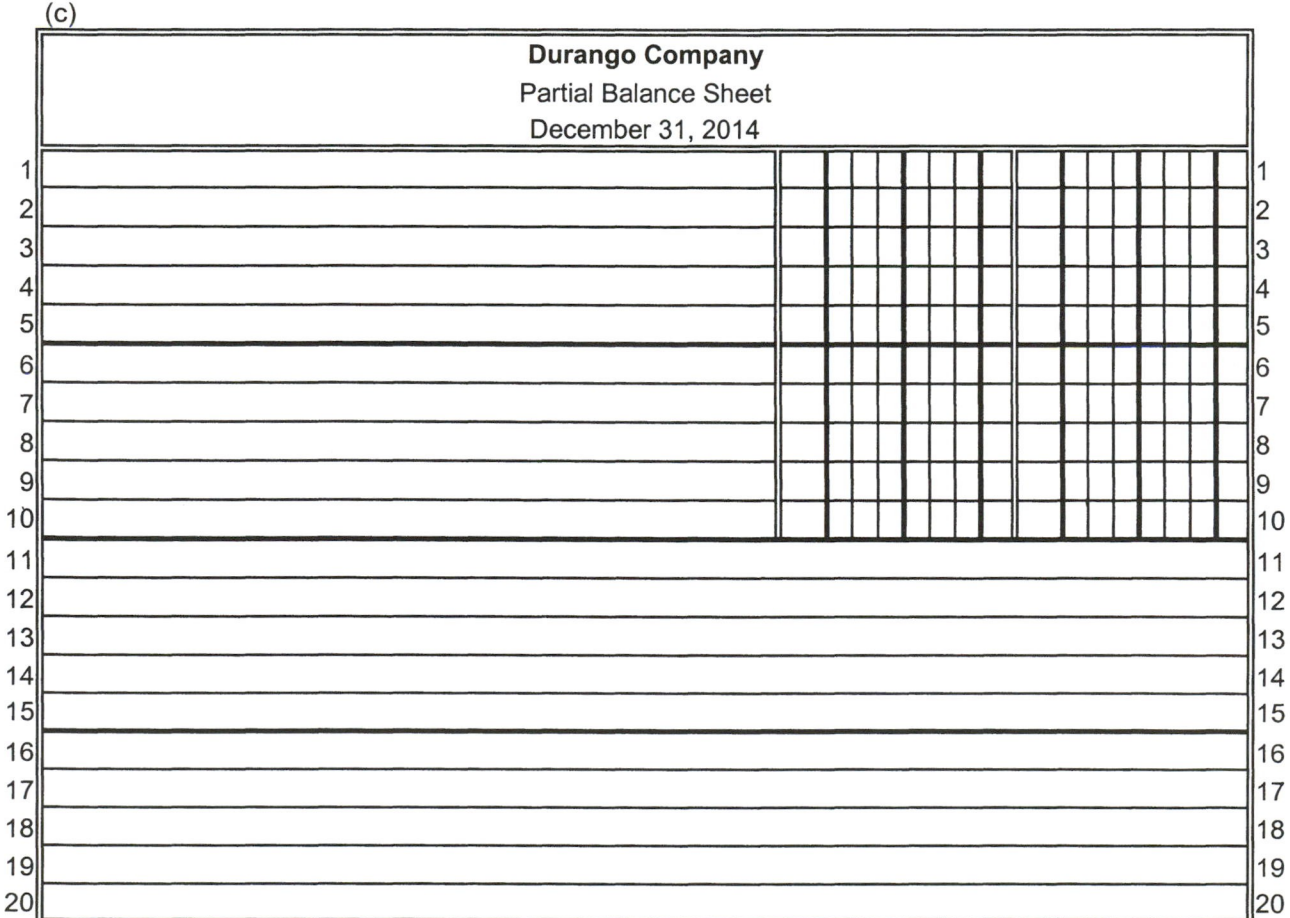

Durango Company
Partial Balance Sheet
December 31, 2014

1				1
2				2
3				3
4				4
5				5
6				6
7				7
8				8
9				9
10				10
11				11
12				12
13				13
14				14
15				15
16				16
17				17
18				18
19				19
20				20

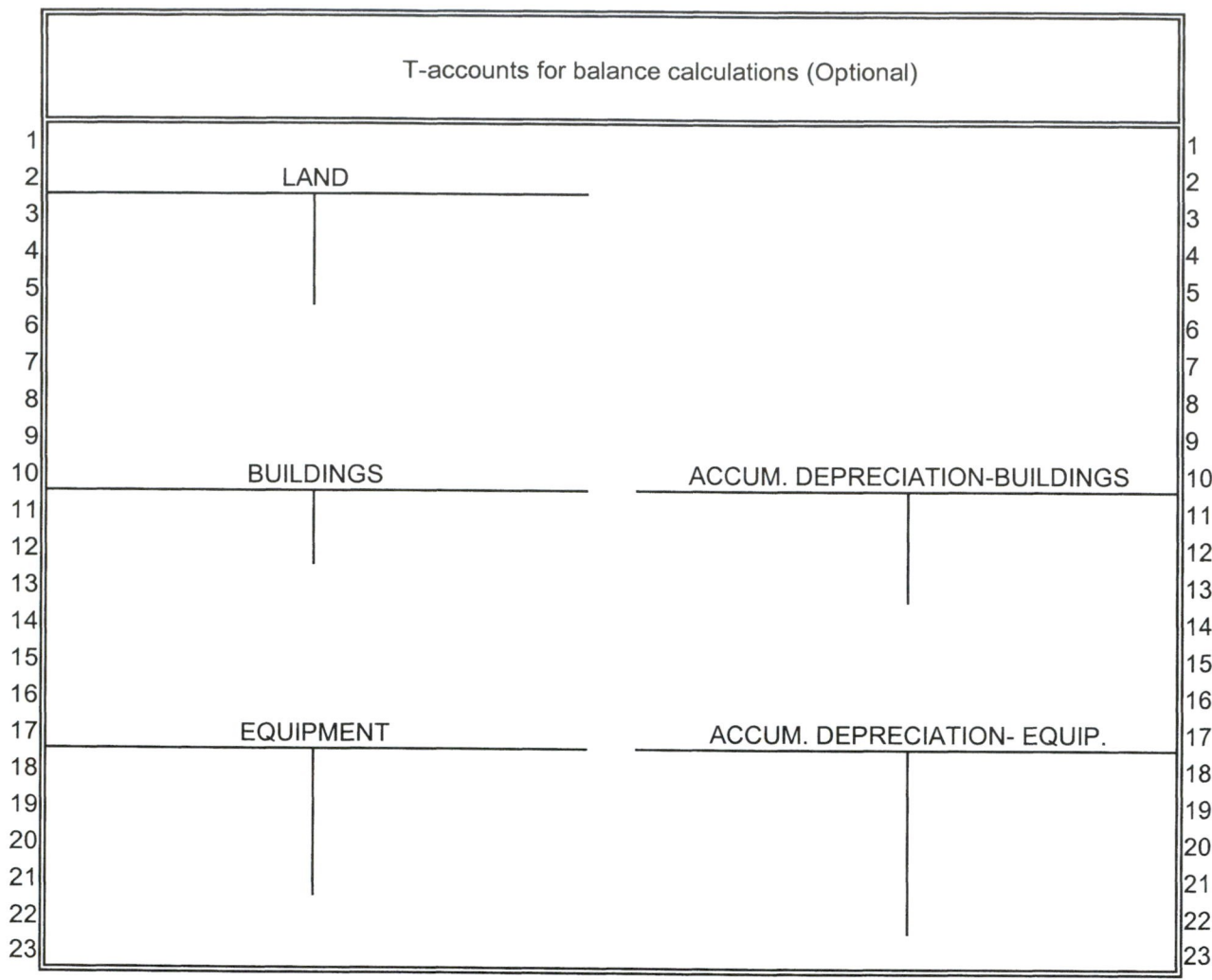

T-accounts for balance calculations (Optional)

LAND

BUILDINGS   ACCUM. DEPRECIATION-BUILDINGS

EQUIPMENT   ACCUM. DEPRECIATION- EQUIP.

	Account Titles	Debit	Credit	
1	(a)			1
2				2
3				3
4				4
5				5
6				6
7				7
8	(b)			8
9				9
10				10
11				11
12				12
13				13
14				14
15				15
16	(c)			16
17				17
18				18
19				19
20				20
21				21
22				22
23				23
24				24
25				25
26				26
27				27
28				28
29				29
30				30
31				31
32				32
33				33
34				34
35				35
36				36
37				37
38				38
39				39
40				40

General Journal

	Date	Account Titles	Debit	Credit	
1	(a)				1
2	Jan. 2				2
3					3
4					4
5	Jan -				5
6	June				6
7					7
8					8
9	Sept. 1				9
10					10
11					11
12					12
13	Oct. 1				13
14					14
15					15
16	(b)				16
17	Dec. 31				17
18					18
19					19
20	31				20
21					21
22					22
23	(c)	Intangible Assets:			23
24					24
25					25
26					26
27					27
28					28
29					29
30					30
31	(d)				31
32					32
33					33
34					34
35					35
36					36
37					37
38					38
39					39
40					40

General Journal

	Account Titles	Debit	Credit	
1	1.			1
2				2
3				3
4				4
5				5
6				6
7				7
8				8
9				9
10	2.			10
11				11
12				12
13				13
14				14
15				15
16				16
17				17
18				18
19				19
20				20
21				21
22				22
23				23
24				24
25				25
26				26
27				27
28				28
29				29
30				30

(a)

		Account Titles	Debit	Credit	
1	1.				1
2					2
3					3
4	2.				4
5					5
6					6
7					7
8					8
9					9
10					10
11					11
12	3.				12
13					13
14					14
15					15
16					16
17					17
18	4.				18
19					19
20					20
21	5.				21
22					22
23					23
24	6.				24
25					25
26					26
27	7.				27
28					28
29					29
30	8.				30
31					31
32					32
33	9.				33
34					34
35					35
36	10.				36
37					37
38					38
39					39
40					40

(a) (Continued)

		Account Titles	Debit	Credit	
1	11.				1
2					2
3					3
4	12.				4
5					5
6					6
7	13.				7
8					8
9					9
10	14.				10
11					11
12					12
13					13
14					14
15					15
16					16
17					17
18					18
19					19
20					20
21					21
22					22
23					23
24					24
25					25
26					26
27					27
28					28
29					29
30					30
31					31
32					32
33					33
34					34
35					35
36					36
37					37
38					38
39					39
40					40

(b)

Raymond Company Trial Balance December 31, 2014	Debits	Credits
1 Cash			1
2 Accounts Receivable			2
3 Notes Receivable			3
4 Interest Receivable			4
5 Inventory			5
6 Prepaid Insurance			6
7 Land			7
8 Buildings			8
9 Equipment			9
10 Patents			10
11 Allowance for Doubtful Accounts			11
12 Accumulated Depreciation - Buildings			12
13 Accumulated Depreciation - Equipment			13
14 Accounts Payable			14
15 Income Taxes Payable			15
16 Salaries and Wages Payable			16
17 Unearned Rent Revenue			17
18 Notes Payable (due in 2015)			18
19 Interest Payable			19
20 Notes Payable (after 2015)			20
21 Common Stock			21
22 Retained Earnings			22
23 Dividends			23
24 Sales Revenue			24
25 Interest Revenue			25
26 Rent Revenue			26
27 Gain on Disposal of Plant Assets			27
28 Bad Debts Expense			28
29 Cost of Goods Sold			29
30 Depreciation Expense			30
31 Income Tax Expense			31
32 Insurance Expense			32
33 Interest Expense			33
34 Other Operating Expenses			34
35 Amortization Expense			35
36 Salaries and Wages Expense			36
37 Totals			37
38			38
39			39

(c)

Raymond Company					
Income Statement					
For the Year Ended December 31, 2014					
1						1
2						2
3						3
4						4
5						5
6						6
7						7
8						8
9						9
10						10
11						11
12						12
13						13
14						14
15						15
16						16
17						17
18						18
19						19
20						20
21						21
22						22
23						23
24						24
25						25

Raymond Company		
Retained Earnings Statement		
For the Year Ended December 31, 2014		
1			1
2			2
3			3
4			4
5			5
6			6
7			7
8			8
9			9
10			10

Name _____

Section _____

Date _____ Raymond Company

(d)

Raymond Company
Balance Sheet
December 31, 2014

Assets

Liabilities and Stockholders' Equity

(a)	Givens Company- Straight-line method				

Runge Company- Double-declining-balance method

Year	Asset	Computation	Annual Depreciation	Accumulated Depreciation
2012	Building			
	Equipment			
2013	Building			
	Equipment			
2014	Building			
	Equipment			

(b) Year	Givens Company Net Income	Runge Co. Net Inc. as Adjusted	Computations for Runge Company
2012	84000		
2013	88400		
2014	90000		
Total	262400		

(c)	

1	(a)	1
2		2
3		3
4		4
5		5
6		6
7		7
8	(b)	8
9		9
10		10
11		11
12		12
13		13
14		14
15		15
16		16
17		17
18		18
19		19
20		20
21	(c)	21
22		Old	22
23		Estimates	23
24			24
25			25
26			26
27			27
28			28
29			29
30		Revised	30
31		Estimates	31
32			32
33			33
34			34
35			35
36			36
37			37
38			38
39			39
40			40

IFRS9-5

		Account Titles	Debit	Credit	
1	(a)				1
2					2
3					3
4					4
5					5
6	(b)				6
7					7
8					8
9					9
10					10
11					11

IFRS9-6

12					12
13					13
14					14
15					15
16					16
17					17
18					18
19					19
20					20
21					21
22					22
23					23
24					24
25					25
26					26
27					27
28					28
29					29
30					30
31					31
32					32
33					33
34					34
35					35
36					36
37					37
38					38
39					39
40					40

IFRS9-7

		Account Titles	Debit	Credit	
1	(a)				1
2					2
3					3
4	(b)				4
5					5
6					6
7	(c)				7
8					8
9					9
10					10
11					11

BE10-2

	Date	Account Titles	Debit	Credit	
1	July 1				1
2					2
3					3
4	Dec 31				4
5					5
6					6
7					7
8					8

BE11-3

9		9
10	Sales tax payable:	10
11		11
12		12
13		13
14		14
15		15
16		16

	Date	Account Titles	Debit	Credit	
17	Date	Account Titles	Debit	Credit	17
18	Mar. 16				18
19					19
20					20
21					21
22					22
23					23
24					24
25					25
26					26
27					27
28					28
29					29
30					30
31					31
32					32
33					33
34					34
35					35
36					36
37					37
38					38
39					39
40					40

BE10-4

	Account Titles	Debit	Credit	
1				1
2				2
3				3
5				5
6				6
7				7
8				8

BE10-5

	Gross earnings:			
9	**BE10-5**			9
10	Gross earnings:			10
11				11
12				12
13				13
14				14
15				15
16				16
17				17
18				18

BE10-6

	Date	Account Titles	Debit	Credit	
19	**BE10-6**				19
20	Date	Account Titles	Debit	Credit	20
21	Jan. 15				21
22					22
23					23
24					24
25					25
26	Jan. 15				26
27					27
28					28

BE10-7

		Issue Stock	Issue Bonds	
29	**BE10-7**	Issue	Issue	29
30		Stock	Bonds	30
31	Income before interest and taxes			31
32	Interest expense from bonds			32
33	Income before income taxes			33
34	Income tax expense			34
35	Net income			35
36				36
37	Outstanding shares			37
38	Earnings per share			38
39				39
40				40
41				41
42				42

BE10-8

	Date	Account Titles	Debit	Credit	
1	(a)				1
2	Jan. 1				2
3					3
4					4
5	(b)				5
6	July 1				6
7					7
8					8
9	(c)				9
10	Dec. 31				10
11					11
12					12
13	**BE10-9**				13
14	(a)				14
15	Jan. 1				15
16					16
17					17
18					18
19	(b)				19
20	Jan. 1				20
21					21
22					22
23					23
24	**BE10-10**				24
25	1.				25
26	Jan. 1				26
27					27
28					28
29	2.				29
30	July 1				30
31					31
32					32
33					33
34	3.				34
35	Sept. 1				35
36					36
37					37
38					38
39					39
40					40

BE10-11

	Date	Account Titles	Debit	Credit	
1	July 1				1
2					2
3					3
4					4
5					5
6					6
7	**BE10-12** See next page				7
8					8
9					9
10	**BE10-13**				10
11	Long-term liabilities				11
12					12
13					13
14					14
15					15
16					16
17					17
18	*BE10-14				18
19	(a)				19
20					20
21					21
22	(b)				22
23					23
24					24
25	*BE10-15				25

		Account Titles	Debit	Credit	
26					26
27	(a)				27
28					28
29					29
30					30
31	(b)				31
32					32
33					33
34					34
35					35
36	(c)				36
37					37
38					38
39					39
40					40

BE10-12

Semiannual Interest Period	(A) Cash Payment	(B) Interest Expense (D) x 5%	(C) Reduction of Principal (A) - (B)	(D) Principal Balance (D) - (C)	
Issue Date					1
1					2
					3
					4
					5
					6
					7
					8
					9

Date	Account Titles	Debit	Credit	
Dec. 31				10
				11
				12
				13
				14
June 30				15
				16
				17
				18
				19
				20
				21
				22
				23

*BE10-16

	Date	Account Titles	Debit	Credit	
1	(a)				1
2	Jan. 1				2
3					3
4					4
5					5
6					6
7	(b)				7
8	July 1				8
9					9
10					10
11					11
12					12
13	***BE10-17**				13
14	(a)				14
15	Jan. 1				15
16					16
17					17
18					18
19					19
20	(b)				20
21	July 1				21
22					22
23					23
24					24
25					25
26					26
27					27
28					28
29					29
30					30
31					31
32					32
33					33
34					34
35					35
36					36
37					37
38					38
39					39
40					40

DO IT! 10-3

(a)	Account Titles	Debit	Credit	
1				1
2				2
3				3
4				4
5	(b) Long-term liabilities:			5
6				6
7				7
8				8
9				9
10				10
11				11

DO IT! 10-4

	Account Titles	Debit	Credit	
13				13
14				14
15				15
16				16
17				17
18				18
19				19

DO IT! 10-5

20				20
21				21
22				22
23				23
24				24
25				25
26				26
27				27
28				28
29				29
30				30
31				31
32				32
33				33
34				34
35				35
36				36
37				37
38				38
39				39
40				40

Account Titles	Debit	Credit
1	July 1, 2014		
2			
3			
4			
5	November 1, 2014		
6			
7			
8			
9	December 31, 2014		
10			
11			
12			
13			
14			
15			
16	February 1, 2015		
17			
18			
19			
20			
21			
22	April 1, 2015		
23			
24			
25			
26			
27			
28			
29			
30			
31			
32			
33			
34			
35			
36			
37			
38			
39			
40			

E10-2

	Date	Account Titles	Debit	Credit	
1	(a)				1
2	June 1				2
3					3
4					4
5	(b)				5
6	June 30				6
7					7
8					8
9	(c)				9
10	Dec. 1				10
11					11
12					12
13					13
14	(d)				14
15					15
16	**E10-3**	**Jackson Company**			16
17	Apr. 10				17
18					18
19					19
20					20
21		**Pearson Company**			21
22	15				22
23					23
24					24
25					25
26					26
27	**E10-4**				27
28	(a) 2014				28
29	Nov. 30				29
30					30
31					31
32	(b)				32
33	Dec. 31				33
34					34
35					35
36	(c) 2015				36
37	Mar. 31				37
38					38
39					39
40					40

E10-5

			Debit	Credit	
1	(a)				1
2					2
3					3
4					4
5					5
6					6
7	(b)	Account Titles	Debit	Credit	7
8					8
9					9
10					10
11					11
12					12
13	(c)				13
14					14
15					15
16	**E10-6**	Account Titles	Debit	Credit	16
17					17
18					18
19					19
20					20
21					21
22	**E10-7**		2010	2009	22
23	(a)				23
24					24
25					25
26					26
27					27
28					28
29					29
30					30
31					31
32					32
33	(b)				33
34					34
35					35
36					36
37					37
38					38
39					39
40					40

E10-9

		Plan One Issue Stock		Plan Two Issue Bonds	
1	Income before interest and taxes				
2	Interest				
3	Income before taxes				
4	Income tax expense				
5	Net income				
6	Outstanding shares				
7	Earnings per share				
8					

E10-10

	Date	Account Titles	Debit	Credit
11	(a)			
12	Jan. 1			
13				
14				
15	(b)			
16	July 1			
17				
18				
19	(c)			
20	Dec.31			
21				
22				

E10-11

24	(a)			
25	Jan. 1			
26				
27				
28	(b)			
29	July 1			
30				
31				
32				
33	(c)			
34	Dec. 31			
35				
36				
37				
38				
39				
40				

E10-12

	Account Titles	Debit	Credit	
1	(a) (1)			1
2				2
3				3
4				4
5				5
6	(2)			6
7				7
8				8
9				9
10				10
11				11
12				12

	Account Titles	Debit	Credit	
13	(b) (1)			13
14				14
15				15
16				16
17				17
18	(2)			18
19				19
20				20
21				21
22				22
23				23

E10-13

	Date	Account Titles	Debit	Credit	
24					24
25	Date	Account Titles	Debit	Credit	25
26	(a)				26
27	Jan. 1				27
28					28
29					29
30	(b)				30
31	Jan. 1				31
32					32
33					33
34					34
35	(c)				35
36	July 1				36
37					37
38					38
39					39
40					40

E10-14

	Date	Account Titles	Debit	Credit	
1	1.				1
2	June 30				2
3					3
4					4
5					5
6					6
7	2.				7
8	June 30				8
9					9
10					10
11					11
12					12
13	3.				13
14	Dec. 31				14
15					15
16					16
17					17
18					18
19	**E10-15**	2014 Issuance of Note			19
20	Dec. 31				20
21					21
22					22
23		2015 First Installment Payment			23
24	June 30				24
25					25
26					26
27					27
28		Second Installment Payment			28
29	Dec. 31				29
30					30
31					31
32					32
33	**E10-16**				33
34	Long-term libilities				34
35					35
36					36
37					37
38					38
39					39
40					40

		1
1		1
2		2
3		3
4		4
5		5
6		6
7		7
8		8
9		9
10		10
11		11
12		12
13		13
14		14
15		15
16		16
17		17
18		18
19		19
20		20
21		21
22		22
23		23
24		24
25		25
26		26
27		27
28		28
29		29
30		30
31		31
32		32
33		33
34		34
35		35
36		36
37		37
38		38
39		39
40		40

Semiannual Interest Periods	(A) Interest to Be Paid	(B) Interest Expense	(C) Discount Amortization	(D) Unamortized Discount	(E) Bond Carrying Value
Issue Date					
1					
2					

	Date	Account Titles	Debit	Credit
1				
2				
3				
4				
5				
6				
7	(a)			
8	Jan. 1			
9				
10				
11				
12				
13	(b)			
14	July 1			
15				
16				
17				
18	(c)			
19	Dec. 31			
20				
21				
22				
23				

Semiannual Interest Periods	(A) Interest to Be Paid	(B) Interest Expense	(C) Premium Amortization	(D) Unamortized Premium	(E) Bond Carrying Value
Issue Date					
1					
2					

	Date	Account Titles	Debit	Credit
7				
8	(a)			
9	Jan. 1			
10				
11				
12				
13	(b)			
14	July 1			
15				
16				
17				
18	(c)			
19	Dec. 31			
20				
21				
22				
23				

*E10-20

	Date	Account Titles	Debit	Credit	
1	(a)				1
2	Jan. 1				2
3					3
4					4
5					5
6	(b)				6
7	July 1				7
8					8
9					9
10					10
11	(c)				11
12	Dec. 31				12
13					13
14					14
15					15
16	(d)	2034			16
17	Jan. 1				17
18					18
19					19
20	***E10-21**				20
21	(a)	2013			21
22	Dec. 31				22
23					23
24					24
25					25
26	(b)	2014			26
27	June 30				27
28					28
29					29
30					30
31	(c)	2014			31
32	Dec. 31				32
33					33
34					34
35					35
36	(d)	2023			36
37	Dec. 31				37
38					38
39					39
40					40

General Journal

	Date	Account Titles	Debit	Credit	
1	(a)				1
2	Jan. 1				2
3					3
4					4
5					5
6	12				6
7					7
8					8
9	14				9
10					10
11					11
12	20				12
13					13
14					14
15					15
16	21				16
17					17
18					18
19	25				19
20					20
21					21
22					22
23	(b)				23
24	Jan. 31				24
25					25
26					26
27					27
28					28

(c)

Shumway Company		
Balance Sheet (Partial)		
January 31, 2014		
1 Current liabilities:			1
2			2
3			3
4			4
5			5
6			6
7			7
8			8

(a)

Date	Account Titles	Debit	Credit
Jan. 2			
Feb. 1			
Mar.31			
Apr. 1			
July 1			
Sept. 30			
Oct. 1			
Dec. 1			
Dec. 31			

(b)

1	1
2	Notes Payable	2
3	3
4	4
5	5
6	6
7	7
8	Interest Payable	8
9	9
10	10
11	11
12	12
13	13
14	Interest Expense	14
15	15
16	16
17	17
18	18
19	19
20	20

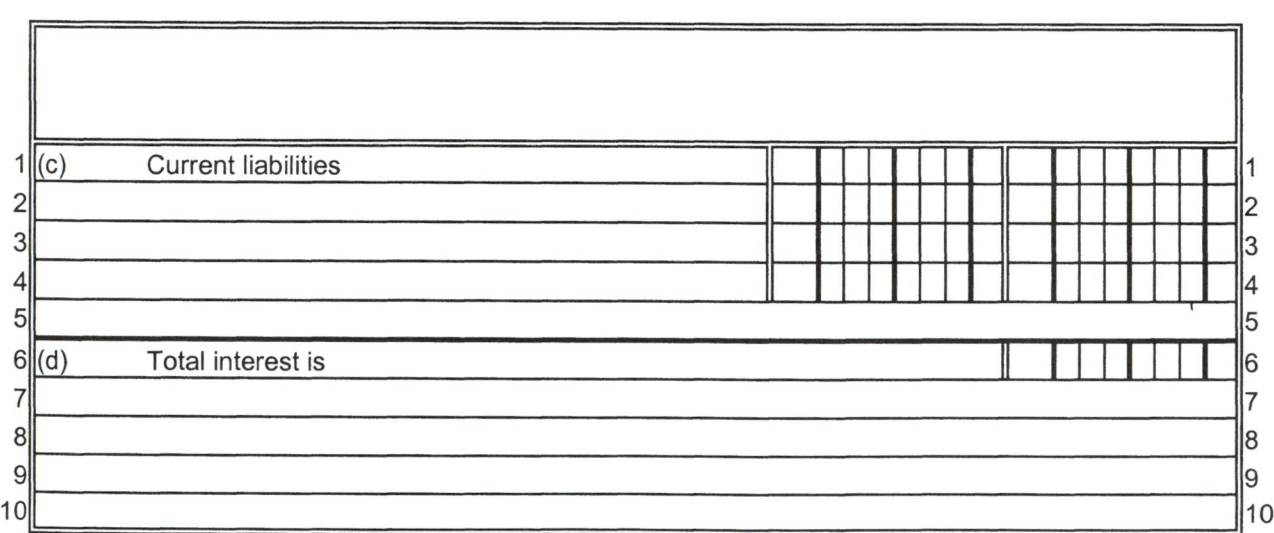

(c) Current liabilities

(d) Total interest is

General Journal

	Date	Account Titles	Debit	Credit	
1	(a)	2014			1
2	May 1				2
3					3
4					4
5	(b)				5
6	Dec. 31				6
7					7
8					8
9					9
10	(d)	2015			10
11	May 1				11
12					12
13					13
14					14
15					15
16	(e)				16
17	Nov. 1				17
18					18
19					19
20	(f)				20
21	Nov. 1				21
22					22
23					23
24					24
25					25
26					26
27					27

(c)

Hopkins Corp.
Balance Sheet (Partial)
December 31, 2014

1		1
2		2
3		3
4		4
5		5
6		6
7		7
8		8

General Journal

	Date	Account Titles	Debit	Credit	
1	(a)	2014			1
2	Jan. 1				2
3					3
4					4
5					5
6					6
7					7
8					8
9					9
10					10
11	(c)	2016			11
12	Jan. 1				12
13					13
14					14
15					15
16					16
17					17
18					18
19					19
20					20
21					21
22					22
23					23
24					24
25					25
26					26
27					27

(b)

	Formosa Electric Balance Sheet (Partial) December 31, 2014			
1				1
2				2
3				3
4				4
5				5
6				6
7				7
8				8

(a)

Semiannual Interest Period	Cash Payment	Interest Expense	Reduction of Principal	Principal Balance
Issue Date				
1				
2				
3				
4				

(b)   General Journal

Date	Account Titles	Debit	Credit
	2013		
Dec. 31			
	2014		
June 30			
Dec. 31			

(c)

	12/31/14

General Journal

	Date	Account Titles	Debit	Credit	
1	(a)	2014			1
2	July 1				2
3					3
4					4
5					5
6	(b)	See next page			6
7					7
8	(c)				8
9	Dec. 31				9
10					10
11					11
12					12
13					13
14	(d)	2015			14
15	July 1				15
16					16
17					17
18					18
19	(e)				19
20	Dec. 31				20
21					21
22					22
23					23
24					24
25					25
26					26
27					27

(b)

Strigel Corporation

Bond Premium Amortization Table

Effective Interest Method - Semiannual Interest Payments

10% Bonds Issued at 8%

Semi-annual Interest Periods	(A) Interest To Be Paid	(B) Interest Expense To Be Recorded	(C) Premium Amortization	(D) Unamortized Premium	(E) Bond Carrying Value
Issue date					
1					
2					
3					

(a)   General Journal

	Date	Account Titles	Debit	Credit	
1	(1)	2014			1
2	July 1				2
3					3
4					4
5					5
6	(2)				6
7	Dec. 31				7
8					8
9					9
10					10
11	(3)	2015			11
12	July 1				12
13					13
14					14
15					15
16	(4)				16
17	Dec. 31				17
18					18
19					19
20					20
21					21
22					22
23					23
24					24
25					25
26					26
27					27

(b)

Kingston Company
Balance Sheet (Partial)
December 31, 2015

1				1
2				2
3				3
4				4
5				5
6				6
7				7
8				8

(c)

General Journal

	Date	Account Titles	Debit	Credit	
1	(a)	2014			1
2	Jan. 1				2
3					3
4					4
5					5
6	(b)	See next page			6
7					7
8	(c)	2014			8
9	July 1				9
10					10
11					11
12					12
13	Dec. 31				13
14					14
15					15
16					16
17		2015			17
18	Jan. 1				18
19					19
20					20
21	July 1				21
22					22
23					23
24					24
25	Dec. 31				25
26					26
27					27
28					28

(d)

	Guehler Electric Partial Balance Sheet December 31, 2015			
1				1
2				2
3				3
4				4
5				5
6				6
7				7

(b)

Semi-annual Interest Periods	(A) Interest To Be Paid	(B) Interest Expense To Be Recorded	(C) Premium Amortization	(D) Unamortized Premium	(E) Bond Carrying Value
Issue date					
1					
2					
3					
4					

General Journal

	Date	Account Titles	Debit	Credit	
1	(a)	2014			1
2	July 1				2
3					3
4					4
5					5
6	Dec. 31				6
7					7
8					8
9					9
10	(b)	2014			10
11	July 1				11
12					12
13					13
14					14
15	Dec. 31				15
16					16
17					17
18					18
19					19
20					20

(c)

1	Premium:	1
2		2
3		3
4		4
5		5
6		6
7	Discount:	7
8		8
9		9
10		10
11		11
12		12
13		13
14		14
15		15

General Journal

	Date	Account Titles	Debit	Credit	
1	(a)				1
2	Jan. 1				2
3					3
4					4
5	(b)				5
6	July 1				6
7					7
8					8
9					9
10	(c)				10
11	July 1				11
12					12
13					13
14					14
15					15
16	(d)				16
17	Dec. 31				17
18					18
19					19
20					20
21					21
22					22
23					23
24					24
25					25
26					26
27					27

General Journal

	Date	Account Titles	Debit	Credit	
1	(a)				1
2	Jan. 1				2
3					3
4					4
5	5				5
6					6
7					7
8					8
9	12				9
10					10
11					11
12	14				12
13					13
14					14
15	20				15
16					16
17					17
18					18
19	25				19
20					20
21					21
22					22
23	(b)				23
24	Jan. 31				24
25					25
26					26
27	Jan 31				27

(c)

	Zaur Company Balance Sheet (Partial) January 31, 2014			
1	Current liabilities:			1
2				2
3				3
4				4
5				5
6				6
7				7
8				8

General Journal

	Date	Account Titles	Debit	Credit	
1	(a)	2014			1
2	June 1				2
3					3
4					4
5	(b)				5
6	Dec. 31				6
7					7
8					8
9					9
10	(d)	2015			10
11	June 1				11
12					12
13					13
14					14
15	(e)				15
16	Dec. 1				16
17					17
18					18
19	(f)				19
20	Dec. 1				20
21					21
22					22
23					23
24					24
25					25
26					26
27					27

(c)

Sator Corp.
Balance Sheet (Partial)
December 31, 2014

1		1
2		2
3		3
4		4
5		5
6		6
7		7
8		8

General Journal

	Date	Account Titles	Debit	Credit	
1	(a)	2014			1
2	Jan. 1				2
3					3
4					4
5					5
6					6
7					7
8					8
9					9
10					10
11	(c)	2016			11
12	Jan. 1				12
13					13
14					14
15					15
16					16
17					17
18					18
19					19
20					20
21					21
22					22
23					23
24					24
25					25
26					26
27					27

(b)

	Booker Co. Balance Sheet (Partial) December 31, 2014			
1				1
2				2
3				3
4				4
5				5
6				6
7				7
8				8

(a)

Semiannual Interest Period	Cash Payment	Interest Expense	Reduction of Principal	Principal Balance
Issue Date				
1				
2				
3				
4				

(b)   General Journal

Date	Account Titles	Debit	Credit
	2014		
Dec. 31			
	2015		
June 30			
Dec. 31			

(c)

Hamilton's Electronics

Partial Balance Sheet

December 31, 2014

General Journal

	Date	Account Titles	Debit	Credit	
1	(a)	2014			1
2	July 1				2
3					3
4					4
5					5
6	(b)	See next page			6
7					7
8	(c)				8
9	Dec. 31				9
10					10
11					11
12					12
13	(d)	2015			13
14	July 1				14
15					15
16					16
17					17
18	(e)				18
19	Dec. 31				19
20					20
21					21
22					22
23					23
24					24
25					25
26					26
27					27

Name

Section

Date

*Problem 10-5B Concluded

Visnak Satellites

(b)

Visnak Satellites

Bond Discount Amortization Table

Effective Interest Method - Semiannual Interest Payments

9% Bonds Issued at 10%

Semi-annual Interest Periods	(A) Interest To Be Paid	(B) Interest Expense	(C) Discount Amortization	(D) Unamortized Discount	(E) Bond Carrying Value
Issue date					
1					
2					
3					

(a)   General Journal

	Date	Account Titles	Debit	Credit	
1	(1)	2014			1
2	July 1				2
3					3
4					4
5					5
6	(2)				6
7	Dec. 31				7
8					8
9					9
10					10
11	(3)	2015			11
12	July 1				12
13					13
14					14
15					15
16	(4)				16
17	Dec. 31				17
18					18
19					19
20					20
21					21
22					22
23					23
24					24
25					25
26					26
27					27

(b)

Keokuk Chemical Company
Balance Sheet (Partial)
December 31, 2015

1				1
2				2
3				3
4				4
5				5
6				6
7				7
8				8

(c)

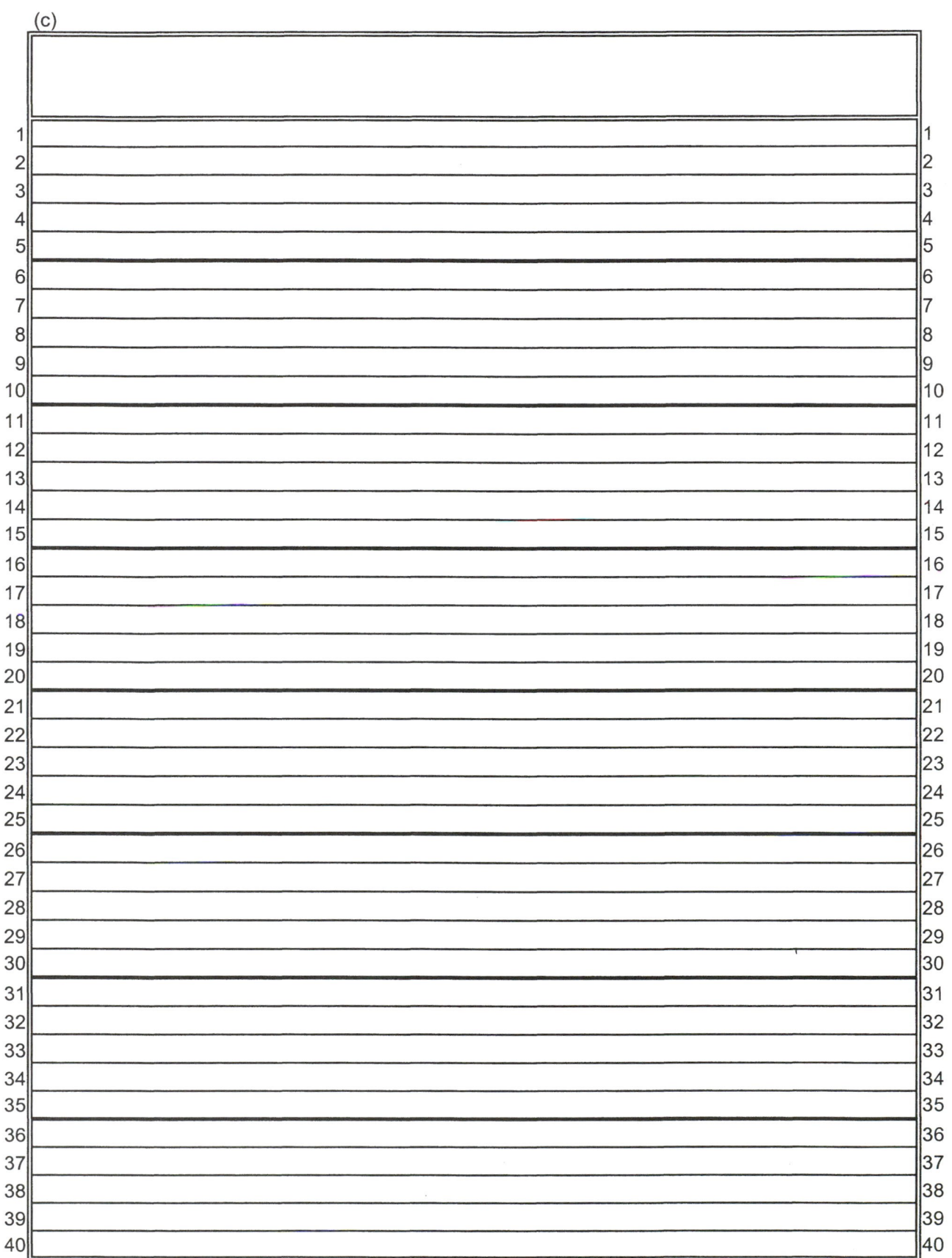

General Journal

	Date	Account Titles	Debit	Credit	
1	(a)	2014			1
2	Jan. 1				2
3					3
4					4
5					5
6	(b)	See next page			6
7					7
8	(c)	2014			8
9	July 1				9
10					10
11					11
12					12
13	Dec. 31				13
14					14
15					15
16					16
17		2015			17
18	Jan. 1				18
19					19
20					20
21	July 1				21
22					22
23					23
24					24
25	Dec. 31				25
26					26
27					27
28					28

(d)

Wilkowski Company
Partial Balance Sheet
December 31, 2015

1			1
2			2
3			3
4			4
5			5
6			6
7			7

(b)

Semi-annual Interest Periods	(A) Interest To Be Paid	(B) Interest Expense To Be Recorded	(C) Discount Amortization	(D) Unamortized Discount	(E) Bond Carrying Value
Issue date					
1					
2					
3					
4					

General Journal

	Date	Account Titles	Debit	Credit	
1	(a)	2014			1
2	Jan. 1				2
3					3
4					4
5					5
6	July 1				6
7					7
8					8
9					9
10	Dec. 31				10
11					11
12					12
13					13
14	(b)	2015			14
15	Jan. 1				15
16					16
17					17
18					18
19	July 1				19
20					20
21					21
22					22
23	Dec. 31				23
24					24
25					25
26					26
27					27

(c)

1 Premium:		
2		
3		
4		
5		
6		
7		
8		
9		
10		
11 Discount:		
12		
13		
14		
15		
16		
17		
18		
19		
20		
21		
22		
23		
24		
25		
26		
27		

General Journal

	Date	Account Titles	Debit	Credit	
1	(a)				1
2	Jan. 1				2
3					3
4					4
5	(b)				5
6	July 1				6
7					7
8					8
9					9
10	(c)				10
11	July 1				11
12					12
13					13
14					14
15					15
16	(d)				16
17	Dec. 31				17
18					18
19					19
20					20
21					21
22					22
23					23
24					24
25					25
26					26
27					27

(a)

		Account Titles	Debit	Credit	
1	1.				1
2					2
3					3
4	2.				4
5					5
6					6
7	3.				7
8					8
9					9
10					10
11					11
12					12
13					13
14	4.				14
15					15
16					16
17	5.				17
18					18
19					19
20	6.				20
21					21
22					22
23	7.				23
24					24
25					25
26	8.				26
27					27
28					28
29	9.				29
30					30
31					31
32	10.				32
33					33
34					34
35					35
36					36
37					37
38					38
39					39
40					40

(a)   (Continued)

		Account Titles	Debit	Credit	
1	11.				1
2					2
3					3
4					4
5		Adjusting Entries			5
6	12.				6
7					7
8					8
9	13.				9
10					10
11					11
12	14.				12
13					13

(b)

James Corporation
Trial Balance
12/31/2014

	Account	Debit	Credit	
1				1
2				2
3				3
4				4
5				5
6				6
7				7
8				8
9				9
10				10
11				11
12				12
13				13
14				14
15				15
16				16
17				17
18				18
19				19
20				20
21				21
22				22

(a) and (b) Optional T accounts

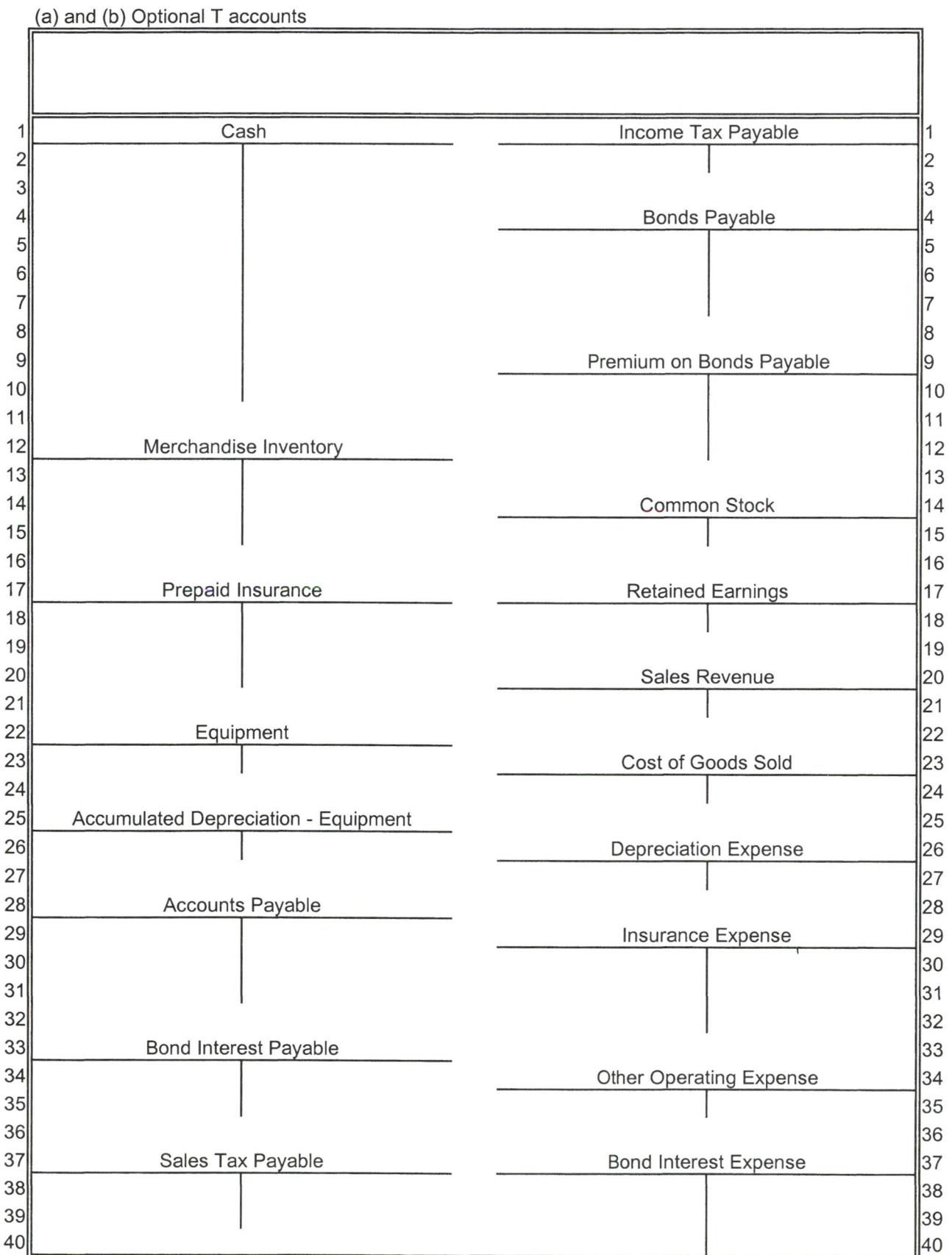

Cash	Income Tax Payable
Merchandise Inventory	Bonds Payable
Prepaid Insurance	Premium on Bonds Payable
Equipment	Common Stock
Accumulated Depreciation - Equipment	Retained Earnings
Accounts Payable	Sales Revenue
Bond Interest Payable	Cost of Goods Sold
Sales Tax Payable	Depreciation Expense
	Insurance Expense
	Other Operating Expense
	Bond Interest Expense

(a) and (b) Optional T accounts (Continued)

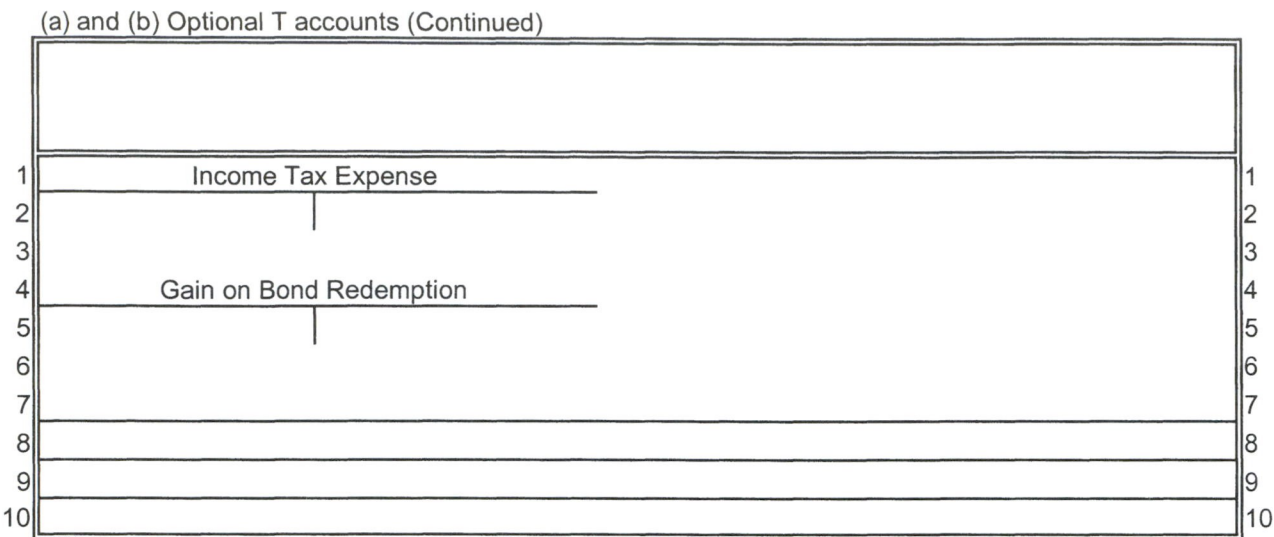

1	Income Tax Expense		1
2			2
3			3
4	Gain on Bond Redemption		4
5			5
6			6
7			7
8			8
9			9
10			10

(c)

James Corporation
Income Statement
For the Year Ending 12/31/14

(c) (Continued)

James Corporation
Retained Earnings Statement
For the Year Ending 12/31/14

1		1
2		2
3		3
4		4
5		5

James Corporation
Balance Sheet
12/31/2014

1		1
2		2
3		3
4		4
5		5
6		6
7		7
8		8
9		9
10		10
11		11
12		12
13		13
14		14
15		15
16		16
17		17
18		18
19		19
20		20
21		21
22		22
23		23
24		24
25		25
26		26
27		27
28		28
29		29
30		30

(a)

	Eastland Company	Westside Company
1 Cash		
2 Accounts Receivable		
3 Allowance for Doubtful Accounts		
4 Inventory		
5 Plant and Equipment		
6 Accumulated Depreciation - Pant and Equipment		
7 Total Assets		
8		
9 Current Liabilities		
10 Long-term Liabilities		
11 Total Liabilities		
12 Stockholders' Equity		
13 Total Liabilities and Stockholders' Equity		
14		
15		

16

17

18

19

20 (b)

21

22

23

24

25

26

27

28

29

30

31

32

33

34

35

36

37

38

39

40

1	(a)
2	
3	
4	
5	(b)
6	
7	
8	
9	
10	(c) (in millions of dollars)
11	
12	
13	
14	
15	
16	
17	
18	(d)
19	
20	
21	
22	
23	
24	
25	
26	
27	
28	(e)
29	
30	
31	
32	
33	
34	
35	
36	
37	
38	
39	
40	

1	(a) Discount on bonds payable:						1
2							2
3							3
4							4
5	Bond discount amortization per year:						5
6							6
7							7
8							8
9							9
10	Carrying value of bonds, January 1, 2014:						10
11							11
12							12
13							13
14							14
15							15
16							16
17							17
18							18
19							19

	(b)	Account Titles	Debit	Credit	
20					20
21	1.				21
22					22
23					23
24					24
25					25
26					26
27	2.				27
28					28
29					29
30					30
31					31
32					32
33					33
34					34
35					35
36					36
37					37
38					38
39					39
40					40

(c)

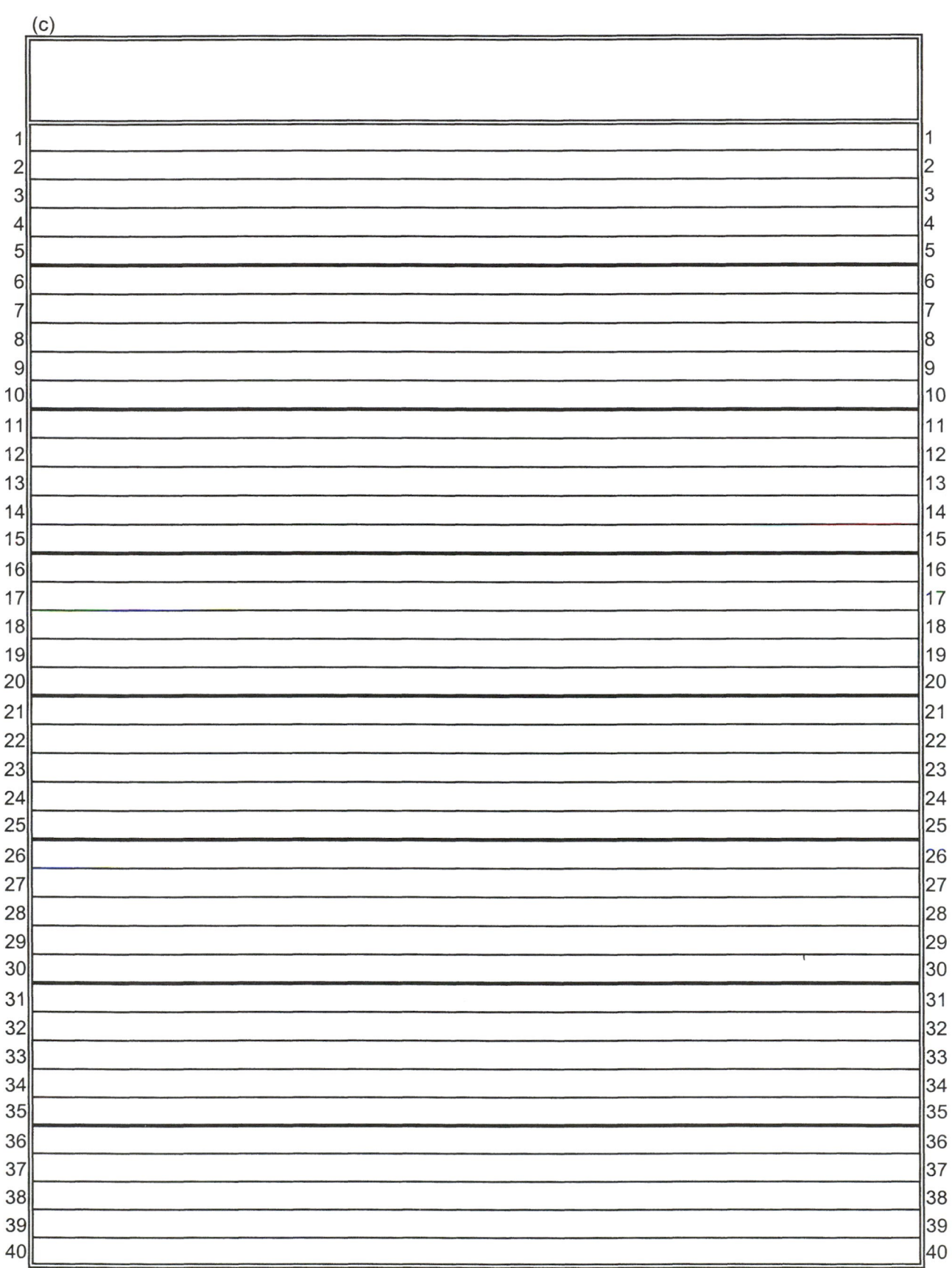

1	(a)	1
2		2
3		3
4		4
5		5
6		6
7		7
8		8
9		9
10	(b)	10
11		11
12	(c)	12
13		13
14		14
15		15
16		16
17		17
18	(d)	18
19		19
20		20
21	(e)	21
22		22
23	(f)	23
24		24
25		25
26		26
27		27
28		28
29		29
30		30
31	Total taxes:	31
32		32
33		33
34		34
35		35
36		36
37		37
38		38

IFRS10-2

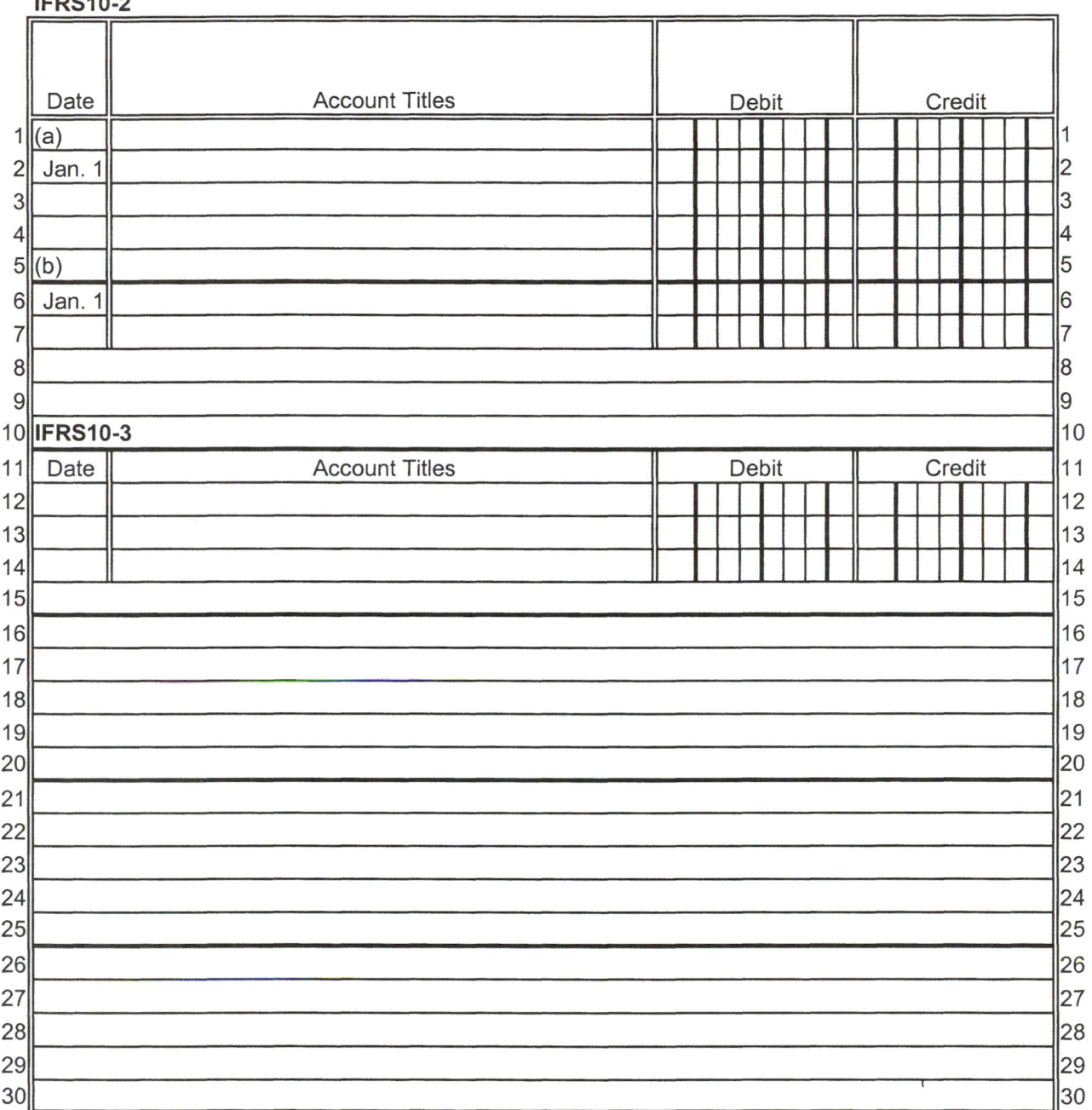

	Date	Account Titles	Debit	Credit	
1	(a)				1
2	Jan. 1				2
3					3
4					4
5	(b)				5
6	Jan. 1				6
7					7
8					8
9					9

IFRS10-3

	Date	Account Titles	Debit	Credit	
11	Date	Account Titles	Debit	Credit	11
12					12
13					13
14					14
15					15
16					16
17					17
18					18
19					19
20					20
21					21
22					22
23					23
24					24
25					25
26					26
27					27
28					28
29					29
30					30

BE11-2

	Date	Account Titles	Debit	Credit	
1	May 10				1
2					2
3					3
4					4
5	**BE11-3**				5
6	June 1				6
7					7
8					8
9					9
10	**BE11-4**				10
11					11
12					12
13					13
14					14
15	**BE11-5**				15
16	July 1				16
17					17
18					18
19	Sept. 1				19
20					20
21					21
22					22
23					23
24	**BE11-6**				24
25					25
26					26
27					27
28					28
29					29
30					30
31					31
32					32
33					33
34					34
35					35
36					36
37					37
38					38
39					39
40					40

BE11-7

	Date	Account Titles	Debit	Credit	
1	Nov. 1				1
2					2
3					3
4	Dec. 31				4
5					5
6					6

BE11-8

	Date	Account Titles	Debit	Credit	
8	Dec. 1				8
9					9
10					10
11					11
12	31				12
13					13
14					14
15					15

BE11-9

		Before Dividend	After Dividend	
17	(a)			17
19	Stockholders' equity			19
20	Paid-in capital			20
21	Common stock, $10 par			21
22	In excess of par value			22
23	Total paid-in capital			23
24	Retained earnings			24
25	Total stockholders' equity			25
27	(b) Outstanding shares			27

BE11-10

Abbott Inc.
Retained Earnings Statement
For the Year Ended December 31, 2014

BE11-11

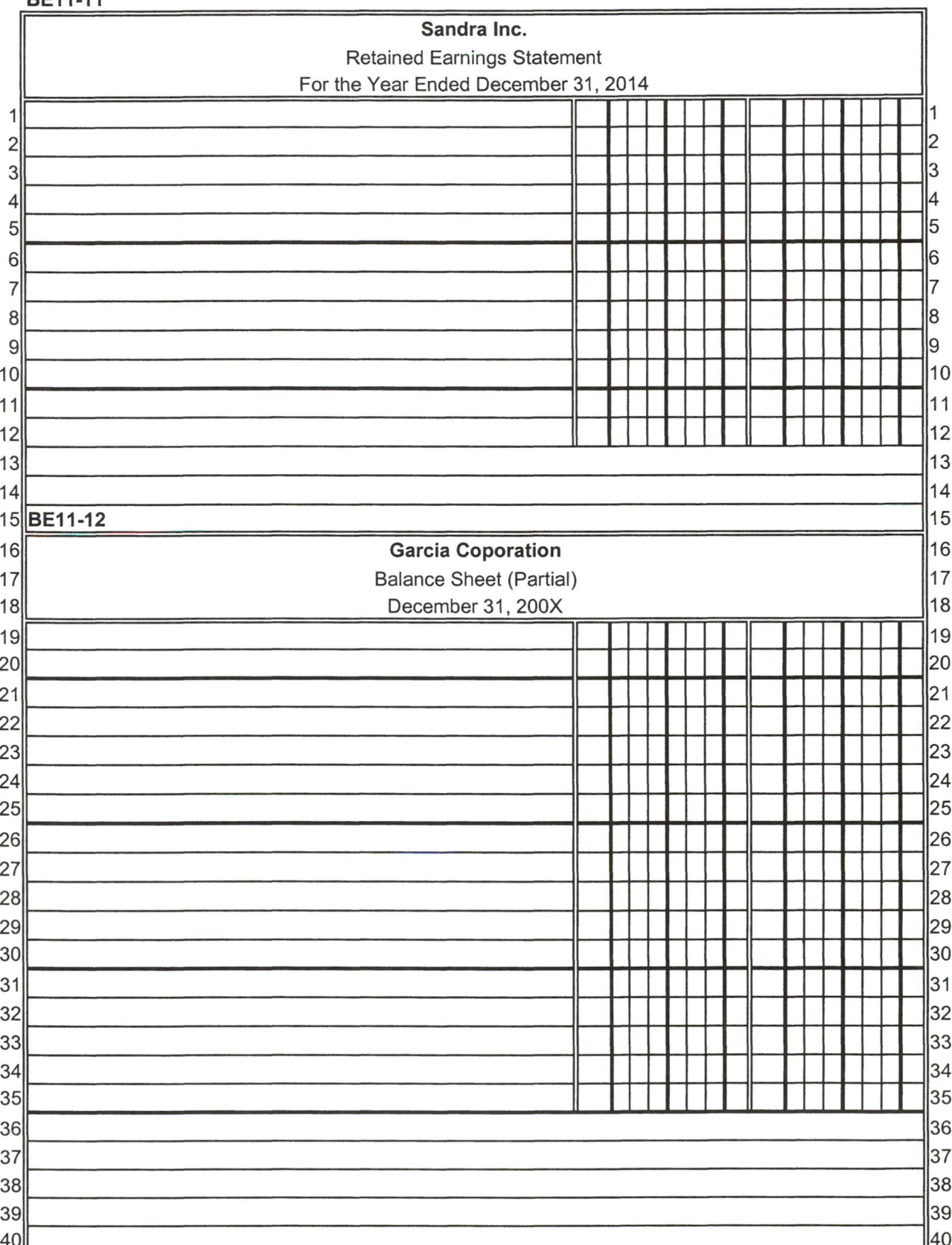

Sandra Inc.

Retained Earnings Statement

For the Year Ended December 31, 2014

BE11-12

Garcia Coporation

Balance Sheet (Partial)

December 31, 200X

DO IT! 11-2

	(a) Account Titles	Debit	Credit	
1				1
2				2
3				3
4				4
5	(b)			5
6				6
7				7
8				8
9				9
10				10

DO IT! 11-3

	Date	Account Titles	Debit	Credit	
11					11
12	Date	Account Titles	Debit	Credit	12
13	Apr 1				13
14					14
15					15
16					16
17					17
18					18
19	Apr 9				19
20					20
21					21
22					22
23					23
24					24
25					25
26					26

DO IT! 11-4

	Date	Account Titles	Debit	Credit	
27					27
28	Date	Account Titles	Debit	Credit	28
29	Aug 1				29
30					30
31					31
32					32
33					33
34	Dec 1				34
35					35
36					36
37					37
38					38
39					39
40					40

DO IT! 11-6

1. (a) 1.

2.

(b)   (1) and (2). The effects on the equity accounts are as follows:

	Original Balances	After Dividend	After Split

DO IT! 11-7

Raymond Corporation
Retained Earnings Statement
For the Year Ended December 31, 2014

E11-3

	Date	Account Titles	Debit	Credit	
1	(a)				1
2	Jan. 10				2
3					3
4					4
5	July 1				5
6					6
7					7
8					8
9	(b)				9
10	Jan. 10				10
11					11
12					12
13					13
14	July 1				14
15					15
16					16
17					17
18					18
19					19
20	**E11-4**				20
21	(a)				21
22					22
23					23
24					24
25	(b)				25
26					26
27					27
28					28
29	(c)				29
30					30
31					31
32	(d)				32
33					33
34					34
35					35
36	(e)				36
37					37
38					38
39					39
40					40

E11-5

	Account Titles	Debit	Credit	
1				1
2				2
3				3
4				4
5				5
6				6
7				7
8				8
9				9
10				10
11				11
12				12
13				13
14				14
15				15
16				16
17				17
18				18
19				19
20	**E11-6**			20
21	(a)			21
22				22
23				23
24				24
25				25
26	(b)			26
27				27
28				28
29				29
30				30
31	(c)			31
32				32
33				33
34				34
35				35
36				36
37				37
38				38
39				39
40				40

E11-7

	Date	Account Titles	Debit	Credit	
1	Mar. 2				1
2					2
3					3
4					4
5	June 12				5
6					6
7					7
8					8
9	July 11				9
10					10
11					11
12					12
13	Nov. 28				13
14					14
15					15
16					16
17					17
18					18
19					19
20	**E11-8**				20
21	1.				21
22					22
23					23
24					24
25					25
26	2.				26
27					27
28					28
29					29
30					30
31					31
32					32
33					33
34					34
35					35
36					36
37					37
38					38
39					39
40					40

	Date	Account Titles	Debit	Credit	
1	(a)				1
2	Mar. 1				2
3					3
4					4
5	July 1				5
6					6
7					7
8					8
9					9
10	Sept. 1				10
11					11
12					12
13					13
14					14
15	(b)				15
16	Sept. 1				16
17					17
18					18
19					19
20					20
21					21
22					22
23					23
24					24
25					25
26					26
27					27
28					28
29					29
30					30
31					31
32					32
33					33
34					34
35					35
36					36
37					37
38					38
39					39
40					40

(a)

General Journal

	Date	Account Titles	Debit	Credit	
1	Feb. 1				1
2					2
3					3
4					4
5					5
6	July 1				6
7					7
8					8
9					9
10					10

(b)

Preferred Stock

Date	Explanation	Ref.	Debit	Credit	Balance

Paid-in Capital in Excess of Par Value-Preferred Stock

Date		Ref.	Debit	Credit	Balance

(c)

1		1
2		2
3		3
4		4
5		5
6		6
7		7
8		8
9		9
10		10

E11-12

	Date	Account Titles	Debit	Credit	
1	May 2				1
2					2
3					3
4					4
5					5
6	10				6
7					7
8					8
9					9
10					10
11	15				11
12					12
13					13
14	31				14
15					15
16					16
17					17
18					18
19	**E11-13**				19
20	(a)				20
21	June 15				21
22					22
23					23
24	July 10				24
25					25
26					26
27	Dec. 15				27
28					28
29					29
30					30
31	(b)				31
32					32
33					33
34					34
35					35
36					36
37					37
38					38
39					39
40					40

E11-14

	Date	Account Titles	Debit	Credit	
1	(a)				1
2					2
3					3
4					4
5					5
6					6
7	(b)				7
8					8
9					9
10					10
11					11
12					12

E11-15

		Before Action	After Stock Dividend	After Stock Split	
13					13
14					14
15					15
16	Stockholders' equity				16
17	Paid-in capital				17
18	Common stock				18
19	In excess of par value				19
20	Total paid-in capital				20
21	Retained Earnings				21
22	Total stockholders' equity				22
23					23
24					24
25	Outstanding shares				25
26					26
27					27
28					28
29					29
30					30
31					31
32					32
33					33
34					34
35					35
36					36
37					37
38					38
39					39
40					40

E11-16

	Date	Account Titles	Debit	Credit	
1	1.				1
2	Dec. 31				2
3					3
4					4
5	2.				5
6	31				6
7					7
8					8
9					9
10					10
11					11
12	3.				12
13	31				13
14					14
15					15

E11-17

	Richard Corporation			
	Retained Earnings Statement			
	For the Year Ended December 31, 2014			
1				1
2				2
3				3
4				4
5				5
6				6
7				7
8				8
9				9
10				10
11				11
12				12
13				13
14				14
15				15
16				16
17				17
18				18
19				19

E11-18

Bindra Company
Retained Earnings Statement
For the Year Ended December 31, 2014

1			
2			
3			
4			
5			
6			
7			
8			
9			
10			
11			
12			
13			
14			
15			

E11-19

	Paid-in Capital			
Account	Capital Stock	Additional Paid-in Capital	Retained Earnings	Other
Common Stock				
Preferred Stock				
Treasury Stock				
Paid-in Capital in Excess of Par				
Value - Preferred Stock				
Paid-in Capital in Excess of				
Stated Value - Common Stock				
Paid-in Capital from Treasury				
Stock				
Retained Earnings				

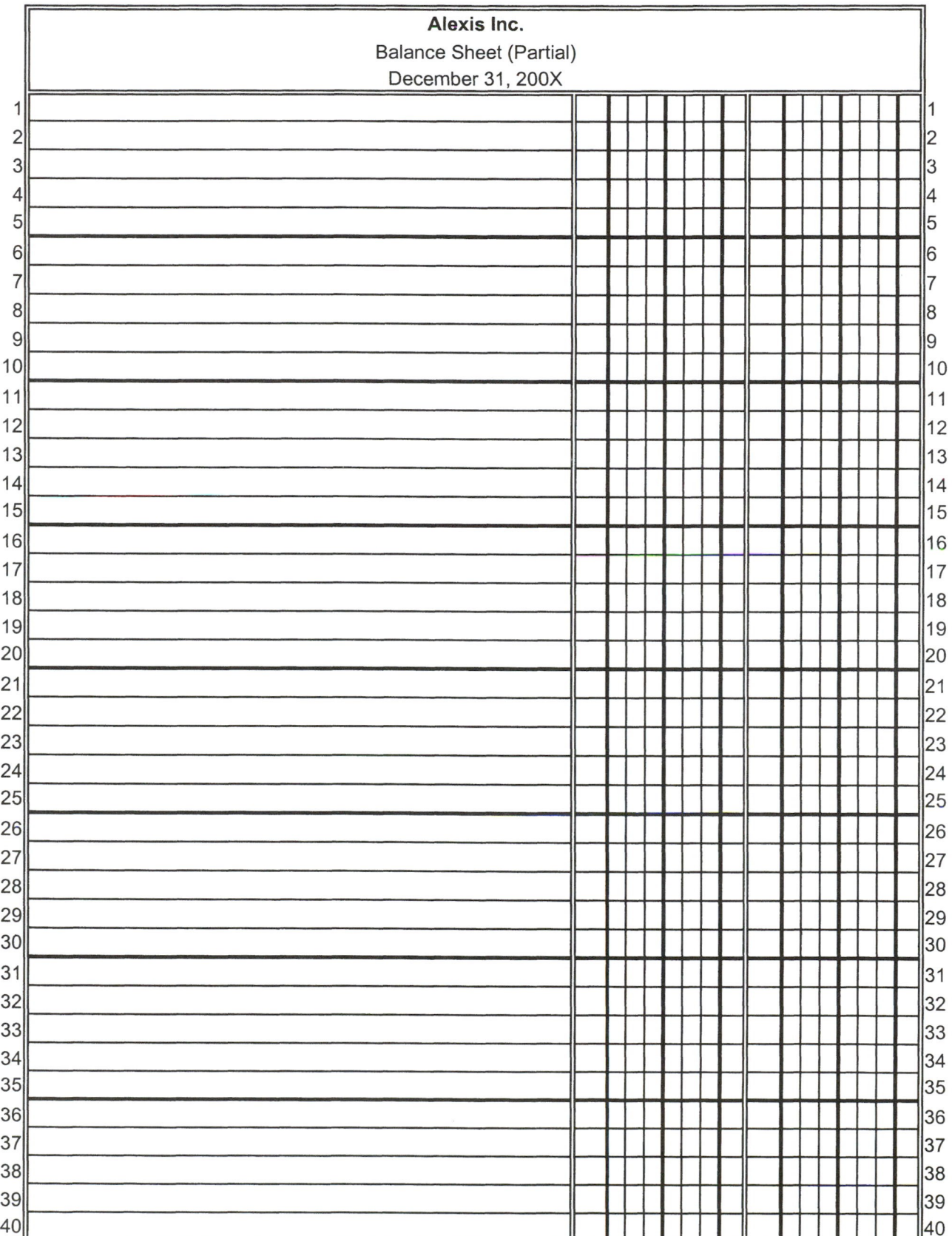

Alexis Inc.

Balance Sheet (Partial)

December 31, 200X

E11-21

Perin Company			
Balance Sheet (Partial)			
December 31, 2014			

1			
2			
3			
4			
5			
6			
7			
8			
9			
10			
11			
12			
13			
14			
15			
16			
17			
18			

E11-22

Reliant Corporation			
Income Statement			
For the Year Ended December 31, 2014			

1			
2			
3			
4			
5			
6			
7			
8			
9			
10			
11			
12 (b)			
13			
14			
15			
16			
17			
18			

(a)

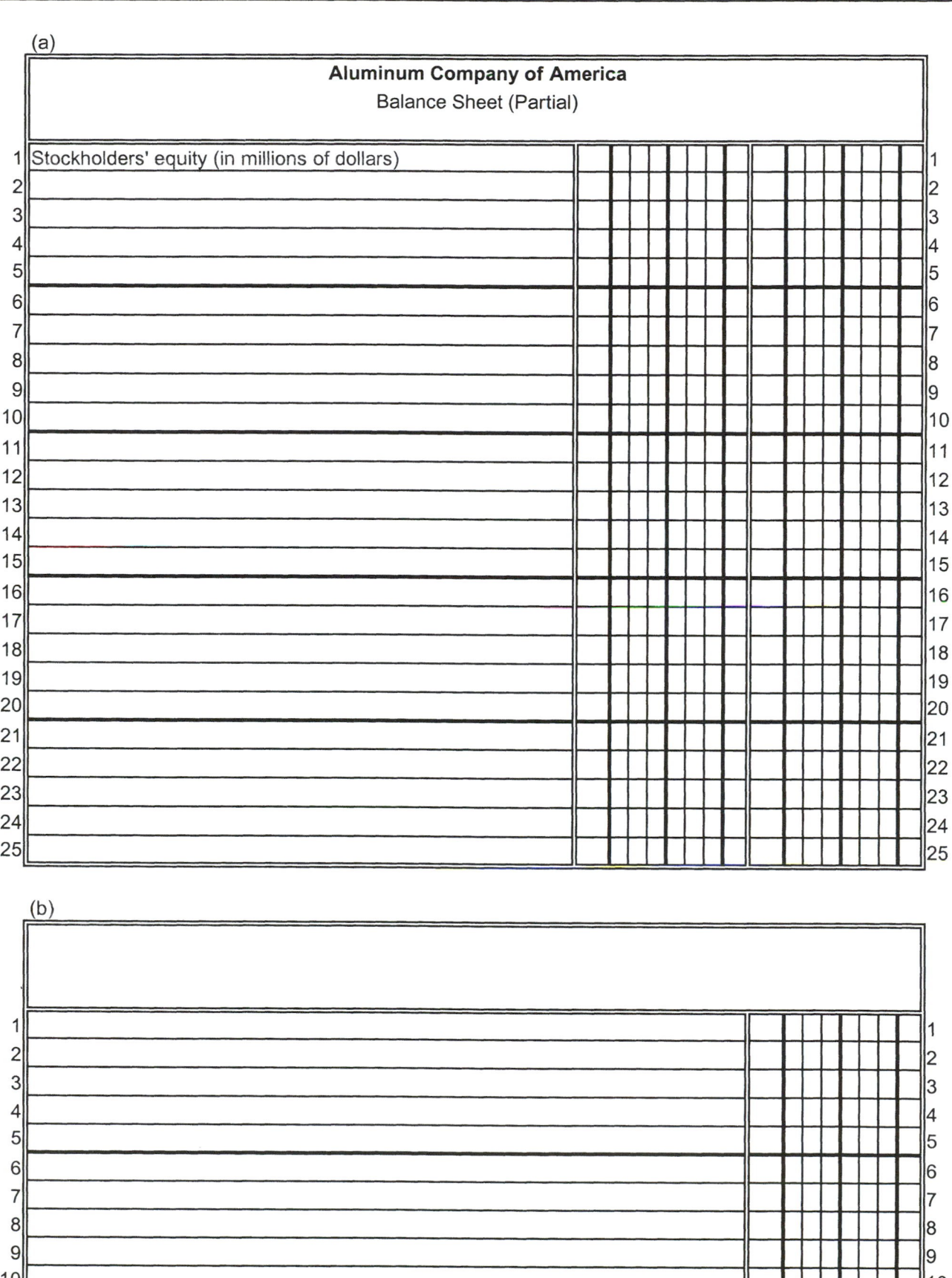

Aluminum Company of America
Balance Sheet (Partial)

1 Stockholders' equity (in millions of dollars)

(b)

*E11-25

	(a)	(b)
1		
2		
3		
4		
5		
6		
7		
8		
9		
10		
11		
12		

*E11-26

(a)

1 (1)	
2	
3	
4 (2)	
5	
6	
7 (b)	
8 Common stock:	
9	
10	
11	
12	
13 Paid-in capital in excess of par value:	
14	
15	
16	
17	
18 Retained earnings:	
19	
20	
21	
22	
23	

(a)

General Journal

J1

	Date	Account Titles	Ref.	Debit	Credit	
1	Jan. 10					1
2						2
3						3
4						4
5						5
6	Mar. 1					6
7						7
8						8
9						9
10						10
11	Apr. 1					11
12						12
13						13
14						14
15						15
16	May 1					16
17						17
18						18
19						19
20						20
21	Aug. 1					21
22						22
23						23
24						24
25						25
26	Sept. 1					26
27						27
28						28
29						29
30						30
31	Nov. 1					31
32						32
33						33
34						34
35						35
36						36
37						37
38						38
39						39
40						40

(b)

Preferred Stock

Date	Explanation	Ref.	Debit	Credit	Balance

Common Stock

Date	Explanation	Ref.	Debit	Credit	Balance

Paid-in Capital in Excess of Par Value - Preferred Stock

Date	Explanation	Ref.	Debit	Credit	Balance

Paid-in Capital in Excess of Stated Value - Common Stock

Date	Explanation	Ref.	Debit	Credit	Balance

(c)

	Burke Corporation																	
	Balance Sheet (Partial)																	
	December 31, 2011																	
1	Stockholders' equity																	1
2																		2
3																		3
4																		4
5																		5
6																		6
7																		7
8																		8
9																		9
10																		10
11																		11
12																		12
13																		13
14																		14
15																		15
16																		16
17																		17
18																		18
19																		19
20																		20
21																		21
22																		22
23																		23
24																		24
25																		25
26																		26
27																		27
28																		28
29																		29
30																		30
31																		31
32																		32
33																		33
34																		34
35																		35
36																		36
37																		37
38																		38
39																		39
40																		40

(a)   General Journal   J12

	Date	Account Titles	Ref.	Debit	Credit	
1	Mar. 1					1
2						2
3						3
4						4
5	June 1					5
6						6
7						7
8						8
9						9
10	Sept. 1					10
11						11
12						12
13						13
14						14
15						15
16	Dec. 1					16
17						17
18						18
19						19
20						20
21	31					21
22						22
23						23
24						24
25						25
26						26
27						27
28						28
29						29
30						30
31						31
32						32
33						33
34						34
35						35
36						36
37						37
38						38
39						39
40						40

(b)

Paid-in Capital from Treasury Stock

Date	Explanation	Ref.	Debit	Credit	Balance

Treasury Stock

Date	Explanation	Ref.	Debit	Credit	Balance

Retained Earnings

Date	Explanation	Ref.	Debit	Credit	Balance
Jan. 1	Balance	√			1 0 0 0 0 0

(c)

	Elston Corporation						
	Balance Sheet (Partial)						
	December 31, 2014						
1	Stockholders' equity						
2							
3							
4							
5							
6							
7							
8							
9							
10							
11							
12							
13							
14							
15							
16							
17							
18							
19							
20							
21							
22							
23							
24							
25							

(a)   General Journal   J1

	Date	Account Titles	Ref.	Debit	Credit
1	Feb. 1				
2					
3					
4					
5					
6					
7	Mar. 20				
8					
9					
10					
11	June 14				
12					
13					
14					
15					
16					
17	Sept. 3				
18					
19					
20					
21					
22					
23	Dec. 31				
24					
25					
26					
27					
28					
29					
30					
31					
32					
33					
34					
35					
36					
37					
38					
39					
40					

(b)

Preferred Stock

Date	Explanation	Ref.	Debit	Credit	Balance
Jan. 1	Balance	√			4 0 0 0 0 0

Common Stock

Date	Explanation	Ref.	Debit	Credit	Balance
Jan. 1	Balance	√			1 0 0 0 0 0 0

Paid-in Capital in Excess of Par Value - Preferred Stock

Date	Explanation	Ref.	Debit	Credit	Balance
Jan. 1	Balance	√			1 0 0 0 0

Paid-in Capital in Excess of Stated Value - Common Stock

Date	Explanation	Ref.	Debit	Credit	Balance
Jan. 1	Balance	√			1 4 5 0 0 0 0

Retained Earnings

Date	Explanation	Ref.	Debit	Credit	Balance
Jan. 1	Balance	√			1 8 1 6 0 0 0

Treasury Stock - Common

Date	Explanation	Ref.	Debit	Credit	Balance
Jan. 1	Balance	√			5 0 0 0 0

Paid-in Capital from Treasury Stock - Common

Date	Explanation	Ref.	Debit	Credit	Balance

(c)

	Terrell Corporation																	
	Balance Sheet (Partial)																	
	December 31, 2014																	
1	Stockholders' equity																	1
2																		2
3																		3
4																		4
5																		5
6																		6
7																		7
8																		8
9																		9
10																		10
11																		11
12																		12
13																		13
14																		14
15																		15
16																		16
17																		17
18																		18
19																		19
20																		20
21																		21
22																		22
23																		23
24																		24
25																		25
26																		26
27																		27
28																		28
29																		29
30																		30
31																		31
32																		32
33																		33
34																		34
35																		35
36																		36
37																		37
38																		38
39																		39
40																		40

(a)

General Journal

	Date	Account Titles	Ref.	Debit	Credit	
1	Feb. 1					1
2						2
3						3
4						4
5	Mar. 1					5
6						6
7						7
8						8
9	Apr. 1					9
10						10
11						11
12						12
13						13
14						14
15						15
16	July 1					16
17						17
18						18
19						19
20						20
21						21
22						22
23	31					23
24						24
25						25
26						26
27						27
28	Dec. 1					28
29						29
30						30
31						31
32	31					32
33						33
34						34
35						35
36						36
37						37
38						38
39						39
40						40

(b)

Common Stock

Date	Explanation	Ref.	Debit	Credit	Balance
Jan. 1	Balance	√			1 200 000

Common Stock Dividends Distributable

Date	Explanation	Ref.	Debit	Credit	Balance

Paid-in Capital in Excess of Par Value

Date	Explanation	Ref.	Debit	Credit	Balance
Jan. 1	Balance	√			200 000

Retained Earnings

Date	Explanation	Ref.	Debit	Credit	Balance
Jan. 1	Balance	√			600 000

Cash Dividends

Date	Explanation	Ref.	Debit	Credit	Balance

Stock Dividends

Date	Explanation	Ref.	Debit	Credit	Balance

(c)

Prasad Corporation						
Balance Sheet (Partial)						
December 31, 2014						
Stockholders' equity						

(a)

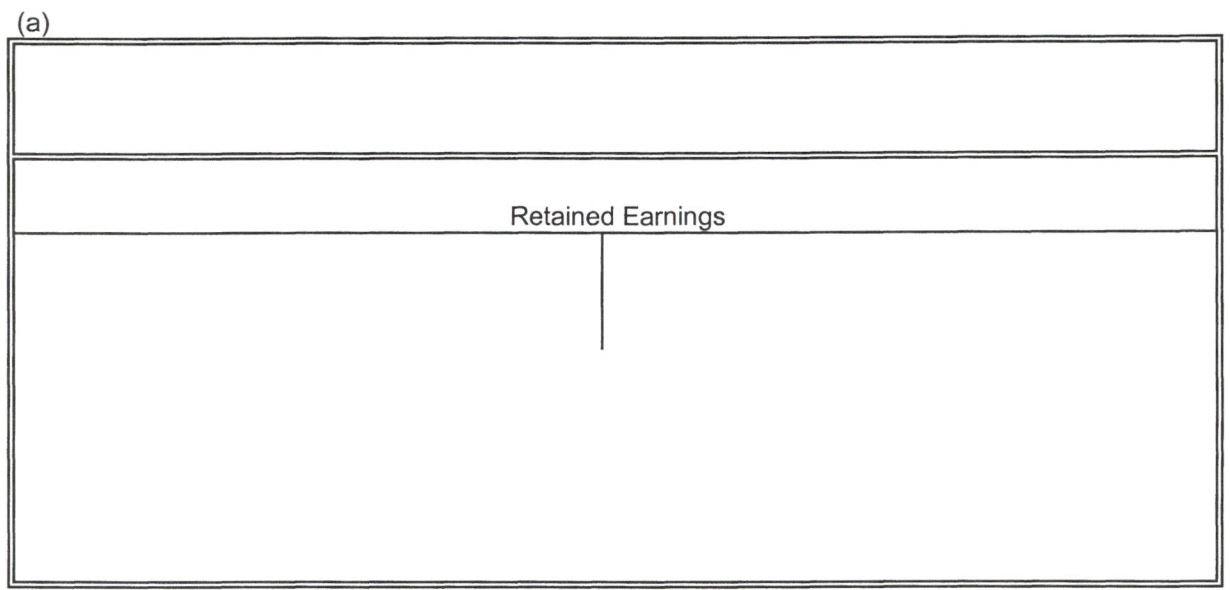

Retained Earnings

(b)

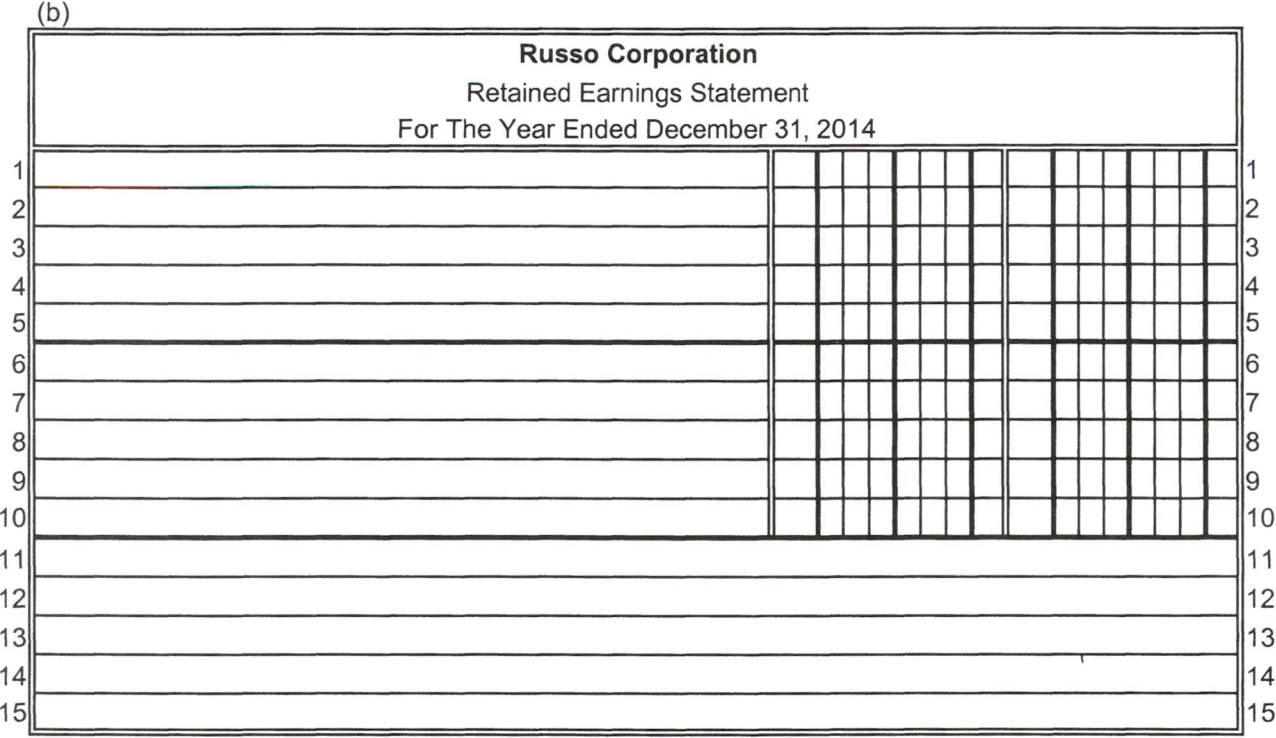

Russo Corporation

Retained Earnings Statement

For The Year Ended December 31, 2014

1		1
2		2
3		3
4		4
5		5
6		6
7		7
8		8
9		9
10		10
11		11
12		12
13		13
14		14
15		15

(c)

	Russo Corporation						
	Partial Balance Sheet						
	December 31, 2014						
1	Stockholders' equity						
2							
3							
4							
5							
6							
7							
8							
9							
10							
11							
12							
13							
14							
15							
16							
17							
18							
19							
20							
21							
22							
23							
24							
25							
26							
27							
28							
29							
30							
31							
32							
33							
34							
35							
36							
37	(d)						
38							
39							
40							

(a)   General Journal

	Date	Account Titles	Ref.	Debit	Credit	
1	(1)					1
2						2
3						3
4						4
5						5
6						6
7	(2)					7
8						8
9						9
10						10
11						11
12						12
13	(3)					13
14						14
15						15
16						16
17	(4)					17
18						18
19						19
20						20
21						21
22						22
23						23
24						24
25						25
26						26
27						27
28						28
29						29
30						30
31						31
32						32
33						33
34						34
35						35
36						36
37						37
38						38
39						39
40						40

(b)

Jude Corporation						
Partial Balance Sheet						
December 31, 2014						
Stockholders' equity						

(a)   General Journal

	Date	Account Titles	Ref.	Debit	Credit	
1	Jan. 15					1
2						2
3						3
4						4
5	Feb 15					5
6						6
7						7
8						8
9	Apr. 15					9
10						10
11						11
12						12
13						13
14						14
15						15
16	May 15					16
17						17
18						18
19						19
20						20
21	July 1					21
22						22
23						23
24						24
25						25
26						26
27						27
28	Dec. 1					28
29						29
30						30
31						31
32	31					32
33						33
34						34
35	31					35
36						36
37						37
38	31					38
39						39
40						40

(b)

Common Stock

Date	Explanation	Ref.	Debit	Credit	Balance
Jan. 1	Balance	√			7 5 0 0 0 0

Paid-in Capital in Excess of Par Value - Common Stock

Date	Explanation	Ref.	Debit	Credit	Balance
Jan. 1	Balance	√			2 0 0 0 0 0

Retained Earnings

Date	Explanation	Ref.	Debit	Credit	Balance
Jan. 1	Balance	√			5 4 0 0 0 0

Cash Dividends

Date	Explanation	Ref.	Debit	Credit	Balance

Stock Dividends

Date	Explanation	Ref.	Debit	Credit	Balance

Common Stock Dividends Distributable

Date	Explanation	Ref.	Debit	Credit	Balance

(c)

Primo Corporation
Balance Sheet (Partial)
December 31, 2014

Stockholders' equity			

(a)

	Westin Corporation Partial Balance Sheet December 31, 2014													
1														
2														
3														
4														
5														
6														
7														
8														
9														
10														
11														
12														
13														
14														
15														
16														
17														
18														
19														
20														
21														
22														
23														
24														
25														
26														
27														
28														
29														
30														
31														
32														
33														
34														
35														

(b)

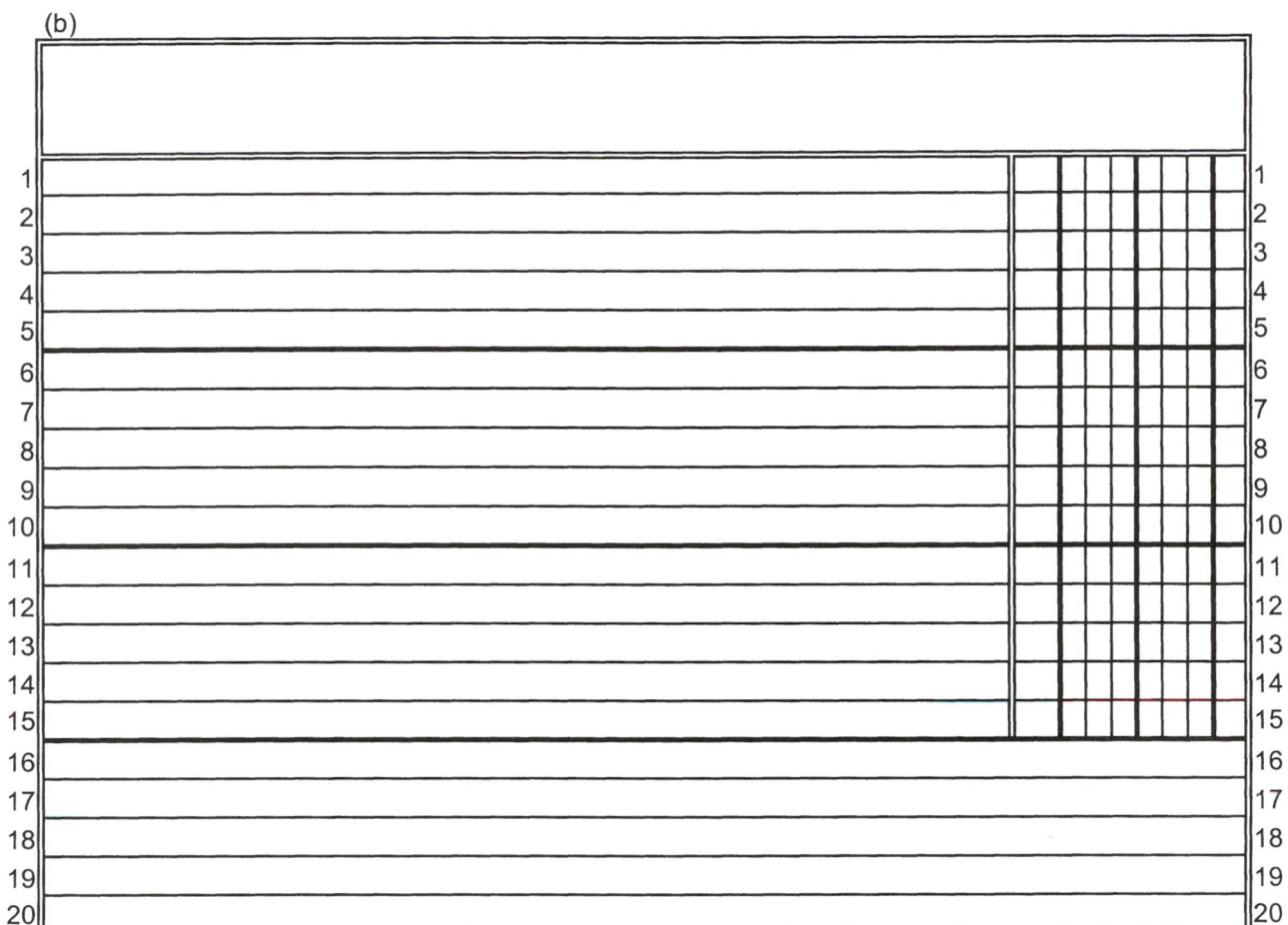

Goodhue Inc.

Stockholders' Equity Statement

For The Year Ended December 31, 2014

(in thousands, except shares)

	Common Stock	Paid-in Capital in Excess of Par Value	Common Stock Dividends Distributable	Treasury Stock	Retained Earnings	Total
1						
2						
3						
4						
5 Balances, Jan. 1	$ 800	$ 500	$ 120	$ 0	$ 600	$ 2020
6						
7						
8						
9						
10						
11						
12						
13						
14						
15						
16						
17						
18						
19						
20						
21						
22						
23						
24						

(a)   General Journal   J5

	Date	Account Titles	Ref.	Debit	Credit	
1	Jan. 10					1
2						2
3						3
4						4
5						5
6	Mar. 1					6
7						7
8						8
9						9
10						10
11	Apr. 1					11
12						12
13						13
14						14
15						15
16	May 1					16
17						17
18						18
19						19
20						20
21	Aug. 1					21
22						22
23						23
24						24
25						25
26	Sept. 1					26
27						27
28						28
29						29
30						30
31	Nov. 1					31
32						32
33						33
34						34
35						35
36						36
37						37
38						38
39						39
40						40

(b)

Preferred Stock

Date	Explanation	Ref.	Debit	Credit	Balance

Common Stock

Date	Explanation	Ref.	Debit	Credit	Balance

Paid-in Capital in Excess of Par Value - Preferred Stock

Date	Explanation	Ref.	Debit	Credit	Balance

Paid-in Capital in Excess of Stated Value - Common Stock

Date	Explanation	Ref.	Debit	Credit	Balance

(c)

Welles Corporation		
Balance Sheet (Partial)		
December 31, 2014		
Stockholders' equity		

(a) General Journal J10

	Date	Account Titles	Ref.	Debit	Credit	
1	Mar. 1					1
2						2
3						3
4						4
5	June 1					5
6						6
7						7
8						8
9						9
10	Sept. 1					10
11						11
12						12
13						13
14						14
15						15
16	Dec. 1					16
17						17
18						18
19						19
20						20
21	31					21
22						22
23						23
24						24
25						25
26						26
27						27
28						28
29						29
30						30
31						31
32						32
33						33
34						34
35						35
36						36
37						37
38						38
39						39
40						40

(b)

Paid-in Capital from Treasury Stock

Date	Explanation	Ref.	Debit	Credit	Balance

Treasury Stock

Date	Explanation	Ref.	Debit	Credit	Balance

Retained Earnings

Date	Explanation	Ref.	Debit	Credit	Balance
Jan. 1	Balance	√			1 0 0 0 0 0

(c)

	Plover Corporation									
	Balance Sheet (Partial)									
	December 31, 2014									
1	Stockholders' equity									
2										
3										
4										
5										
6										
7										
8										
9										
10										
11										
12										
13										
14										
15										
16										
17										
18										
19										
20										
21										
22										
23										
24										
25										
26										
27										
28										
29										
30										
31										
32										
33										
34										
35										
36										
37										
38										
39										
40										

(a)   General Journal   J5

	Date	Account Titles	Ref.	Debit	Credit	
1	Feb. 1					1
2						2
3						3
4						4
5						5
6						6
7	Apr. 14					7
8						8
9						9
10						10
11						11
12						12
13	Sept. 3					13
14						14
15						15
16						16
17						17
18						18
19	Nov. 10					19
20						20
21						21
22						22
23	Dec. 31					23
24						24
25						25
26						26
27						27
28						28
29						29
30						30
31						31
32						32
33						33
34						34
35						35
36						36
37						37
38						38
39						39
40						40

(b)

Preferred Stock

Date	Explanation	Ref.	Debit	Credit	Balance
Jan. 1	Balance	√			300000

Common Stock

Date	Explanation	Ref.	Debit	Credit	Balance
Jan. 1	Balance	√			660000

Paid-in Capital in Excess of Par Value - Preferred Stock

Date	Explanation	Ref.	Debit	Credit	Balance
Jan. 1	Balance	√			20000

Paid-in Capital in Excess of Stated Value - Common Stock

Date	Explanation	Ref.	Debit	Credit	Balance
Jan. 1	Balance	√			396000

Retained Earnings

Date	Explanation	Ref.	Debit	Credit	Balance
Jan. 1	Balance	√			488000

Treasury Stock - Common

Date	Explanation	Ref.	Debit	Credit	Balance
Jan. 1	Balance	√			30000

Paid-in Capital from Treasury Stock - Common

Date	Explanation	Ref.	Debit	Credit	Balance

(c)

Marya Corporation						
Balance Sheet (Partial)						
December 31, 2014						
Stockholders' equity						

(a)   General Journal

	Date	Account Titles	Ref.	Debit	Credit	
1	Feb. 1					1
2						2
3						3
4						4
5	Mar. 1					5
6						6
7						7
8						8
9	Apr. 1					9
10						10
11						11
12						12
13						13
14						14
15						15
16	July 1					16
17						17
18						18
19						19
20						20
21						21
22						22
23	31					23
24						24
25						25
26						26
27						27
28	Dec. 1					28
29						29
30						30
31						31
32	31					32
33						33
34						34
35	31					35
36						36
37						37
38	31					38
39						39
40						40

(b)

Common Stock

Date	Explanation	Ref.	Debit	Credit	Balance
Jan. 1	Balance	√			1 0 0 0 0 0 0

Common Stock Dividends Distributable

Date	Explanation	Ref.	Debit	Credit	Balance

Paid-in Capital in Excess of Par Value - Common Stock

Date	Explanation	Ref.	Debit	Credit	Balance
Jan. 1	Balance	√			2 0 0 0 0 0

Retained Earnings

Date	Explanation	Ref.	Debit	Credit	Balance
Jan. 1	Balance	√			8 4 0 0 0 0

Cash Dividends

Date	Explanation	Ref.	Debit	Credit	Balance

Stock Dividends

Date	Explanation	Ref.	Debit	Credit	Balance

(c)

	Dixon Corporation						
	Balance Sheet (Partial)						
	December 31, 2014						
1	Stockholders' equity						
2							
3							
4							
5							
6							
7							
8							
9							
10							
11							
12							
13							
14							
15							
16							
17							
18							
19							
20							
21							
22							
23							
24							
25							
26							
27							
28							
29							
30							
31							
32							
33							
34							
35							
36							
37							
38							
39							
40							

(a)

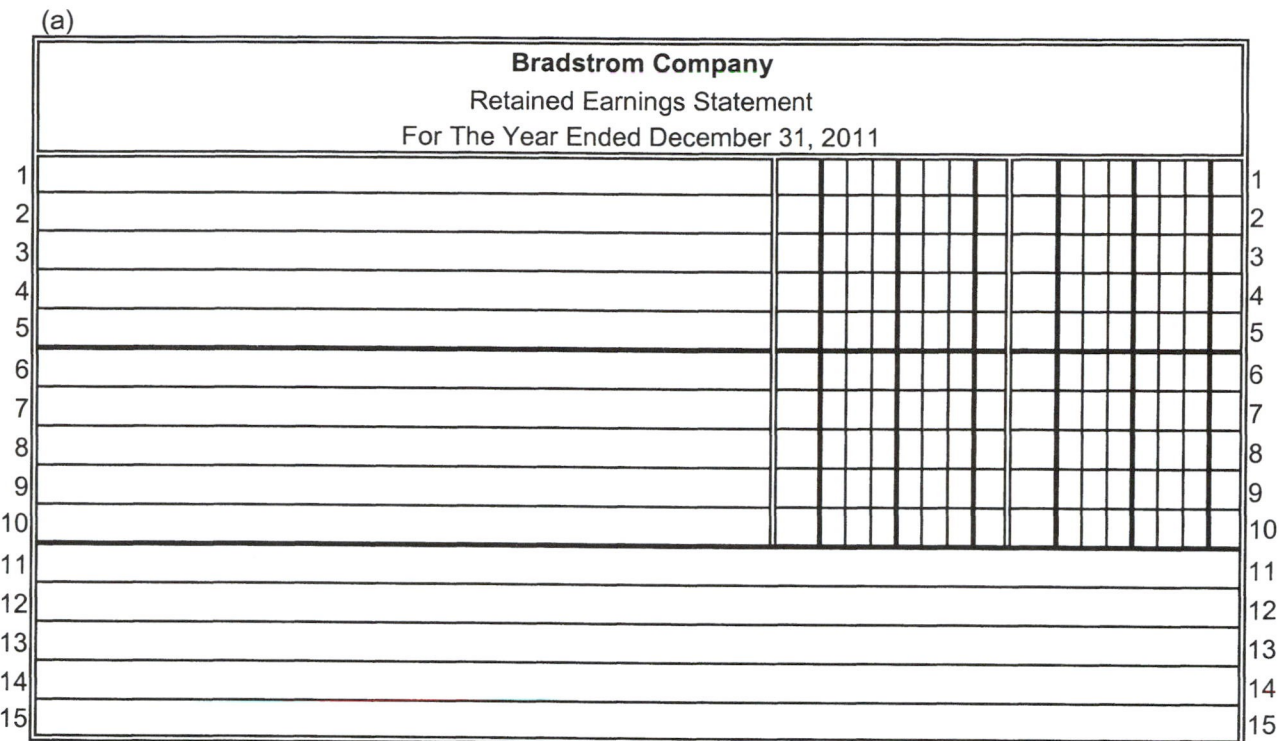

Bradstrom Company
Retained Earnings Statement
For The Year Ended December 31, 2011

(b)

	Andes Company																
	Partial Balance Sheet																
	December 31, 2014																

Stockholders' equity

(a)

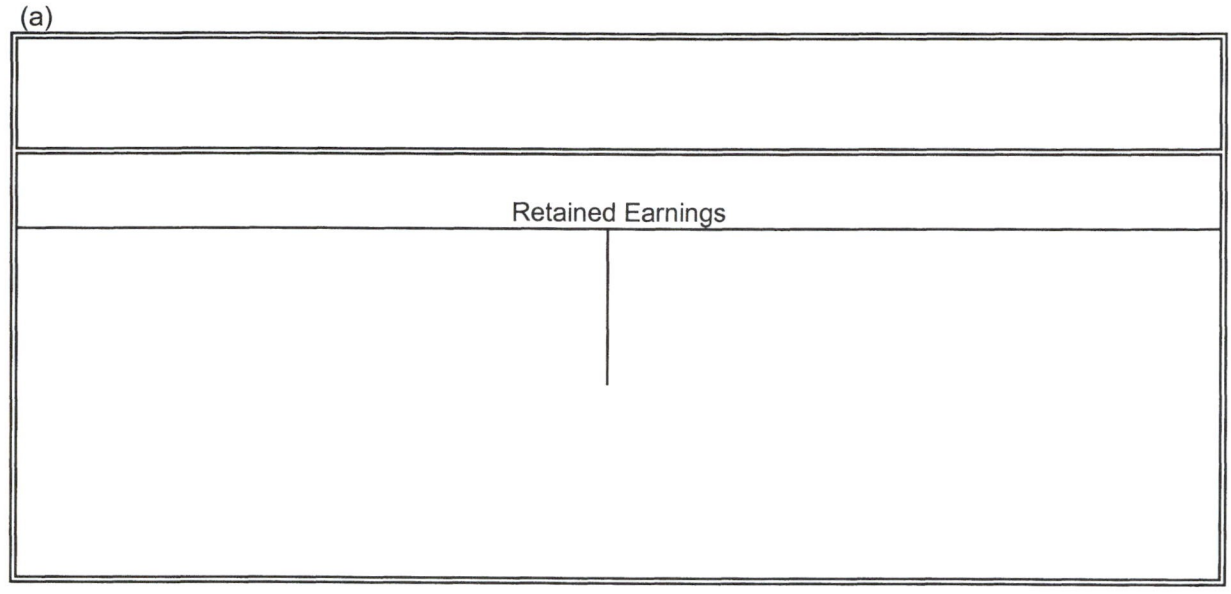

Retained Earnings

(b)

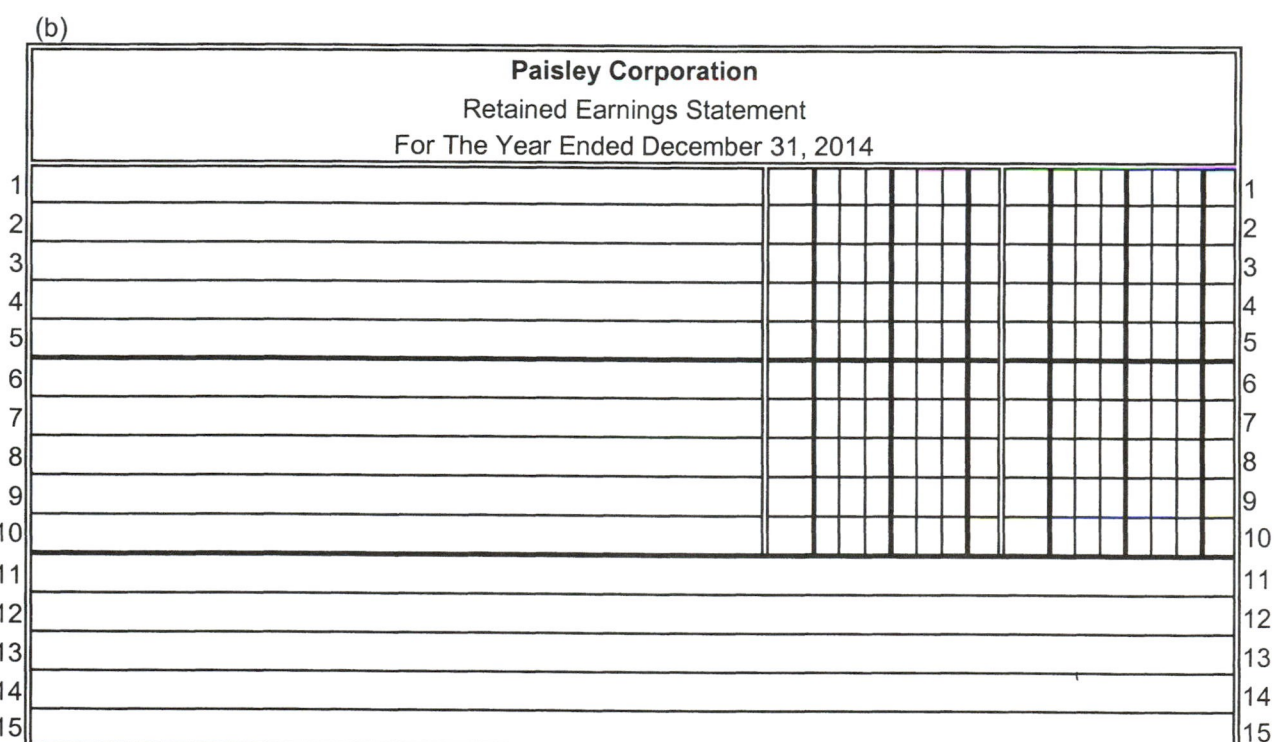

Paisley Corporation
Retained Earnings Statement
For The Year Ended December 31, 2014

1		
2		
3		
4		
5		
6		
7		
8		
9		
10		
11		
12		
13		
14		
15		

(c)

	Paisley Corporation Partial Balance Sheet December 31, 2014							
1	Stockholders' equity								1
2									2
3									3
4									4
5									5
6									6
7									7
8									8
9									9
10									10
11									11
12									12
13									13
14									14
15									15
16									16
17									17
18									18
19									19
20									20
21									21
22									22
23									23
24									24
25									25
26									26
27									27
28									28
29									29
30									30
31									31
32									32
33									33
34	(d)								34
35									35
36									36
37									37
38									38
39									39
40									40

(a)

Crivello Corporation
Partial Balance Sheet
December 31, 2014

(b)

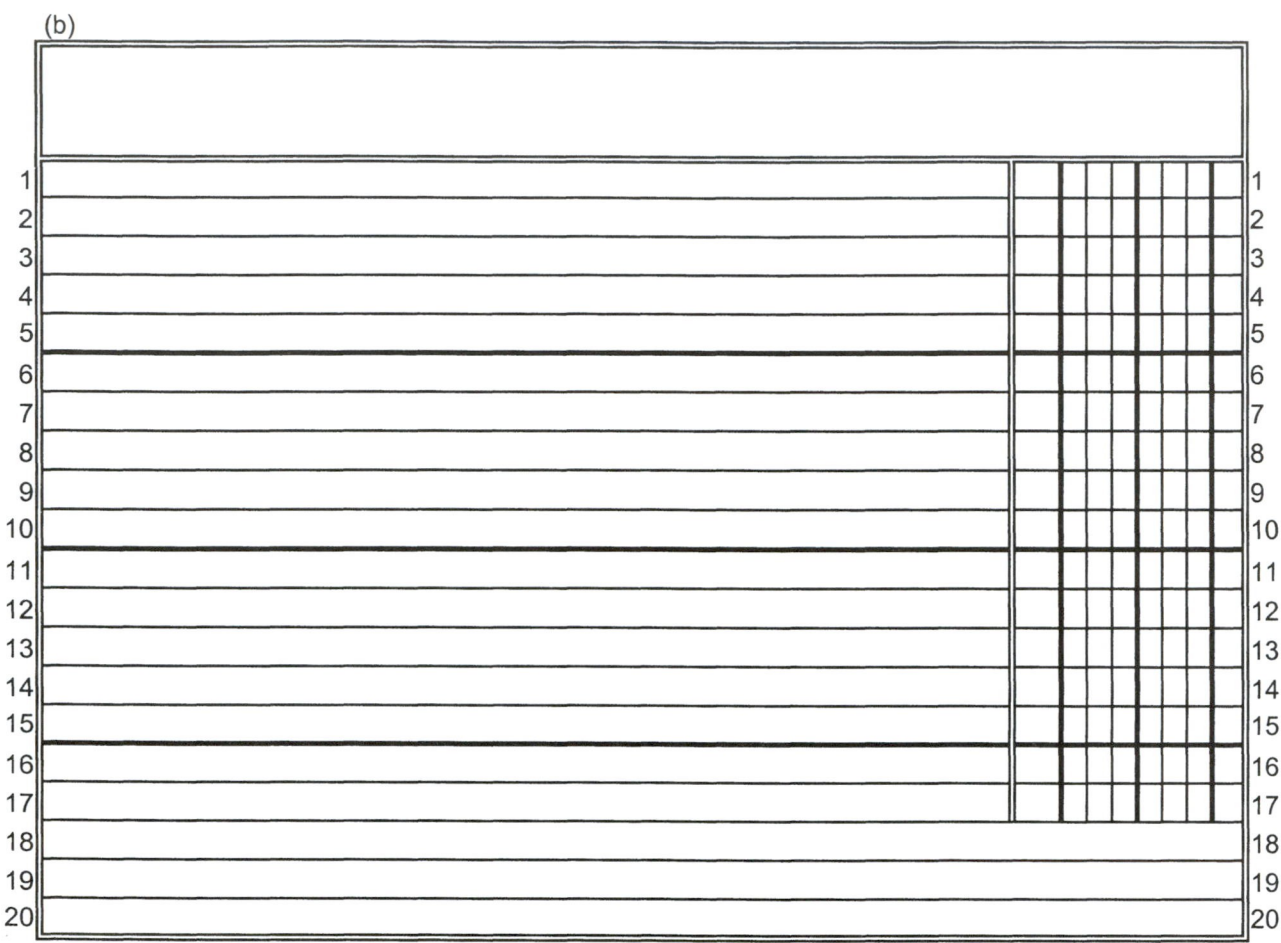

(a)

		Account Titles	Debit	Credit	
1	1.				1
2					2
3					3
4					4
5	2.				5
6					6
7					7
8					8
9	3.				9
10					10
11					11
12	4.				12
13					13
14					14
15	5.				15
16					16
17					17
18	6.				18
19					19
20					20
21	7.				21
22					22
23					23
24	8.				24
25					25
26					26
27	9.				27
28					28
29					29
30	10.				30
31					31
32					32
33	11.				33
34					34
35					35
36					36
37					37
38					38
39					39
40					40

(a)   (Continued)

		Account Titles	Debit	Credit	
1		Adjusting Entries			1
2	1.				2
3					3
4					4
5	2.				5
6					6
7					7
8	3.				8
9					9
10					10
11	4.				11
12					12
13					13
14	5.				14
15					15
16					16
17					17
18					18
19					19
20					20
21					21
22					22
23					23
24					24
25					25
26					26
27					27
28					28
29					29
30					30
31					31
32					32
33					33
34					34
35					35
36					36
37					37
38					38
39					39
40					40

(b)

Voltaire Corporation
Adjusted Trial Balance
12/31/14

Account	Debit	Credit

(c)   Optional T Accounts

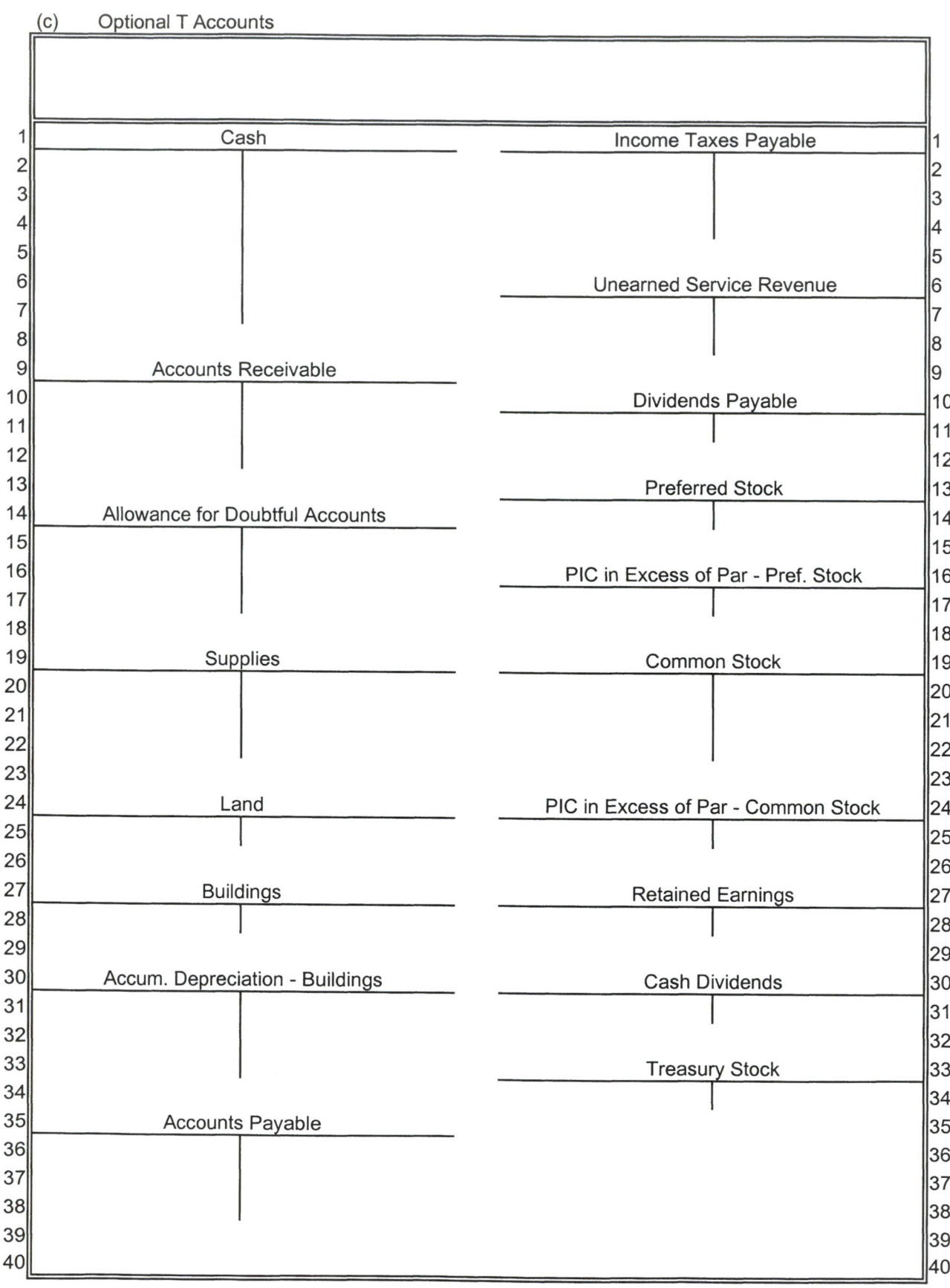

	Cash		Income Taxes Payable
1			
2			
3			
4			
5			
6			Unearned Service Revenue
7			
8			
9	Accounts Receivable		
10			Dividends Payable
11			
12			
13			Preferred Stock
14	Allowance for Doubtful Accounts		
15			
16			PIC in Excess of Par - Pref. Stock
17			
18			
19	Supplies		Common Stock
20			
21			
22			
23			
24	Land		PIC in Excess of Par - Common Stock
25			
26			
27	Buildings		Retained Earnings
28			
29			
30	Accum. Depreciation - Buildings		Cash Dividends
31			
32			
33			Treasury Stock
34			
35	Accounts Payable		
36			
37			
38			
39			
40			

(c)   Optional T Accounts (Continued)

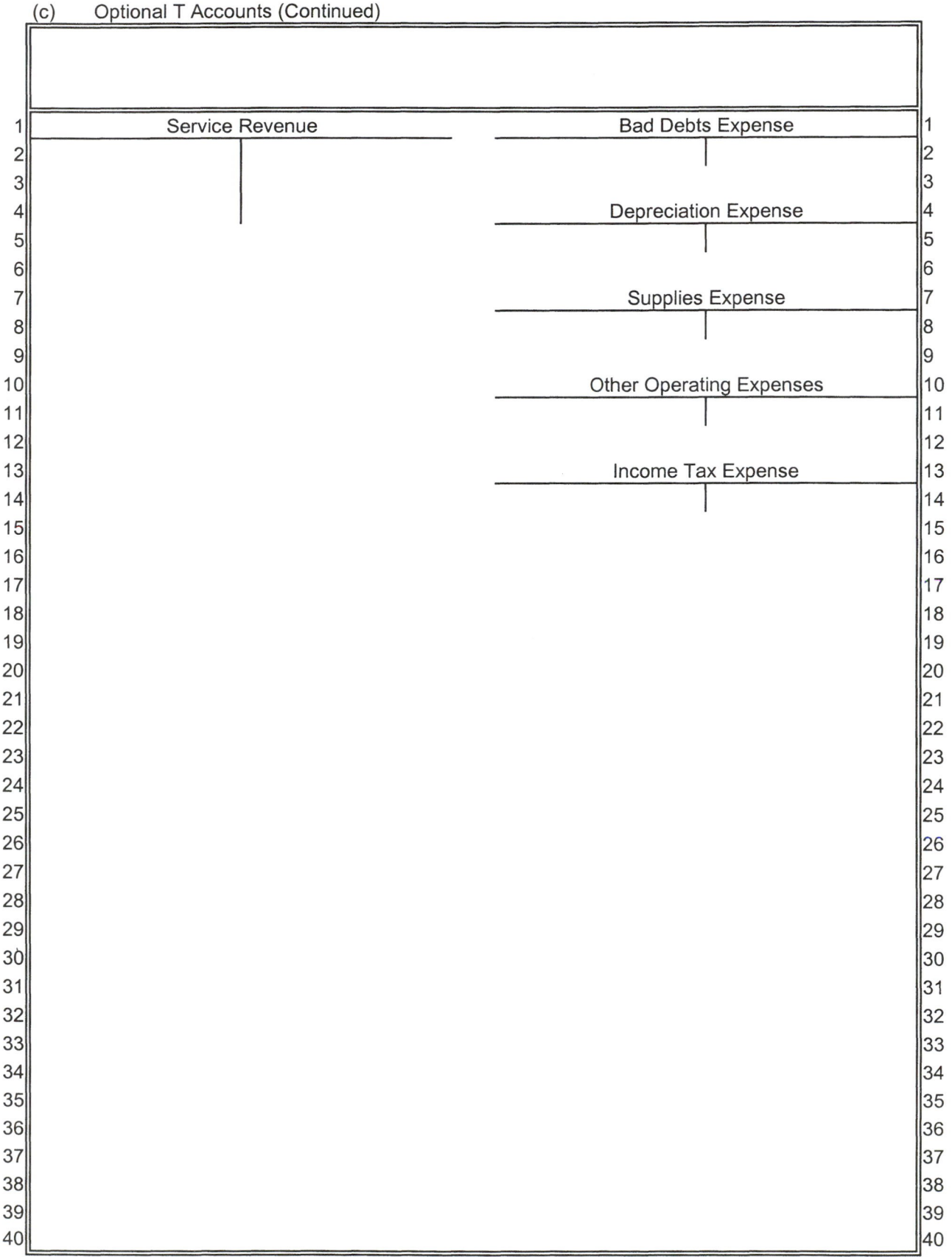

Service Revenue

Bad Debts Expense

Depreciation Expense

Supplies Expense

Other Operating Expenses

Income Tax Expense

(d)

Voltaire Corporation
Income Statement
For the Year Ending 12/31/14

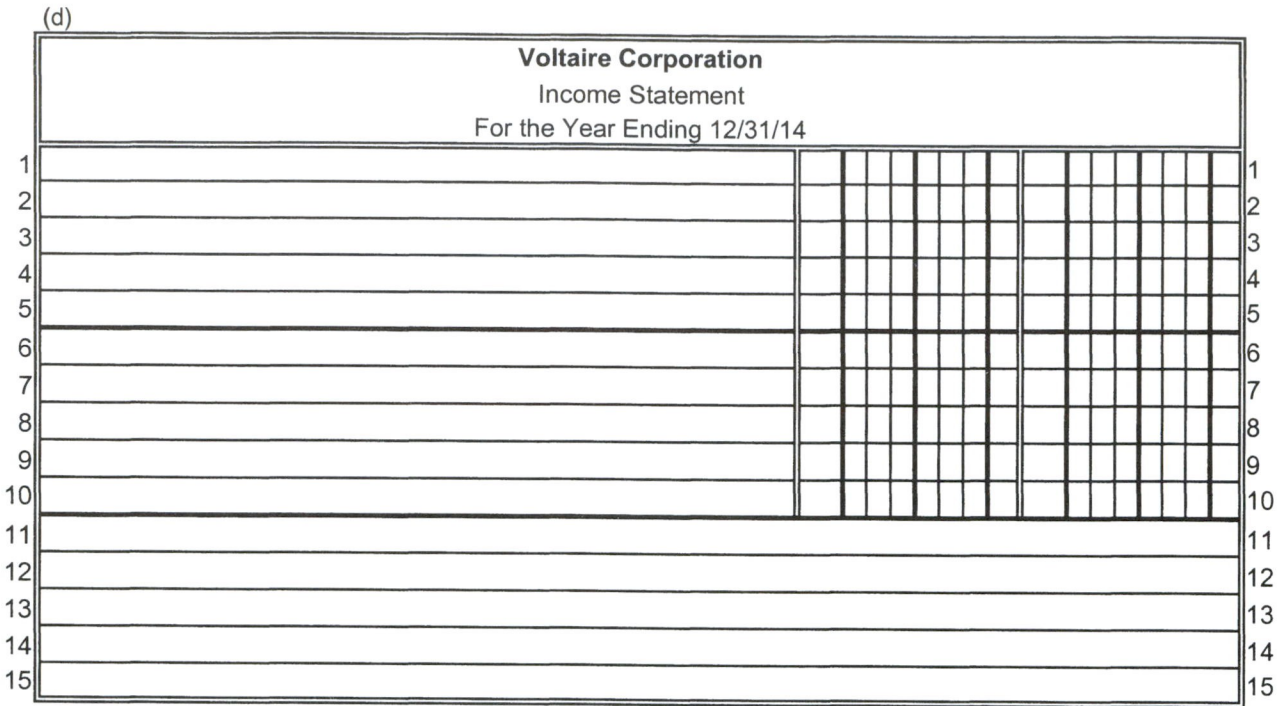

Voltaire Corporation
Retained Earnings Statement
For the Year Ending 12/31/14

(d)   (Continued)

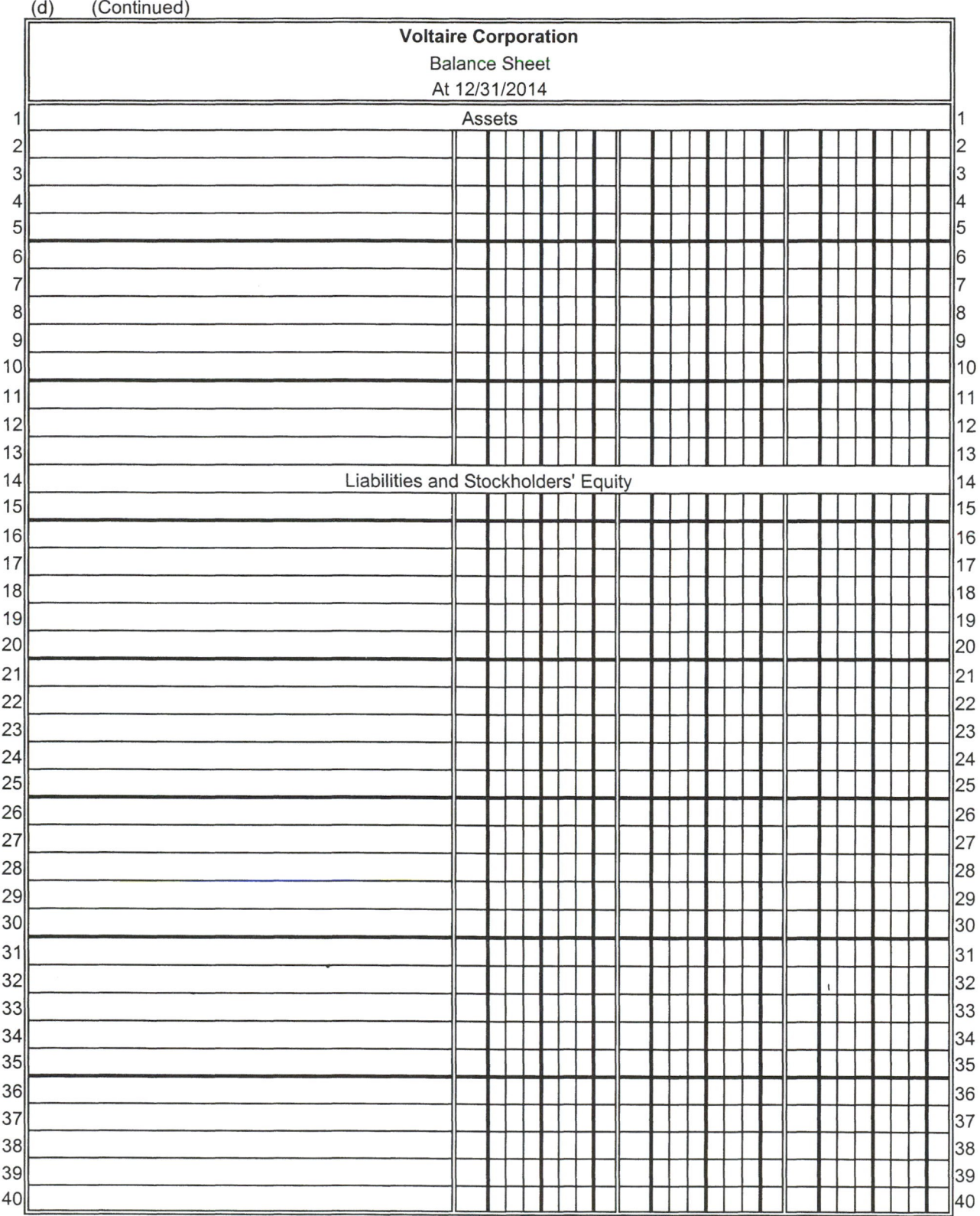

Voltaire Corporation
Balance Sheet
At 12/31/2014

Assets

Liabilities and Stockholders' Equity

		2010	2009
(a)			
(b)			
(c)		2010	2009
*(d)		2010	2009
(e)			

IFRS11-1

	Date	Account Titles	Debit	Credit	
1	May 10				1
2					2
3					3
4					4

IFRS11-2

5			5

Ingram Corporation

Partial Statement of Financial Position

December 31, 2014

9	Equity		9
10			10
11			11
12			12
13			13
14			14
15			15
16			16
17			17

IFRS11-3

	Date	Account Titles	Debit	Credit	
20	Mar. 2				20
21					21
22					22
23					23
24	June 12				24
25					25
26					26
27					27
28	July 11				28
29					29
30					30
31					31
32	Nov. 28				32
33					33
34					34
35					35
36					36
37					37
38					38
39					39
40					40

IFRS11-4

	Account Titles	Debit	Credit	
1	(a)			1
2				2
3				3
4				4

	(b)	IFRS	GAAP	
5	(b)	IFRS	GAAP	5
6				6
7				7
8				8
9				9
10				10
11				11
12				12

13	(c)		13
14			14
15			15
16			16
17	(d)	Return on ordinary shareholders' equity:	17
18			18
19			19
20			20
21			21
22			22
23			23
24			24
25	(e)	Earnings per share:	25
26			26
27			27
28			28
29			29
30			30
31			31
32			32
33			33
34			34
35			35
36			36
37			37
38			38
39			39
40			40

BE12-1

	Date	Account Titles	Debit	Credit	
1					1
2	Jan 1				2
3					3
4					4
5	July 1				5
6					6
7					7
8	**BE12-2**				8
9	Aug 1				9
10					10
11					11
12	Dec 1				12
13					13
14					14
15					15
16	**BE12-3**				16
17	Dec 31				17
18					18
19					19
20	31				20
21					21
22					22
23	**BE12-4**				23
24	Dec 31				24
25					25
26					26
27					27
28	**BE12-5**	Balance Sheet			28
29					29
30					30
31					31
32		Income Statement			32
33					33
34					34
35					35
36	**BE12-6**				36
37	Date	Account Titles	Debit	Credit	37
38	Dec 31				38
39					39
40					40

BE12-7

Balance Sheet

1		1
2		2
3		3
4		4
5		5
6		6
7		7
8		8
9		9

BE12-8

Balance Sheet

10		10
11		11
12		12
13		13
14		14
15		15
16		16
17		17
18		18
19		19
20		20
21		21
22		22
23		23
24		24
25		25
26		26
27		27
28		28
29		29
30		30
31		31
32		32
33		33
34		34
35		35
36		36
37		37
38		38
39		39
40		40

*BE12-9

	Paula Company	Shannon Company	Eliminations		Consolidated Data
			Debit	Credit	
1 Investment in Shannon Common Stock					
2 Common Stock					
3 Retained Earnings					
4					
5					

*BE12-10

	Paula Company	Shannon Company	Eliminations		Consolidated Data
			Debit	Credit	
1 Investment in Shannon Common Stock					
2 Excess of Cost Over Book Value					
3 Common Stock					
4 Retained Earnings					
5					
6					
7					
8					
9					
10					

DO IT! 12-1

	Date	Account Titles	Debit	Credit	
1	(a)				1
2	Jan 1				2
3					3
4					4
5	July 1				5
6					6
7					7
8	1				8
9					9
10					10
11					11
12	(b)				12
13	Dec 31				13
14					14
15					15
16					16
17	**DO IT! 12-2**				17
18	1.				18
19	June 17				19
20					20
21					21
22	Sept 3				22
23					23
24					24
25	2.				25
26	Jan 1				26
27					27
28					28
29	May 15				29
30					30
31					31
32	Dec 31				32
33					33
34					34
35					35
36					36
37					37
38					38
39					39
40					40

DO IT! 12-3

	Account Titles	Debit	Credit	
1	Trading Securities:			1
2				2
3				3
4				4
5				5
6	Non-trading Securities:			6
7				7
8				8
9				9
10				10

DO IT! 12-4

	Item	Financial Statement	Category	
14				14
15	1. Loss on sale of investments in stock			15
16				16
17				17
18	2. Unrealized gain on non-trading securities			18
19				19
20	3. Market adjustment - trading			20
21				21
22	4. Interest earned on investments in bonds			22
23				23
24	5. Unrealized loss on trading securities			24
25				25

E12-2

	Date	Account Titles	Debit	Credit	
1	(a)				1
2	Jan 1				2
3					3
4					4
5	July 1				5
6					6
7					7
8	1				8
9					9
10					10
11					11
12	(b)				12
13	Dec 31				13
14					14
15					15

E12-3

		Account Titles	Debit	Credit	
1		January 1, 2011			1
2					2
3					3
4					4
5		July 1, 2011			5
6					6
7					7
8					8
9		December 31, 2011			9
10					10
11					11
12					12
13		January 1, 2012			13
14					14
15					15
16					16
17		January 1, 2012			17
18					18
19					19
20					20

E12-4

	Date	Account Titles	Debit	Credit	
1	(a)				1
2	Feb 1				2
3					3
4					4
5	July 1				5
6					6
7					7
8	Sept 1				8
9					9
10					10
11					11
12	Dec 1				12
13					13
14					14
15					15
16	(b)				16
17					17
18					18

E12-5

	Date	Account Titles	Debit	Credit	
1	Jan 1				1
2					2
3					3
4	July 1				4
5					5
6					6
7	Dec 1				7
8					8
9					9
10					10
11	31				11
12					12
13					13
14					14
15					15

E12-6

	Account Titles	Debit	Credit	
1	February 1			1
2				2
3				3
4				4
5	March 20			5
6				6
7				7
8				8
9				9
10	April 25			10
11				11
12				12
13				13
14	June 15			14
15				15
16				16
17				17
18				18
19	July 28			19
20				20
21				21

E12-7

	Date	Account Titles	Debit	Credit	
1	(a)				1
2	Jan 1				2
3					3
4					4
5	Dec 31				5
6					6
7					7
8	31				8
9					9
10					10
11	(b)				11
12					12
13					13
14					14

	Date	Account Titles	Debit	Credit	
1	(a)				1
2	Mar 18				2
3					3
4					4
5	June 30				5
6					6
7					7
8	Dec 31				8
9					9
10					10
11	(b)				11
12	Jan 1				12
13					13
14					14
15	June 15				15
16					16
17					17
18	Dec 31				18
19					19
20					20

E12-10

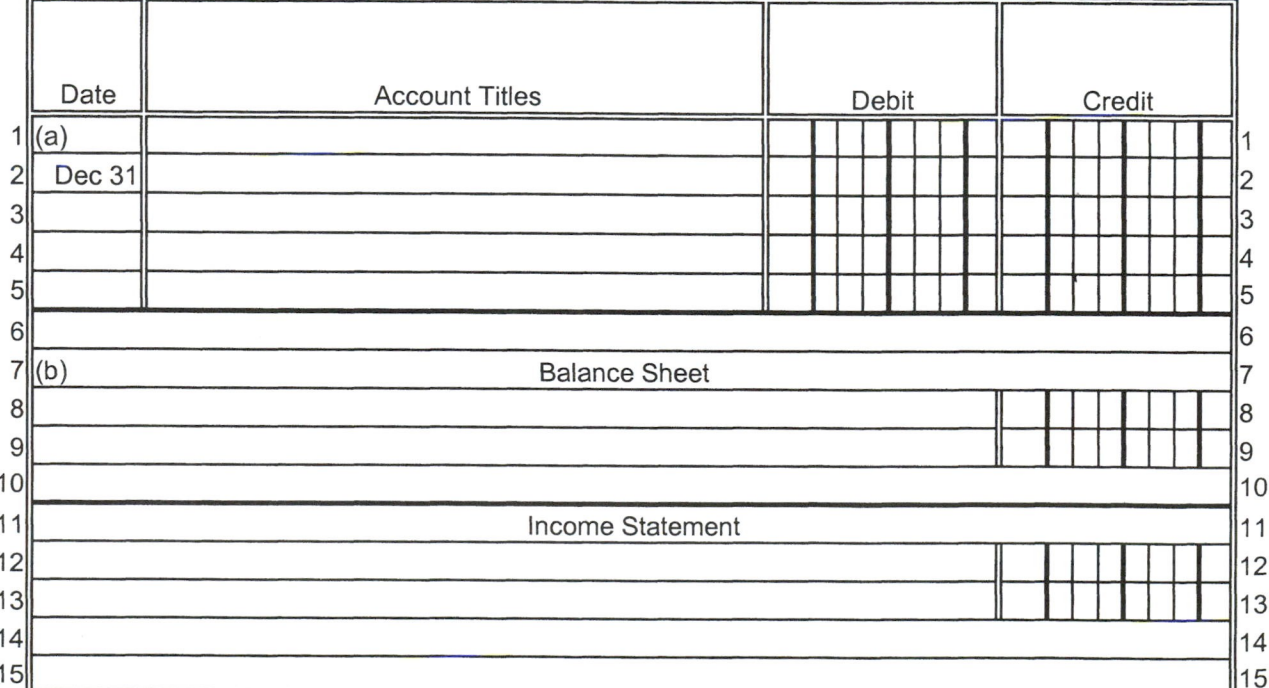

	Date	Account Titles	Debit	Credit	
1	(a)				1
2	Dec 31				2
3					3
4					4
5					5
6					6
7	(b)	Balance Sheet			7
8					8
9					9
10					10
11		Income Statement			11
12					12
13					13
14					14
15					15

(a)

	Date	Account Titles	Debit	Credit	
1	Dec 31				1
2					2
3					3
4					4
5					5

(b)

	Balance Sheet		
1			1
2			2
3			3
4			4
5			5
6			6

(c)

1		1
2		2
3		3
4		4
5		5
6		6
7		7
8		8
9		9
10		10
11		11
12		12
13		13
14		14
15		15
16		16
17		17
18		18
19		19

(a)

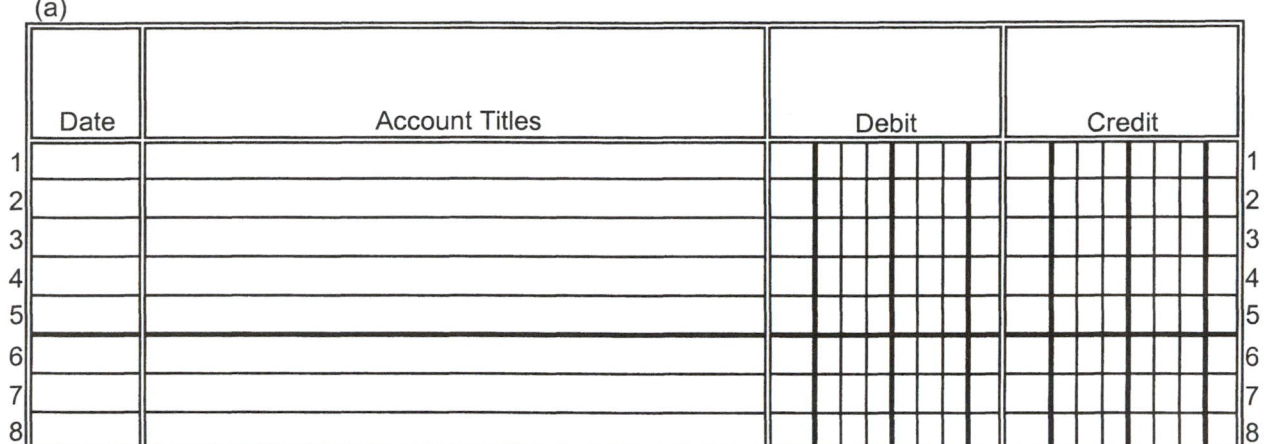

	Date	Account Titles	Debit	Credit	
1					1
2					2
3					3
4					4
5					5
6					6
7					7
8					8

(b)

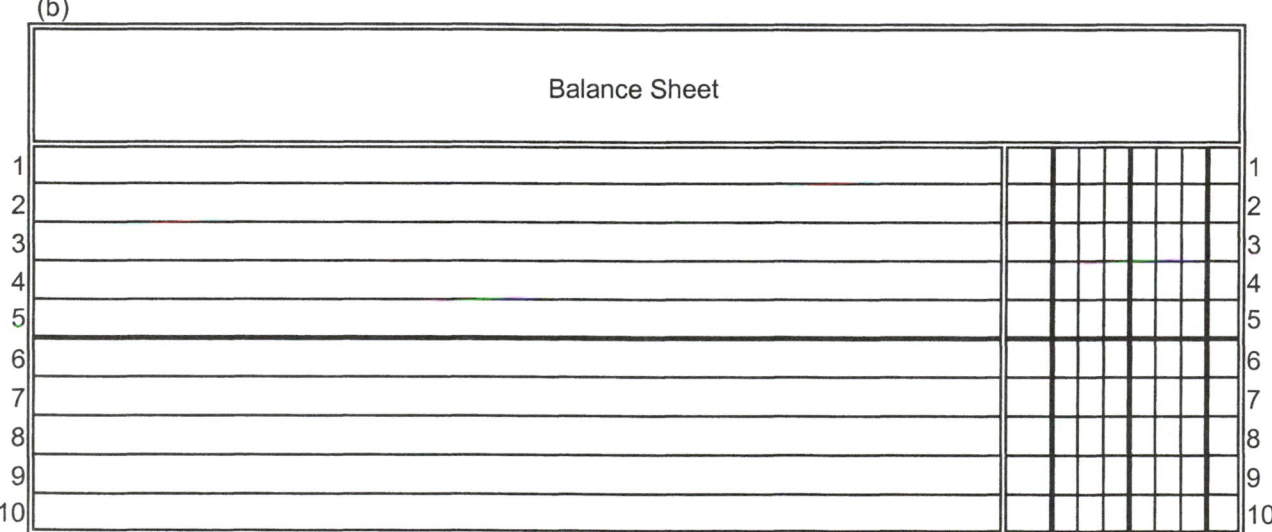

Balance Sheet

1		1
2		2
3		3
4		4
5		5
6		6
7		7
8		8
9		9
10		10

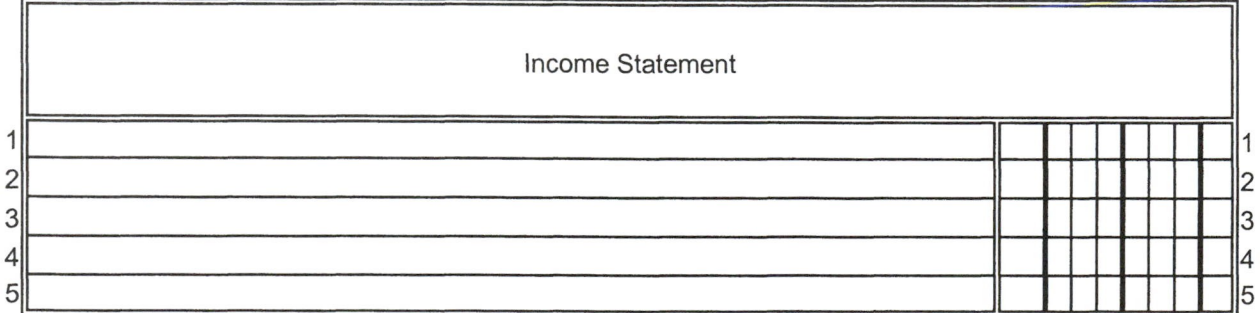

Income Statement

1		1
2		2
3		3
4		4
5		5

Lennon Corporation and Subsidiary
Worksheet - Consolidated Balance Sheet
January 1, 2014

	Lennon Corporation	Ono Inc.	Eliminations Dr.	Eliminations Cr.	Consolidated Data
Assets					
1 Current assets	600000	500000			
2 Investment in Ono Inc. common stock	2200000				
3 Plant and equipment (net)	3000000	2200000			
4 Totals	5800000	2700000			
5					
6 **Liabilities and Stockholders' Equity**					
7 Current liabilities	1800000	500000			
8 Common stock - Lennon Corp.	2300000				
9 Common Stock - Ono Inc.		800000			
10 Retained earnings - Lennon Corp.	1700000				
11 Retained earnings - Ono Inc.		1400000			
12 Totals	5800000	2700000			
13					
14					
15					
16					
17					
18					
19					
20					
21					

Lennon Corporation and Subsidiary

Work Sheet - Consolidated Balance Sheet

January 1, 2014

	Lennon Corporation	Ono Inc.	Eliminations Dr.	Eliminations Cr.	Consolidated Data	
Assets						
1 Current assets	5 5 0 0 0 0	5 0 0 0 0				1
2 Investment in Ono Inc. common stock	2 2 5 0 0 0					2
3 Plant and equipment (net)	3 0 0 0 0 0	2 2 0 0 0 0				3
4 Excess of cost over book value						4
5 Totals	5 8 0 0 0 0	2 7 0 0 0 0				5
6						6
7 Liabilities and Stockholders' Equity						7
8 Current liabilities	1 8 0 0 0 0	5 0 0 0 0				8
9 Common stock - Lennon Corp.	2 3 0 0 0 0					9
10 Common stock - Ono Inc.		8 0 0 0 0				10
11 Retained earnings - Lennon Corp.	1 7 0 0 0 0 0					11
12 Retained earnings - Ono Inc.		1 4 0 0 0 0				12
13 Totals	5 8 0 0 0 0	2 7 0 0 0 0				13
14						14
15						15
16						16
17						17
18						18
19						19
20						20

(a) & (b)

	Date	Account Titles	Debit	Credit	
1	(a) 2014				1
2	Jan 1				2
3					3
4					4
5	July 1				5
6					6
7					7
8	Dec 31				8
9					9
10					10
11	2017				11
12	Jan 1				12
13					13
14					14
15	1				15
16					16
17					17
18					18
19	July 1				19
20					20
21					21
22	Dec 31				22
23					23
24					24
25	(b) 2014				25
26	Dec 31				26
27					27

(c)

Pagnucci Carecenters Inc.
Balance Sheet (Partial)
December 31, 2014

1		1
2		2
3		3
4		4
5		5
6		6
7		7
8		8

(a)

	Date	Account Titles	Debit	Credit	
1	Feb 1				1
2					2
3					3
4	Mar 1				4
5					5
6					6
7	Apr 1				7
8					8
9					9
10	July 1				10
11					11
12					12
13	Aug 1				13
14					14
15					15
16					16
17	Sept 1				17
18					18
19					19
20	Oct 1				20
21					21
22					22
23	1				23
24					24
25					25
26					26
27					27
28					28
29					29
30					30

STOCK INVESTMENTS	DEBT INVESTMENTS

(b)

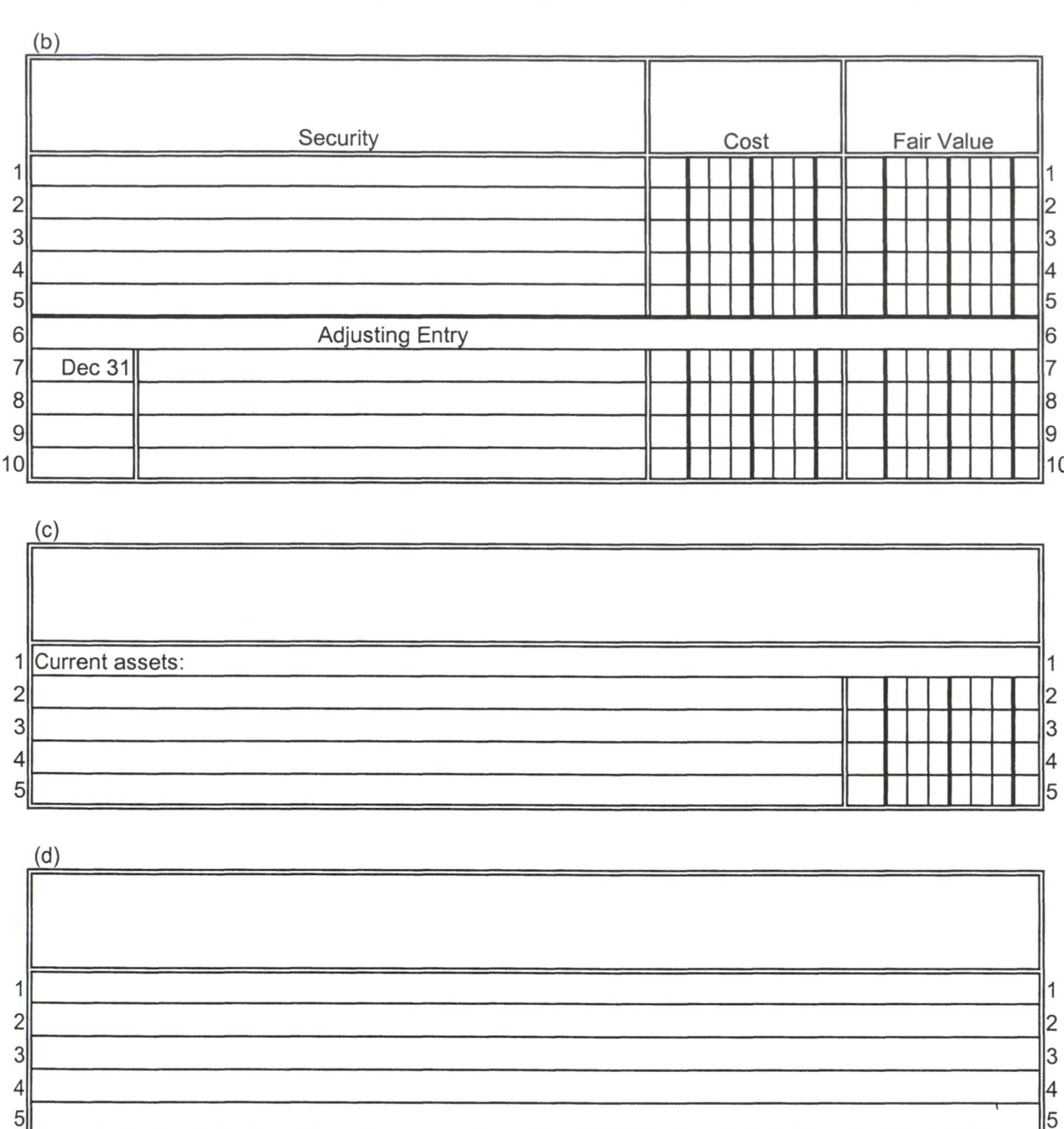

	Security	Cost	Fair Value	
1				1
2				2
3				3
4				4
5				5
6	Adjusting Entry			6
7	Dec 31			7
8				8
9				9
10				10

(c)

1	Current assets:		1
2			2
3			3
4			4
5			5

(d)

1		1
2		2
3		3
4		4
5		5

(a)

	Date	Account Titles	Debit	Credit	
1	July 1				1
2					2
3					3
4	Aug 1				4
5					5
6					6
7	Sept 1				7
8					8
9					9
10					10
11	Oct 1				11
12					12
13					13
14					14
15	Nov 1				15
16					16
17					17
18	Dec 15				18
19					19
20					20
21	31				21
22					22
23					23
24					24
25					25

STOCK INVESTMENTS

1/1/15 Bal   135,000

(b)

Security	Cost	Fair Value
1		
2		
3		
4		
5		
6		
7		

	Adjusting Entry		
9	Dec 31		
10			
11			
12			

(c)

Ogallala Associates
Balance Sheet (Partial)
December 31, 2015

Assets		
Investments		

Liabilities and Stockholders' Equity		
Stockholders' equity		

	Date	Account Titles	Debit	Credit	
1	(a)				1
2	Jan 1				2
3					3
4					4
5	Mar 15				5
6					6
7					7
8	June 15				8
9					9
10					10
11	Sept 15				11
12					12
13					13
14	Dec 15				14
15					15
16					16
17	31				17
18					18
19					19
20	(b)				20
21	Jan 1				21
22					22
23					23
24	Mar 15				24
25					25
26					26
27	June 15				27
28					28
29					29
30	Sept 15				30
31					31
32					32
33	Dec 15				33
34					34
35					35
36	31				36
37					37
38					38
39					39
40					40

(c)

	Cost Method	Equity Method
1		
2		
3		
4		
5		
6		
7		
8		
9		
10		
11		
12		
13		
14		
15		
16		
17		
18		
19		
20		
21		
22		
23		
24		
25		
26		
27		
28		
29		
30		
31		
32		
33		
34		
35		

(a)

	Date	Account Titles	Debit	Credit	
1	Jan 20				1
2					2
3					3
4					4
5	28				5
6					6
7					7
8	30				8
9					9
10					10
11	Feb 8				11
12					12
13					13
14	18				14
15					15
16					16
17					17
18	July 30				18
19					19
20					20
21	Sept 6				21
22					22
23					23
24	Dec 1				24
25					25
26					26
27					27

(b)

INVESTMENT IN REGINALD CORPORATION
COMMON STOCK

1/1 Bal 52,000

INVESTMENT IN ELDERBERRY CORPORATION
COMMON STOCK

1/1 Bal 84,000

(b) (Continued)

INVESTMENT IN MATTOON CORPORATION
PREFERRED STOCK

| 1/1 Bal | 33,600 | |

INVESTMENT IN HACHITO CORPORATION
COMMON STOCK

(c)

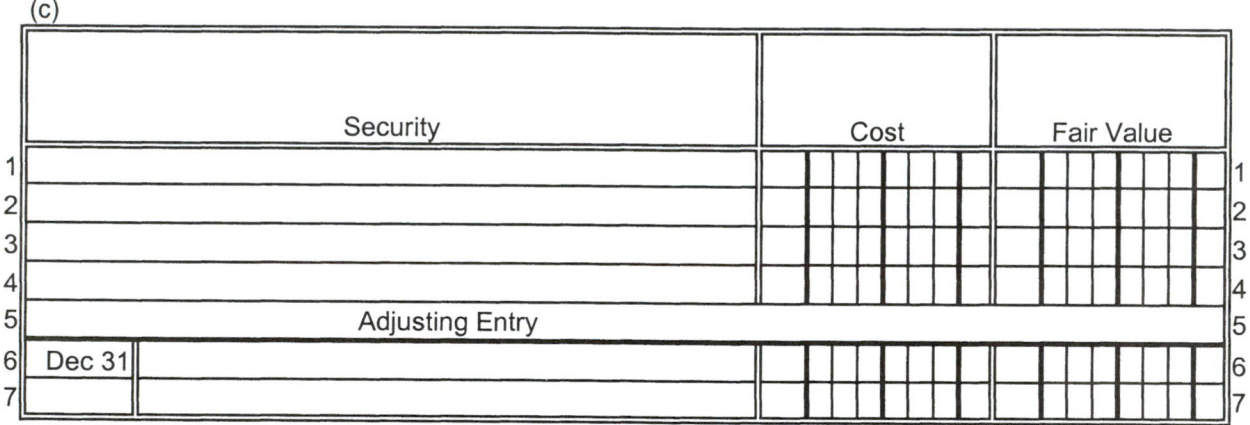

Security	Cost	Fair Value
1		
2		
3		
4		
5 Adjusting Entry		
6 Dec 31		
7		

(d)

Amberwood Company
Balance Sheet (Partial)
December 31, 2014

Assets	
Investments	
Liabilities and Stockholder's Equity	
Stockholders' Equity	

	Radar Corporation																		
	Balance Sheet																		
	December 31, 2014																		
1	Assets																		1
2																			2
3																			3
4																			4
5																			5
6																			6
7																			7
8																			8
9																			9
10																			10
11																			11
12																			12
13																			13
14																			14
15																			15
16																			16
17																			17
18																			18
19																			19
20																			20
21																			21
22																			22
23																			23
24																			24
25																			25
26																			26
27																			27
28																			28
29																			29
30																			30
31																			31
32																			32
33																			33
34																			34
35																			35
36																			36
37																			37
38																			38
39																			39
40																			40

Radar Corporation							
Balance Sheet (continued)							
December 31, 2014							
Liabilities and Stockholders' Equity							

(a)

General Journal

Date	Account Titles		Debit	Credit
2014				
Dec. 31		1		
		2		
		3		
		4		
		5		

(b)

Robinson Corporation and Subsidiary
Work Sheet - Consolidated Balance Sheet
December 31, 2014

	Robinson Corporation	Hoffman Plastics	Eliminations Dr.	Eliminations Cr.	Consolidated Data	
Assets						
Current assets	255000	435500				1
Investment in Hoffman Plastics common stock	1225000					2
Plant and equipment (net)	2100000	676000				3
Excess of cost over book value of subsidiary						4
Totals	3580000	1111500				5
						6
Liabilities and Stockholders' Equity						7
Current liabilities	578000	92500				8
Common stock - Robinson Corporation	1950000					9
Common stock - Hoffman Plastics		525000				10
Retained earnings - Robinson Corporation	1052000					11
Retained earnings - Hoffman Plastics		494000				12
Totals	3580000	1111500				13
						14

Robinson Corporation and Subsidiary

Condensed Balance Sheet

December 31, 2014

Assets			

Liabilities and Stockholders' Equity			

(a) & (b)

	Date	Account Titles	Debit	Credit	
1	(a) 2014				1
2	Jan 1				2
3					3
4					4
5	July 1				5
6					6
7					7
8	Dec 31				8
9					9
10					10
11	2017				11
12	Jan 1				12
13					13
14					14
15	1				15
16					16
17					17
18					18
19	July 1				19
20					20
21					21
22	Dec 31				22
23					23
24					24
25	(b) 2014				25
26	Dec 31				26
27					27

(c)

(a)

	Date	Account Titles	Debit	Credit	
1	Feb 1				1
2					2
3					3
4	Mar 1				4
5					5
6					6
7	Apr 1				7
8					8
9					9
10	July 1				10
11					11
12					12
13	Aug 1				13
14					14
15					15
16					16
17	Sept 1				17
18					18
19					19
20	Oct 1				20
21					21
22					22
23	1				23
24					24
25					25
26					26
27					27
28					28
29					29
30					30

STOCK INVESTMENTS	DEBT INVESTMENTS

(b)

Security	Cost	Fair Value
Adjusting Entry		
Dec 31		

(c)

Current assets:	

(d)

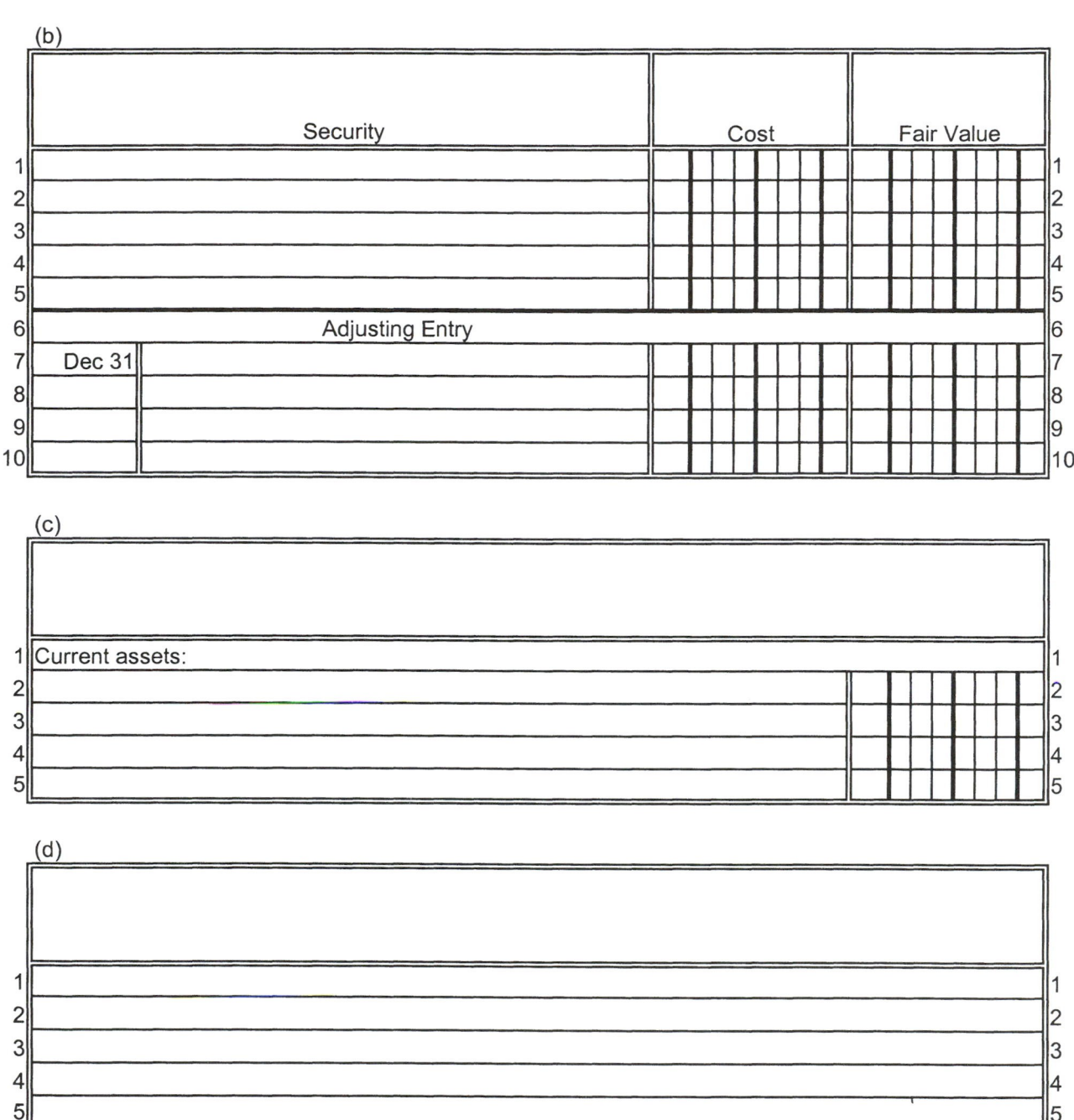

(a)

	Date	Account Titles	Debit	Credit	
1	July 1				1
2					2
3					3
4	Aug 1				4
5					5
6					6
7	Sept 1				7
8					8
9					9
10					10
11	Oct 1				11
12					12
13					13
14					14
15	Nov 1				15
16					16
17					17
18	Dec 15				18
19					19
20					20
21	31				21
22					22
23					23
24					24
25					25

STOCK INVESTMENTS

1/1/15 Bal 190,000

(b)

Security	Cost	Fair Value
1			1
2			2
3			3
4			4
5			5
6			6
7			7

	Adjusting Entry		
9	Dec 31			9
10				10
11				11
12				12

(c)

Eli Associates
Balance Sheet (Partial)
December 31, 2014

Assets		
2	Investments		2
3			3
4			4
5			5
6			6

Liabilities and Stockholders' Equity		
8	Stockholders' equity		8
9			9
10			10
11			11
12			12
13			13
14			14
15			15

	Date	Account Titles	Debit	Credit	
1	(a) 2014				1
2	Jan 1				2
3					3
4					4
5	June 30				5
6					6
7					7
8	Dec 31				8
9					9
10					10
11					11
12	31				12
13					13
14					14
15					15
16					16
17					17
18					18
19					19
20	(b) 2014				20
21	Jan 1				21
22					22
23					23
24	June 30				24
25					25
26					26
27	Dec 31				27
28					28
29					29
30	31				30
31					31
32					32
33					33
34					34
35					35
36					36
37					37
38					38
39					39
40					40

(c)

	Cost Method	Equity Method
1		
2		
3		
4		
5		
6		
7		
8		
9		
10		
11		
12		
13		
14		
15		
16		
17		
18		
19		
20		
21		
22		
23		
24		
25		
26		
27		
28		
29		
30		
31		
32		
33		
34		
35		

(a)

	Date	Account Titles	Debit	Credit	
1	Jan 7				1
2					2
3					3
4					4
5	10				5
6					6
7					7
8	26				8
9					9
10					10
11	Feb 2				11
12					12
13					13
14	10				14
15					15
16					16
17					17
18	July 1				18
19					19
20					20
21	Sept 1				21
22					22
23					23
24	Dec 15				24
25					25
26					26
27					27

(b)

INVESTMENT IN SASHA CORPORATION
COMMON STOCK

1/1 Bal	35,000	

INVESTMENT IN UKRAINE CORPORATION
COMMON STOCK

1/1 Bal	42,000	

(b) (Continued)

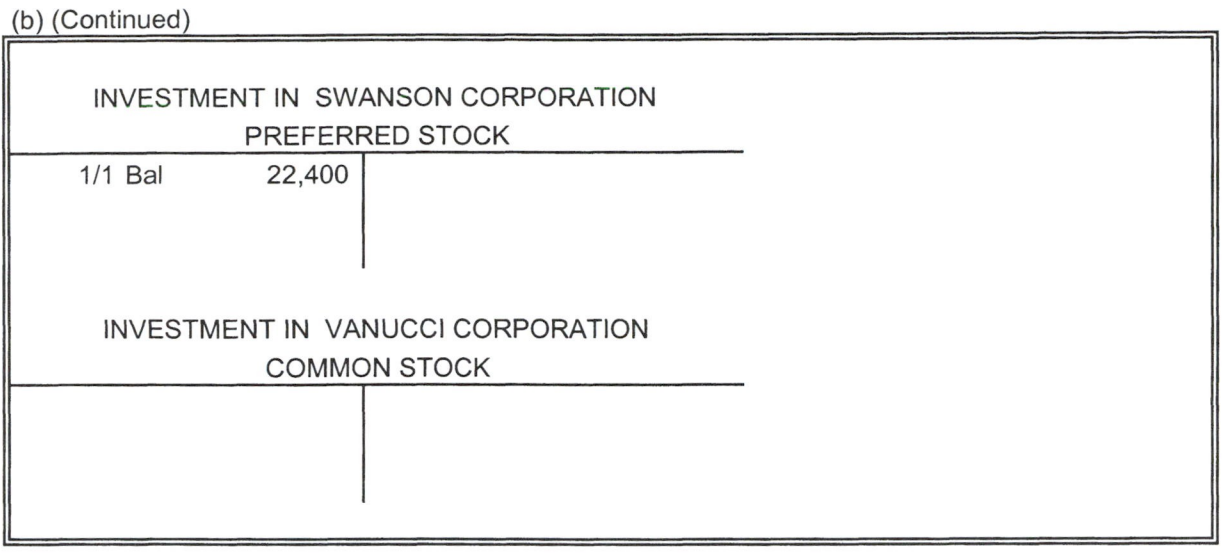

INVESTMENT IN SWANSON CORPORATION
PREFERRED STOCK

1/1 Bal   22,400

INVESTMENT IN VANUCCI CORPORATION
COMMON STOCK

(c)

	Security	Cost	Fair Value	
1				1
2				2
3				3
4				4
5	Adjusting Entry			5
6	Dec 31			6
7				7

(d)

	Verbitsky's Company BalanceSheet (Partial) December 31, 2014		
1	Assets		1
2	Investments		2
3			3
4			4
5			5
6	Liabilities and Stockholder's Equity		6
7	Stockholders' Equity		7
8			8
9			9
10			10
11			11
12			12

Redlands Corporation

Balance Sheet

December 31, 2014

Assets

	Redlands Corporation										
	Balance Sheet (continued)										
	December 31, 2014										
1	Liabilities and Stockholders' Equity										

*Problem 12-7B

Patel Company and Subsidiary

(a)

General Journal

	Date	Account Titles	Debit	Credit	
1	Dec. 31				1
2					2
3					3
4					4
5					5

(b)

Patel Company and Subsidiary
Work Sheet - Consolidated Balance Sheet
31-Dec-14

		Patel Company	Singh Company	Eliminations Debit	Eliminations Credit	Consolidated Data	
1	Current assets	768000	379000				1
2	Investment in Singh Company common stock	710000					2
3	Plant and equipment (net)	1882000	351000				3
4	Excess of cost over book value of subsidiary						4
5	Totals	3360000	730000				5
6							6
7	Liabilities and Stockholders' Equity						7
8	Current liabilities	870000	90000				8
9	Common stock - Patel Company	1947000					9
10	Common stock - Singh Company		360000				10
11	Retained earnings - Patel Company	543000					11
12	Retained earnings - Singh Company		280000				12
13	Totals	3360000	730000				13
14							14

Patel Company and Subsidiary

Condensed Balance Sheet

December 31, 2014

Assets

Liabilities and Stockholders' Equity

Part I

1	(a)	1
2		2
3		3
4		4
5		5
6		6
7		7
8		8
9		9
10		10
11		11
12		12
13		13
14		14
15		15
16		16
17		17
18		18
19		19
20		20
21		21
22		22
23		23
24		24
25		25
26		26
27		27
28		28
29		29
30		30
31		31
32		32
33		33
34		34
35		35
36		36
37		37
38		38
39		39
40		40

(a) (Continued)

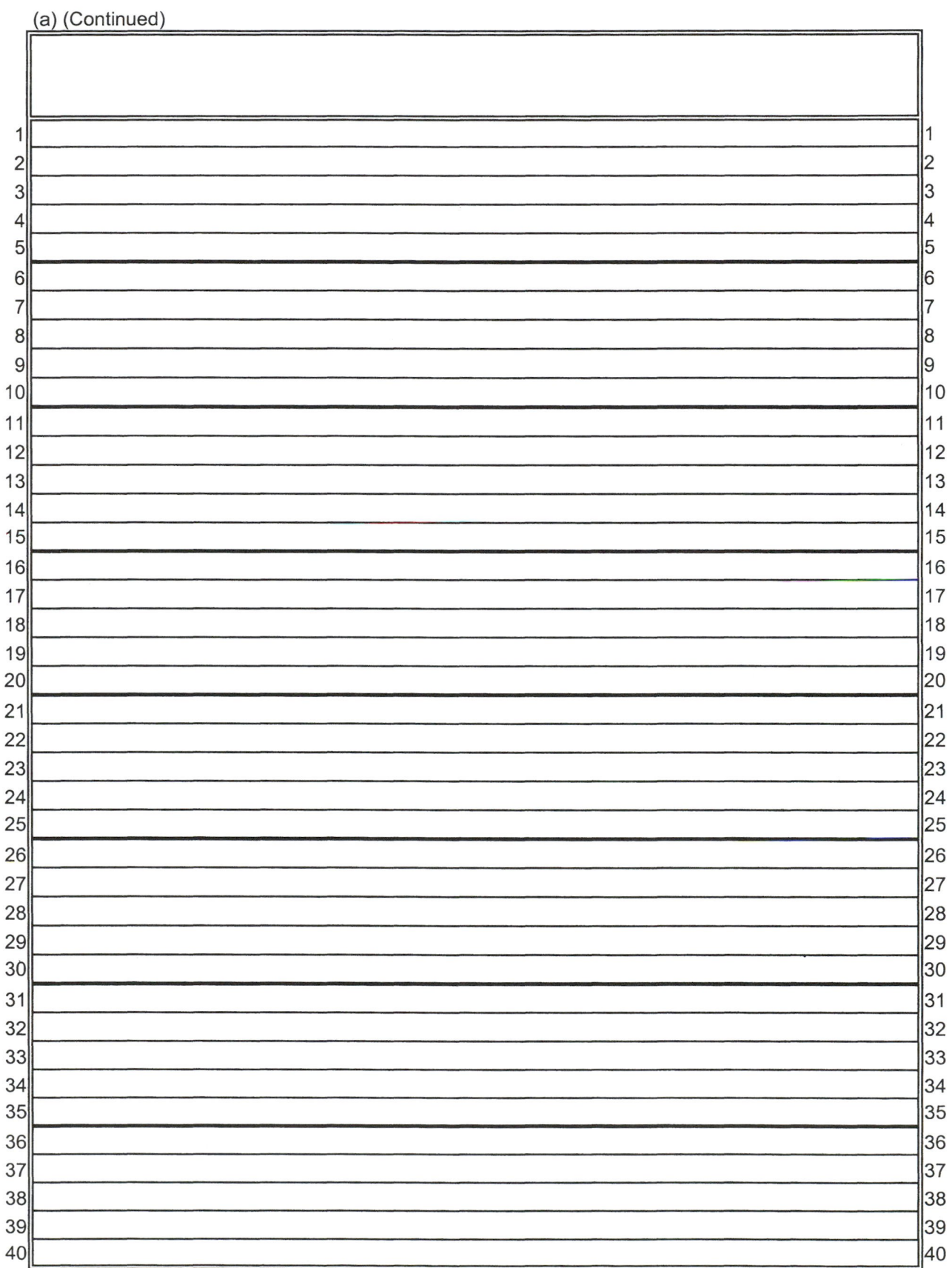

Part II

1	(b) Equity financing option:		1
2			2
3	Positives	Negatives	3
4			4
5			5
6			6
7			7
8			8
9			9
10	Debt financing option:		10
11			11
12	Positives	Negatives	12
13			13
14			14
15			15
16			16
17			17
18			18
19	Shares outstanding before financing		19
20			20

		Equity Financing	Debt Financing	
21				21
22				22
23	Income before interest and taxes			23
24	Interest expense			24
25	Income before taxes			25
26	Tax expense			26
27	Net income			27
28	Shares outstanding after financing			28
29	Earnings per share			29
30				30
31				31

Part III

	Date	Account Titles	Debit	Credit	
33					33
34	(c) (1)				34
35	6/12/13				35
36					36
37					37
38					38
39					39
40					40

Part III (Continued)

	Date	Account Titles	Debit	Credit	
1	7/21/13				1
2					2
3					3
4					4
5	7/27/14				5
6					6
7					7
8					8
9	7/31/14				9
10					10
11	8/15/14				11
12					12
13					13
14	12/4/14				14
15					15
16					16
17	12/14/14				17
18					18
19	12/24/14				19
20					20
21					21

	(2) Shares Issued and Outstanding		Number of Shares Issued	Total Shares Issued and Outstanding	
22					22
23					23
24					24
25	Date	Event			25
26	6/12/13				26
27	7/21/13				27
28	8/15/14				28
29					29

Part IV

	Date	Account Titles	Debit	Credit	
31	Date	Account Titles	Debit	Credit	31
32	(d) (1)				32
33	6/1/15				33
34					34
35					35
36					36
37					37
38					38
39					39
40					40

Part IV (Continued)

	Date	Account Titles	Debit	Credit	
1	(2)				1
2	12/1/15				2
3					3
4					4
5					5
6	(3)				6
7	12/31/15				7
8					8
9					9
10					10
11	(4)				11
12	6/1/16				12
13					13
14					14
15					15
16					16
17	Part V				17
18	(e) (1)				18
19	2013				19
20					20
21					21
22					22
23					23
24					24
25					25
26					26
27					27
28	2014				28
29					29
30					30
31					31
32					32
33					33
34	2015				34
35					35
36					36
37					37
38					38
39					39
40					40

Part V (Continued)

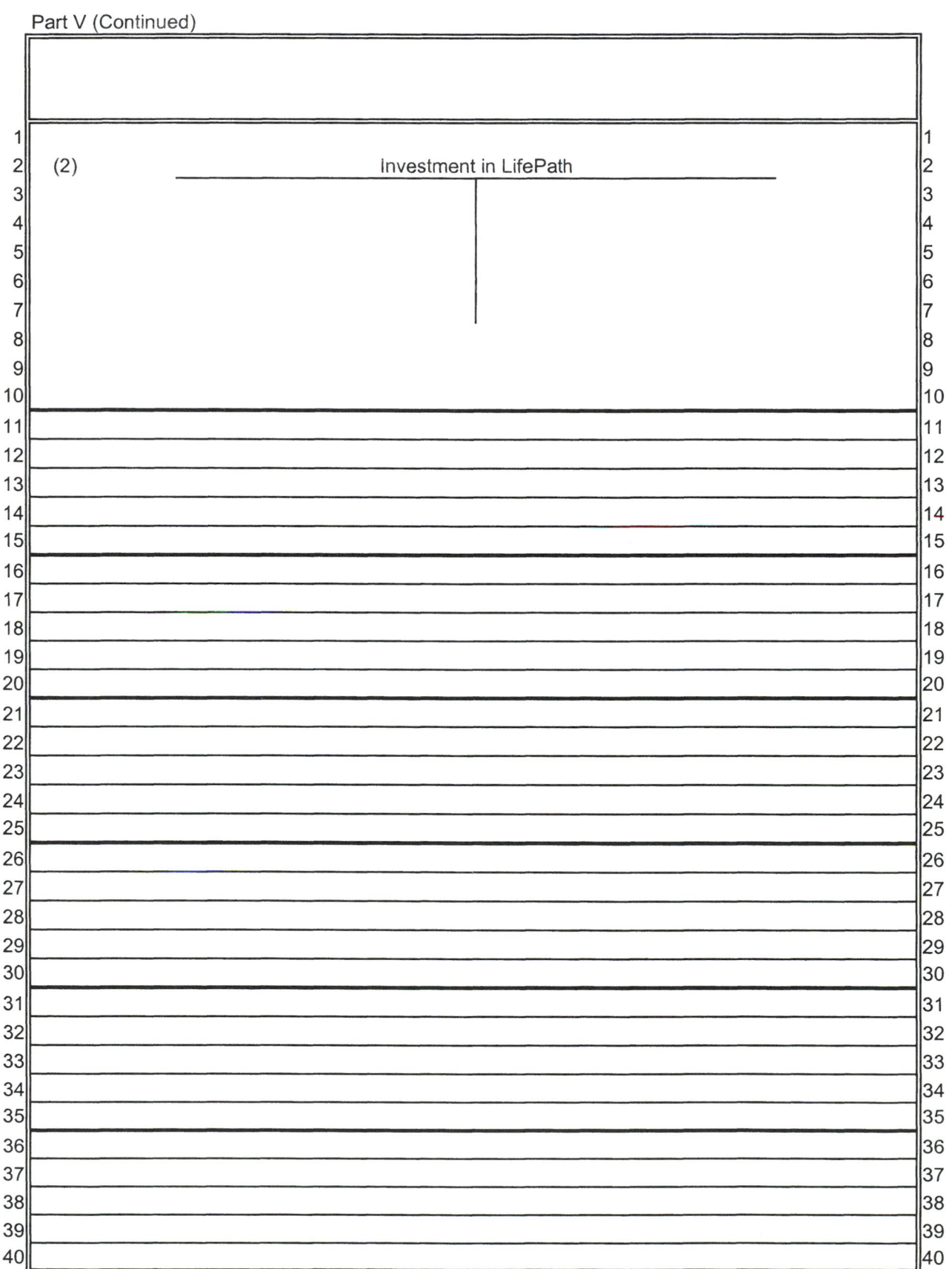

(2)   Investment in LifePath

(a)	(in millions)	PepsiCo	Coca-Cola
1.	Cash used for investing activities		
2.	Cash used for capital expenditures (spending)		

(b)

(a) & (b)

			1
			2
			3
			4
			5
			6
			7
			8
			9
			10
			11
			12
			13
			14
			15
			16
			17
			18
			19

Supporting Calculations

Entries for investment in UMW Company:

Account Titles	Debit	Credit
Acquisition		
Previous Years - Equity Method		
This Year - Equity Method		

(a) & (b) (Continued)

	Account Titles	Debit	Credit	
1				1
2	Sale of the UMW Company Stock			2
3				3
4				4
5				5
6				6
7				7
8				8
9				9
10				10
11				11
12				12
13				13
14				14
15				15
16				16
17				17
18				18
19				19
20				20
21				21
22				22
23				23
24				24
25				25
26				26
27				27
28				28
29				29
30				30
31				31
32				32
33				33
34				34
35				35
36				36
37				37
38				38
39				39
40				40

BE13-3

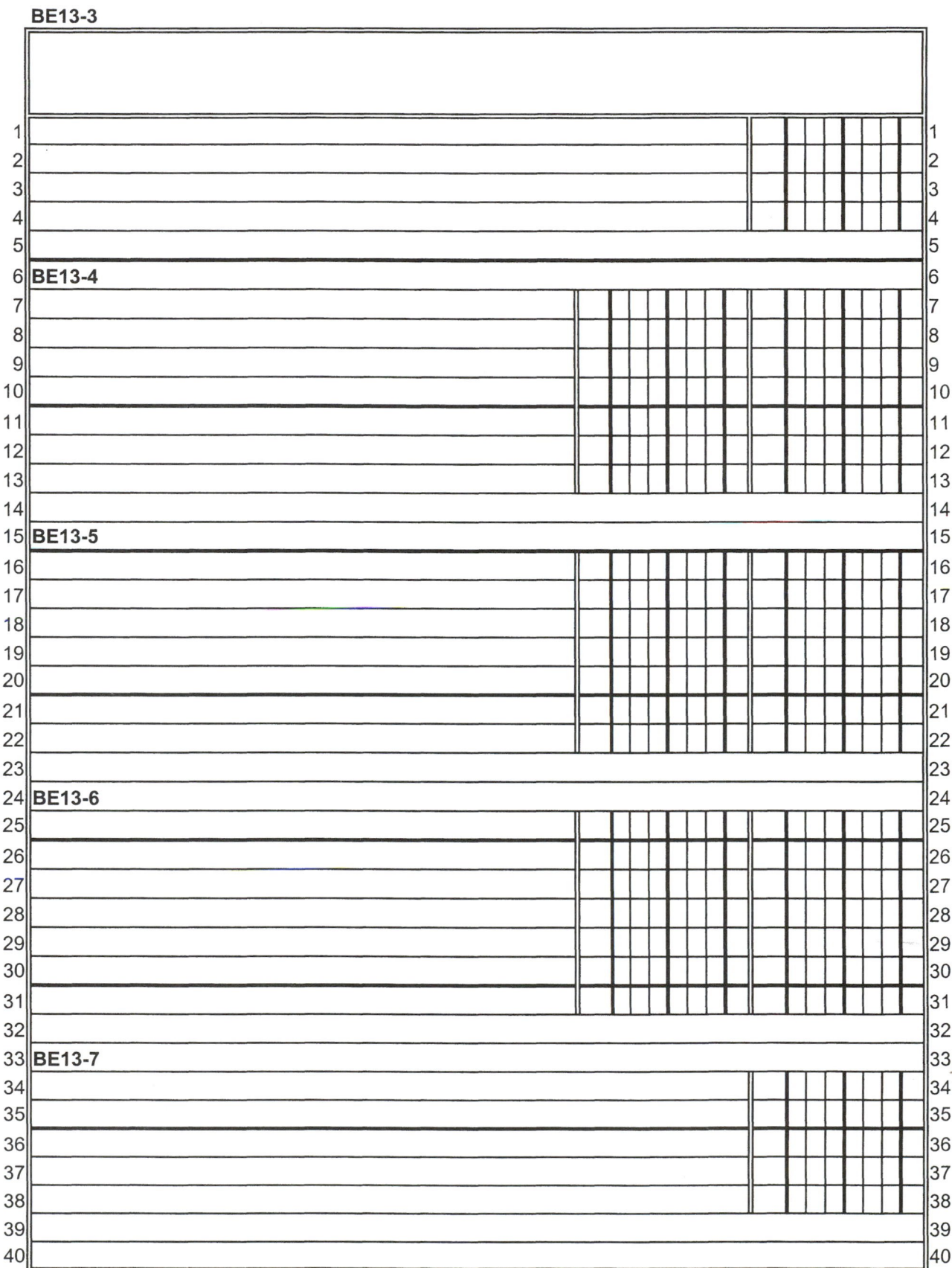

BE13-4

BE13-5

BE13-6

BE13-7

*BE13-12

		Balance 1/1/14		Reconciling Items		Balance 12/31/14	
				Debit	Credit		
1	Balance Sheet Accounts						1
2	Prepaid expenses	$	1 8 6 0 0				2
3	Accrued exp. payable		8 2 0 0				3
4							4
5							5
6	Statement of Cash Flow						6
7	Effects						7
8							8
9							9
10							10

		1
1		1
2		2
3		3
4		4
5		5
6		6
7		7
8		8
9		9
10		10
11		11
12		12
13		13
14		14
15		15
16		16
17		17
18		18
19		19
20		20
21		21
22		22
23		23
24		24
25		25
26		26
27		27
28		28
29		29
30		30
31		31
32		32
33		33
34		34
35		35
36		36
37		37
38		38
39		39
40		40

	Account Titles	Debit	Credit	
1	1.(a)			1
2				2
3				3
4				4
5	(b)			5
6				6
7				7
8	2.(a)			8
9				9
10				10
11	(b)			11
12				12
13				13
14	3.(a)			14
15				15
16				16
17	(b)			17
18				18
19				19
20	4.(a)			20
21				21
22				22
23	(b)			23
24				24
25				25
26				26
27				27
28				28
29				29
30				30
31				31
32				32

E13-3 (Continued)

		Account Titles	Debit	Credit	
1	5.(a)				1
2					2
3					3
4					4
5	(b)				5
6					6
7					7
8					8
9					9
10	6.(a)				10
11					11
12					12
13					13
14					14
15	(b)				15
16					16
17					17
18					18
19					19
20					20

E13-4

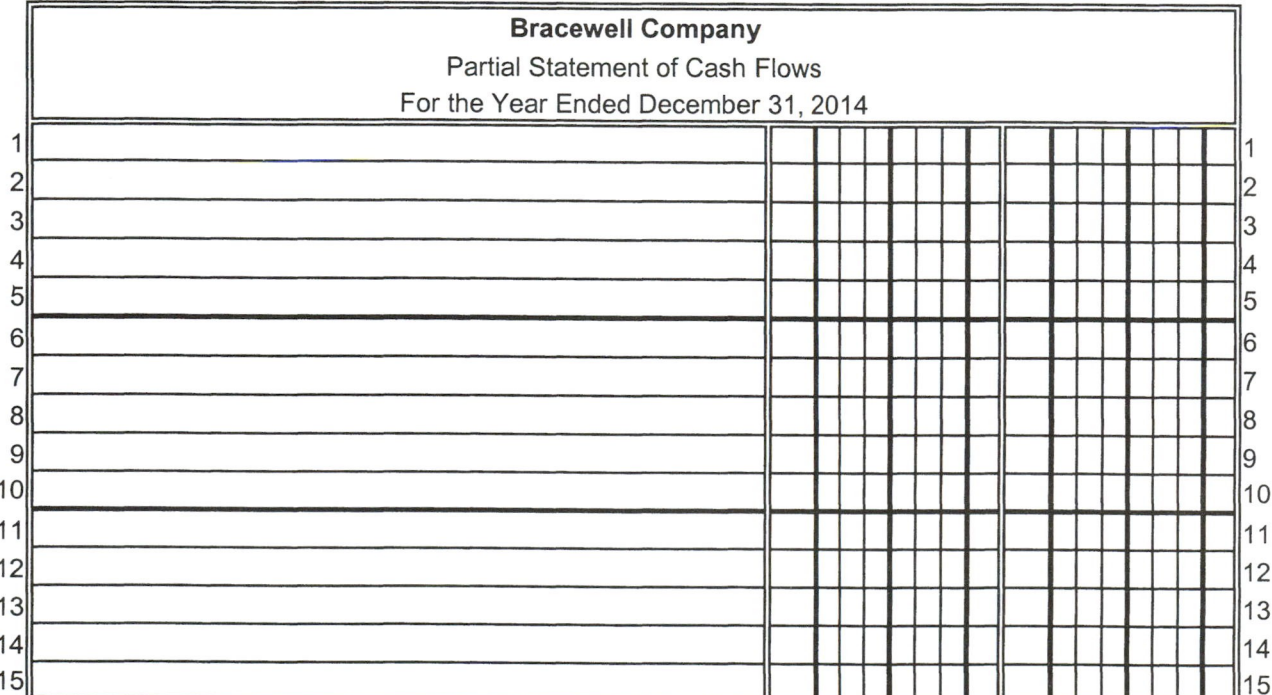

Bracewell Company

Partial Statement of Cash Flows

For the Year Ended December 31, 2014

E13-5   Indirect

Nasreen Inc.

Partial Statement of Cash Flows

For the Year Ended December 31, 2014

1		
2		
3		
4		
5		
6		
7		
8		
9		
10		
11		
12		

E13-6   Indirect

Chaudry Corp.

Partial Statement of Cash Flows

Foe the Year Ended December 31, 2014

1		
2		
3		
4		
5		
6		
7		
8		
9		
10		
11		
12		
13		
14		
15		
16		
17		
18	Cash proceeds from sale of equipment calculations:	
19		
20		
21		
22		
23		

(a)   Indirect

Meera Corporation			
Statement of Cash Flows			
For the Year Ended December 31, 2014			

1			
2			
3			
4			
5			
6			
7			
8			
9			
10			
11			
12			
13			
14			
15			
16			
17			
18			
19			
20			
21			
22			
23			
24			
25			
26			
27			
28			
29			
30			

(b)   Free cash flow:

Indirect

Syal Company Statement of Cash Flows For the Year Ended December 31, 2014			
1			
2			
3			
4			
5			
6			
7			
8			
9			
10			
11			
12			
13			
14			
15			
16			
17			
18			
19			
20			
21			
22			
23			
24			
25			
26			
27			
28			
29			
30			
31			
32			
33			
34			
35			
36			
37			
38			
39			
40			

(a)   Indirect

Cassandra Corporation

Statement of Cash Flows

For the Year Ended December 31, 2014

1		
2		
3		
4		
5		
6		
7		
8		
9		
10		
11		
12		
13		
14		
15		
16		
17		
18		
19		
20		
21		
22		
23		
24		
25		
26		
27		
28		
29		
30		
31		
32		
33		
34		
35 (b)	Free cash flow:	
36		
37		
38		
39		
40		

Erisa Magambo Company

Worksheet - Statement of Cash Flows

For the Year Ended December 31, 2014

Bal. Sheet Accounts	Balance 12/31/13	Reconciling Items Debit	Reconciling Items Credit	Balance 12/31/14
Debits				
Cash	22 000			58 000
Accounts receivable	76 000			85 000
Inventory	187 000			180 000
Land	100 000			75 000
Equipment	200 000			250 000
Totals	585 000			648 000
Credits				
Accum. depr. - equip.	42 000			66 000
Accts. Pay.	45 000			34 000
Bonds payable	200 000			150 000
Common stock	164 000			214 000
Retained earnings	134 000			184 000
Totals	585 000			648 000
Stmt. of Cash Flows				
Effects				

*E13-11

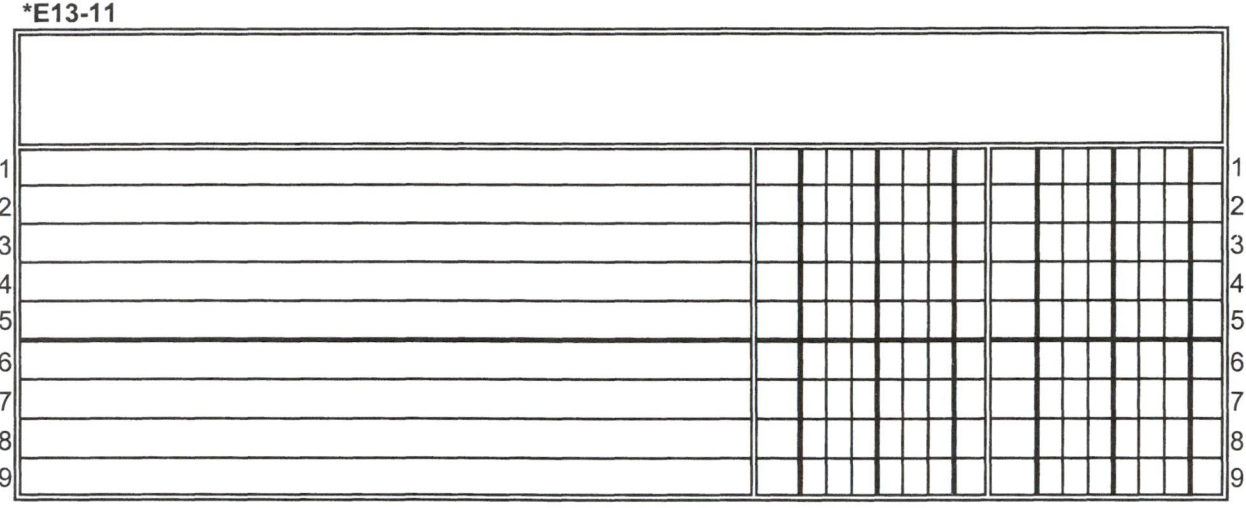

Helpful T-accounts:

Accounts Receivable

Accounts Payable

*E13-13   Direct

Liz Ten Transport
Partial Statement of Cash Flows
For the Year Ended December 31, 2014

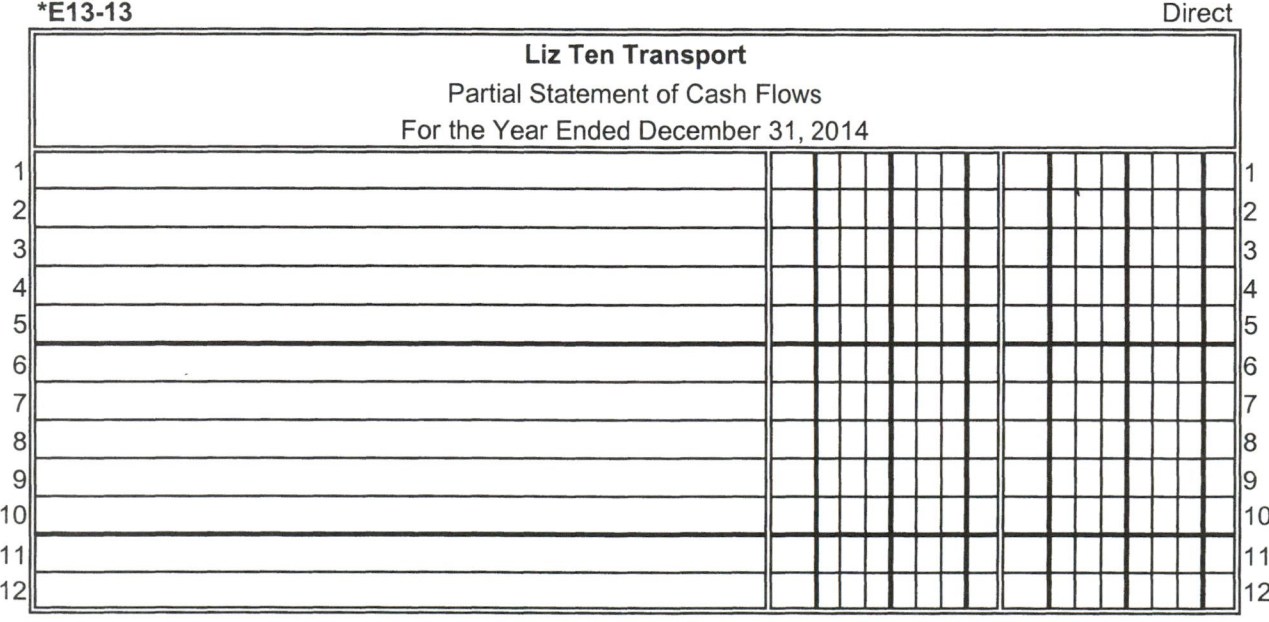

*E13-12

	$ in millions	
(a) Cash payments to suppliers		
(b) Cash payments for operating expenses		

*E13-14

Cash payments for rent:		
Cash payments for salaries:		
Cash receipts from customers:		

(a)

(b)

Common Stock

(c)

Indirect

Toby Zed Company

Partial Statement of Cash Flows

For the Year Ended November 30, 2014

	Cash flows from operating activities		
1	Cash flows from operating activities		
2			
3			
4			
5			
6			
7			
8			
9			
10			
11			
12			
13			
14			
15			
16			
17			
18			
19			
20			
21			
22			
23			
24			
25			
26			
27			
28			
29			
30			
31			
32			
33			
34			
35			
36			
37			
38			
39			
40			

Direct

Toby Zed Company				
Partial Statement of Cash Flows				
For the Year Ended November 30, 2014				
1	Cash flows from operating activities			
2				
3				
4				
5				
6				
7				
8				
9	Computations-			
10	(1) Cash receipts from customers:			
11				
12				
13				
14				
15	(2) Cash payments to suppliers:			
16				
17				
18				
19				
20				
21				
22	(3) Cash payments for operating expenses:			
23				
24				
25				
26				
27				
28				
29				
30				
31				
32				
33				
34				
35				
36				
37				
38				
39				
40				

Indirect

	Rattigan Company				
	Partial Statement of Cash Flows				
	For the Year Ended December 31, 2014				
1	Cash flows from operating activities				
2					
3					
4					
5					
6					
7					
8					
9					
10					
11					
12					
13					
14					
15					
16					
17					
18					
19					
20					
21					
22					
23					
24					
25					
26					
27					
28					
29					
30					
31					
32					
33					
34					
35					
36					
37					
38					
39					
40					

Direct

Rattigan Company				
Partial Statement of Cash Flows				
For the Year Ended December 31, 2014				
1	Cash flows from operating activities				1
2					2
3					3
4					4
5					5
6					6
7					7
8	Computations-				8
9	(1) Cash receipts from customers:				9
10					10
11					11
12					12
13					13
14					14
15	(2) Cash payments for operating expenses:				15
16					16
17					17
18					18
19					19
20					20
21					21
22					22
23	(3) Cash payments for income taxes:				23
24					24
25					25
26					26
27					27
28					28
29					29
30					30
31					31
32					32
33					33
34					34
35					35
36					36
37					37
38					38
39					39
40					40

(a)

Indirect

Rajesh Company

Statement of Cash Flows

For the Year Ended December 31, 2014

(b)   Free cash flow:

(a)   Direct

Rajesh Company

Statement of Cash Flows

For the Year Ended December 31, 2014

1	Cash Flows from operating activities:		
2			
3			
4			
5			
6			
7			
8			
9			
10			
11			
12			
13			
14			
15			
16			
17			
18			
19			
20			
21			
22			
23			
24			
25			
26			
27			
28			
29			
30	Computations:		
31	(1) Cash receipts from customers:		
32			
33			
34			
35			
36			
37			
38			
39			
40			

(a) (Continued)

Rajesh Company
Statement of Cash Flows
For the Year Ended December 31, 2014

1	Computations (continued):	
2	(2) Cash payments to suppliers:	
3		
4		
5		
6		
7		
8		
9		
10	(3) Cash payment for operating expenses:	
11		
12		
13		
14		
15		
16	(4) Cash payments for income taxes:	
17		
18		
19		
20		
21		

(b)

1	Free cash flow:	
2		
3		
4		
5		

Indirect

Sinjh Inc.
Statement of Cash Flows
For the Year Ended December 31, 2014

1			
2			
3			
4			
5			
6			
7			
8			
9			
10			
11			
12			
13			
14			
15			
16			
17			
18			
19			
20			
21			
22			
23			
24			
25			
26			
27			
28			
29			
30			
31			
32			
33			
34			
35			

(b)

Direct

Sinjh Inc.			
Statement of Cash Flows			
For the Year Ended December 31, 2014			

#	Cash Flows from operating activities:			
1	Cash Flows from operating activities:			
2				
3				
4				
5				
6				
7				
8				
9				
10				
11				
12				
13				
14				
15				
16				
17				
18				
19				
20				
21				
22				
23				
24				
25				
26				
27				
28				
29				
30	Computations:			
31	(1) Cash receipts from customers:			
32				
33				
34				
35				
36				
37				
38				
39				
40				

Sinjh Inc.		
Statement of Cash Flows		
For the Year Ended December 31, 2014		
1	Computations (continued):	
2	(2) Cash payments to suppliers:	
3		
4		
5		
6		
7		
8		
9		
10	(3) Cash payments for operating expenses:	
11		
12		
13		
14		
15		
16		
17		
18		
19		
20		
21		

Indirect

Strackman Lux Company		
Statement of Cash Flows		
For the Year Ended December 31, 2014		

1				
2				
3				
4				
5				
6				
7				
8				
9				
10				
11				
12				
13				
14				
15				
16				
17				
18				
19				
20				
21				
22				
23				
24				
25				
26				
27				
28				
29				
30				
31				
32				
33				
34				
35				
36				
37				
38				
39				
40				

	Jhutti Company					
	Worksheet - Statement of Cash Flows					
	For the Year Ended December 31, 2014					

		Balance 12/31/13	Reconciling Items		Balance 12/31/14
	Bal. Sheet Accounts		Debit	Credit	
1	Debits				
2	Cash	47250			90300
3	Accounts receivable	57000			80900
4	Inventory	102650			121900
5	Investments	87000			84000
6	Plant assets	205000			250000
7	Totals	498900			627100
8					
9	Credits				
10	Accum. depr. -				
11	plant assets	40000			46600
12	Accts. payable	48280			53400
13	Acc. expenses pay.	18830			12100
14	Bonds payable	70000			100000
15	Common stock	200000			240000
16	Retained Earnings	121790			175000
17	Totals	498900			627100
18					
19	Stmt of Cash Flows				
20	Effects				
21					
22					
23					
24					
25					
26					
27					
28					
29					
30					
31					
32					
33					
34					
35					
36					
37					
38					
39					
40					

(a)		

(a)

Accumulated Depreciation - Equipment

Optional journal entries:

Account Titles	Debit	Credit

(b) Cash Flow	Classification-Inflow (Outflow)

Indirect

Asquith Company						
Partial Statement of Cash Flows						
For the Year Ended December 31, 2014						
1	Cash flows from operating activities						1
2							2
3							3
4							4
5							5
6							6
7							7
8							8
9							9
10							10
11							11
12							12
13							13
14							14
15							15
16							16
17							17
18							18
19							19
20							20
21							21
22							22
23							23
24							24
25							25
26							26
27							27
28							28
29							29
30							30
31							31
32							32
33							33
34							34
35							35
36							36
37							37
38							38
39							39
40							40

Direct

Asquith Company			
Partial Statement of Cash Flows			
For the Year Ended December 31, 2014			
1 Cash flows from operating activities			
2			
3			
4			
5			
6			
7			
8			
9 Computations-			
10 (1) Cash receipts from customers:			
11			
12			
13			
14			
15 (2) Cash payments to suppliers:			
16			
17			
18			
19			
20			
21			
22 (3) Cash payments for operating expenses:			
23			
24			
25			
26			
27			
28			
29			
30			
31			
32			
33			
34			
35			
36			
37			
38			
39			
40			

Indirect

Anne Droid Inc.						
Partial Statement of Cash Flows						
For the Year Ended December 31, 2014						
1	Cash flows from operating activities					
2						
3						
4						
5						
6						
7						
8						
9						
10						
11						
12						
13						
14						
15						
16						
17						
18						
19						
20						
21						
22						
23						
24						
25						
26						
27						
28						
29						
30						
31						
32						
33						
34						
35						
36						
37						
38						
39						
40						

Direct

Anne Droid Inc.

Partial Statement of Cash Flows

For the Year Ended December 31, 2014

1	Cash flows from operating activities		
2			
3			
4			
5			
6			
7			
8	Computations-		
9	(1) Cash receipts from customers:		
10			
11			
12			
13			
14			
15	(2) Cash payments for operating expenses:		
16			
17			
18			
19			
20			
21			
22			
23	(3) Cash payments for income taxes:		
24			
25			
26			
27			
28			
29			
30			
31			
32			
33			
34			
35			
36			
37			
38			
39			
40			

(a)

Indirect

Rocastle Company
Statement of Cash Flows
For the Year Ended December 31, 2014

1		
2		
3		
4		
5		
6		
7		
8		
9		
10		
11		
12		
13		
14		
15		
16		
17		
18		
19		
20		
21		
22		
23		
24		
25		
26		
27		
28		
29		
30		
31		
32		
33		
34		
35		

(b) Free cash flow:

(a)   Direct

Rocastle Company

Statement of Cash Flows

For the Year Ended December 31, 2014

	Cash Flows from operating activities:				
1	Cash Flows from operating activities:				
2					
3					
4					
5					
6					
7					
8					
9					
10					
11					
12					
13					
14					
15					
16					
17					
18					
19					
20					
21					
22					
23					
24					
25					
26					
27					
28					
29					
30	Computations:				
31	(1) Cash receipts from customers:				
32					
33					
34					
35					
36					
37					
38					
39					
40					

Rocastle Company	
Statement of Cash Flows	
For the Year Ended December 31, 2014	

1	Computations (continued):	1
2	(2) Cash payments to suppliers:	2
3		3
4		4
5		5
6		6
7		7
8		8
9		9
10	(3) Cash payments for income taxes:	10
11		11
12		12
13		13
14		14
15		15
16		16
17		17
18		18
19		19
20		20
21		21

Indirect

Minnie Hooper Company
Statement of Cash Flows
For the Year Ended December 31, 2014

(b)

Direct

	Minnie Hooper Company Statement of Cash Flows For the Year Ended December 31, 2014		
1	Cash Flows from operating activities:			1
2				2
3				3
4				4
5				5
6				6
7				7
8				8
9				9
10				10
11				11
12				12
13				13
14				14
15				15
16				16
17				17
18				18
19				19
20				20
21				21
22				22
23				23
24				24
25				25
26				26
27				27
28				28
29				29
30	Computations:			30
31	(1) Cash receipts from customers:			31
32				32
33				33
34				34
35				35
36				36
37				37
38				38
39				39
40				40

Minnie Hooper Company
Statement of Cash Flows
For the Year Ended December 31, 2014

1	Computations (continued):	
2	(2) Cash payments to suppliers:	
3		
4		
5		
6		
7		
8		
9		
10	(3) Cash payment for operating expenses:	
11		
12		
13		
14		
15		
16		
17		
18		
19		
20		
21		

Indirect

Vernet Company				
Statement of Cash Flows				
For the Year Ended December 31, 2014				

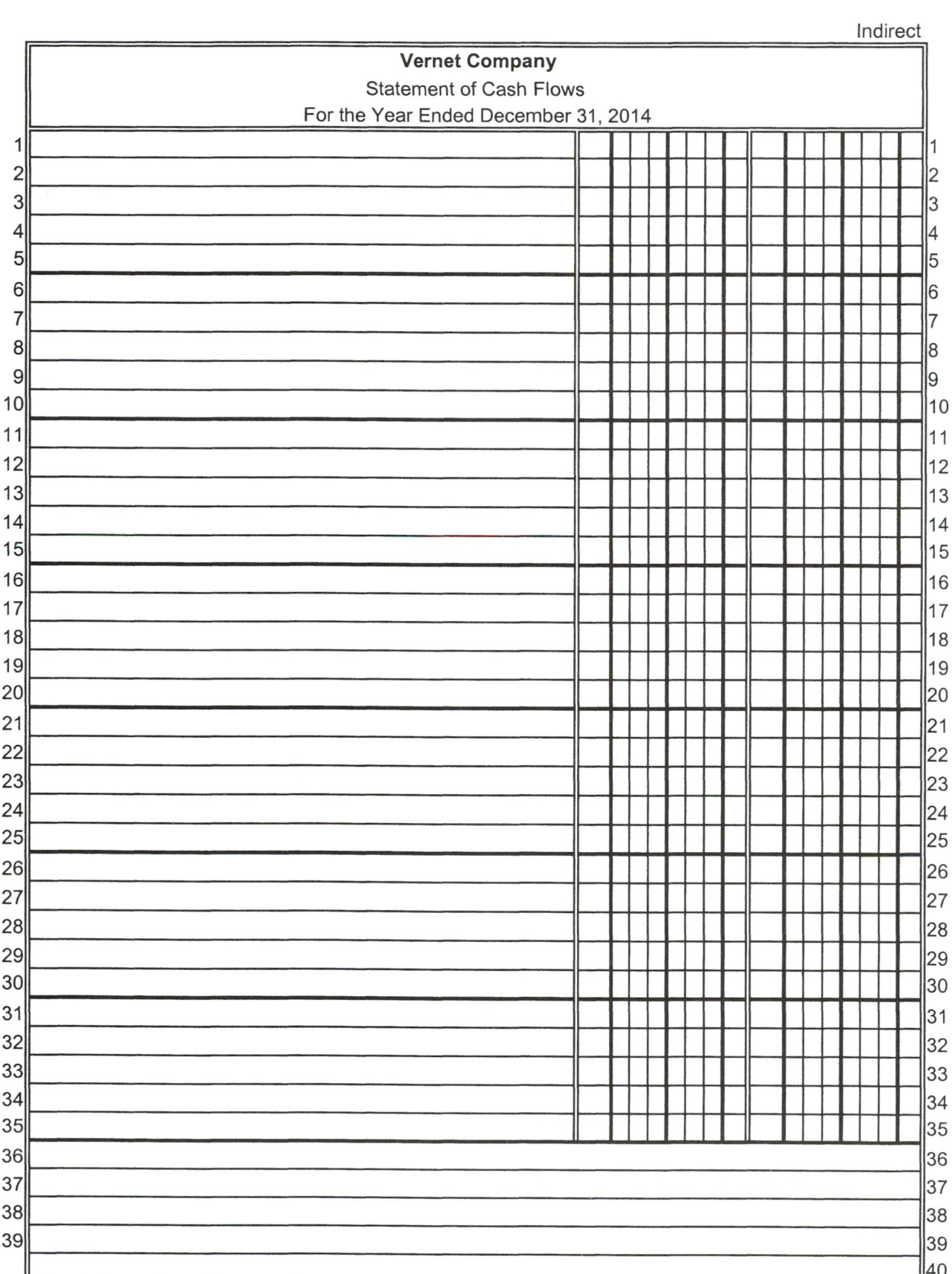

		$ Amounts in millions	
		2010	2009
1	(a) Net cash provided by operating activities		
2			
3			
4			
5			
6	(b) Increase (decrease) in cash and cash equivalents		
7			
8			
9			
10			
11	(c)		
12			
13			
14			
15			
16	(d)		
17			
18			
19			
20			
21	(e)		
22			
23			
24			
25			
26	(f)		
27			
28			
29			
30			
31			
32			
33			
34			
35			
36			
37			
38			
39			
40			

	PepsiCo	Coca-Cola
(a) Free cash flow (in millions):		
(b)		

(a)

Del Carpio Company
Statement of Cash Flows
For the Year Ended January 31, 2014

1			
2			
3			
4			
5			
6			
7			
8			
9			
10			
11			
12			
13			
14			
15			
16			
17			
18			
19			
20			
21			
22			
23			
24			
25			
26			
27			
28			
29			
30 Computation of net income (loss):			
31			
32			
33			
34			
35			
36			
37			
38			
39			
40			

(b)

1	1
2	2
3	3
4	4
5	5
6	6
7	7
8	8
9	9
10	10
11	11
12	12
13	13
14	14
15	15
16	16
17	17
18	18
19	19
20	20
21	21
22	22
23	23
24	24
25	25
26	26
27	27
28	28
29	29
30	30
31	31
32	32
33	33
34	34
35	35
36	36
37	37
38	38
39	39
40	40

IFRS13-4

1 (a)

3 (b)

8 (c)

12 (d)   Components of the "net movement in working capital":

BE14-3   Horizontal Analysis

	Dec. 31, 2014	Dec. 31, 2013	Increase or (Decrease) Amount	Percentage	
1 Accounts receivable	$ 5 2 0 0 0 0	$ 3 5 0 0 0 0			1
2 Inventory	8 4 0 0 0 0	5 0 0 0 0 0			2
3 Total assets	2 5 0 0 0 0 0	3 0 0 0 0 0 0			3

BE15-4   Vertical Analysis

	Dec. 31, 2014		Dec. 31, 2013		
	Amount	Percentage	Amount	Percentage	
13 Accounts receivable	$ 5 2 0 0 0 0		$ 3 5 0 0 0 0		13
14 Inventory	8 4 0 0 0 0		5 0 0 0 0 0		14
15 Total assets	2 5 0 0 0 0 0		3 0 0 0 0 0 0		15

BE15-5

	2014	2013	2012		
25 Net income	$ 5 2 2 0 0 0	$ 4 5 0 0 0 0	$ 5 0 0 0 0 0		25

		Increase (Decrease)		
		Amount	Percentage	
31 (a) 2012 - 2013				31
32 (b) 2013 - 2014				32

BE14-6

	2014	2013	Increase
1			
2 Net income			4 0 %
3			
4			
5			
6			
7			
8			
9			
10			

BE14-8	2014	2013	2012
12 Sales	1 0 0 .0	1 0 0 .0	1 0 0 .0
13 Cost of goods sold	5 9 .2	6 2 .4	6 4 .5
14 Expenses	2 5 .0	2 5 .6	2 7 .5
15			
16			

BE14-9

22 (a)   Working capital

27 (b)   Current ratio

30 (c)   Acid-test ratio

BE14-14

	Reeves Corporation									
	Partial Income Statement									
1	Income before income taxes	$	5	0	0	0	0	0		1
2										2
3										3
4										4
5										5
6										6
7										7

8 BE14-15

	Blevins Corporation				
	Partial Income Statement				
9					9
10					10
11					11
12	Discontinued operations:				12
13					13
14					14
15					15
16					16
17					17
18					18
19					19
20					20
21					21

DO IT! 14-1

		Increase (Decrease) in 2014		
		Amount		Percent
1	Current assets			
2	Plant assets			
3	Total assets			

DO IT! 14-3

Grinders Corporation

Income Statement (Partial)

E14-1   Horizontal Analysis

	Gallup Inc.																	
	Condensed Balance Sheets																	
	December 31,																	
1										Increase or (Decrease)								1
2	Assets		2014				2013			Amount					Percent			2
3	Current assets	$	1 2 8 0 0 0			$	1 0 0 0 0 0											3
4	Plant assets (net)		3 9 6 0 0 0				3 3 0 0 0 0											4
5	Total assets																	5
6																		6
7	Liabilities																	7
8	Current liabilities	$	9 1 0 0 0			$	7 0 0 0 0											8
9	Long-term liabilities		1 3 8 7 0 0				9 5 0 0 0											9
10	Total liabilities																	10
11																		11
12	Stockholders' Equity																	12
13	Common stock, $1 par		1 5 9 0 0 0				1 1 5 0 0 0											13
14	Retained earnings		1 3 5 3 0 0				1 5 0 0 0 0											14
15	Total stockholders' equity																	15
16	Total liabilities and																	16
17	stockholders' equity																	17
18																		18

E14-2   Vertical Analysis

	Conrad Corporation											
	Condensed Income Statements											
	For the Years Ended December 31,											
1			2014					2013				1
2		Amount			Percent		Amount			Percent		2
3	Sales	$	7 5 0 0 0 0			$	6 0 0 0 0 0					3
4	Cost of goods sold		4 8 0 0 0 0				4 0 8 0 0 0					4
5	Gross profit											5
6	Selling expenses		1 0 5 0 0 0				8 4 0 0 0					6
7	Administrative expenses		7 5 0 0 0				5 4 0 0 0					7
8	Total operating expenses											8
9	Income before income taxes											9
10	Income tax expense		3 6 0 0 0				1 8 0 0 0					10
11	Net income	$	5 4 0 0 0			$	3 6 0 0 0					11
12												12
13												13
14												14
15												15
16												16
17												17

(a)   Horizontal Analysis

Garcia Corporation

Comparative Balance Sheets

December 31,

					Increase or (Decrease)	
	Assets	2014	2013		Amount	Percent
3	Current assets	$ 76000	$ 80000			
4	Prop., plant, & equip. (net)	100000	90000			
5	Intangibles	24000	40000			
6	Total assets	$ 200000	$ 210000			
7						
8	Liabilities & Stockholders'					
9	Equity					
10	Current liabilities	$ 40000	$ 48000			
11	Long-term liabilities	140000	150000			
12	Stockholders' equity	20000	12000			
13	Total liabilities and					
14	stockholders' equity	$ 200000	$ 210000			

(b)   Vertical Analysis

Garcia Corporation

Condensed Balance Sheets

December 31, 2014

	Assets	Amount	Percent
2	Current assets	$ 76000	
3	Property, plant, and equipment (net)	100000	
4	Intangibles	24000	
5	Total assets	$ 200000	
6			
7	Liabilities and Stockholders' Equity		
8	Current liabilities	$ 40000	
9	Long-term liabilities	140000	
10	Stockholders' equity	20000	
11	Total liabilities and stockholders' equity	$ 200000	

Hendi Corporation

Condensed Income Statements

For the Years Ended December 31,

(a) Horizontal Analysis

	2014	2013	Increase or (Decrease) Amount	Percent
Net sales	$ 600000	$ 500000		
Cost of goods sold	468000	400000		
Gross profit	132000	100000		
Operating expenses	60000	54000		
Net income	$ 72000	$ 46000		

(b) Vertical Analysis

	2014 Amount	Percent	2013 Amount	Percent
Net sales	$ 600000		$ 500000	
Cost of goods sold	468000		400000	
Gross profit	132000		100000	
Operating expenses	60000		54000	
Net income	$ 72000		$ 46000	

	Quick Assets +	Inventory +	Prepaid Expenses =	Total Current Assets	Total Current Liabilities	(a) Current Ratio	(b) Acid-test Ratio
1 Feb 1 Bal		$ 1 0 0 0 0	$ 5 0 0 0	$ 1 4 0 0 0 0	$ 5 0 0 0 0		
2							
3 Feb 3							
4							
5 Bal							
6							
7 Feb 7							
8							
9 Bal							
10							
11 Feb 11							
12							
13 Bal							
14							
15 Feb 14							
16							
17 Bal							
18							
19 Feb 18							
20							
21 Bal							
22							
23							

(a)

Douglas Corporation						
Partial Income Statement						
For The Year Ended October 31, 2011						
1	Income before income taxes	$	5	5	0	0 0 0	1
2							2
3							3
4							4
5							5
6							6
7							7
8							8
9							9
10							10

(b)

1	1
2	2
3	3
4	4
5	5
6	6
7	7
8	8
9	9
10	10
11	11
12	12
13	13
14	14
15	15
16	16
17	17
18	18
19	19
20	20
21	21
22	22
23	23
24	24
25	25

(a)

Maulder Corporation

Partial Income Statement

For the Year Ended December 31, 2014

1	Income from continuing operations	$ 290000
2		
3		
4		
5		
6		
7		
8		
9		
10		
11		
12		
13		
14		
15		

(b)

1	
2	
3	
4	
5	
6	
7	
8	
9	
10	
11	
12	
13	
14	
15	
16	
17	
18	
19	
20	

(a)

		COMPARATIVE VERTICAL ANALYSIS				
		Condensed Income Statement				
		For the Year Ended December 31, 2014				
		Lionel Company		Barrymore Company		
		Dollars	Percent	Dollars	Percent	
1	Net sales	$1 549 035		$ 339 038		1
2	Cost of goods sold	1 053 345		237 325		2
3	Gross profit					3
4	Operating expenses	278 825		77 979		4
5	Income from operations					5
6	Other expenses and losses:					6
7	Interest expense	7 745		2 034		7
8	Income before income taxes					8
9	Income tax expense	61 960		8 476		9
10	Net income	$		$		10
11						11
12						12
13						13
14						14
15						15

(b)

1	1
2	2
3	3
4	4
5	5
6	6
7	7
8	8
9	9
10	10
11	11
12	12
13	13
14	14
15	15
16	16
17	17

(b) (Continued)

1			1
2			2
3			3
4			4
5			5
6			6
7			7
8			8
9			9
10			10
11			11
12			12
13			13
14			14
15			15
16			16
17			17
18			18
19			19
20			20
21			21
22			22
23			23
24			24
25			25
26			26
27			27
28			28
29			29
30			30
31			31
32			32
33			33
34			34
35			35
36			36
37			37
38			38
39			39
40			40

Bondi Corporation									
Income Statement									
For the Year Ended December 31, 2014									
1									1
2 Sales	$	10	5	0	0	0	0	0	2
3 Cost of goods sold									3
4 Gross profit									4
5 Operating expenses		1	5	0	0	0	0	0	5
6 Income from operations									6
7 Other expenses and losses:									7
8 Interest expense									8
9 Income before income taxes									9
10 Income tax expense			5	5	0	0	0	0	10
11 Net income	$								11

Bondi Corporation																	
Balance Sheets																	
December 31																	
1	**Assets**		2014								2013							1
2	Current Assets																	2
3	Cash	$	4	8	0	0	0	0		$	3	7	5	0	0	0		3
4	Accounts receivable (net)										9	5	0	0	0	0		4
5	Inventory									1	7	2	0	0	0	0		5
6	Total current assets									3	0	4	5	0	0	0		6
7	Plant assets (net)		4	6	2	0	0	0	0		4	4	5	5	0	0	0	7
8	Total assets	$								$7	5	0	0	0	0	0		8
9																		9
10	**Liabilities and Stockholders' Equity**																	10
11	Current liabilities									$	8	2	5	0	0	0		11
12	Long-term notes payable									3	3	0	0	0	0	0		12
13	Total liabilities									4	1	2	5	0	0	0		13
14	Common stock, $1 par		3	0	0	0	0	0	0		3	0	0	0	0	0	0	14
15	Retained earnings			4	0	0	0	0	0			3	7	5	0	0	0	15
16	Total stockholders' equity		3	4	0	0	0	0	0		3	3	7	5	0	0	0	16
17	Total liabilities and stockholders' equity	$								$7	5	0	0	0	0	0		17

Computations:

1	1
2	2
3	3
4	4
5	5
6	6
7	7
8	8
9	9
10	10
11	11
12	12
13	13
14	14
15	15
16	16
17	17
18	18
19	19
20	20
21	21
22	22
23	23
24	24
25	25
26	26
27	27
28	28
29	29
30	30
31	31
32	32
33	33
34	34
35	35
36	36
37	37
38	38
39	39
40	40

Computations:

1	1
2	2
3	3
4	4
5	5
6	6
7	7
8	8
9	9
10	10
11	11
12	12
13	13
14	14
15	15
16	16
17	17
18	18
19	19
20	20
21	21
22	22
23	23
24	24
25	25
26	26
27	27
28	28
29	29
30	30
31	31
32	32
33	33
34	34
35	35
36	36
37	37
38	38
39	39
40	40

Violet Bick Corporation
Condensed Income Statement
For the Year Ended December 31, 2014

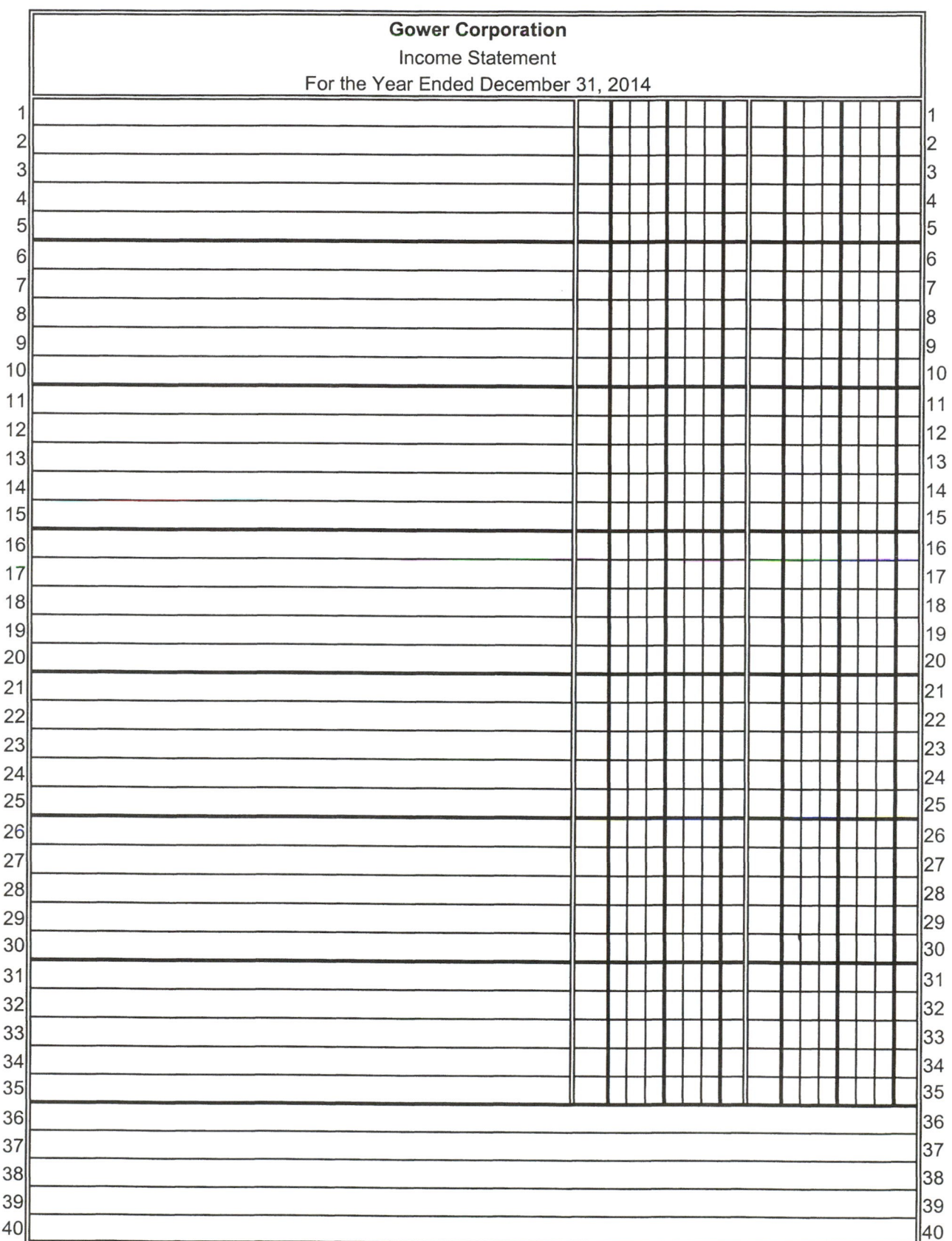

Gower Corporation

Income Statement

For the Year Ended December 31, 2014

(a)

PepsiCo, Inc.
Trend Analysis of Net Sales and Net Income
For the Five Years Ended 2008

Base Period 2001 - (in millions)	2010	2009	2008	2007	2006
1 (1) Net sales					
2					
3 Trend					
4					
5 (2) Net income					
6					
7 Trend					
8					
9 Analysis:					
10					
11					
12					

Chapter 14 Financial Reporting Problem Continued

PepsiCo, Inc.

(b)   (dollar amounts in millions)

PepsiCo, Inc.
2010 and 2009 Ratio Analysis: Profitability

	2010	2009
1 (1) Profit margin:		
2		
3		
4		
5		
6 (2) Asset turnover:		
7		
8		
9		
10		
11		
12 (3) Return on assets:		
13		
14		
15		
16		
17		
18 (4) Return on common stockholders' equity:		
19		
20		
21		
22		
23 Analysis:		
24		

Name

Section

Date   PepsiCo, Inc.

(c)   (dollar amounts in millions)

PepsiCo, Inc.

2010 and 2009 Ratio Analysis: Solvency

	2010	2009
(1) Debt to total assets:		
(2) Times interest earned:		
Analysis:		

(d)

IFRS14-1

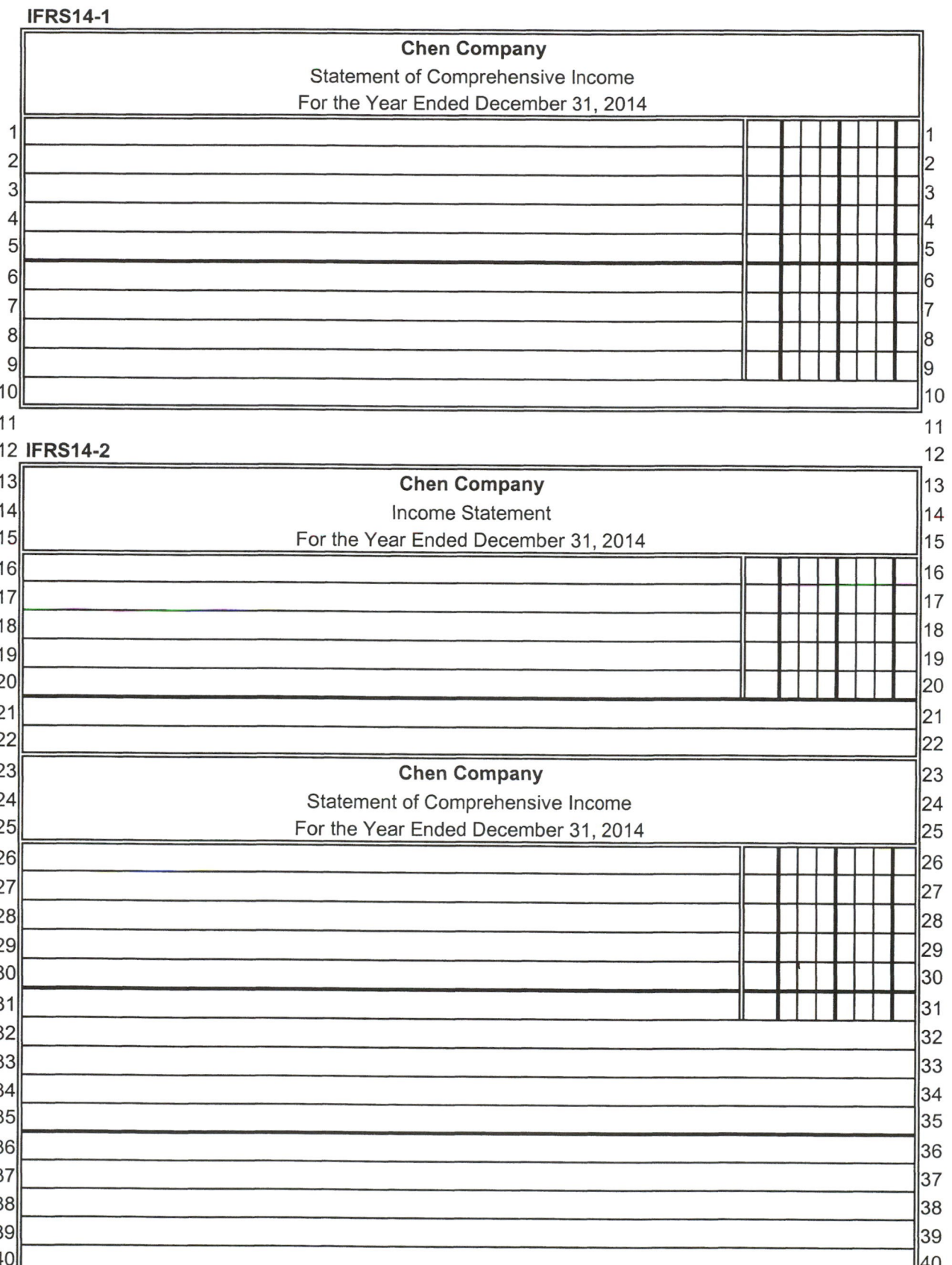

Chen Company

Statement of Comprehensive Income

For the Year Ended December 31, 2014

IFRS14-2

Chen Company

Income Statement

For the Year Ended December 31, 2014

Chen Company

Statement of Comprehensive Income

For the Year Ended December 31, 2014

BED-3

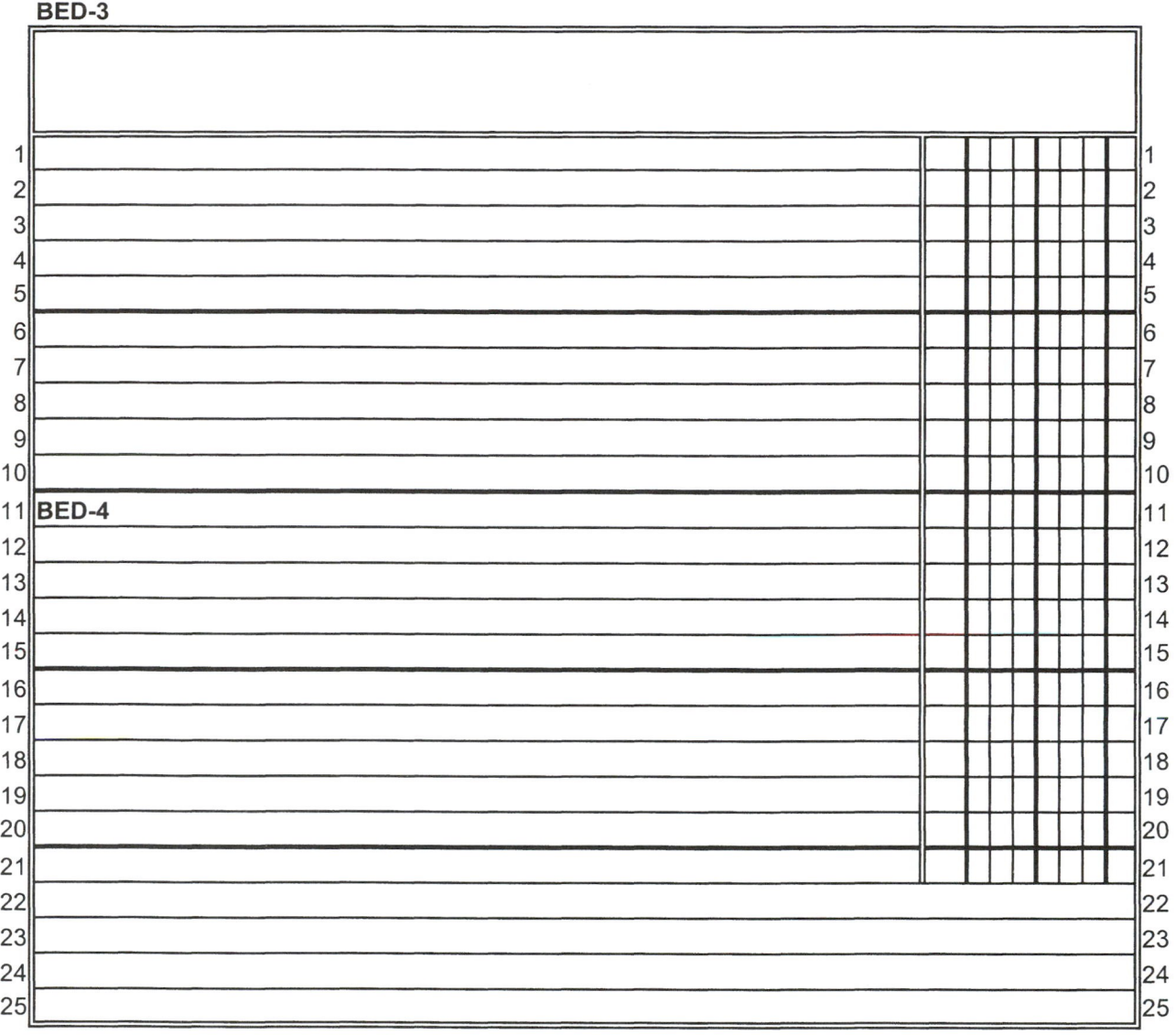

BED-4

BED-5

1		1
2		2
3		3
4		4
5		5
6		6
7		7
8		8
9		9
10	**BED-6**	10
11		11
12		12
13		13
14		14
15		15
16		16
17		17
18		18
19		19
20	**BED-8**	20
21	(a)	21
22		22
23		23
24		24
25	(b)	25
26		26
27		27
28		28
29		29
30		30
31		31
32		32
33		33
34		34
35		35
36		36
37		37
38		38
39		39
40		40

BED-9

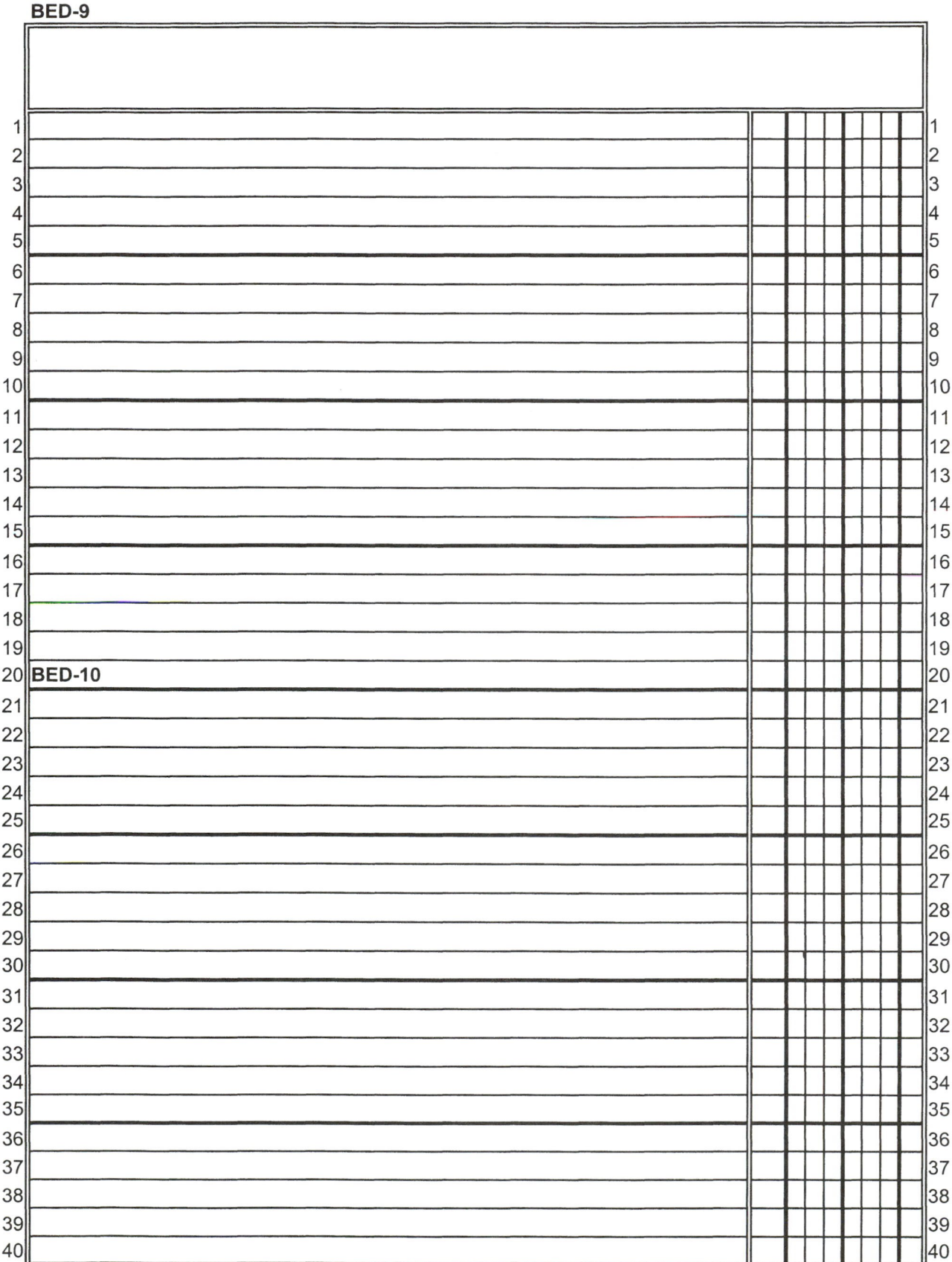

BED-10

BED-11

			1
1			1
2			2
3			3
4			4
5			5
6			6
7			7
8			8
9			9
10			10
11			11
12			12
13			13
14			14
15			15
16			16
17	**BED-12**		17
18			18
19			19
20			20
21			21
22			22
23			23
24			24
25			25
26			26
27			27
28			28
29			29
30			30
31			31
32	**BED-13**		32
33			33
34			34
35			35
36			36
37			37
38			38
39			39
40			40

BED-14

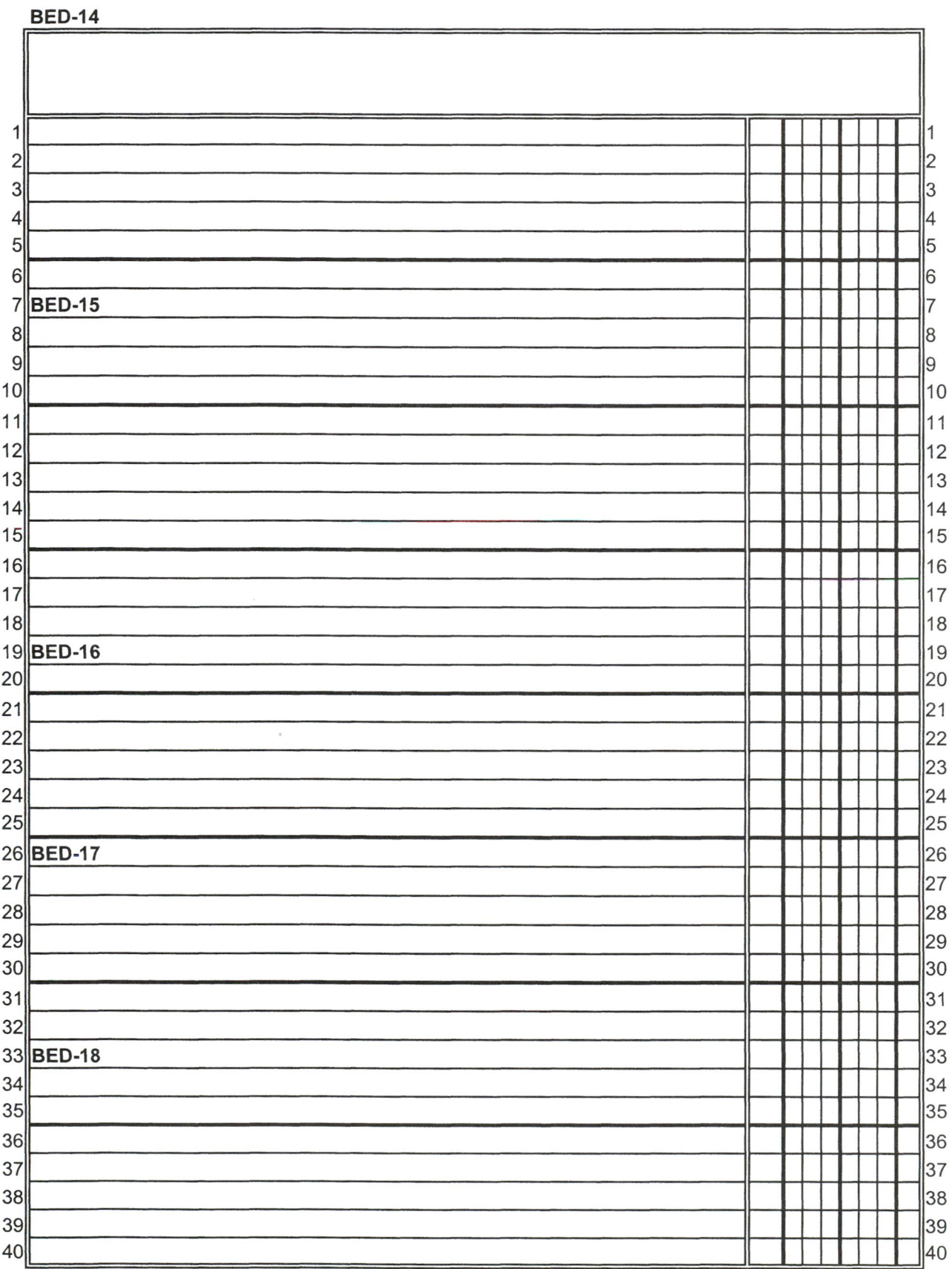

BED-15

BED-16

BED-17

BED-18

BED-19

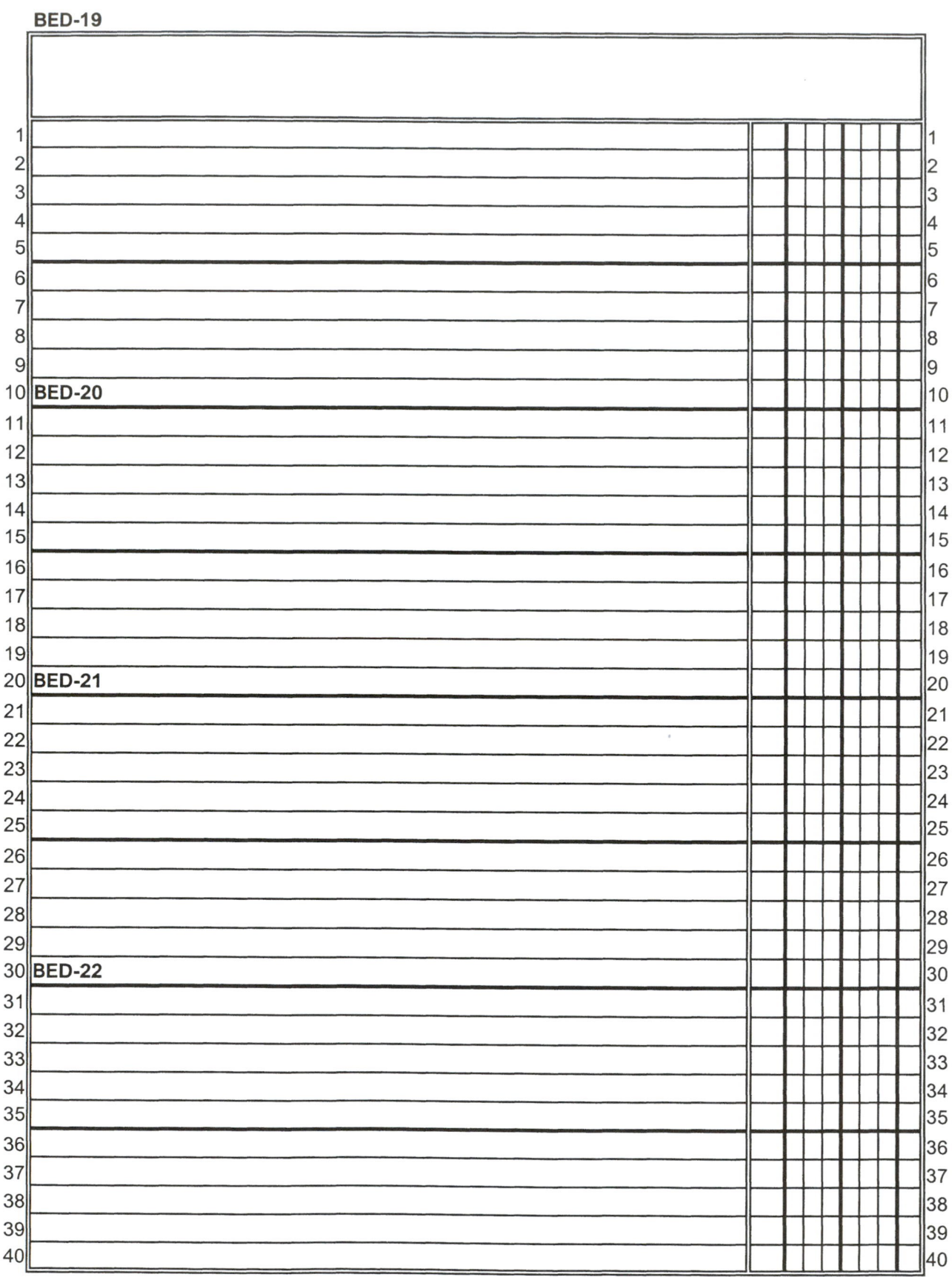

BED-20

BED-21

BED-22

BED-23

BED-24

BED-25

BEE-2

	Debit	Credit
1		
2		
3		
4		
5		
6		
7		
8		
9		
10		
11		

BEE-3

Date	Account Titles	Debit	Credit
Jan. 15			
Jan. 15			

BEE-4

Date	Account Titles	Debit	Credit
Jan. 31			

1	(a) (1)		1
2			2
3			3
4			4
5	(2)		5
6	(3)		6
7	(4)		7
8	(5)		8
9			9
10			10
11			11
12			12
13			13
14			14
15	(b)	Account Titles	Debit	Credit	15
16					16
17					17
18					18
19					19
20					20
21					21
22			22
23			23
24			24
25			25
26			26
27			27
28			28
29			29
30			30
31			31
32			32
33			33
34			34
35			35
36			36
37			37
38			38
39			39
40			40

(a)

Welstead Company

Payroll Register

For the Week Ending January 31

Employee	Total Hours	Earnings Regular	Earnings Overtime	Gross Pay	
1 W. Jeong					1
2					2
3 C. Garrison					3
4					4
5 J. Buss					5
6					6
7 Totals					7

(a) Continued

Welstead Company

Payroll Register (continued)

For the Week Ending January 31

Employee	Deductions FICA Taxes	Federal Income Taxes	Health Insurance	Total	Net Pay	
1 W. Jeong						1
2						2
3 C. Garrison						3
4						4
5 J. Buss						5
6						6
7 Totals						7

(b)

General Journal

	Date	Account Titles	Debit	Credit	
1	Jan. 31				1
2					2
3					3
4					4
5					5
6					6
7					7
8	Jan. 31				8
9					9
10					10
11					11
12					12
13					13
14					14
15					15
16					16
17					17
18					18
19					19
20					20
21					21
22					22
23					23
24					24
25					25

	(a)					
1	Gross earnings:					1
2	Regular	$		8 9 0 0		2
3	Overtime					3
4	Total					4
5	Deductions:					5
6	FICA taxes			7 6 5		6
7	Federal income taxes			1 3 9 5		7
8	State income taxes					8
9	Union dues			1 0 0		9
10	Total deductions					10
11	Net pay				7 3 4 0	11
12	Accounts debited:					12
13	Warehouse wages					13
14	Store wages				4 0 0 0	14
15						15
16	(b)					16

	Date	Account Titles	Debit	Credit	
17					17
18	Feb. 28				18
19					19
20					20
21					21
22					22
23					23
24					24
25					25
26					26
27	28				27
28					28
29					29
30					30
31					31
32					32
33					33
34					34
35					35
36					36
37					37
38					38
39					39
40					40

(a)

	Debit	Credit
1		
2		
3		
4		
5		
6		

(b)

Date	Account Titles	Debit	Credit
8			
9			
10			
11			
12			
13			
14			
15			

(a)

Ethridge Drug Store

Payroll Register

For the Week Ending February 15, 2014

Employee	Hours	Earnings		
		Regular	Overtime	Gross Pay
1 A. Joseph				
2 J. Wilgus				
3 P. Kirk				
4 L. Zhang				
5 Totals				

(a) (Continued)

Ethridge Drug Store

Payroll Register (continued)

For the Week Ending February 15, 2014

Employee	Deductions				
	FICA Taxes	Federal Income Taxes	State Income Taxes	United Fund	Total
1 A. Joseph					
2 J. Wilgus					
3 P. Kirk					
4 L. Zhang					
5 Totals					

(a) (Continued)

Ethridge Drug Store

Payroll Register (concluded)

For the Week Ending February 15, 2014

Employee	Net Pay	Store Wages Expense	Office Wages Expense
1 A. Joseph			
2 J. Wilgus			
3 P. Kirk			
4 L. Zhang			
5 Totals			

(b) - (d)   General Journal

	Date	Account Titles	Debit	Credit	
1	(b)				1
2	Feb. 15				2
3					3
4					4
5					5
6					6
7					7
8					8
9					9
10					10
11					11
12	15				12
13					13
14					14
15					15
16					16
17					17
18					18
19					19
20	(c)				20
21	Feb. 16				21
22					22
23					23
24					24
25	(d)				25
26	Feb. 28				26
27					27
28					28
29					29
30					30
31					31
32					32
33					33
34					34
35					35
36					36
37					37
38					38
39					39
40					40

(a)   General Journal

	Date	Account Titles	Debit	Credit	
1	Jan. 10				1
2					2
3					3
4					4
5	12				5
6					6
7					7
8					8
9	15				9
10					10
11					11
12	17				12
13					13
14					14
15	20				15
16					16
17					17
18					18
19					19
20					20
21	31				21
22					22
23					23
24					24
25					25
26					26
27					27
28					28
29					29
30					30
31					31
32					32
33	31				33
34					34
35					35
36					36
37					37
38					38
39					39
40					40

(b) General Journal

	Date	Account Titles	Debit	Credit	
1	Jan. 31				1
2					2
3					3
4					4
5					5
6					6
7					7
8					8
9					9
10					10
11					11
12					12
13					13
14					14
15					15
16					16
17					17
18					18
19					19
20					20
21					21
22					22
23					23
24					24
25					25
26					26
27					27
28					28
29					29
30					30
31					31
32					32
33					33
34					34
35					35
36					36
37					37
38					38
39					39
40					40

General Journal

	Date	Account Titles	Debit	Credit	
1	(a)				1
2					2
3					3
4					4
5					5
6					6
7					7
8					8
9					9
10					10
11					11
12					12
13					13
14					14
15	(b)				15
16					16
17					17
18					18
19					19
20					20
21					21
22					22
23					23
24					24
25					25
26					26
27					27
28					28
29					29
30					30
31					31
32					32
33					33
34					34
35					35
36					36
37					37
38					38
39					39
40					40

Problem E-3A Concluded

Pienkos Company

(c)

Employee	Wages, Tips, Other Compensation	Federal Income Taxes Withheld	State Income Tax Withheld	FICA Wages	FICA Tax Withheld
1 S. Brand					
2					
3 R. Morin					
4					
5					
6					
7					

(a)

Ralph's Hardware

Payroll Register

For the Week Ending March 15, 2014

Employee	Total Hours	Earnings		Gross Pay
		Regular	Overtime	
1 K. Litwack					1
2 E. Burgess					2
3 R. Perez					3
4 H. Hosseini					4
5 Totals					5

(a) (Continued)

Ralph's Hardware

Payroll Register (continued)

For the Week Ending March 15, 2014

Employee	Deductions				
	FICA Taxes	Federal Income Taxes	State Income Taxes	United Fund	Total
1 K. Litwack						1
2 E. Burgess						2
3 R. Perez						3
4 H. Hosseini						4
5 Totals						5

(a) (Continued)

Ralph's Hardware

Payroll Register (concluded)

For the Week Ending March 15, 2014

Employee	Net Pay	Store Wages Expense	Office Wages Expense
1 K. Litwack				1
2 E. Burgess				2
3 R. Perez				3
4 H. Hosseini				4
5 Totals				5

(b) - (d)   General Journal

	Date	Account Titles	Debit	Credit	
1	(b)				1
2	Mar. 15				2
3					3
4					4
5					5
6					6
7					7
8					8
9					9
10					10
11					11
12	15				12
13					13
14					14
15					15
16					16
17					17
18					18
19					19
20	(c)				20
21	Mar. 15				21
22					22
23					23
24					24
25	(d)				25
26	Mar. 31				26
27					27
28					28
29					29
30					30
31					31
32					32
33					33
34					34
35					35
36					36
37					37
38					38
39					39
40					40

(a)   General Journal

	Date	Account Titles	Debit	Credit	
1	Jan. 10				1
2					2
3					3
4					4
5	12				5
6					6
7					7
8					8
9	15				9
10					10
11					11
12	17				12
13					13
14					14
15	20				15
16					16
17					17
18					18
19					19
20					20
21	31				21
22					22
23					23
24					24
25					25
26					26
27					27
28					28
29					29
30					30
31					31
32					32
33	31				33
34					34
35					35
36					36
37					37
38					38
39					39
40					40

(b)   General Journal

	Date	Account Titles	Debit	Credit	
1	Jan. 31				1
2					2
3					3
4					4
5					5
6					6
7					7
8					8
9					9
10					10
11					11
12					12
13					13
14					14
15					15
16					16
17					17
18					18
19					19
20					20
21					21
22					22
23					23
24					24
25					25
26					26
27					27
28					28
29					29
30					30
31					31
32					32
33					33
34					34
35					35
36					36
37					37
38					38
39					39
40					40

General Journal

	Date	Account Titles	Debit	Credit	
1	(a)				1
2					2
3					3
4					4
5					5
6					6
7					7
8					8
9					9
10					10
11					11
12					12
13					13
14					14
15	(b)				15
16					16
17					17
18					18
19					19
20					20
21					21
22					22
23					23
24					24
25					25
26					26
27					27
28					28
29					29
30					30
31					31
32					32
33					33
34					34
35					35
36					36
37					37
38					38
39					39
40					40

Problem E-3B Concluded

Grayson Electrical Repair Company

(c)

Employee	Wages, Tips, Other Compensation	Federal Income Taxes Withheld	State Income Tax Withheld	FICA Wages	FICA Tax Withheld
1 Jin Chien					
2					
3 Nina Harris					
4					
5					
6					
7					

(a)

Oxford Services, Inc.				
Schedules: Comparative Employee Costs				
Annual Estimates				
OXFORD SERVICES, INC.				
Month	Number of Employees	Days Worked	Daily Rate	Cost
1 January - March				
2 April - May				
3 June - October				
4 November - December				
5 Total cost				
6				

PERMANENT EMPLOYEES		
1 Salaries		
2 Additional payroll costs:		
3		
4		
5		
6		
7		
8		
9		
10		

(b)

1
2
3
4
5
6
7
8
9
10
11
12
13
14

BEF-1

Accounts Receivable Subsidiary Ledger

Austin Co.

Date	Explanation	Ref.	Debit	Credit	Balance

Diaz Co.

Date	Explanation	Ref.	Debit	Credit	Balance

Nichols Co.

Date	Explanation	Ref.	Debit	Credit	Balance

General Ledger

Accounts Receivable

Date	Explanation	Ref.	Debit	Credit	Balance

1	Sudsidiary balances:										1
2	Gorst Company										2
3											3
4											4
5											5
6											6
7	Maddoy Company										7
8											8
9											9
10											10
11											11
12	Tian Company										12
13											13
14											14
15											15
16											16
17	General ledger Accounts Payable balance										17
18											18
19											19
20											20

(a) & (b)   *General Ledger*

Accounts Receivable

Date	Explanation	Ref.	Debit	Credit	Balance
9/1	Balance	√			1 1 0 9 6 0

Accounts Receivable Subsidiary Ledger

Bohn

Date	Explanation	Ref.	Debit	Credit	Balance
9/1	Balance	√			2 0 6 0

Cao

Date	Explanation	Ref.	Debit	Credit	Balance
9/1	Balance	√			4 8 2 0

Han

Date	Explanation	Ref.	Debit	Credit	Balance

Lahr

Date	Explanation	Ref.	Debit	Credit	Balance
9/1	Balance	√			2 6 4 0

Lahr

Date	Explanation	Ref.	Debit	Credit	Balance
9/1	Balance	√			1 4 4 0

EF-3 (c)

	Thone Company
	Schedule of Customers
	As of September 30, 2014

EF-4

(a)

(b)

(c)

(d)

	1		1
1	(a)		1
2			2
3	(b)		3
4			4
5			5
6			6
7	(c)		7
8			8
9			9
10			10
11			11
12			12
13			13
14	(d)		14
15			15
16			16
17			17
18			18
19			19
20			20
21			21
22			22
23			23
24			24
25			25

(a) & (b)   S1

Pashak Company

Sales Journal

	Date	Account Debited	Invoice No.	Ref.	Accounts Receiv. Dr. Sales Rev. Cr.	COGS Dr. Inventory Cr.	
1	2014						1
2							2
3							3
4							4
5							5

P1

Pashak Company

Purchases Journal

	Date	Account Credited	Terms	Ref	Inventory (Dr.) Acc. Pay (Cr.)	
1	2014					1
2						2
3						3
4						4
5						5

(a) & (b)

CR1

Newell Co.

Cash Receipts Journal

Date	Account Credited	Ref.	Cash Dr.	Sales Discounts Dr.	Accounts Receivable Cr.	Sales Revenue Cr.	Other Accounts Cr.	COGS Dr. Inventory Cr.
2014								1
								2
								3
								4
								5

CP1

Newell Co.

Cash Payments Journal

Date	Check Number	Account Debited	Ref	Other Accounts Dr.	Accounts Payable Dr.	Cash Cr.
2014						1
						2
						3
						4

(a)

	Date	Account Titles	Debit	Credit	
1	Mar 2				1
2					2
3					3
4	5				4
5					5
6					6
7	7				7
8					8
9					9
10					10
11					11
12					12

(b)

1		1
2		2
3		3
4		4
5		5
6		6
7		7
8		8
9		9
10		10
11		11
12		12
13		13
14		14
15		15
16		16
17		17
18		18
19		19
20		20
21		21
22		22
23		23

EF-12 (a)

P1

	Date	Account Credited	Ref.	Inventory (Dr.) Acc. Pay. (Cr.)	
1	July 3				1
2	12				2
3	14				3
4	17				4
5	20				5
6	21				6
7	29				7
8					8
9					9

Purchases Journal

(b)   General Journal

	Date	Account Titles	Ref	Debit	Credit	
1	July 1					1
2						2
3						3
4						4
5	15					5
6						6
7						7
8						8
9	18					9
10						10
11						11
12	25					12
13						13

EF-13

1			1
2			2
3			3
4			4
5			5
6			6

1	(a) Accounts Payable		1
2			2
3			3
4			4
5			5
6			6
7	(b) Accounts Receivable		7
8			8
9			9
10			10
11			11
12			12
13	(c) Cash		13
14			14
15			15
16			16
17			17
18			18
19	(d) Inventory		19
20			20
21			21
22			22
23			23
24			24
25			25
26	(e) Sales		26
27			27
28			28
29			29
30			30

(a)

Cash Receipts Journal

CR1

Date	Account Credited	Ref.	Cash Dr.	Sales Discounts Dr.	Accounts Receivable Cr.	Sales Revenue Cr.	Other Accounts Cr.	COGS Dr. Inventory Cr.	
									1
									2
									3
									4
									5
									6
									7
									8
									9
									10
									11
									12
									13
									14
									15
									16
									17

(b)

General Ledger

Accounts Receivable   No. 112

Date	Explanation	Ref	Debit	Credit	Balance
Apr. 1	Balance	√			7 4 5 0

Accounts Receivable Subsidiary Ledger

Siem

Date	Explanation	Ref	Debit	Credit	Balance
Apr.1	Balance	√			1 5 5 0

Milkie

Date	Explanation	Ref	Debit	Credit	Balance
Apr. 1	Balance	√			1 2 0 0

Jury Co,

Date	Explanation	Ref	Debit	Credit	Balance
Apr. 1	Balance	√			2 9 0 0

Afzal

Date	Explanation	Ref	Debit	Credit	Balance
Apr. 1	Balance	√			1 8 0 0

(c)

1	
2	
3	
4	
5	
6	

Gatske Company

(a)

CP1

Cash Payments Journal

Date	Ck. No.	Account Debited	Ref.	Other Accounts Dr.	Accounts Payable Dr.	Inventory Cr.	Cash Cr.
1							
2							
3							
4							
5							
6							
7							
8							
9							
10							
11							
12							
13							
14							
15							
16							
17							
18							
19							
20							

(b)

General Ledger

Accounts Payable   No. 201

Date	Explanation	Ref	Debit	Credit	Balance
Oct. 1	Balance	√			1 1 0 0 0

Accounts Payable Subsidiary Ledger

Deavers Co.

Date	Explanation	Ref	Debit	Credit	Balance
Oct. 1	Balance	√			2 7 0 0

Greer Co.

Date	Explanation	Ref	Debit	Credit	Balance
Oct. 1	Balance	√			2 5 0 0

May Co.

Date	Explanation	Ref	Debit	Credit	Balance
Oct. 1	Balance	√			2 1 0 0

Snell Company

Date	Explanation	Ref	Debit	Credit	Balance
Oct. 1	Balance	√			3 7 0 0

(c)

1	Accounts payable balance:	1
2		2
3	Subsidiary account balances:	3
4		4
5		5
6		6

(a)   P1

			Purchases Journal			
				Accounts Payable Cr.	Inventory Dr.	Orther Accounts Dr.
	Date	Account Credited (Debited)	Ref.			
1						
2						
3						
4						
5						
6						
7						
8						
9						
10						
11						
12						
13						
14						
15						
16						
17						
18						

		Sales Journal			
				Accounts Receiv. Dr. Sales Cr.	COGS Dr. Merchandise Inventory Cr.
	Date	Account Debited	Ref.		
1					
2					
3					
4					
5					
6					
7					
8					
9					
10					

S1

(a) (Continued)

General Journal G1

	Date	Account Titles	Ref.	Debit	Credit	
1	July 8					1
2						2
3						3
4						4
5						5
6	22					6
7						7
8						8
9						9
10						10
11						11
12						12

(b)

General Ledger

Accounts Receivable No. 112

Date	Explanation	Ref.	Debit	Credit	Balance

Inventory No. 120

Date	Explanation	Ref.	Debit	Credit	Balance

Supplies No. 126

Date	Explanation	Ref.	Debit	Credit	Balance

Equipment No. 157

Date	Explanation	Ref.	Debit	Credit	Balance

(b)(Continued)

Accounts Payable   No. 201

Date	Explanation	Ref.	Debit	Credit	Balance

Sales Revenue   No. 401

Date	Explanation	Ref.	Debit	Credit	Balance

Sales Returns and Allowances   No. 412

Date	Explanation	Ref.	Debit	Credit	Balance

Cost of Goods Sold   No. 505

Date	Explanation	Ref.	Debit	Credit	Balance

Advertising Expense   No. 610

Date	Explanation	Ref.	Debit	Credit	Balance

(b)(Continued)

Accounts Receivable Subsidiary Ledger

Pitas Bros.

Date	Explanation	Ref.	Debit	Credit	Balance

Effron Company

Date	Explanation	Ref.	Debit	Credit	Balance

Felber Company

Date	Explanation	Ref.	Debit	Credit	Balance

Musky Company

Date	Explanation	Ref.	Debit	Credit	Balance

(b)(Continued)   *Accounts Payable Subsidiary Ledger*

Bowe Supply

Date	Explanation	Ref.	Debit	Credit	Balance

Pegasus Shipping

Date	Explanation	Ref.	Debit	Credit	Balance

Chad Company

Date	Explanation	Ref.	Debit	Credit	Balance

Kivlin Company

Date	Explanation	Ref.	Debit	Credit	Balance

Wei Advertisements

Date	Explanation	Ref.	Debit	Credit	Balance

Goran Company

Date	Explanation	Ref.	Debit	Credit	Balance

(c)

1	Accounts receivable balance:	1
2		2
3		3
4		4
5		5
6	Subsidiary account balances:	6
7		7
8		8
9		9
10		10
11		11
12		12
13		13
14		14
15		15
16		16
17	Accounts payable balance:	17
18		18
19		19
20		20
21	Subsidiary account balances:	21
22		22
23		23
24		24
25		25
26		26
27		27
28		28
29		29
30		30
31		31
32		32
33		33
34		34
35		35
36		36
37		37
38		38
39		39
40		40

(a), (b), & (c)   S1

	Sales Journal					
Date	Account Debited	Invoice No.	Ref.	Accounts Receivable Dr. Sales Rev. Cr.	COGS Dr. Inventory Cr.	
1						1
2						2
3						3
4						4
5						5
6						6
7						7

P1

	Purchases Journal			
Date	Account Credited	Ref.	Inventory (Dr.) Acc. Pay (Cr.)	
1				1
2				2
3				3
4				4
5				5
6				6
7				7
8				8

G1

	General Journal				
Date	Account Titles	Ref.	Debit	Credit	
1					1
2					2
3					3
4					4
5					5
6					6

(a), (b), (c) (Continued)

Cash Receipts Journal

CR1

Date	Account Credited	Ref.	Cash Dr.	Sales Discounts Dr.	Accounts Receivable Cr.	Sales Revenue Cr.	Other Accounts Cr.	COGS Dr. Inventory Cr.
1								
2								
3								
4								
5								
6								
7								
8								
9								
10								
11								
12								
13								
14								
15								

(a), (b), (c) (Continued)

Cash Payments Journal

Date	Account Debited	Ref.	Other Accounts Dr.	Accounts Payable Dr.	Inventory Cr.	Cash Cr.
1						
2						
3						
4						
5						
6						
7						
8						
9						
10						
11						
12						
13						
14						
15						

CP1

(a), (d) & (g)   General Ledger

Cash   No. 101

Date	Explanation	Ref.	Debit	Credit	Balance

Accounts Receivable   No. 112

Date	Explanation	Ref.	Debit	Credit	Balance

Inventory   No. 120

Date	Explanation	Ref.	Debit	Credit	Balance

Supplies   No. 127

Date	Explanation	Ref.	Debit	Credit	Balance

Prepaid Rent   No. 131

Date	Explanation	Ref.	Debit	Credit	Balance

Accounts Payable   No. 201

Date	Explanation	Ref.	Debit	Credit	Balance

Common Stock   No. 311

Date	Explanation	Ref.	Debit	Credit	Balance

(a), (d) & (g) (Continued)

Cash Dividends
No. 332

Date	Explanation	Ref.	Debit	Credit	Balance

Sales Revenue
No. 401

Date	Explanation	Ref.	Debit	Credit	Balance

Sales Discounts
No. 414

Date	Explanation	Ref.	Debit	Credit	Balance

Cost of Goods Sold
No. 505

Date	Explanation	Ref.	Debit	Credit	Balance

Supplies Expense
No. 631

Date	Explanation	Ref.	Debit	Credit	Balance

Rent Expense
No. 729

Date	Explanation	Ref.	Debit	Credit	Balance

(b)

			Sales Journal		
					S1
Date	Account Debited	Ref.	Accounts Receivable Dr. Sales Rev. Cr.	COGS Dr. Inventory Cr.	
1					1
2					2
3					3
4					4
5					5
6					6

(a), (b), (c) (Continued)

CR1

Cash Receipts Journal

Date	Account Credited	Ref.	Cash Dr.	Sales Discounts Dr.	Accounts Receivable Cr.	Sales Revenue Cr.	Other Accounts Cr.	COGS Dr. Inventory Cr.
1								
2								
3								
4								
5								
6								
7								
8								
9								
10								
11								
12								
13								
14								
15								

(c)

Accounts Receivable Subsidiary Ledger

Dorfner Co.

Date	Explanation	Ref.	Debit	Credit	Balance

M. Putzi

Date	Explanation	Ref.	Debit	Credit	Balance

L. Ortiz

Date	Explanation	Ref.	Debit	Credit	Balance

Bonilha

Date	Explanation	Ref.	Debit	Credit	Balance

Accounts Payable Subsidiary Ledger

D. Tablert

Date	Explanation	Ref.	Debit	Credit	Balance

K. Emmons

Date	Explanation	Ref.	Debit	Credit	Balance

G. Young

Date	Explanation	Ref.	Debit	Credit	Balance

T. Cigale

Date	Explanation	Ref.	Debit	Credit	Balance

(c) (Continued)

M. Huang

Date	Explanation	Ref.	Debit	Credit	Balance

(e)

Rosalez Co.
Trial Balance
July 31, 2014

		Debit	Credit	
1				1
2				2
3				3
4				4
5				5
6				6
7				7
8				8
9				9
10				10
11				11
12				12
13				13
14				14
15				15

(f)

1	Accounts receivable balance:	
2		
3	Subsidiary accounts balance:	
4		
5		
6		
7	Accounts payable balance:	
8		
9	Subsidiary accounts balance:	
10		
11		
12		

(g)

General Journal   G1

	Date	Account Titles	Ref.	Debit	Credit	
1						1
2						2
3						3
4						4
5						5
6						6

(h)

Rosalez Co. Adjusted Trial Balance July 31, 2014	Debit	Credit	
1 Cash			1
2 Accounts Receivable			2
3 Inventory			3
4 Supplies			4
5 Prepaid Rent			5
6 Accounts Payable			6
7 Common Stock			7
8 Dividends			8
9 Sales Revenue			9
10 Sales Discounts			10
11 Cost of Goods Sold			11
12 Supplies Expense			12
13 Rent Expense			13
14			14
15			15
16			16

(b) & (c)

CR1

Cash Receipts Journal

Date	Account Credited	Ref.	Cash Dr.	Sales Discounts Dr.	Accounts Receivable Cr.	Sales Revenue Cr.	Other Accounts Cr.	COGS Dr. Inventory Cr.
1								
2								
3								
4								
5								
6								

CP1

Cash Payments Journal

Date	Account Debited	Ref.	Other Accounts Dr.	Accounts Payable Dr.	Inventory Cr.	Cash Cr.
1						
2						
3						
4						
5						
6						
7						
8						

(b) & (c) (Continued)

S1

| | | | Accounts | COGS Dr. |
| | Account | | Receivable Dr. | |
Date	Debited	Ref.	Sales Rev. Cr.	Inventory Cr.
1				
2				
3				
4				
5				

Sales Journal

P1

Purchases Journal

Date	Account Credited	Ref.	Inventory Dr. Acc. Pay. Cr.
1			
2			
3			
4			
5			

General Journal

G1

Date	Account Titles	Ref.	Debit	Credit
1				
2				
3				
4				
5				
6				
7				
8				
9				
10				
11				
12				
13				

(a) and (c)   *General Ledger*

Cash   No. 101

Date	Explanation	Ref.	Debit	Credit	Balance
Jan. 1	Balance	√			4 1 5 0 0

Accounts Receivable   No. 112

Date	Explanation	Ref.	Debit	Credit	Balance
Jan. 1	Balance	√			1 5 0 0 0

Notes Receivable   No. 115

Date	Explanation	Ref.	Debit	Credit	Balance
Jan. 1	Balance	√			4 5 0 0 0

Inventory   No. 120

Date	Explanation	Ref.	Debit	Credit	Balance
Jan. 1	Balance	√			2 0 0 0 0

Equipment   No. 157

Date	Explanation	Ref.	Debit	Credit	Balance
Jan. 1	Balance	√			7 5 0 0

Accumulated Depreciation - Equipment   No. 158

Date	Explanation	Ref.	Debit	Credit	Balance
Jan. 1	Balance	√			1 5 0 0

(a) and (c) (Continued)

Notes Payable   No. 200

Date	Explanation	Ref.	Debit	Credit	Balance

Accounts Payable   No. 201

Date	Explanation	Ref.	Debit	Credit	Balance
Jan. 1	Balance	√			4 3 0 0 0

Common Stock   No. 311

Date	Explanation	Ref.	Debit	Credit	Balance
Jan. 1	Balance	√			8 4 5 0 0

Sales Revenue   No. 401

Date	Explanation	Ref.	Debit	Credit	Balance

Sales Returns and Allowances   No. 412

Date	Explanation	Ref.	Debit	Credit	Balance

Sales Discounts   No. 414

Date	Explanation	Ref.	Debit	Credit	Balance

Cost of Goods Sold   No. 505

Date	Explanation	Ref.	Debit	Credit	Balance

(a) and (c) (Continued)

Salaries and Wages Expense   No. 726

Date	Explanation	Ref.	Debit	Credit	Balance

Rent Expense   No. 729

Date	Explanation	Ref.	Debit	Credit	Balance

Accounts Receivable Subsidiary Ledger

M. Barajas

Date	Explanation	Ref.	Debit	Credit	Balance
Jan. 1	Balance	√			2500

J. Clare

Date	Explanation	Ref.	Debit	Credit	Balance
Jan. 1	Balance	√			7500

E. Divine

Date	Explanation	Ref.	Debit	Credit	Balance
Jan. 1	Balance	√			5000

T. Payton

Date	Explanation	Ref.	Debit	Credit	Balance

(a) and (c) (Continued)

Accounts Payable Subsidiary Ledger

E. Monty

Date	Explanation	Ref.	Debit	Credit	Balance

B. Forrest

Date	Explanation	Ref.	Debit	Credit	Balance
Jan. 1	Balance	√			1 0 0 0 0

L. Gold

Date	Explanation	Ref.	Debit	Credit	Balance
Jan. 1	Balance	√			1 8 0 0 0

A. Qazi

Date	Explanation	Ref.	Debit	Credit	Balance
Jan. 1	Balance	√			1 5 0 0 0

B. Yang

Date	Explanation	Ref.	Debit	Credit	Balance

(d)

Amland Co. Trial Balance January 31, 2014	Debit	Credit
1 Cash		
2 Accounts Receivable		
3 Notes Receivable		
4 Inventory		
5 Equipment		
6 Accumulated Depreciation - Equipment		
7 Notes Payable		
8 Accounts Payable		
9 Common Stock		
10 Sales Revenue		
11 Sales Returns and Allowances		
12 Sales Discounts		
13 Cost of Goods Sold		
14 Salaries and Wages Expense		
15 Rent Expense		
16		
17		
18		

(e)

1 Accounts receivable subsidiary ledger:		
2		
3		
4		
5		
6		
7 Account receivable control:		
8		
9 Accounts payable subsidiary ledger:		
10		
11		
12		
13		
14		
15 Accounts payable control:		
16		

Caspari Company

(a)

Cash Receipts Journal

CR1

Date	Account Credited	Ref.	Cash Dr.	Sales Discounts Dr.	Accounts Receivable Cr.	Sales Revenue Cr.	Other Accounts Cr.	COGS Dr. Inventory Cr.	
									1
									2
									3
									4
									5
									6
									7
									8
									9
									10
									11
									12
									13
									14
									15
									16
									17

(b)

General Ledger

Accounts Receivable   No. 112

Date	Explanation	Ref	Debit	Credit	Balance
June 1	Balance	√			7 5 0 0

Accounts Receivable Subsidiary Ledger

Detwiler & Son

Date	Explanation	Ref	Debit	Credit	Balance
June 1	Balance	√			2 5 0 0

Flores Co.

Date	Explanation	Ref	Debit	Credit	Balance
June 1	Balance	√			1 9 0 0

Glaimo Bros.

Date	Explanation	Ref	Debit	Credit	Balance
June 1	Balance	√			1 6 0 0

Loomi's Co.

Date	Explanation	Ref	Debit	Credit	Balance
June 1	Balance	√			1 5 0 0

(c)

1		1
2		2
3		3

(a)

Cash Payments Journal

CP1

Date	Ck. No.	Account Debited	Ref.	Other Accounts Dr.	Accounts Payable Dr.	Inventory Cr.	Cash Cr.
1							
2							
3							
4							
5							
6							
7							
8							
9							
10							
11							
12							
13							
14							
15							
16							
17							
18							
19							
20							

(b)

General Ledger

Accounts Payable   No. 201

Date	Explanation	Ref	Debit	Credit	Balance
Nov. 1	Balance	√			9 3 5 0

Accounts Payable Subsidiary Ledger

C. Holt & Co.

Date	Explanation	Ref	Debit	Credit	Balance
Nov. 1	Balance	√			4 5 0 0

O. Kroll

Date	Explanation	Ref	Debit	Credit	Balance
Nov. 1	Balance	√			2 3 5 0

K. Radaj

Date	Explanation	Ref	Debit	Credit	Balance
Nov. 1	Balance	√			1 0 0 0

Weber Bros.

Date	Explanation	Ref	Debit	Credit	Balance
Nov. 1	Balance	√			1 5 0 0

(c)

1	Accounts payable balance:							1
2								2
3								3
4	Subsidiary account balances:							4
5								5
6								6
7								7
8								8
9								9
10								10

(a)

Purchases Journal

	Date	Account Credited (Debited)	Ref.	Accounts Payable Cr.	Inventory Dr.	Other Accounts Dr.	
1							1
2							2
3							3
4							4
5							5
6							6
7							7
8							8
9							9
10							10
11							11
12							12
13							13
14							14
15							15
16							16
17							17
18							18

Sales Journal

	Date	Account Debited	Ref.	Accounts Receiv. Dr. Sales Rev. Cr.	COGS Dr. Inventory Cr.	
1						1
2						2
3						3
4						4
5						5
6						6
7						7
8						8
9						9
10						10

(a) (Continued)

General Journal   G1

	Date	Account Titles	Ref.	Debit	Credit	
1						1
2						2
3						3
4						4
5						5
6						6
7						7
8						8
9						9
10						10
11						11
12						12

(b)

General Ledger

Accounts Receivable   No. 112

Date	Explanation	Ref.	Debit	Credit	Balance

Inventory   No. 120

Date	Explanation	Ref.	Debit	Credit	Balance

Supplies   No. 126

Date	Explanation	Ref.	Debit	Credit	Balance

Equipment   No. 157

Date	Explanation	Ref.	Debit	Credit	Balance

(b)(Continued)

Accounts Payable   No. 201

Date	Explanation	Ref.	Debit	Credit	Balance

Sales Revenue   No. 401

Date	Explanation	Ref.	Debit	Credit	Balance

Sales Returns and Allowances   No. 412

Date	Explanation	Ref.	Debit	Credit	Balance

Cost of Goods Sold   No. 505

Date	Explanation	Ref.	Debit	Credit	Balance

Advertising Expense   No. 610

Date	Explanation	Ref.	Debit	Credit	Balance

(b)(Continued)

Accounts Receivable Subsidiary Ledger

Eder

Date	Explanation	Ref.	Debit	Credit	Balance

Dixon Bros.

Date	Explanation	Ref.	Debit	Credit	Balance

Lamb Company

Date	Explanation	Ref.	Debit	Credit	Balance

(b)(Continued)   *Accounts Payable Subsidiary Ledger*

Porter Freight

Date	Explanation	Ref.	Debit	Credit	Balance

Yan Company

Date	Explanation	Ref.	Debit	Credit	Balance

Rizio Supply

Date	Explanation	Ref.	Debit	Credit	Balance

Quirk Company

Date	Explanation	Ref.	Debit	Credit	Balance

Zamora Company

Date	Explanation	Ref.	Debit	Credit	Balance

Anshus Advertising

Date	Explanation	Ref.	Debit	Credit	Balance

(c)

1	Accounts receivable balance:	1
2		2
3		3
4		4
5		5
6	Subsidiary account balances:	6
7		7
8		8
9		9
10		10
11		11
12		12
13		13
14		14
15		15
16		16
17	Accounts payable balance:	17
18		18
19		19
20		20
21	Subsidiary account balances:	21
22		22
23		23
24		24
25		25
26		26
27		27
28		28
29		29
30		30
31		31
32		32
33		33
34		34
35		35
36		36
37		37
38		38
39		39
40		40

(a), (b), & (c)

S1

					Accounts Receivable Dr. Sales Rev. Cr.	COGS Dr. Inventory Cr.	
	Date	Account Debited	Invoice No.	Ref.			
1							1
2							2
3							3
4							4
5							5
6							6
7							7

Sales Journal

P1

Purchases Journal

	Date	Account Credited	Ref.	Inventory (Dr.) Acc. Pay (Cr.)	
1					1
2					2
3					3
4					4
5					5
6					6
7					7
8					8

G1

General Journal

	Date	Account Titles	Ref.	Debit	Credit	
1						1
2						2
3						3
4						4
5						5
6						6

(a), (b), (c) (Continued)

CR1

Cash Receipts Journal

	Date	Account Credited	Ref.	Cash Dr.	Sales Discounts Dr.	Accounts Receivable Cr.	Sales Revenue Cr.	Other Accounts Cr.	COGS Dr. Inventory Cr.
1									
2									
3									
4									
5									
6									
7									
8									
9									
10									

(a), (b), (c) (Continued)

Cash Payments Journal CP1

Date	Account Debited	Ref.	Other Accounts Dr.	Accounts Payable Dr.	Inventory Cr.	Cash Cr.
1						
2						
3						
4						
5						
6						
7						
8						
9						
10						
11						

Name

Section

Date

Problem F-5B

Wesley Co.

(b)

Purchases Journal

P1

Date	Account Credited	Ref.	Inventory (Dr) Acc Pay (Cr)	
1				1
2				2
3				3
4				4
5				5
6				6
7				7

Cash Payments Journal

CP1

Date	Account Debited	Ref.	Other Accounts Dr.	Accounts Payable Dr.	Inventory Cr.	Cash Cr.	
1							1
2							2
3							3
4							4
5							5
6							6
7							7
8							8
9							9
10							10

(a), (d), & (g)

General Ledger

Cash   No. 101

Date	Explanation	Ref.	Debit	Credit	Balance

Accounts Receivable   No. 112

Date	Explanation	Ref.	Debit	Credit	Balance

Inventory   No. 120

Date	Explanation	Ref.	Debit	Credit	Balance

Supplies   No. 126

Date	Explanation	Ref.	Debit	Credit	Balance

Equipment   No. 157

Date	Explanation	Ref.	Debit	Credit	Balance

Accumulated Depreciation - Equipment   No. 158

Date	Explanation	Ref.	Debit	Credit	Balance

(a), (d) and (g) (Continued)

Accounts Payable   No. 201

Date	Explanation	Ref.	Debit	Credit	Balance

Common Stock   No. 311

Date	Explanation	Ref.	Debit	Credit	Balance

Cash Dividends   No. 332

Date	Explanation	Ref.	Debit	Credit	Balance

Sales Revenue   No. 401

Date	Explanation	Ref.	Debit	Credit	Balance

Sales Discounts   No. 414

Date	Explanation	Ref.	Debit	Credit	Balance

Cost of Goods Sold   No. 505

Date	Explanation	Ref.	Debit	Credit	Balance

Supplies Expense   No. 631

Date	Explanation	Ref.	Debit	Credit	Balance

Depreciation Expense   No. 711

Date	Explanation	Ref.	Debit	Credit	Balance

(c

Accounts Receivable Subsidiary Ledger

S. Armour

Date	Explanation	Ref.	Debit	Credit	Balance

V. Ciatti

Date	Explanation	Ref.	Debit	Credit	Balance

M. Barajas

Date	Explanation	Ref.	Debit	Credit	Balance

A. Dobbs

Date	Explanation	Ref.	Debit	Credit	Balance

Accounts Payable Subsidiary Ledger

D. Hachey

Date	Explanation	Ref.	Debit	Credit	Balance

T. Valentine

Date	Explanation	Ref.	Debit	Credit	Balance

B. Kucera

Date	Explanation	Ref.	Debit	Credit	Balance

(c) (Continued)
E. Nicks

Date	Explanation	Ref.	Debit	Credit	Balance

(e)

Wesley Co.
Trial Balance
February 28, 2014

		Debit	Credit	
1	Cash			1
2	Accounts Receivable			2
3	Inventory			3
4	Supplies			4
5	Equipment			5
6	Accounts Payable			6
7	Common Stock			7
8	Cash Dividends			8
9	Sales			9
10	Sales Discounts			10
11	Cost of Goods Sold			11
12				12
13				13

(f)

1	Accounts receivable control account:		1
2			2
3	Accounts receivable subsidiary accounts:		3
4			4
5			5
6			6
7			7
8	Accounts payable control account:		8
9			9
10	Accounts payable subsidiary accounts:		10
11			11
12			12
13			13

(g)

	Date	Account Titles	Ref.	Debit	Credit	
General Journal					G1	
1	Feb 28					1
2						2
3						3
4						4
5						5
6	28					6
7						7
8						8
9						9
10						10

(h)

Wesley Co.
Adjusted Trial Balance
February 28, 2014

		Debit	Credit	
1	Cash			1
2	Accounts Receivable			2
3	Inventory			3
4	Supplies			4
5	Equipment			5
6	Accumulated Depreciation - Equipment			6
7	Accounts Payable			7
8	Common Stock			8
9	Cash Dividends			9
10	Sales			10
11	Sales Discounts			11
12	Cost of Goods Sold			12
13	Supplies Expense			13
14	Depreciation Expense			14
15				15
16				16
17				17
18				18
19				19
20				20
21				21

(a)   S1

Sales Journal

	Date	Account Debited	Invoice No.	Ref.	Accounts Receiv. Dr. Sales Rev. Cr.	
1						1
2						2
3						3
4						4
5						5
6						6
7						7
8						8
9						9
10						10
11						11
12						12

P1

Purchases Journal

	Date	Account Credited	Terms	Ref.	Purchases Dr. Acc. Pay Cr.	
1						1
2						2
3						3
4						4
5						5
6						6
7						7
8						8
9						9
10						10
11						11
12						12

Comprehensive Problem: Chapters 3 to 6 and Appendix F Continued

Zweifel Company

(a) (Continued)

CR1

Cash Receipts Journal

Date	Account Credited	Ref.	Cash Dr.	Accounts Receivable Cr.	Sales Revenue Cr.	Other Accounts Cr.
1						
2						
3						
4						
5						
6						
7						
8						
9						
10						
11						
12						
13						
14						
15						

Comprehensive Problem: Chapters 3 to 6 and Appendix F Continued

Zweifel Company

CP1

(a) (Continued)

Cash Payments Journal

Date	Account Debited	Ref.	Other Accounts Dr.	Accounts Payable Dr.	Supplies Dr.	Cash Cr.

(a) and (e)

	General Journal				G1
Date	Account Titles	Ref	Debit	Credit	
1					1
2					2
3					3
4					4
5					5
6					6
7					7
8					8
9					9
10					10
11					11
12					12
13	Adjusting Entries				13
14					14
15					15
16					16
17					17
18					18
19					19
20					20
21					21
22					22
23					23
24					24
25					25
26					26
27					27
28					28
29					29
30					30
31					31
32					32
33					33
34					34
35					35
36					36
37					37
38					38
39					39
40					40

(a) and (e) (Continued)

General Journal   G1

	Date	Account Titles	Ref	Debit	Credit	
1		Closing Entries				1
2						2
3						3
4						4
5						5
6						6
7						7
8						8
9						9
10						10
11						11
12						12
13						13
14						14
15						15
16						16
17						17
18						18
19						19
20						20
21						21
22						22
23						23
24						24
25						25
26						26
27						27
28						28
29						29
30						30
31						31
32						32
33						33
34						34
35						35
36						36
37						37
38						38
39						39
40						40

(b) and (e)

General Ledger

Cash   No. 101

Date	Explanation	Ref.	Debit	Credit	Balance
Jan. 1	Balance	√			3 2 7 5 0

Accounts Receivable   No. 112

Date	Explanation	Ref.	Debit	Credit	Balance
Jan. 1	Balance	√			1 3 0 0 0

Notes Receivable   No. 115

Date	Explanation	Ref.	Debit	Credit	Balance
Jan. 1	Balance	√			4 2 0 0 0

Inventory   No. 120

Date	Explanation	Ref.	Debit	Credit	Balance
Jan. 1	Balance	√			2 0 0 0 0

Supplies   No. 125

Date	Explanation	Ref.	Debit	Credit	Balance
Jan. 1	Balance	√			1 0 0 0

Prepaid Insurance   No. 130

Date	Explanation	Ref.	Debit	Credit	Balance
Jan. 1	Balance	√			2 0 0 0

(b) and (e) (Continued)

Equipment   No. 157

Date	Explanation	Ref.	Debit	Credit	Balance
Jan. 1	Balance	√			6450

Accumulated Depreciation - Equipment   No. 158

Date	Explanation	Ref.	Debit	Credit	Balance
Jan. 1	Balance	√			1500

Notes Payable   No. 200

Date	Explanation	Ref.	Debit	Credit	Balance

Accounts Payable   No. 201

Date	Explanation	Ref.	Debit	Credit	Balance
Jan. 1	Balance	√			35000

Interest Payable   No. 230

Date	Explanation	Ref.	Debit	Credit	Balance

Common Stock   No. 311

Date	Explanation	Ref.	Debit	Credit	Balance
Jan. 1	Balance	√			70000

Retained Earnings   No. 320

Date	Explanation	Ref.	Debit	Credit	Balance
Jan. 1	Balance	√			10700

Cash Dividends   No. 332

Date	Explanation	Ref.	Debit	Credit	Balance

(b) and (e) (Continued)

Income Summary   No. 350

Date	Explanation	Ref.	Debit	Credit	Balance

Sales Revenue   No. 401

Date	Explanation	Ref.	Debit	Credit	Balance

Sales Returns and Allowances   No. 412

Date	Explanation	Ref.	Debit	Credit	Balance

Purchases   No. 510

Date	Explanation	Ref.	Debit	Credit	Balance

Purchase Returns and Allowances   No. 512

Date	Explanation	Ref.	Debit	Credit	Balance

Freight-in   No. 516

Date	Explanation	Ref.	Debit	Credit	Balance

Salaries AND Wages Expense   No. 627

Date	Explanation	Ref.	Debit	Credit	Balance

(b) and (e) (Continued)

Depreciation Expense   No. 711

Date	Explanation	Ref.	Debit	Credit	Balance

Interest Expense   No. 718

Date	Explanation	Ref.	Debit	Credit	Balance

Insurance Expense   No. 722

Date	Explanation	Ref.	Debit	Credit	Balance

Supplies Expense   No. 728

Date	Explanation	Ref.	Debit	Credit	Balance

Rent Expense   No. 729

Date	Explanation	Ref.	Debit	Credit	Balance

(b) and (e) (Continued)

Accounts Receivable Subsidiary Ledger

G.Dukes

Date	Explanation	Ref.	Debit	Credit	Balance
Jan. 1	Balance	√			1800

M. Fischer

Date	Explanation	Ref.	Debit	Credit	Balance

M. Hall

Date	Explanation	Ref.	Debit	Credit	Balance
Jan. 1	Balance	√			7200

L.Longhini

Date	Explanation	Ref.	Debit	Credit	Balance
Jan. 1	Balance	√			4000

W. Rayms

Date	Explanation	Ref.	Debit	Credit	Balance

(b) and (e) (Continued)

Accounts Payable Subsidiary Ledger

J. Liotta

Date	Explanation	Ref.	Debit	Credit	Balance

O. Kisten

Date	Explanation	Ref.	Debit	Credit	Balance
Jan. 1	Balance	√			9000

D. Markoff

Date	Explanation	Ref.	Debit	Credit	Balance
Jan. 1	Balance	√			15000

L. Quinn

Date	Explanation	Ref.	Debit	Credit	Balance
Jan. 1	Balance	√			11000

K. Zapfel

Date	Explanation	Ref.	Debit	Credit	Balance

Comprehensive Problem: Chapters 3 to 6 and Appendix F

Zweifel Company

You will find this working paper at the end of this work book

(d)

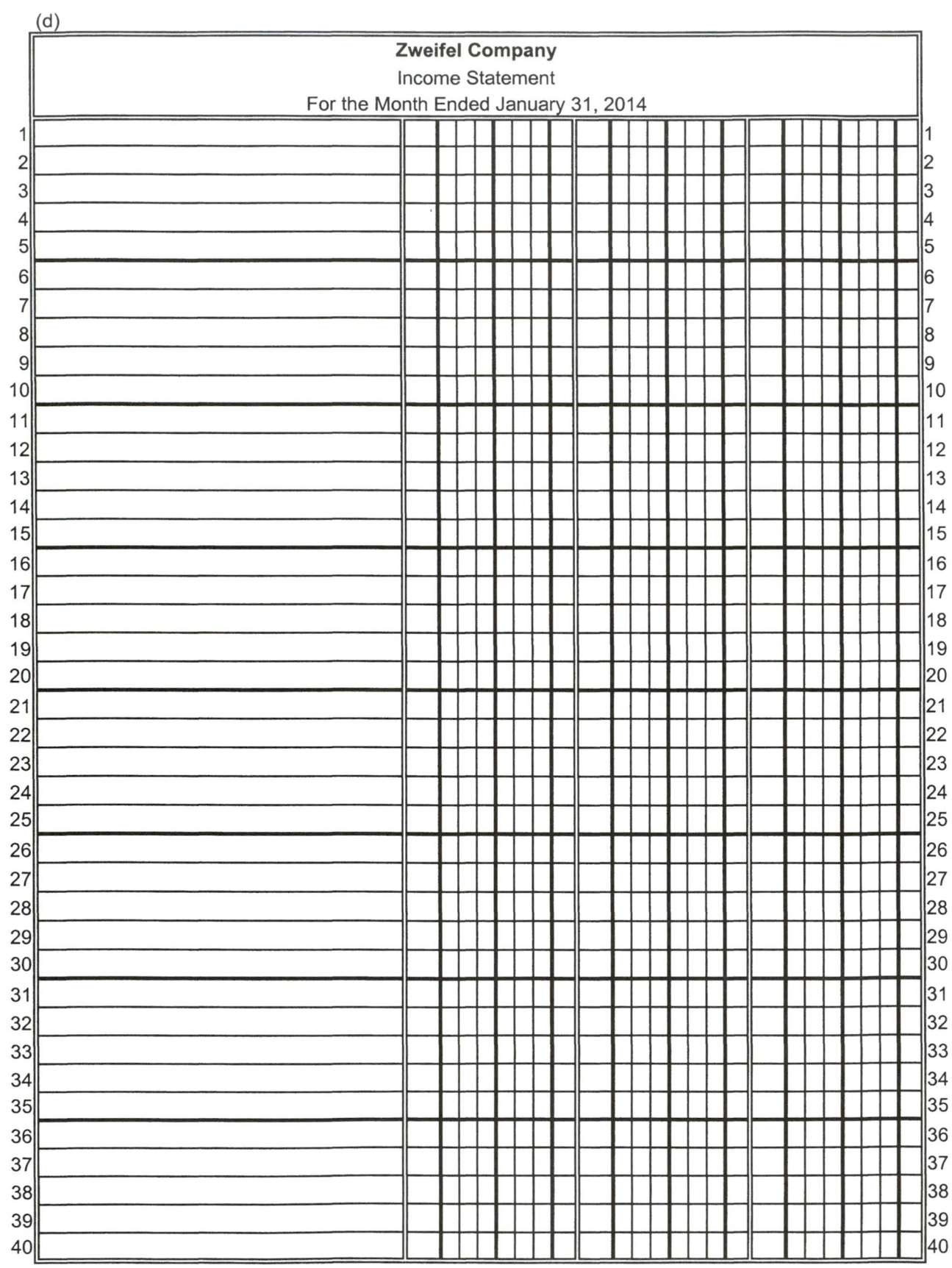

Zweifel Company

Income Statement

For the Month Ended January 31, 2014

(d) (Continued)

Zweifel Company

Statement of Retained Earnings

For the Month Ended January 31, 2014

Zweifel Company

Balance Sheet

January 31, 2014

Assets

Liabilities and Stockholders' Equity

(f)

Zweifel Company	Debit	Credit	
Post-Closing Trial Balance			
January 31, 2014			
1 Cash			1
2 Notes Receivable			2
3 Accounts Receivable			3
4 Inventory			4
5 Supplies			5
6 Prepaid Insurance			6
7 Equipment			7
8 Accumulated Depreciation - Equipment			8
9 Notes Payable			9
10 Accounts Payable			10
11 Interest Payable			11
12 Common Stock			12
13 Retained Earnings			13
14			14

1 Accounts Receivable balance:		1
2		2
3 Subsidiary account balances:		3
4		4
5		5
6		6
7		7
8		8
9		9
10 Accounts Payable balance:		10
11		11
12 Subsidiary account balances:		12
13		13
14		14
15		15
16		16
17		17

S1

Sales Journal

	Date	Account Debited	Invoice No.	Ref.	Accounts Receiv. Dr. Sales Rev. Cr.	COGS Dr. Inventory Cr.	
1							1
2							2
3							3
4							4
5							5
6							6
7							7
8							8
9							9
10							10
11							11
12							12

P1

Purchases Journal

	Date	Account Credited	Terms	Ref.	Inventory (Dr.) Acc. Pay (Cr.)	
1						1
2						2
3						3
4						4
5						5
6						6
7						7
8						8
9						9
10						10
11						11
12						12

(a) (Continued)

CR1

Cash Receipts Journal

Date	Account Credited	Ref.	Cash Dr.	Sales Discounts Dr.	Accounts Receivable Cr.	Sales Revenue Cr.	Other Accounts Cr.	COGS Dr. Inventory Cr.
1								
2								
3								
4								
5								
6								
7								
8								
9								
10								
11								
12								
13								
14								
15								

Appendix F Financial Reporting Problem Continued

Bryant Co.

CP1

(a) (Continued)

Cash Payments Journal

	Date	Account Debited	Ref.	Other Accounts Dr.	Accounts Payable Dr.	Supplies Dr.	Inventory Cr.	Cash Cr.
1								
2								
3								
4								
5								
6								
7								
8								
9								
10								
11								
12								
13								
14								
15								

(a) and (e)

General Journal   G1

	Date	Account Titles	Ref	Debit	Credit	
1						1
2						2
3						3
4						4
5						5
6						6
7						7
8						8
9						9
10						10
11						11
12						12
13						13
14						14
15						15
16						16
17						17
18						18
19						19
20		Adjusting Entries				20
21	31					21
22						22
23						23
24						24
25	31					25
26						26
27						27
28						28
29	31					29
30						30
31						31
32						32
33	31					33
34						34
35						35
36						36
37						37
38						38
39						39
40						40

(a) and (e) (Continued)

General Journal   G1

	Date	Account Titles	Ref	Debit	Credit	
1		Closing Entries				1
2	Jan. 31					2
3						3
4						4
5	31					5
6						6
7						7
8						8
9						9
10						10
11						11
12						12
13						13
14						14
15						15
16						16
17						17
18	31					18
19						19
20						20
21	31					21
22						22
23						23
24						24
25						25
26						26
27						27
28						28
29						29
30						30
31						31
32						32
33						33
34						34
35						35
36						36
37						37
38						38
39						39
40						40

(b) and (e)

General Ledger

Cash
No. 101

Date	Explanation	Ref.	Debit	Credit	Balance
Jan. 1	Balance	√			3 5 7 5 0

Accounts Receivable
No. 112

Date	Explanation	Ref.	Debit	Credit	Balance
Jan. 1	Balance	√			1 3 0 0 0

Notes Receivable
No. 115

Date	Explanation	Ref.	Debit	Credit	Balance
Jan. 1	Balance	√			3 9 0 0 0

Inventory
No. 120

Date	Explanation	Ref.	Debit	Credit	Balance
Jan. 1	Balance	√			1 8 0 0 0

Supplies
No. 125

Date	Explanation	Ref.	Debit	Credit	Balance
Jan. 1	Balance	√			1 0 0 0

Prepaid Insurance
No. 130

Date	Explanation	Ref.	Debit	Credit	Balance
Jan. 1	Balance	√			2 0 0 0

(b) and (e) (Continued)

Equipment   No. 157

Date	Explanation	Ref.	Debit	Credit	Balance
Jan. 1	Balance	√			6450

Accumulated Depreciation - Equipment   No. 158

Date	Explanation	Ref.	Debit	Credit	Balance
Jan. 1	Balance	√			1500

Notes Payable   No. 200

Date	Explanation	Ref.	Debit	Credit	Balance

Accounts Payable   No. 201

Date	Explanation	Ref.	Debit	Credit	Balance
Jan. 1	Balance	√			35000

Interest Payable   No. 230

Date	Explanation	Ref.	Debit	Credit	Balance

Common Stock   No. 311

Date	Explanation	Ref.	Debit	Credit	Balance
Jan. 1	Balance	√			70000

Retained Earnings   No. 320

Date	Explanation	Ref.	Debit	Credit	Balance
Jan. 1	Balance	√			8700

Cash Dividends   No. 332

Date	Explanation	Ref.	Debit	Credit	Balance

(b) and (e) (Continued)

Income Summary   No. 350

Date	Explanation	Ref.	Debit	Credit	Balance

Sales Revenue   No. 401

Date	Explanation	Ref.	Debit	Credit	Balance

Sales Returns and Allowances   No. 412

Date	Explanation	Ref.	Debit	Credit	Balance

Sales Discounts   No. 414

Date	Explanation	Ref.	Debit	Credit	Balance

Cost of Goods Sold   No. 505

Date	Explanation	Ref.	Debit	Credit	Balance

Salaries and Wages Expense   No. 627

Date	Explanation	Ref.	Debit	Credit	Balance

Depreciation Expense   No. 711

Date	Explanation	Ref.	Debit	Credit	Balance

(b) and (e) (Continued)

Interest Expense   No. 718

Date	Explanation	Ref.	Debit	Credit	Balance

Insurance Expense   No. 722

Date	Explanation	Ref.	Debit	Credit	Balance

Supplies Expense   No. 728

Date	Explanation	Ref.	Debit	Credit	Balance

Rent Expense   No. 729

Date	Explanation	Ref.	Debit	Credit	Balance

(b) and (e) (Continued)

Accounts Receivable Subsidiary Ledger

C. Dunlap

Date	Explanation	Ref.	Debit	Credit	Balance
Jan. 1	Balance	√			1500

J. Fieber

Date	Explanation	Ref.	Debit	Credit	Balance

S. Grady

Date	Explanation	Ref.	Debit	Credit	Balance
Jan. 1	Balance	√			7500

A. Naker

Date	Explanation	Ref.	Debit	Credit	Balance
Jan. 1	Balance	√			4000

K. Rai

Date	Explanation	Ref.	Debit	Credit	Balance

(b) and (e) (Continued)

Accounts Payable Subsidiary Ledger

W. Lachey

Date	Explanation	Ref.	Debit	Credit	Balance

T. Joosten

Date	Explanation	Ref.	Debit	Credit	Balance
Jan. 1	Balance	√			9 0 0 0

A. Mangrich

Date	Explanation	Ref.	Debit	Credit	Balance
Jan. 1	Balance	√			1 5 0 0 0

I. Maida

Date	Explanation	Ref.	Debit	Credit	Balance
Jan. 1	Balance	√			1 1 0 0 0

D. Vang

Date	Explanation	Ref.	Debit	Credit	Balance

Appendix F Financial Reporting Problem

Bryant Co.

You will find this working paper at the end of this work book

(d)

Bryant Co.

Income Statement

For the Month Ended January 31, 2014

(d) (Continued)

Bryant Co.

Retained Earnings Statement

For the Month Ended January 31, 2014

1					1
2					2
3					3
4					4
5					5
6					6

Bryant Co.

Balance Sheet

January 31, 2014

	Assets			
1				1
2				2
3				3
4				4
5				5
6				6
7				7
8				8
9				9
10				10
11				11
12				12
13				13
14				14
15				15
16	Liabilities and Stockholders' Equity			16
17				17
18				18
19				19
20				20
21				21
22				22
23				23
24				24
25				25
26				26
27				27
28				28
29				29
30				30

(f)

	Bryant Co. Post-Closing Trial Balance January 31, 2014	Debit	Credit	
1	Cash			1
2	Notes Receivable			2
3	Accounts Receivable			3
4	Inventory			4
5	Supplies			5
6	Prepaid Insurance			6
7	Equipment			7
8	Accumulated Depreciation - Equipment			8
9	Notes Payable			9
10	Accounts Payable			10
11	Interest Payable			11
12	Common Stock			12
13	Retained Earnings			13
14				14
15				15

1	Accounts Receivable balance:		1
2			2
3	Subsidiary account balances:		3
4			4
5			5
6			6
7			7
8			8
9			9
10	Accounts Payable balance:		10
11			11
12	Subsidiary account balances:		12
13			13
14			14
15			15
16			16
17			17
18			18
19			19

BEG-1

	Date	Account Titles	Debit	Credit	
1	Dec. 31				1
2					2
3					3
4					4
5					5
6					6
7					7
8					8
9					9
10	**BEG-2**				10
11					11
12	a.				12
13					13
14					14
15					15
16	b.				16
17					17
18					18
19					19
20	**BEG-3**				20
21	Jan. 31				21
22					22
23					23
24					24
25					25
26					26
27					27
28					28
29					29
30					30
31					31
32					32
33					33
34					34
35					35
36					36
37					37
38					38
39					39
40					40

	Date	Account Titles	Debit	Credit	
1	(a)				1
2					2
3					3
4					4
5					5
6					6
7	(b)				7
8					8
9					9
10					10
11					11
12					12
13					13
14					14
15					15
16					16
17					17
18					18
19					19
20					20
21					21
22					22
23					23
24					24
25					25
26					26
27					27
28					28
29					29
30					30
31					31
32					32
33					33
34					34
35					35
36					36
37					37
38					38
39					39
40					40

EG-1

(a) Estimated warranties outstanding:

Month	Estimate	Units Defective	Outstanding

Date	Account Titles	Debit	Credit
(b)			
(c)			

EG-2

Kesete Online Company

Partial Balance Sheet

(a)

Current liabilities:

(b)

EG-3

General Journal

	Date	Account Titles	Debit	Credit	
1	(a)				1
2					2
3					3
4					4
5	(b)				5
6	Jan. 1				6
7					7
8					8
9					9
10	**EG-4**				10
11	Mar. 31				11
12					12
13					13
14					14
15	31				15
16					16
17					17
18					18
19					19
20					20
21					21
22					22
23					23
24					24
25					25
26					26
27					27
28					28
29					29
30					30
31					31
32					32
33					33
34					34
35					35
36					36
37					37
38					38
39					39
40					40

General Journal

	Date	Account Titles	Debit	Credit	
1	(a)				1
2	Jan. 1				2
3					3
4					4
5	5				5
6					6
7					7
8					8
9					9
10	12				10
11					11
12					12
13	14				13
14					14
15					15
16	20				16
17					17
18					18
19					19
20					20
21	25				21
22					22
23					23
24					24
25					25
26	(b) (1)				26
27	Jan. 31				27
28					28
29					29
30					30
31	(2)				31
32	Jan. 31				32
33					33
34					34
35					35
36					36
37					37
38					38
39					39
40					40

(c)

	Current liabilities:							
1								1
2								2
3								3
4								4
5								5
6								6
7								7
8								8
9								9
10								10
11								11
12								12
13								13
14								14
15								15
16								16
17								17
18								18
19								19
20								20
21								21
22								22
23								23
24								24
25								25
26								26
27								27
28								28
29								29
30								30
31								31
32								32
33								33
34								34
35								35
36								36
37								37
38								38
39								39
40								40

(a)

(b)

	Account Titles	Debit	Credit

(c)

	Account Titles	Debit	Credit

General Journal

	Date	Account Titles	Debit	Credit	
1	(a)				1
2	Jan. 5				2
3					3
4					4
5					5
6					6
7	12				7
8					8
9					9
10	14				10
11					11
12					12
13	20				13
14					14
15					15
16					16
17					17
18	21				18
19					19
20					20
21	25				21
22					22
23					23
24					24
25					25
26	(b) (1)				26
27	Jan. 31				27
28					28
29					29
30					30
31	(2)				31
32	Jan. 31				32
33					33
34					34
35					35
36					36
37					37
38					38
39					39
40					40

(c)

1	Current liabilities:			
2				
3				
4				
5				
6				
7				
8				
9				
10				
11				
12				
13				
14				
15				
16				
17				
18				
19				
20				
21				
22				
23				
24				
25				
26				
27				
28				
29				
30				
31				
32				
33				
34				
35				
36				
37				
38				
39				
40				

(a)

(b)

Account Titles	Debit	Credit

(c)

Account Titles	Debit	Credit

(a)

	Kinney's Repair Inc.													
	Assets						=	Liabilities	+			Stockholders' Equity		
Trans-actions	Cash	+	Accounts Receivable	+	Supplies	+	Equipment	=	Accounts Payable	+	Common Stock	+	Retained Earnings		
													Revenues	−	Expenses	−	Dividends
1.															
2.															
3.															
4.															
5.															
6.															
7.															
8.															
9.															
10															
11.															

(a)

Donahue Veterinary Clinic

Trans-actions		Assets							=		Liabilities			+		Stockholders' Equity								
		Cash	+		Accounts Receivable	+		Supplies	+		Office Equipment	=		Notes Payable	+		Accounts Payable	+		Common Stock	+		Retained Earnings	+	Revenues	-	Expenses	-	Dividends
1. Bal.	$	9000		$	1700		$	600		$	6000					$	3600		$	13000		$	700					
2. 1.																											
3.																											
4. 2.																											
5.																											
6. 3.																											
7.																											
8. 4.																											
9.																											
10. 5.																											
11.																											
12.																											
13.																											
14. 6.																											
15.																											
16. 7.																											
17.																											
18. 8.																											
19.																											
20.																											

(a)

		Stiner Deliveries												
		Assets		=	Liabilities		+	Stockholders' Equity						
Date	Cash	+	Accounts Receivable	+	Supplies	+	Equipment	=	Notes Payable	+	Accounts Payable	+	Common Stock	+	Retained Earnings
														Revenues	-	Expenses	-	Dividends
1	June 1														
2	2														
3															
4	3														
5															
6	5														
7															
8	9														
9															
10	12														
11															
12	15														
13															
14	17														
15															
16	20														
17															
18	23														
19															
20	26														
21															
22	29														
23															
24	30														
25															

(a)

	Holiday Travel Agency																
	Assets						=	Liabilities				+	Stockholders' Equity				
Trans-actions	Cash	+	Accounts Receivable	+	lies	+	Equipment	=	Notes Payable	+	Accounts Payable	+	Common Stock	+	Retained Earnings	+	Revenues	−	Expenses	−	Dividends
1.																	
2.																	
3.																	
4.																	
5.																	
6.																	
7.																	
8.																	
9.																	
10																	
11.																	

(a)

		Assets			=	Liabilities	+			Stockholders' Equity				
Trans-actions	Cash	+	Accounts Receivable	+	Supplies	+	Equipment	=	Notes Payable	+	Accounts Payable	+	Common Stock	+	Retained Earnings	+	Revenues	−	Expenses	−	Dividends
Bal.	$ 4000		$ 1500		$ 500		$ 5000				$ 4200		$ 6000		$ 800						
1.																					
2.																					
3.																					
4.																					
5.																					
6.																					
7.																					
8.																					

(a)

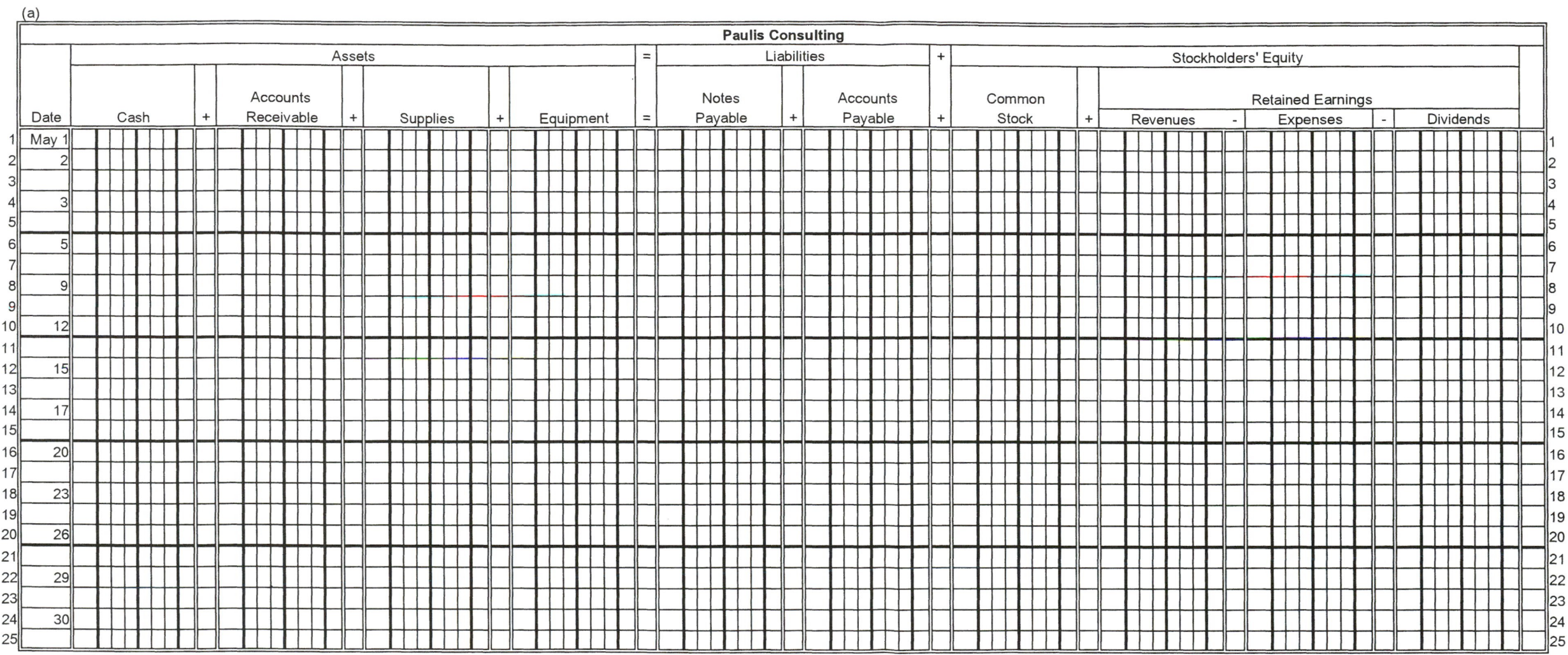

		Paulis Consulting												
		Assets				=	Liabilities			+	Stockholders' Equity			
Date	Cash	+	Accounts Receivable	+	Supplies	+	Equipment	=	Notes Payable	+	Accounts Payable	+	Common Stock	+	Retained Earnings
														Revenues	-	Expenses	-	Dividends
May 1														
2														
3														
5														
9														
12														
15														
17														
20														
23														
26														
29														
30														

BE4-2

	Keo Company										
	Worksheet										
Account Titles	Trial Balance		Adjustments		Adjusted Trial Balance		Income Statement		Balance Sheet	
	Debit	Credit	Debit	Credit	Debit	Credit	Debit	Credit	Debit	Credit
1 Prepaid Insurance	3000										1
2 Service Revenue		61000									2
3 Salaries and Wages											3
4 Expense	25000										4
5 Accounts Receivable											5
6 Salaries and Wages											6
7 Payable											7
8 Insurance Expense											8
9											9
10											10

Cajon Company
Worksheet
For The Month Ended June 30, 2014

	Account Titles	Trial Balance		Adjustments		Adjusted Trial Balance		Income Statement		Balance Sheet		
		Dr.	Cr.	Dr.	Cr.	Dr.	Cr.	Dr.	Cr.	Dr.	Cr.	
1	Cash	4020										1
2	Accounts Receivable	2440										2
3	Supplies	1900										3
4	Accounts Payable		1120									4
5	Unearned Service Rev.		240									5
6	Common Stock		5000									6
7	Service Revenue		3100									7
8	Salaries & Wages Exp	860										8
9	Miscellaneous Expense	240										9
10	Totals	9460	9460									10
11	Supplies Expense											11
12	Salaries & Wages Pay											12
13	Totals											13
14	Net Income											14
15	Totals											15
16												16
17												17
18												18
19												19
20												20

(a)

Sherlock Holmes, P.I., Inc.
Worksheet
For the Quarter Ended March 31, 2014

	Account Titles	Trial Balance Dr.	Trial Balance Cr.	Adjustments Dr.	Adjustments Cr.	Adjusted Trial Balance Dr.	Adjusted Trial Balance Cr.	Income Statement Dr.	Income Statement Cr.	Balance Sheet Dr.	Balance Sheet Cr.	
1	Cash	11410										1
2	Account Receivable	5920										2
3	Supplies	1250										3
4	Prepaid Insurance	2400										4
5	Equipment	30000										5
6	Notes Payable		10000									6
7	Accounts Payable		12350									7
8	Common Stock		20000									8
9	Dividends	600										9
10	Service Revenue		14200									10
11	Sal. & Wages Expense	2240										11
12	Travel Expense	1300										12
13	Rent Expense	1200										13
14	Miscellaneous Expense	230										14
15	Totals	56550	56550									15
16												16
17	Supplies Expense											17
18	Depreciation Expense											18
19	Accum. Depreciation											19
20	Interest Expense											20
21	Interest Payable											21
22	Insurance Expense											22
23	Totals											23
24	Net Income											24
25	Totals											25
26	Totals											26

(a)

Excelsior Amusement Park
Worksheet
For The Year Ended September 30, 2014

	Account Titles	Trial Balance		Adjustments		Adjusted Trial Balance		Income Statement		Balance Sheet		
		Dr.	Cr.	Dr.	Cr.	Dr.	Cr.	Dr.	Cr.	Dr.	Cr.	
1	Cash	34400				34400						1
2	Supplies	18600				2200						2
3	Prepaid Insurance	29900				10900						3
4	Land	80000				80000						4
5	Equipment	120000				120000						5
6	Accum. Depr. - Equip.		36200				42200					6
7	Accounts Payable		14600				14600					7
8	Unearned Ticket Revenue		3900				1000					8
9	Mortgage Payable		50000				50000					9
10	Common Stock		60000				60000					10
11	Retained Earnings		36100				36100					11
12	Dividends	14000				14000						12
13	Ticket Revenue		277900				280800					13
14	Salaries & Wages Exp.	98000				98000						14
15	Maint. & Repairs Exp	30500				30500						15
16	Advertising Expense	9400				9400						16
17	Utilities Expense	16900				16900						17
18	Property Taxes Expense	21000				24000						18
19	Interest Expense	6000				8000						19
20	Totals	478700	478700									20
21	Insurance Expense					19000						21
22	Supplies Expense					16400						22
23	Interest Payable						2000					23
24	Depreciation Expense					6000						24
25	Property Taxes Payable						3000					25
26	Totals					489700	489700					26
27	Net Income											27
28	Totals											28

(b) & (c)

	Fresh Step Carpet Cleaners									
	Worksheet									
	For the Month Ended March 31, 2014									
Account Titles	Trial Balance		Adjustments		Adjusted Trial Balance		Income Statement		Balance Sheet	
	Dr.	Cr.	Dr.	Cr.	Dr.	Cr.	Dr.	Cr.	Dr.	Cr.
1 Cash										
2 Accounts Receivable										
3 Supplies										
4 Prepaid Insurance										
5 Equipment										
6 Accounts Payable										
7 Common Stock										
8 Dividends										
9 Service Revenue										
10 Gasoline Expense										
11 Salaries & Wages Expense										
12 Totals										
13 Depreciation Expense										
14 Accum. Depreciation - Equip.										
15 Insurance Expense										
16 Supplies Expense										
17 Salaries & Wages Payable										
18 Totals										
19 Net Income										
20 Totals										
21										

(a)

Info Cable									
(1) Incorrect Entry			(2) Correct Entry			(3) Correcting Entry			
Account Titles	Dr.	Cr.	Account Titles	Dr.	Cr.	Account Titles	Dr.	Cr.	
1.									1
									2
									3
2.									4
									5
									6
3.									7
									8
									9
									10
									11
4.									12
									13
									14
5.									15
									16
									17
									18
									19
									20

(a)

	Firmament Roofing Worksheet For The Month Ended March 31, 2014										
Account Titles	Trial Balance		Adjustments		Adjusted Trial Balance		Income Statement		Balance Sheet		
	Dr.	Cr.	Dr.	Cr.	Dr.	Cr.	Dr.	Cr.	Dr.	Cr.	
1 Cash	2720										1
2 Accounts Receivable	2700										2
3 Supplies	1500										3
4 Equipment	11000										4
5 Accum. Depr. - Equip.		1250									5
6 Accounts Payable		2500									6
7 Unearned Service Rev		550									7
8 Common Stock		10000									8
9 Dividends	1100										9
10 Service Revenue		6300									10
11 Sal. & Wages Exp.	1300										11
12 Misc. Expense	280										12
13 Totals	20600	20600									13
14 Supplies Expense											14
15 Depr. Expense											15
16 Sal. & Wages Pay.											16
17 Totals											17
18 Net Income											18
19 Totals											19
20											20

(a)

Kumar Management Services, Inc.
Worksheet
For the Year Ended December 31, 2014

Account Titles	Trial Balance Dr.	Trial Balance Cr.	Adjustments Dr.	Adjustments Cr.	Adjusted Trial Balance Dr.	Adjusted Trial Balance Cr.	Income Statement Dr.	Income Statement Cr.	Balance Sheet Dr.	Balance Sheet Cr.
1 Cash	13800				13800					
2 Accounts Receivable	26300				26300					
3 Prepaid Insurance	3600				1800					
4 Land	67000				67000					
5 Buildings	127000				127000					
6 Equipment	59000				59000					
7 Accounts Payable		12500				12500				
8 Unearned Rent Revenue		8000				3500				
9 Mortgage Payable		120000				120000				
10 Common Stock		80000				80000				
11 Retained Earnings		54000				54000				
12 Dividends	16000				16000					
13 Service Revenue		90700				90700				
14 Rent Revenue		26000				30500				
15 Salaries & Wages Expense	42000				42000					
16 Advertising Expense	17500				17500					
17 Utilities Expense	19000				19000					
18 Totals	391200	391200								
19 Insurance Expense					1800					
20 Depr. Expense					6600					
21 Accum. Depreciation - Bldg.						3000				
22 Accum. Depreciation - Equip.						3600				
23 Interest Expense					9600					
24 Interest Payable						9600				
25										
26 Totals					407400	407400				
27 Net Income										
28 Totals										
29										

(b) and (c)

	Brennan's Cleaning Services									
	Worksheet									
	For The Month Ended July 31, 2014									
Account Titles	Trial Balance		Adjustments		Adjusted Trial Balance		Income Statement		Balance Sheet	
	Dr.	Cr.	Dr.	Cr.	Dr.	Cr.	Dr.	Cr.	Dr.	Cr.
1 Cash										
2 Accounts Receivable										
3 Supplies										
4 Prepaid Insurance										
5 Equipment										
6 Accounts Payable										
7 Common Stock										
8 Dividends										
9 Service Revenue										
10 Gasoline Expense										
11 Salaries & Wages Exp.										
12 Totals										
13										
14 Depreciation Expense										
15 Accum. Depr. - Equip.										
16 Insurance Expense										
17 Supplies Exp.										
18 Salaries & Wages Pay.										
19 Totals										
20 Net Income										
21 Totals										
22										

(b) & (c)

	Mary's Maids Cleaning Service									
	Worksheet									
	For the Month Ended July 31, 2014									
Account Titles	Trial Balance		Adjustments		Adjusted Trial Balance		Income Statement		Balance Sheet	
	Dr.	Cr.	Dr.	Cr.	Dr.	Cr.	Dr.	Cr.	Dr.	Cr.
1 Cash										
2 Accounts Receivable										
3 Supplies										
4 Prepaid Insurance										
5 Equipment										
6 Accounts Payable										
7 Common Stock										
8 Dividends										
9 Service Revenue										
10 Gasoline Expense										
11 Salaries & Wages Expense										
12 Totals										
14 Depreciation Expense										
15 Accum. Depreciation - Equip.										
16 Insurance Expense										
17 Supplies Expense										
18 Salaries & Wages Payable										
19 Totals										
20 Net Income										
21 Totals										
22										
23										
24										

Adelle Company

Worksheet

For the Month Ended June 30, 2014

	Account Titles	Trial Balance Dr.	Trial Balance Cr.	Adjustments Dr.	Adjustments Cr.	Adjusted Trial Balance Dr.	Adjusted Trial Balance Cr.	Income Statement Dr.	Income Statement Cr.	Balance Sheet Dr.	Balance Sheet Cr.	
1	Cash	2120										1
2	Accounts Receivable	2440										2
3	Inventory	11640										3
4	Accounts Payable		1120									4
5	Common Stock		4000									5
6	Sales		42500									6
7	Cost of Goods Sold	20560										7
8	Operating Expenses	10860										8
9	Totals	47620	47620									9
10	Net Income											10
11	Totals											11
12												12
13												13
14												14
15												15
16												16

(a)

Mr. Rosiak Fashion Center
Worksheet
For the Year Ended November 30, 2014

	Account Titles	Trial Balance Dr.	Trial Balance Cr.	Adjustments Dr.	Adjustments Cr.	Adjusted Trial Balance Dr.	Adjusted Trial Balance Cr.	Income Statement Dr.	Income Statement Cr.	Balance Sheet Dr.	Balance Sheet Cr.	
1	Cash	8700										1
2	Accounts Receivable	27700										2
3	Inventory	44700										3
4	Supplies	6200										4
5	Equipment	133000										5
6	Accum. Depr. - Equip.		23000									6
7	Notes Payable		51000									7
8	Accounts Payable		48500									8
9	Common Stock		50000									9
10	Retained Earnings		38000									10
11	Dividends	8000										11
12	Sales Revenue		755200									12
13	Sales Returns and Allow.	12800										13
14	Cost of Goods Sold	497400										14
15	Sal. And Wages Expense	136000										15
16	Advertising Expense	24400										16
17	Utilities Expense	14000										17
18	Maint. & Repairs Expense	12100										18
19	Freight-out	16700										19
20	Rent Expense	24000										20
21	Totals	965700	965700									21
22	Supplies Expense											22
23	Depreciation Expense											23
24	Interest Expense											24
25	Interest Payable											25
26	Totals											26
27	Net Loss											27
28	Totals											28
29												29
30												30
31												31

(c)

	Zweifel Company										
	Work Sheet										
	For the Month Ended January 31, 2014										
Account Titles	Trial Balance		Adjustments		Adjusted Trial Balance		Income Statement		Balance Sheet		
	Dr.	Cr.	Dr.	Cr.	Dr.	Cr	Dr.	Cr	Dr.	Cr.	
1 Cash											1
2 Accounts Receivable											2
3 Notes Receivable											3
4 Inventory											4
5 Supplies											5
6 Prepaid Insurance											6
7 Equipment											7
8 Accum. Depr. - Equip.											8
9 Notes Payable											9
10 Accounts Payable											10
11 Interest Payable											11
12 Common Stock											12
13 Retained Earnings											13
14 Cash Dividends											14
15 Sales Revenue											15
16 Sales Rtns. and Allow.											16
17 Purchases											17
18 Purch. Rtns and Allow.											18
19 Freight-In											19
20 Salaries & Wages Exp.											20
21 Rent Expense											21
22 Totals											22
23											23
24 Supplies Exp.											24
25 Insurance Exp.											25
26 Depreciation Exp.											26
27 Interest Exp.											27
28 Totals											28
29 Net Income											29
30 Totals											30

(c)

	Bryant Co. Work Sheet For the Month Ended January 31, 2014									
Account Titles	**Trial Balance**		**Adjustments**		**Adjusted Trial Balance**		**Income Statement**		**Balance Sheet**	
	Dr.	Cr.	Dr.	Cr.	Dr.	Cr	Dr.	Cr	Dr.	Cr.
1 Cash										
2 Accounts Receivable										
3 Notes Receivable										
4 Inventory										
5 Supplies										
6 Prepaid Insurance										
7 Equipment										
8 Accum. Depr. - Equip.										
9 Notes Payable										
10 Accounts Payable										
11 Interest Payable										
12 Common Stock										
13 Retained Earnings										
14 Cash Dividends										
15 Sales Revenue										
16 Sales Rtns. and Allow.										
17 Sales Discounts										
18 Cost of Goods Sold										
19 Salaries & Wages Exp.										
20 Rent Exp.										
21 Totals										
22										
23 Supplies Exp.										
24 Insurance Exp.										
25 Depreciation Exp.										
26 Interest Exp.										
27 Totals										
28 Net Income										
29 Totals										
30										